T2-AJN-400

The Supreme Court
Justice and the Law

THIRD EDITION

CONGRESSIONAL QUARTERLY INC.
1414 22nd STREET, N.W.
WASHINGTON, D.C. 20037

Congressional Quarterly Inc.

Congressional Quarterly Inc., an editorial research service and publishing company, serves clients in the fields of news, education, business and government. It combines specific coverage of Congress, government and politics by Congressional Quarterly with the more general subject range of an affiliated service, Editorial Research Reports.

Congressional Quarterly was founded in 1945 by Henrietta and Nelson Poynter. Its basic periodical publication was and still is the *Congressional Quarterly Weekly Report,* mailed to clients every Saturday. A cumulative index is published quarterly.

CQ also publishes a variety of books including college political science texts, public affairs paperbacks and reference volumes. The latter include the *CQ Almanac,* a compendium of legislation for one session of Congress that is published each spring, and *Congress and the Nation,* a record of government for a presidential term that is published every four years.

The public affairs books are designed as timely reports to keep journalists, scholars and the public abreast of developing issues, events and trends. They include such recent titles as *How Congress Works, Regulation: Process and Politics,* the fourth edition of *The Washington Lobby* and the third edition of *Dollar Politics.*

College textbooks, prepared by outside scholars and published under the CQ Press imprint, include such recent titles as *Goodbye to Good-time Charlie: The American Governorship Transformed, Second Edition,* and *Interest Group Politics.*

In addition, CQ publishes *The Congressional Monitor,* a daily report on current and future activities of congressional committees. This service is supplemented by *The Congressional Record Scanner,* an abstract of each day's *Congressional Record,* and *Congress in Print,* a weekly listing of committee publications. CQ also publishes newsletters including *Congressional Insight,* a weekly analysis of congressional action, and *Campaign Practices Reports,* a bi-monthly update on campaign laws and developments.

CQ conducts seminars and conferences on Congress, the legislative process, the federal budget, national elections and politics, and other current issues. CQ Direct Research is a consulting service that performs contract research and maintains a reference library and query desk for clients.

Editorial Research Reports covers subjects beyond the specialized scope of Congressional Quarterly. It publishes reference material on foreign affairs, business, education, cultural affairs, national security, science and other topics of news interest. Service to clients includes a 6,000-word report four times a month, bound and indexed semi-annually. Editorial Research Reports publishes paperback books in its field of coverage. Founded in 1923, the service merged with Congressional Quarterly in 1956.

Copyright © 1983 Congressional Quarterly Inc.

All rights reserved. No part of this publication may be reproduced or transmitted in any form or by any means, electronic or mechanical, including photocopy, recording, or any information storage and retrieval system, without permission in writing from the publisher.

Printed in the United States of America

Library of Congress Cataloging in Publication Data

Main entry under title:

The Supreme Court, justice and the law.

Bibliography: p.
Includes indexes.
1. United States. 2. Supreme Court. 3. Justice, Administration of — United States. I. Congressional Quarterly, inc.
KF8742.C65 1983   347.73'26'2   83-2120
ISBN 0-87187-253-6   AACR2

KF
8742
.S92
1983

Editor: Michael D. Wormser
Major Contributor: Elder Witt
Contributors: Nadine Cohodas, Carolyn H. Crowley
Design: Mary L. McNeil
Cover: Richard A. Pottern;
      A. Pierce Bounds/UNIPHOTO
Graphics: Bob Redding, Belle T. Burkhart
Index: Elizabeth Furbush

Book Department

David R. Tarr *Director*
Joanne D. Daniels *Director, CQ Press*
John L. Moore *Assistant Director*
Michael D. Wormser *Associate Editor*
Martha V. Gottron *Associate Editor*
Barbara R. de Boinville *Senior Editor, CQ Press*
Sari Horwitz *Senior Editor*
Nancy Lammers *Senior Editor*
Susan D. Sullivan *Developmental Editor, CQ Press*
Margaret C. Thompson *Senior Writer*
Carolyn Goldinger *Project Editor*
Janet E. Hoffman *Project Editor*
Mary L. McNeil *Project Editor*
Robert S. Mudge *Project Editor*
Patricia M. Russotto *Editorial Assistant*
Esther D. Wyss *Editorial Assistant*
Mary Ames Booker *Editorial Assistant*
Barbara Corry *Editorial Assistant*
Dirk Olin *Editorial Assistant*
Judith Aldock *Editorial Assistant*
Elizabeth Summers *Editorial Assistant*
Calvin Chin *Editorial Assistant*
Mark White *Editorial Assistant*
Nancy A. Blanpied *Indexer*
Jodean Marks *Indexer*
Barbara March *Secretary*
Patricia Ann O'Connor *Contributing Editor*
Elder Witt *Contributing Editor*

Congressional Quarterly Inc.

Eugene Patterson *Editor and President*
Wayne P. Kelley *Publisher*
Peter A. Harkness *Executive Editor*
Robert E. Cuthriell *Director, Research and Development*
Robert C. Hur *General Manager*
I.D. Fuller *Production Manager*
Maceo Mayo *Assistant Production Manager*
Sydney E. Garriss *Computer Services*
Richard A. Pottern *Director, Art Department*

Table of Contents

Editor's Note. *The Supreme Court, Justice and the Law, Third Edition,* concentrates on the court during the era of Chief Justice Warren E. Burger — the period beginning in 1969 — to illustrate the operation of the separation of powers in the federal government and the system of checks and balances. The first chapter introduces the contemporary court — the current concerns of the justices and trends as reflected in recent decisions, membership changes and a comparison with the court under Chief Justice Earl Warren. Chapter 2 examines the relationship between the court and the chief executive, particularly the ebb and flow of presidential influence during the court's 194-year history. Chapter 3 looks at the court's relations with Congress, the powers of each over the other. It discusses the powers Congress possesses to overturn decisions of the court and traces the history of the court's influence, particularly its use of judicial review to judge the constitutionality of legislation passed by Congress. The last chapter probes the positions and concerns of the sitting justices through quotes from some of their most important decisions. The chapter contains summaries of some of the important rulings of the court affecting every facet of American life over the past 14 years. An appendix contains excerpts from *Marbury v. Madison* and more recent landmark court decisions, a list of all nominations to the court since 1789, the acts of Congress declared unconstitutional, biographies of all justices since 1969, the text of the U.S. Constitution and all ratified amendments, a glossary of common legal terms and a selected bibliography. Both a subject index and a case index are provided. *The Supreme Court, Justice and the Law* is one of CQ's public affairs books, which are designed as timely reports to keep journalists, scholars and the public informed about national issues, events and trends.

The Supreme Court
Justice and the Law

The Contemporary Court

The United States came into being as a protest against tyranny. To preclude a recurrence of the sort of autocratic rule that sparked the American Revolution, the men who drafted the outlines of the new national government in Philadelphia during the steamy summer of 1787 divided national power among three branches — the executive, headed by the president; the legislative, embodied in Congress; and the judicial, a national court system headed by the Supreme Court.

Congress was given authority to make the laws; the president, to see that they were faithfully executed; and the Supreme Court, to interpret and apply the law and to resolve disputes between certain specified parties.

The Weakest Branch ...

Writing in *The Federalist Papers* in 1788, during the campaign for ratification of the new Constitution by the states, Alexander Hamilton described the court as "beyond comparison the weakest of the three departments of power ... it can never attack with success either of the other two; and ... all possible care is requisite to enable it to defend against their attacks." Hamilton added:

> Whoever attentively considers the different departments of power must perceive that, in a government in which they are separated from each other, the judiciary, from the nature of its functions, will always be the least dangerous to the political rights of the Constitution; because it will be least in a capacity to annoy or injure them. The executive not only dispenses the honors but holds the sword of the community. The legislature not only commands the purse but prescribes the rules by which the duties and rights of every citizen are to be regulated. The judiciary, on the contrary, has no influence over either the sword or the purse; no direction either of the strength or of the wealth of the society, and can take no active resolution whatever. It may truly be said to have neither FORCE nor WILL but merely judgment; and must ultimately depend upon the aid of the executive arm even for the efficacy of its judgments.

Concluding this unflattering description of the court, Hamilton added that "from the natural feebleness of the judiciary, it is in continual jeopardy of being overpowered, awed, or influenced by its co-ordinate branches," and thus, Hamilton argued, life tenure for its members was essential to protect its independence.

Notwithstanding this pathetic portrait of the judiciary, Hamilton then went on to claim for this weakest branch the power and duty "to declare all acts contrary to the manifest tenor of the Constitution void."

Nothing in the Constitution gave the court this power of judicial review, and scholars still wrangle over whether or not it was in the original scheme of things for the court to have such authority.

To all intents and purposes, however, the debate has been irrelevant ever since 1803 when the court first exercised this power to strike down an act of Congress, declaring that "it is, emphatically, the province and duty of the judicial department to say what the law is," The significance for American government of this ruling in *Marbury v. Madison* cannot be overestimated.

It is in *Marbury* that the court, in addition to exercising for the first time its power vis-a-vis Congress, also put the president on notice that his actions, too, were subject to judicial review. Chief Justice John Marshall's opinion reprimanded President Thomas Jefferson for failing to deliver commissions to certain judicial officers who had been nominated by his predecessor, John Adams, and confirmed before Jefferson took office.

... And the Most Powerful Court

It is this extraordinary power, wielded with care, that has enabled the weakest branch of the federal government to become the most powerful court of law in history.

The Supreme Court's orders are enforced by little power other than that of public opinion. Yet the court can override the will of the majority embodied in acts of Congress. It can forcefully remind the president that in the United States all persons are subject to the rule of law. It can require the states to redistribute political power among their citizens. And it can persuade the nation's citizens that the fabric of their society must be rewoven into new and fairer patterns.

The court's rulings have done much to shape the character of the federal government and the manner in which it relates to the states and to individual citizens. One view of its effect was set out early in the 20th century by constitutional historian Charles Warren. Warren wrote that without the court's power to check Congress,

[T]he Nation could never have remained a Federal Republic. Its government would have become a consolidated and centralized autocracy. Congress would have attained supreme, final and unlimited power over the Executive and the Judiciary branches, and the States and the individual citizens could have possessed only such powers and rights as Congress chose to leave or grant to them.

The Balance Wheel

The court is the nation's balance wheel, continually tilting the flow of power away from one sufficiently powerful branch of the national government to another and to or from the individual and the states.

In his published lectures, *The Supreme Court in the American System of Government*, Justice Robert H. Jackson, a member of the court from 1941 to 1954, made this point with particular clarity:

In a society in which rapid changes tend to upset all equilibrium, the court, without exceeding its own limited powers must strive to maintain the great system of balances upon which our free government is based. Whether those balances and checks are essential to liberty elsewhere in the world is beside the point; they are indispensable to the society we know. Chief of these balances are: first, between the Executive and Congress; second, between the central government and the States; third, between state and state; fourth, between authority, be it state or national, and the liberty of the citizen, or between the rule of the majority and the rights of the individual.

Recent Court Trends

It is not difficult to apply Jackson's categories to some of the major rulings issued by the court since 1969. The balance between the executive branch and Congress was adjusted with the court's ruling in a 1975 decision holding that the president could not impound (refuse to spend) funds approved by Congress for specific programs, and it could be altered again when the court rules on issues raised by the so-called legislative veto. *(Details, box, p. 52)*

The balance between national power and the rights of the states is at the heart of numerous modern-day rulings. Considered the most notable of these is the court's 1976 decision that Congress may not require states to compensate their own employees at salary levels dictated by the federal minimum wage law. As it has done since 1790, the court resolves disputes between states over land, water and, more recently, energy.

The most controversial of the court's decisions in the 1969-82 period, however, have been those that readjusted the balance between the authority of the government and the liberty of the individual. Among these opinions were the 1973 decision guaranteeing women a right of privacy in deciding whether or not to have an abortion, and the series of decisions in the late 1970s on the issue of "affirmative action." *(Details, pp. 113, 114)*

The Post-Warren Court

The court of the 1970s is often referred to as the Burger court, but for a variety of reasons the label has not stuck. A more accurate label might be the post-Warren court.

Chief Justice Warren E. Burger took his seat in June 1969, upon the retirement of Chief Justice Earl Warren. To all outward appearances it was a smooth transition, but the court was a different place without Warren, whose personality had dominated it during his 16-year tenure.

Burger differed from Warren in many ways; each had his own strengths and his own view of the duties and responsibilities of the chief justice.

Earl Warren, who had a long career in politics before he was appointed chief justice, focused his energy and considerable political skill upon his colleagues on the court, encouraging a creative exchange of views among the eight other independent justices and working to cajole or reason an effective court majority into being.

Warren was not the greatest intellect on the court in the 1950s and 1960s, but no one questioned his role as its chief, its leader, and the first among equals.

Warren Burger had been a judge, not a politician, when he was chosen to be chief justice. Often a dissenter himself in his earlier judicial career, he was content to speak and vote as one of the nine justices, eschewing the Warren role of consensus-maker. One result was an increase in the number of splintered rulings — those without the backing of even a solid five-member majority on the court — and multiple opinions, factors that sometimes generated more confusion than clarity on the issues involved.

Burger views himself primarily as the head of the federal judicial system, and he devotes a considerable amount of time and energy to questions of judicial administration and efficiency. He frequently speaks out to Congress and legal groups urging action to modernize the courts and better equip them to deal with the ever-growing volume of cases coming before them. This role for the chief justice is not without precedent, but Burger has been criticized for some of his activities. *(Details, box, pp. 70-71)*

Controversy and Stability

The 1970s began for the court amid bitter controversy. Abe Fortas had resigned as an associate justice in May 1969, a month before Burger was sworn in.

Liberal resentment at the circumstances that forced Fortas to resign flared into a fierce confirmation battle later in the year, culminating in the Senate's rejection of President Richard M. Nixon's choice of Clement F. Haynsworth, a noted appeals court judge, as Fortas' successor. Not since 1930 had a president's nominee to the court been rejected outright.

Matters went from bad to worse the next year. In April 1970 the Senate, after another brutal confirmation fight, also rejected Nixon's misguided choice of G. Harrold Carswell to fill the Fortas seat.

Both of the rejected nominees were Southern conservatives.

But peace finally was restored when the Senate then confirmed Nixon's third choice for the seat — Harry A. Blackmun, a court of appeals judge and close friend of Chief Justice Burger's.

The court, now with two Nixon appointees as members, soon issued a decision that set off a drive in Congress to enact a constitutional amendment to lower the voting age to 18. In December 1970 the justices agreed with the administration's argument that Congress lacked the power to lower, by statute, the voting age in state and local elections. This decision, in the case of *Oregon v. Mitchell*, led directly to approval and ratification of the 26th Amendment on July 1, 1971.

The 1970 court term was an eventful one in other ways. In February the court issued a ruling in the case of *Harris v. New York* indicating that it might indeed be ready to back off somewhat from the strict requirements of the controversial 1966 *Miranda v. Arizona* decision denying prosecutors the use of evidence obtained from a suspect who had not been warned of his constitutional rights.

In April the court ruled unanimously in the case of *Swann v. Charlotte-Mecklenburg County Board of Education* that busing was a permissible interim means of desegregating the nation's public schools, a position directly at odds with that of the Nixon administration. And in June the court found itself head-to-head with the White House in the so-called Pentagon Papers case. The administration ultimately lost its bid for injunctions to halt publication of articles based on a classified history of U.S. military involvement in Vietnam. *(Details, pp. 27, 131)*

In September 1971, just days before the beginning of the new court term, veteran Justices Hugo L. Black and John Marshall Harlan retired in poor health. Black's retirement marked the end of an era; he had been President Franklin D. Roosevelt's first appointee to the Supreme Court in 1937.

After the earlier confirmation battles, Nixon acted more cautiously in selecting his nominees to fill these seats. In October he named former American Bar Association President Lewis F. Powell Jr. and Assistant Attorney General William F. Rehnquist. Both men were approved with little controversy. Powell glided through the confirmation process; the path was bumpier for Rehnquist, but Senate approval was never in doubt.

The remaining years of the post-Warren period saw other major developments. In the October 1971 term it issued the first in a long line of rulings striking down state and federal laws that discriminated unfairly between men and women. The next year was notable for the court's decision that effectively struck down all existing state capital punishment laws. In 1973, the first year of Nixon's second term, the court issued its landmark abortion decision — *Roe v. Wade*. The following year brought the Watergate tapes ruling and the premature end of the Nixon presidency.

In November 1975 Justice William O. Douglas retired. He had been appointed in 1939. In serving on the court for more than 36 years, Douglas easily surpassed all previous justices in length of service.

Douglas' retirement brought the post-Warren era to an end. His departure now reduced the number of Warren court justices to fewer than a majority; only Justices William J. Brennan Jr., Potter Stewart, Thurgood Marshall and Byron R. White had served with Warren.

President Gerald R. Ford, who once led an abortive attempt to impeach Douglas, appointed his successor — John Paul Stevens, a federal appeals court judge from Chicago. Stevens was easily confirmed and took his seat in December 1975.

From left: Harry A. Blackmun, Thurgood Marshall, William J. Brennan Jr., Chief Justice Warren E. Burger, Sandra Day O'Connor, Byron R. White, Lewis F. Powell Jr., William H. Rehnquist, John Paul Stevens

Federal Judicial System

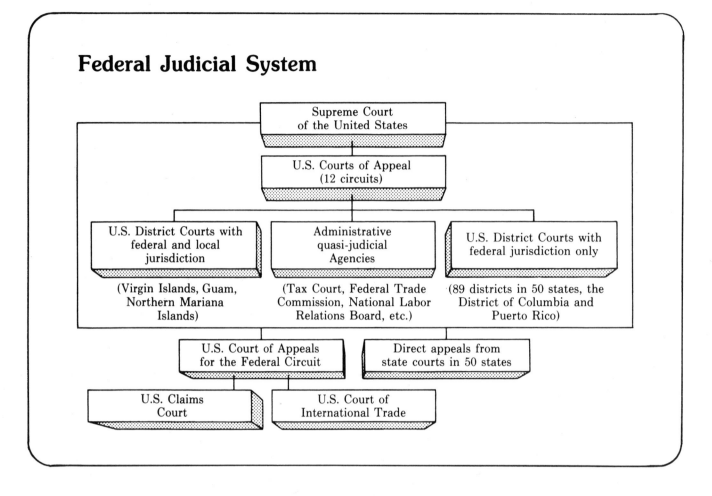

The Contemporary Court

Three major rulings in the first half of 1976 set the tone for the work of the Supreme Court for the remainder of the 1970s and the early 1980s.

The care with which the contemporary court examines its cases and draws distinctions was evident in two of these. In *Buckley v. Valeo*, the court considered a challenge to the constitutionality of a long list of provisions of the federal campaign finance law that Congress approved in 1974. The court upheld some of the challenged sections of that law, including provisions limiting campaign contributions, while striking down others, including spending ceilings; the court ruled that the latter violated the First Amendment guarantee of free speech.

Five months later, the court upheld some revised state death penalty laws that were enacted in the wake of its 1972 ruling. However, it struck down others on constitutional grounds. *(Details, p. 100-101)*

When it struck down a 1974 law that required states to pay their employees according to the dictates of the federal minimum wage law, the court put Congress on notice that states' rights arguments would once again receive a sympathetic hearing at the "marble palace." *(Details, p. 51)*

During this period, the court was presented with numerous challenges to acts of Congress and decisions of the president. It upheld a 1977 federal strip mining law, struck down one portion of the 1970 federal occupational safety and health law, backed the decision of Congress to exclude

women from the military draft, invalidated a key portion of a 1978 bankruptcy reform law, and upheld the legality of the extraordinary 1981 Iran agreements resolving the American hostage crisis.

While refusing to grant absolute immunity to public officials faced with civil damage suits from individuals who claimed they have been injured by official action, the court in 1982 again affirmed the special position of the president by granting him that immunity. *(Details, box, p. 28)*

In other areas, the court reaffirmed its support of women's efforts to be treated equally before the law, striking down various statutes and regulations that unfairly treated men and women differently. And it upheld the major landmarks of the Warren era: the decisions on civil rights and criminal law as well as the laws passed by Congress designed to realize for the nation's black citizens the constitutional promise of equal protection. In that area the court did more than stand pat. For example, it expanded the scope of civil rights protections to include aliens as well as native-born residents. The court ruled in 1982 that states could not deny a public education to alien children illegally living in the United States.

There were no changes in the membership of the court after the Stevens' appointment in 1975 until July 1981, when Justice Potter Stewart retired. To succeed Stewart, President Ronald Reagan picked Sandra Day O'Connor, the first woman ever nominated to be a Supreme Court justice. She was confirmed by the Senate in time to begin the October 1981 term. *(Details, p. 37)*

The Court and the President

To travel from the White House to the Supreme Court building, one must cross or circumvent Capitol Hill. The massive marble dome topping the legislative chambers of Congress stands between the president's offices and the marble edifice east of the Capitol where the justices work.

The president selects the members of the court as vacancies occur. To an outsider, this would seem to make the Supreme Court simply an adjunct of the executive, a rubber stamp in the president's hip pocket. History quickly dispels such an image.

Before Supreme Court nominees can take their seat on the court, they must be confirmed by the Senate. Once they become justices, they are insulated from presidential pressure by life tenure — subject to good behavior — and no justice has ever behaved so badly that Congress felt it necessary to remove him from office. An additional guarantee of independence is the Constitution's assurance that Congress cannot reduce the justices' salaries while they remain on the bench.

In the landmark 1803 ruling claiming for the court the power to hold acts of Congress unconstitutional, Chief Justice John Marshall chided President Thomas Jefferson for withholding commissions from certain justices of the peace. One hundred and seventy-one years later, in the Watergate coverup case, President Richard M. Nixon was ordered by the court to comply with a prosecutor's subpoena, an order that eventually forced him to resign his office in disgrace. The man Nixon had chosen to be chief justice wrote that decision.

From time to time the court reviews particular actions or claims by the president, as in the Watergate case and the Iran agreements case of 1981. This is another aspect of the court's power of judicial review, first used to nullify an act of Congress 180 years ago. It is the court's primary task, Chief Justice Warren E. Burger reminded President Nixon in 1974, "to say what the law is" and to apply it to the other two branches of the national government when they overstep its bounds.

An Arms-Length Relationship

The court reviews presidential actions far less frequently than it considers challenges to acts of Congress. But when presidential claims and decisions do come up for review, a critical element in the court's consideration of the matter is the position of Congress.

When Congress, explicitly or implicitly, backs the president — as in the Iran agreements case — the president is quite likely to win his case. But when Congress is silent, or clearly at odds with the president's position, the chief executive is on shaky ground, as Nixon discovered in the Watergate case.

When Washington was a new town, and the federal government was composed of a small group of bureaucrats without a great deal to do, it was not unusual for the justices to be frequent guests at the White House, and many were unofficial advisers to the president. Chief Justice John Jay often filled such a role for President Washington, who sent Jay, while he was still chief justice, on a diplomatic mission to Europe. In those days the justices did not move their families to Washington, but came to the capital only for the duration of the court's relatively short term.

But since the Civil War and the accompanying growth in the size of the national government, such familiarity has become the exception rather than the rule. Today, justices and presidents are seldom on more than polite speaking terms. There are exceptions, but these tend to draw particular attention and usually generate controversy. Recent examples include the relationships between Justice Felix Frankfurter and Franklin D. Roosevelt and between Justice Abe Fortas and Lyndon B. Johnson.

In October 1982 President Ronald Reagan revived the custom of meeting with the members of the court before the beginning of each term on the first Monday in October. He used the occasion to tell the justices he recognized the inevitable tension underlying the relationship between the two branches. "It's neither surprising nor disturbing that our citizens may at times side with the dissenters," he said. "It's even rumored that presidents sometimes disagree with particular Supreme Court decisions." But Reagan added that on "one point, at least, there can be no disagreement whatsoever: the Supreme Court must continue to demonstrate the independence and integrity that have always been its hallmarks. . . ."

During the term that followed, Reagan's own policies were before the court in numerous cases as diverse as abortion and tax policy.

History provided little doubt that the court, in dealing with those cases, would continue to display the independence to which Reagan referred.

Supreme Court Membership, 1969-83*

Name	State	Date of Birth	Nominated By	To Replace	Date of Appointment	Date Confirmed	Date Retired
Hugo L. Black	Ala.	2/27/1886	Roosevelt	Van Devanter	8/12/37	8/17/37	9/17/71
William O. Douglas	Conn.	10/16/1898	Roosevelt	Brandeis	3/20/39	4/4/39	11/12/75
Earl Warren**	Calif.	3/19/1891	Eisenhower	Vinson	9/30/53	3/1/54	6/23/69
John M. Harlan	N.Y.	5/20/1899	Eisenhower	Jackson	1/10/55	3/16/55	9/23/71
William J. Brennan Jr.	N.J.	4/25/1906	Eisenhower	Minton	11/14/57†	3/19/57	
Potter Stewart	Ohio	1/23/1915	Eisenhower	Burton	1/17/59††	5/5/59	7/3/81
Byron R. White	Colo.	6/8/1917	Kennedy	Whittaker	3/30/62	4/11/62	
Abe Fortas	Tenn.	6/19/1910	Johnson	Goldberg	7/28/65	8/11/65	5/14/69†††
Thurgood Marshall	N.Y.	7/2/1908	Johnson	Clark	6/13/67	8/30/67	
Warren E. Burger**	D.C.	9/17/1907	Nixon	Warren	5/21/69	6/9/69	
Harry A. Blackmun	Minn.	11/12/1908	Nixon	Fortas	4/14/70	5/12/70	
Lewis F. Powell Jr.	Va.	9/19/1907	Nixon	Black	10/21/71	12/6/71	
William H. Rehnquist	Ariz.	10/1/1924	Nixon	Harlan	10/21/71	12/10/71	
John Paul Stevens	Ill.	4/20/1920	Ford	Douglas	11/28/75	12/17/75	
Sandra Day O'Connor	Ariz.	3/26/1930	Reagan	Stewart	8/19/81	9/21/81	

* as of March 10, 1983
** chief justice
† following recess appointment on 10/16/56

†† following recess appointment on 10/14/58
††† resigned, did not retire

The Political Factor

Politics invariably plays a part in the selection of all Supreme Court nominees. The fact that a president serves for a limited term while justices may serve for a lifetime makes it inevitable that politics will be involved in these choices. Every president has his own ideas about how the government should operate, and he wants to see his policies perpetuated in government decisions for as long as possible. This sometimes can be accomplished by the appointment of relatively young men to the court who share that same view and may serve for decades after the appointing president leaves office.

Washington left the White House in 1797, but one of the justices he appointed remained on the court until 1811. Even more notable was John Adams' selection of John Marshall as chief justice in 1801, near the end of Adams' only term as president. Adams was the last Federalist president, but Marshall, committed to the Federalist viewpoint, served as chief justice until 1835. In that post he exercised a vast influence upon the development of the new nation through a long list of court decisions encouraging the development of federal power and authority.

As already noted, however, presidents often are disappointed in the rulings their hand-picked justices produce. Nixon's conservative nominees did indeed provide the votes for some conservative rulings to Nixon's liking, but on some critical issues — including the death penalty and abortion — the court rejected Nixon's positions.

The Power Factor

As the power of the president has grown, an increasing number of challenges to the manner of its exercise have come before the court. The president comes to the court in a position of strength. Generally, he is a popular — and thus influential — figure. The justices approach challenges to his power with caution, well aware that the effective enforcement of their rulings depends heavily upon public opinion and that a president is able to mobilize that power far more effectively than the Supreme Court.

When possible, the justices usually sidestep a head-on collision with the chief executive by separating the person from his policy, thus hoping to avoid alienating the former even while invalidating the latter.

Twice in modern times that distinction became impossible. When the controversy over President Harry S Truman's seizure of the steel mills reached the court in 1952 and when Nixon's claim of privilege to withhold the White House tape recordings demanded by the Watergate special prosecutor came before the court 22 years later, both presidents' deep personal involvement was clearly evident.

Both times, the court ruled against the chief executive. Truman dropped his effort to take over the steel mills, and Nixon complied with the prosecutor's subpoena. Compliance by these immensely powerful men with the decision of nine black-robed judges backed by the Constitution affirmed once again the rule of law and the pre-eminent role of the court in saying what that rule requires.

PRESIDENTS, POLITICS AND JUSTICES

It is the president's prerogative to nominate justices for the Supreme Court whenever vacancies occur. The only road to a career on that bench is through the White House.

Presidents select justices with a variety of considerations in mind, but invariably it is a highly political and very personal choice. This power gives the president a major opportunity to influence the philosophical leanings and performance of the court, and presidents have been well aware that the justices they select may have an immeasurable impact on the shape of public policy.

Few chief executives have been willing to delegate that responsibility, realizing that the persons appointed may sit on the court for many years after they leave the White House.

The number of Supreme Court nominations a president makes is entirely a matter of chance. A vacancy occurs on the average about every two years, but both Franklin D. Roosevelt and Jimmy Carter served an entire four-year term without any change occurring in the membership of the court.

The performance of a Supreme Court justice is rarely predictable, as president after president has learned. Despite great care in selecting individuals who seemed to share their views, many presidents have been disappointed as their nominees, once confirmed, displayed a staunch independence of mind.

Political scientist Robert M. Scigliano, in his 1971 book, *The Supreme Court and the Presidency*, describes the intersecting relationship between the court and the president:

> In their contemporary relationship, the Presidency has gained considerable influence over the Supreme Court.
>
> Yet the President cannot be said to dominate the Court. . . .
>
> Tension continues to exist between the two institutions. . . . A President cannot be sure that he is getting what he thinks he is getting in his appointments, a person may change his views after joining the Court,

and the judicial obligation calls upon a justice to heed the Constitution and the laws, and not Presidential positions.

The Selection Process

Presidents consider a variety of criteria in selecting justices. Among the most consistently weighed factors in these selections have been merit, friendship, geographical and religious balance, and ideology.

Presidents as a rule have been in agreement that a nominee for the court should have some legal training, but judicial experience has not been considered particularly important. Many distinguished appointees — including eight chief justices of the United States — had no prior judicial experience.

Of the modern presidents, Franklin D. Roosevelt appointed six men who had no judicial experience: Chief Justice Harlan Fiske Stone and Associate Justices Stanley F. Reed, Felix Frankfurter, William O. Douglas, James F. Byrnes and Robert H. Jackson. President Eisenhower, after appointing Earl Warren as chief justice, insisted that all future nominees have judicial experience. (Warren had none.)

Harry S Truman appointed two men without judicial experience: Harold H. Burton and Tom C. Clark. Neither of President John F. Kennedy's two appointees, Byron R. White and Arthur J. Goldberg, had judicial experience; nor did Abe Fortas, Lyndon B. Johnson's appointee, or William H. Rehnquist and Lewis F. Powell Jr., Nixon nominees.

Merit

Almost every one of the 102 persons who have served on the Supreme Court had some record of public service prior to their appointment. Many had held offices in the executive branch or had served as state or federal judges, U.S. senators, members of the House of Representatives, governors or law professors.

High ethical standards, as well as experience in public life, usually are criteria presidents seek in a nominee. Louis D. Brandeis' nomination successfully weathered a challenge that stemmed from charges he had engaged in improper practices as an attorney. But the nominations of

The only road to a career on the Supreme Court is through the White House.

Clement F. Haynsworth as associate justice and Abe Fortas as chief justice failed to win Senate approval mainly because of questions involving possible conflicts of interest.

Friendship, Geography

Personal friendship has been a key factor in several nominations to the court. William Howard Taft's nomination of Horace H. Lurton, Woodrow Wilson's selection of Brandeis, Truman's choice of Harold H. Burton and John F. Kennedy's preference for Byron R. White all had some basis in personal friendships. President Johnson selected a reluctant Abe Fortas for the bench in 1965 on the basis of a long friendship.

Justices of the Supreme Court have come from 31 of the 50 states (as of 1983). States have not been represented in any substantially equal pattern. New York has been the home of 15 justices, Pennsylvania has had 11 residents nominated to the court, Massachusetts 10, Ohio nine, and Virginia and Kentucky six. No other states have been so frequently represented.

Early in the court's history, geographical balance was a major consideration in selecting nominees. Because of the justices' function as circuit judges, it was usually felt that each geographic area should have a spokesman on the court. Until the Civil War, this resulted in a "New England seat," a "Virginia seat," a "New York seat" and a "Pennsylvania seat." With the nation's post-Civil War expansion and the end of the justices' circuit-riding duties, this tradition faded.

Religious Balance

The notion of sectarian religious representation on the court developed out of the fact that Americans are a pluralistic society and a politically group-conscious people. Thus the idea of a "Roman Catholic seat" and a "Jewish seat" on the court developed as a way of acknowledging the role of these religious minority groups in the nation.

The 'Catholic Seat.' Chief Justice Roger B. Taney was the first to hold the "Catholic seat." Since Grover Cleveland appointed Edward D. White to that seat in 1894, it has been held by Joseph McKenna, Pierce Butler, Frank Murphy and William J. Brennan Jr.

Truman's appointment of Tom C. Clark in 1949 after Murphy's death interrupted the tradition, but Eisenhower's appointment of Brennan in 1956 restored the notion of a "Catholic seat." The selection was regarded, in part, as an appeal to Catholic voters.

The 'Jewish Seat.' The "Jewish seat," established in 1916 with the appointment of Louis D. Brandeis, was filled by Justices Felix Frankfurter (1938), Arthur J. Goldberg (1963) and Abe Fortas (1965). (Benjamin N. Cardozo, also a Jew, served along with Brandeis.)

In 1969 President Nixon again broke the tradition by nominating three Protestants in succession to the seat Fortas vacated.

Other Factors

The special representational concerns of the Republican and Democratic parties govern, to some extent, the choice of nominees to the court.

Black and Jewish support for the Democratic Party enhances the likelihood that Democratic presidents will continue to consider those groups in making their selections.

In 1967 President Lyndon B. Johnson nominated Thurgood Marshall to be the first black justice of the Supreme Court. Marshall had been counsel for the National Association for the Advancement of Colored People (NAACP) and one of the attorneys responsible for arguing successfully the case of *Brown v. Board of Education* — the landmark 1954 school desegregation case. Marshall served as solicitor general of the United States before his appointment to the court.

Women's groups had been urging the appointment of a woman to the court for more than a decade before President Ronald Reagan in 1981 selected Sandra Day O'Connor. Reagan had promised during his campaign for the White House in 1980 to place a woman on the court, if given the opportunity.

Such a pledge coming from a conservative candidate was clear evidence of the increasing political clout that women's groups could wield over candidates for national office.

Ideology has been a significant factor in many presidents' appointments to the high bench. President Theodore Roosevelt wrote to Sen. Henry Cabot Lodge, R-Mass., that he was considering a Democrat, Horace H. Lurton, to fill a vacancy on the court, explaining that Lurton was "right" on all the important issues:

> The nominal politics of the man has nothing to do with his actions on the bench. His real politics are all important.... On every question that would come before the bench, he has so far shown himself to be in much closer touch with the policies in which you and I believe.

Lodge agreed, but wondered why a Republican who held the same opinions could not be found for the post. He suggested William H. Moody, the attorney general, and Roosevelt in 1906 agreed to appoint Moody. Lurton subsequently was nominated to the court in 1909 by William Howard Taft.

Party Loyalty

Although presidents generally nominate members of their own party to the court, members of the opposition party occasionally are nominated.

Republican presidents have appointed nine Democratic justices, and Democratic presidents have named three Republicans to the court. Whig President John Tyler appointed Democrat Samuel Nelson. Republican Presidents Abraham Lincoln, Benjamin Harrison, William Howard Taft, Warren G. Harding, Herbert Hoover, Dwight D. Eisenhower and Richard M. Nixon appointed nominal Democrats.

Taft appointed Democrats Horace H. Lurton, Edward D. White (promoted to chief justice) and Joseph R. Lamar. The other GOP presidents who nominated Democrats were Lincoln (Stephen J. Field), Benjamin Harrison (Howell E. Jackson), Harding (Pierce Butler), Hoover (Benjamin Cardozo), Eisenhower (William J. Brennan Jr.) and Nixon (Lewis F. Powell Jr.).

Democratic presidents who selected Republican justices were Woodrow Wilson, who appointed Louis D. Brandeis, Franklin D. Roosevelt, who promoted Justice Harlan Fiske Stone to the chief justiceship, and Harry S Truman, who chose Republican Sen. Harold H. Burton, R-Ohio, for the court. *(List of members of Congress who have been appointed to the court, box, p. 21)*

Presidential Nominees to the Court Often Fail to Live Up to Expectations

Despite their best efforts to name persons to the court who share their views, presidents frequently have been disappointed. Once on the court, justices often display an independence in their court opinions that frequently diverges from the political philosophy of the president who appointed them.

Donning the court robe does seem to make a difference in the appointees' views. Justice Felix Frankfurter, when asked if a person changed his views once he was appointed to the court, allegedly retorted: "If he is any good he does."[1]

Chief Justice Earl Warren, reflecting on his 16 years on the court, did not see "how a man could be on the Court and not change his views substantially over a period of years ... for change you must if you are to do your duty on the Supreme Court."[2]

Charles Warren, historian of the court, wrote that "nothing is more striking in the history of the Court than the manner in which the hopes of those who expected a judge to follow the political views of the President appointing him are disappointed."[3]

Jefferson and Marshall

Presidents Thomas Jefferson and James Madison would have agreed. They repeatedly registered their disappointment at the failure of the judges they appointed to the court to resist the powerful and dominating influence of Chief Justice John Marshall.

Madison failed to heed Jefferson's advice not to appoint Joseph Story to the court. Jefferson warned that Story would side with Marshall on important legal issues, which proved to be correct.

Roosevelt and Holmes

Theodore Roosevelt named Oliver Wendell Holmes Jr. to the court in 1902; Holmes then voted against the administration's antitrust efforts — most notably in the 1904 *Northern Securities v. United States* case. Holmes' dissent left the government with a narrow 5-4 majority upholding the dissolution of the Northern Securities railroad conglomerate.

After the decision, Roosevelt, referring to Holmes' defection, said that he "could carve out of a banana a Judge with more backbone than that!" Holmes reportedly smiled when told of the remark. Later, at a White House dinner, Holmes remarked to a labor leader and fellow guest: "What you want is favor, not justice. But when I am on my job, I don't give a damn what you or Mr. Roosevelt want."[4]

Woodrow Wilson had reason to regret the appointment of James C. McReynolds to the bench when that justice proved to hold the opposite of Wilson's viewpoint on almost every question.

Calvin Coolidge's sole appointee, Harlan F. Stone, within a year of his appointment sided with the liberal Holmes-Brandeis wing of the court.

President Harry S Truman noted that "packing the Supreme Court simply can't be done ... I've tried and it won't work.... Whenever you put a man on the Supreme Court he ceases to be your friend."[5]

And Truman knew from experience. In the *Steel Seizure Case* of 1952, the four Truman appointees divided 2-2 in the case, which ruled the president's seizure of the steel mills to be unconstitutional.

Eisenhower and Warren

President Eisenhower later described as a "mistake" his decision to appoint Earl Warren chief justice. Warren's leadership commenced a judicial "revolution" that greatly disturbed the president.

But Warren's appointment made good political sense in 1953. Warren had delivered California delegates to "Ike" at the Republican national nominating convention in 1952. Warren's removal from the California political scene, where he had proven an immensely popular three-term governor, placated conservative California Republican leaders, including Vice President Richard M. Nixon and Senate Majority Leader William F. Knowland, both of whom disliked Warren's progressive Republican views.

But when Eisenhower was asked if he had made any mistakes during his presidency he quipped, "Yes, two, and they are both sitting on the Supreme Court." The former president thus registered his disappointment at the liberalism of Earl Warren and Justice William J. Brennan Jr.[6]

Nixon and Watergate

Former President Richard M. Nixon had ample cause to disagree with the decisions of the court to which he appointed four men. Although the justices Nixon selected held views consonant with his on many issues, some of them voted to reject Nixon's positions on abortion, aid to parochial schools, school desegregation, busing and electronic surveillance.

Nixon's most dramatic confrontation with the court came in 1974, when it ruled against his claim of an absolute executive privilege to withhold White House tapes sought as evidence in the trial of his former aides. The vote was 8-0. The ruling led to Nixon's resignation two weeks later.

---

[1] Henry J. Abraham, *Justices and Presidents: A Political History of Appointments to the Supreme Court* (New York: Oxford University Press, 1974), p. 63.

[2] Anthony Lewis, "A Talk with Warren on Crime, the Court, the Country," *New York Times Magazine*, Oct. 19, 1969, pp. 128-129.

[3] Charles Warren, *The Supreme Court in United States History*, rev. ed., 2 vols. (Boston: Little, Brown & Co., 1922, 1926), I:22.

[4] Abraham, *Justices and Presidents*, p. 62.

[5] Ibid., p. 63.

[6] Ibid., p. 246.

Taft: Champion Kingmaker

William Howard Taft was the only president to become chief justice of the United States, thus enjoying a unique double opportunity to influence the personnel and work of the court. As president, Taft named six justices, including his promotion of associate justice Edward White to chief justice. Then, during Warren G. Harding's presidency, Taft either suggested or gave his approval to three of the four men Harding appointed to the court — George Sutherland, Pierce Butler and Edward T. Sanford.

Taft also had lobbied for his own appointment as chief justice. In 1920 the former president let it be known to newly elected President Harding that he wanted the job. Taft had named White chief justice and, Taft told Harding, "many times in the past ... [White] had said he was holding the office for me and that he would give it back to a Republican administration." On June 30, 1921, Harding nominated Taft as chief justice, succeeding White, who had died in office.

Taft's most prodigious subsequent lobbying effort on presidential appointments resulted in Pierce Butler's appointment to the court. He orchestrated a letter-writing campaign recommending Butler, who was from Minnesota, and played down the talents of other potential nominees. Taft dismissed the candidacy of Judge Benjamin N. Cardozo of the New York Court of Appeals because, Taft wrote, Cardozo was "a Jew and a Democrat ... [and] ... a progressive judge." Judge Learned Hand, Taft warned, "would almost certainly herd with Brandeis and be a dissenter."

The chief justice sought and obtained endorsements for Butler from the Minnesota congressional delegation, members of the church hierarchy — Butler was a Roman Catholic — and from local bar associations across the nation. Harding succumbed to the pressure and sent Butler's nomination to the Senate where, despite considerable opposition from Senate progressives, he won approval.

When Mahlon Pitney resigned in 1922, Taft heartily approved of Harding's choice, Edward T. Sanford. Taft and Sanford had been acquaintances since Theodore Roosevelt's administration. Some observers felt that Sanford was so close to Taft that the chief justice had two votes on the bench. Their friendship and judicial affinity had a final coincidence: they died on the same day in 1930.

Chief Justice Taft's influence over Harding's appointments to the court gave that body a decidedly conservative majority during the 1920s and 1930s — ending only with Franklin D. Roosevelt's appointments to the court beginning in 1937.

Outside Influences

The appointment of a justice to the Supreme Court involves a complex pattern of personal and political transactions between the president and the individuals and interest groups seeking to influence that nomination.

Among the more important centers of influence are the members of the president's administration, the sitting justices of the Supreme Court and the legal community.

The Attorney General

The president normally seeks the advice of his chief legal officer, the attorney general. In 1840 the attorney general assumed responsibility for judicial appointments, taking over that function from the secretary of state. Since then, the attorney general has become the president's liaison with the principal interest groups, members of Congress and other citizens involved in the screening and selection of qualified candidates for appointment to the court.

The Justices

Sitting justices rarely have hesitated to voice their suggestions of especially qualified nominees for vacant seats. Some justices have offered negative advice. Joseph P. Bradley, in the 1890s, prepared a report about those who would be qualified to succeed him and concluded that no candidate from his native New Jersey possessed the necessary qualifications.

In the 19th century justices often lobbied presidents to urge appointment of certain candidates. Justices John Catron and Benjamin R. Curtis, for example, succeeded in convincing President Franklin Pierce to nominate John A. Campbell to the court. Their representations to Pierce included letters of support for Campbell from all the other sitting justices.

Other justices who successfully urged presidents to appoint certain individuals to the court were: Robert C. Grier in support of William Strong in 1870, Noah H. Swayne for Joseph P. Bradley in 1870, Morrison R. Waite for William B. Woods in 1880, Samuel F. Miller for David J. Brewer in 1889 and Henry B. Brown for Howell E. Jackson in 1893.

William Howard Taft, president and later chief justice (1921-30), was by all measures the most successful of the court's members at influencing presidential court nominations.

Chief Justice Charles Evans Hughes counseled three presidents on appointments. Herbert Hoover sought Hughes' advice in naming a replacement for Oliver Wendell Holmes in 1931. The president was interested particularly in Hughes' opinion of fellow New Yorker Benjamin N. Cardozo.

In 1941 Hughes wanted President Franklin D. Roosevelt to name Harlan Fiske Stone his successor as chief justice. President Truman also consulted Hughes in 1946 on his choice of a chief justice after Stone's death that year.

Hoover also had sought and obtained Stone's advice on filling the Holmes seat. Stone was so convinced of Cardozo's qualifications that he sent several memorandums to Hoover recommending Cardozo in preference to alternate candidates. Stone tried to overcome Hoover's reservations about appointing another Jewish justice, even offering his own resignation from the court to make room for Cardozo.

Hoover nominated Cardozo on Feb. 15, 1932, and he

was confirmed by the Senate nine days later. Of the Cardozo nomination one authority on the court has written:

> The appointment and confirmation of Benjamin Cardozo . . . violated nearly all the 'rules of the game.' Judge Cardozo was a New Yorker, and there were already two judges from that state on the bench — Stone and Hughes. He was a nominal Democrat, and his 'real' politics, highly tinged with liberalism, differed sharply from those of President Hoover. Moreover, he was a Jew and there was already one Jewish judge in the person of Louis Brandeis. Cardozo's selection is inexplicable except in terms of his pre-eminent position among American jurists and the overwhelming pressures on his behalf from leaders of the bench and bar throughout the land.

The Role of the ABA

Since World War II the American Bar Association (ABA) — through its standing committee on the federal judiciary — has played a role in the selection process by assessing the legal and intellectual qualifications of those nominated as Supreme Court justices.

Established in 1945-46, the committee, beginning with the nomination of William J. Brennan Jr. in 1956, rated prospective justices as professionally qualified or unqualified. This system of rating nominees continued with every nomination until Harry A. Blackmun's appointment in 1970.

The ABA's judiciary committee had come under heavy criticism after the Senate's rejection of Nixon nominees Clement F. Haynsworth Jr. in 1969 and G. Harrold Carswell in 1970. Most of the criticism was directed at the Carswell case, with the committee insisting that its investigation of the judge had been sound and that the "qualified" rating given him had been justified. But critics charged that the rating had been based on inadequate information. The committee itself, composed of a large number of corporate lawyers, had come under criticism for its alleged conservative bias. As a result of these events, the ABA changed its rating system to three categories — "highly qualified," "not opposed" and "not qualified."

Attorney General John N. Mitchell wrote the chairman of the committee in July 1970 to say that the Nixon administration would submit names of potential Supreme Court nominees to the ABA for preliminary screening before sending the president's choice for the seat to the Senate.

But the agreement dissolved almost immediately when names of prospective Nixon nominees to fill the vacant seats occasioned by the retirements of Justices John Marshall Harlan and Hugo L. Black reached the press while the ABA committee was studying their qualifications. The administration, suspecting a news leak in the committee, withdrew its support of the practice.

Despite this rebuff, the ABA conducted its own investigation of the qualifications of Lewis F. Powell Jr. and William H. Rehnquist, the Nixon administration's choices to succeed Harlan and Black.

The ABA submitted the findings to the Senate Judiciary Committee. The ABA approved both men, Powell unanimously as "one of the best lawyers available." Rehnquist received nine votes for a highly qualified rating, but three ABA committee members said merely that they were "not opposed" to his appointment to the court.

Politics and Appointments

Politics is somewhat less a factor in the selection of modern Supreme Court justices than it was in the early days of the republic. Then, the court often was an open political battlefield between the competing political parties, as each sought to impose its ideology on the government of the new nation.

Political affinities still are perhaps the prevailing factor in a president's choice of a nominee, but the political element has become less openly partisan as the court has become an equal and independent branch of the federal system.

Marshall, McLean and Taney

President John Adams appointed John Marshall chief justice in 1801 because he wanted to place a loyal Federalist in the chief justice's seat who would preserve the party's principles in the wake of Jefferson's election as president in 1800 and the foreseeable decline in Federalist political power.

The Senate approved Marshall, although without a great deal of enthusiasm. No other single appointment affected the young nation more profoundly. From the court, Marshall championed the principles of federalism for 34 years, establishing firmly certain principles upon which a strong national government could be built.

Unlike many of his successors in the White House, Adams was proud of his choice to his dying day. In 1826 he wrote that "my gift of John Marshall to the people of the United States was the proudest act of my life. . . ."

President Andrew Jackson's selection of John McLean as a Supreme Court justice in 1829 illustrates the reasons a president may decide to ignore political loyalty in making such nominations.

McLean, postmaster general under Presidents Monroe and John Quincy Adams, was a constant and persistent aspirant to high office, especially the White House. He held the same Cabinet post under Jackson, who defeated Adams in 1828.

Hoping to end a potential rivalry for the presidency, Jackson named McLean to the court in return for which McLean agreed to abandon his presidential aspirations.

McLean did not live up to his end of the bargain, becoming a presidential candidate from the bench on four more occasions. He was never successful and continued to serve on the court until his death in 1861.

In contrast to the expediency of the McLean nomination was Jackson's persistence in naming Roger B. Taney, the president's faithful supporter and Treasury secretary, to the court.

When an associate justice's seat became vacant early in 1835, Jackson named Taney to the seat. Taney had complied with Jackson's controversial order to remove government deposits from the Bank of the United States during Jackson's war against the bank. The Senate killed the nomination and tried to abolish the vacant seat by reducing the size of the court — a move in which the House did not concur.

Several months later, in mid-1835, Chief Justice John Marshall died. Now Jackson had two seats to fill. In December he named Taney to succeed Marshall as chief justice. Taney was confirmed in March 1836 and served in that post for 28 years, earning a reputation as a great champion of states' rights. His best known opinion came in the *Dred Scott* case — one of the court's most vigorously and justifiably criticized decisions.

Chase and the Currency

Chief Justice Taney died on Oct. 12, 1864, with the nation in the midst of civil war. In weighing a successor to Taney, President Lincoln sought a man who would support him on matters of war policy and who also would help close the widening breach in the Republican Party over Lincoln's conduct of the war.

Salmon P. Chase, who had served as governor and senator from Ohio and as Lincoln's secretary of the Treasury, was Lincoln's choice. Chase was a political character, like McLean, and had sought the Republican presidential nomination in 1856 and 1860, and would do so again from the bench in 1868.

But Chase, notwithstanding his own political ambitions, steered the court on a neutral course in the difficult postwar years. He presided over the court as it dealt with challenges both to Lincoln's wartime policies and his postwar plans for reconciliation of the nation. His reluctance to preside at the treason trial of former Confederate President Jefferson Davis contributed to the eventual dismissal of those charges. And Chase's fair handling of the impeachment trial of President Andrew Johnson is considered an important factor in Johnson's eventual acquittal by the Senate.

In one major legal controversy growing out of the war, however, Chase rejected a key decision of Lincoln's, one in which he had played an important role in formulating as Treasury secretary. During the war, Congress, at the urging of the Lincoln administration, had passed legislation making paper money legal tender. When the war had ended, this law was challenged as unconstitutional, and when the court first acted on this challenge in 1870 Chase delivered the court's opinion holding the legal tender law unconstitutional.

'Court-Packing' — 1870 Style

The decision in the 1870 Legal Tender Case set the stage for the most efficient and successful use by a president of his power to reverse a decision of the Supreme Court through the nomination power.

In 1869 Congress had increased the size of the court from eight to nine members; at the same time, an associate justice had resigned, giving President Ulysses S. Grant the opportunity to fill two seats on the court.

Grant quickly chose two men for those vacancies; one was confirmed but died within four days of confirmation, the other was rejected by the Senate.

In February 1870 — even while Chief Justice Chase was announcing the court's 4-3 ruling that the Legal Tender Act was unconstitutional — Grant sent two new nominations to the Senate: Joseph P. Bradley and William Strong. Both were quickly confirmed. Soon after they took their seats, the court agreed to hear another legal tender case argued.

A year later the court, by a 5-4 vote, overruled its 1870 decision and upheld the power of Congress to make paper money legal tender. Bradley and Strong, the new justices, joined the three dissenting justices in the 1870 case to bring about one of the quickest reversals of a court decision in history.

Scholars still debate whether Grant intentionally "packed" the court to bring about that result. But intentional or not, it was the most successful "court-packing" in history.

'Court-Packing' — 1937 Style

Almost 70 years later, Franklin D. Roosevelt successfully used a court-packing proposal to convince the court to change its anti-New Deal direction.

Roosevelt's action was the most transparent example to date of a president bringing political pressure to bear on the court, and it temporarily landed Roosevelt in considerable political hot water.

In 1935 and 1936 the Supreme Court held unconstitutional almost every major New Deal measure proposed by the Roosevelt administration and approved by Congress to restructure the nation's staggering economy. Four members of the court, who often were joined by one or two others to form a majority, were totally antagonistic to the New Deal philosophy that called for government spending and programs to help farmers, laborers and businesses survive the Depression. *(Acts declared unconstitutional, p. 159)*

In 1936 Roosevelt won a stunning re-election victory. With that political mandate, he resolved to deal head-on with the obstructionist court. The court at that time was made up of older men who had served for some time; there had been no retirements or resignations during his first term.

Roosevelt proposed a "court reform" measure permitting a president to appoint a justice to the Supreme Court for every justice over 70 years of age who continued to serve, effectively expanding the court to a maximum of 18. At that time, there were six justices 70 or older, which would have given Roosevelt, under this plan, the opportunity to expand the court to 15 members.

The import of his proposal was clear, and even some of Roosevelt's most ardent supporters were outraged. The measure received an antagonistic reception on Capitol Hill and was voted down — unfavorably reported — by the Senate Judiciary Committee.

But within two months of the proposal, the court began to signal a more hospitable attitude toward New Deal policies, voting three times in the spring of 1937 to uphold major New Deal statutes. In May one of the four justices most adamantly opposed to the administration's New Deal policies — Willis Van Devanter — announced that he would retire, giving Roosevelt his first chance to name a member of the court.

These developments halted any remaining momentum behind the court-packing move. Roosevelt named a full-fledged New Deal advocate, Alabama Sen. Hugo L. Black, to the seat vacated by Van Devanter. During the remainder of his presidency Roosevelt named eight more justices, more than any other president in history except George Washington.

As a result of this confrontation, and FDR's appointments, the focus of the court's concerns and the nature of its rulings changed dramatically. In the next decade, the court acquiesced in the unprecedented increase in federal power over economic matters and social concerns and shifted its own forcus to matters of individual rights and liberties and away from its long preoccupation with private property rights and economic questions. All of the decisions holding New Deal measures unconstitutional were nullified, in most cases through acceptance by the court of substitute laws that Congress approved.

Modern Nomination Strategies

Modern presidents have continued in the tradition of Adams and Jackson and Grant and Franklin D. Roosevelt, sometimes even managing to create a court vacancy, as did Lyndon B. Johnson in 1965. Johnson wanted to place his friend and trusted adviser Abe Fortas on the Supreme Court — with an eye to making Fortas chief justice when Earl Warren relinquished the position. But there was no vacancy on the court, and its members were all relatively youthful.

Creating a Vacancy

Johnson, fresh from a landslide victory in the 1964 general election, was not deterred. He decided to convince the most junior justice, Arthur J. Goldberg, whom President Kennedy had appointed to the court in 1962, to leave the bench.

Goldberg did not wish to do so; he liked being a justice and described his three years on the bench as "the richest and most satisfying period" of his career. But Johnson appealed to Goldberg's sense of duty, telling him he was needed as U.S ambassador to the United Nations and encouraging Goldberg's hope that he could use that position to help end the war in Vietnam. Goldberg was persuaded to resign, whereupon he accepted the ambassadorial nomination.

Johnson then tried to convince Fortas, a successful Washington lawyer who enjoyed his practice and his role as presidential confidant, to accept a nomination to the court. Fortas was not enthusiastic.

Johnson finally had to use a pretext. He called Fortas to the White House, saying that he needed his advice on some matter of state. When Fortas arrived, Johnson told him they were about to hold a press conference, where the president would announce that he was nominating Fortas to the Supreme Court. Fortas was nominated and confirmed, but Johnson's plans for Fortas to become chief justice and Fortas' career on the court ended unhappily.

Saving the Seat

Throughout history, it has been difficult for lame-duck presidents to win confirmation of their Supreme Court nominees. The party that does not hold the White House has every reason — when a general election is near — to try to delay an impending court vacancy, or to block confirmation of the lame duck's nominee, in order to save the seat for their candidate if he should win the election.

Lyndon B. Johnson already was a lame-duck chief executive when Warren announced in 1968 that he intended to retire. Nevertheless, Johnson named Fortas as Warren's successor.

The Senate refused to confirm Fortas, in large part because Republican senators hoped that a Republican president would be elected and that he could then fill that prestigious post. The Republican strategy, plus concern about Fortas' continuing role as an unofficial presidential adviser and his acceptance of large fees for participating in university seminars while on the court, were enough to forestall confirmation. When a move to end the filibuster against him failed, Fortas asked Johnson to withdraw his nomination.

Richard Nixon won the presidency in 1968. In May 1969 he chose Warren E. Burger as chief justice, fulfilling the hopes of the Republicans who had worked to block confirmation of Fortas.

1969 Fortas Resignation

With his resignation in May 1969, Abe Fortas became the first man to leave the Supreme Court under the threat of impeachment. Despite other incipient attempts, only one justice has ever been impeached.

Fortas resigned less than a year after President Lyndon B. Johnson sent his name to the Senate for elevation to the chief justiceship. In October 1968 his nomination was withdrawn after it became clear the Senate would not confirm him.

Fortas resigned May 14. Ten days earlier, *Life* magazine had reported that in January 1966 — when he already was on the court — Fortas had accepted a $20,000 check from a family foundation set up by multimillionaire industrialist Louis E. Wolfson. Fortas had agreed to act as an adviser to the foundation, which worked to improve community relations. In September 1966 Wolfson was indicted (and later convicted) for selling unregistered securities. The article said Fortas returned the $20,000 to Wolfson in December 1966 and severed his connection with the foundation.

The same day the *Life* article was published, Fortas issued a statement declaring that he did not feel the fee implied any inducement for him to try to influence Wolfson's case.

His statement did not reassure many lawmakers, who felt Fortas had violated Canon 25 of the Canons of Judicial Ethics, which said a "judge should avoid giving any ground for any reasonable suspicion that he is utilizing the power or prestige of his office to persuade or coerce others to patronize or contribute, either to the success of private business, or to charitable enterprises."

On May 11 Rep. H. R. Gross, R-Iowa (1949-75), announced he had prepared articles of impeachment against Fortas to present to the House within a "reasonable" time if the justice did not resign. The articles, Gross said, accused Fortas of malfeasance, misconduct and impropriety. Calls for resignation began to come not only from the conservative Republicans and Southern Democrats in the Senate who had blocked his confirmation as chief justice but also from liberal Democrats who had supported him in the earlier fight.

On May 13 Rep. Clark MacGregor, R-Minn. (1961-71), apparently with the blessing of the administration, proposed a preliminary inquiry into the affair by the House Judiciary Committee. Fortas submitted his resignation the next day.

In a letter to Chief Justice Warren, Fortas maintained he had done nothing wrong. But he said he feared that continued controversy over his association with the foundation would "adversely affect the work" of the court and that his resignation "will enable the Court to proceed with its vital work free from extraneous stress."

Even before Burger was nominated, Fortas had left the court. In May 1969 *Life* magazine, in a story later believed to have been leaked to that publication by the Nixon administration, reported that Fortas in 1966 had accepted a large fee from the family foundation of Louis E. Wolfson. Millionaire Wolfson later went to prison for illegal stock manipulations. Rather than face a full-scale impeachment inquiry, Fortas resigned from the court May 15, 1969. It was a premature and ignominious ending for the Supreme Court career of the able, if reluctant, justice. *(Details, box, p. 13; biography, p. 171)*

The Nixon Nominations

Since the Adams-Jefferson contest of 1800, the Supreme Court, its personnel as well as its decisions, has been a recurring issue in presidential campaigns.

The 1968 presidential campaign, conducted while many of the court's liberal rulings on criminal law, school prayer and reapportionment were fresh in the public's mind, — was something of a referendum on the Warren court. While Hubert H. Humphrey, the Democratic contender, approved most of those rulings, Nixon made it plain that he did not.

He said that if he were elected, he would appoint "strict constructionists" to the court who would cast it in a more conservative image. Nixon's most severe criticism of the court focused on its criminal law rulings. In a campaign that often was characterized as a "law-and-order" election strategy, he charged that the court's decisions — intended to preserve the constitutional rights of criminal suspects — were "seriously hamstringing the peace forces in our society and strengthening the criminal forces."

Nixon's first nomination to the court, Warren E. Burger, was right in line with his campaign rhetoric. Burger, since 1956 a conservative member of an increasingly liberal U.S. circuit court of appeals in the District of Columbia, had come to Nixon's attention precisely because of his criticism of the Warren court on criminal matters. "This seeming anxiety of judges to protect every accused person from every consequence of his voluntary utterances is giving rise to myriad rules, subrules, variations and exceptions which even the most alert and sophisticated lawyers and judges are taxed to follow," Burger had written. He warned that "we are approaching the predicament of the centipede on the fly paper — each time one leg is placed to give support for relief of a leg already 'stuck,' another becomes captive and soon all are securely immobilized."

Burger was confirmed easily as chief justice, but Nixon's efforts to appoint a conservative judge to replace Fortas ran into Senate opposition.

In his campaign for Southern votes, Nixon had promised that he would name a conservative Southerner to the court. His first choice for Fortas' seat — Judge Clement F. Haynsworth Jr. of South Carolina, a distinguished court of appeals judge — fit that description. But the bitterness among Fortas supporters in the Senate, who felt that Fortas had been forced to leave the court merely because of the appearance of possible conflict of interest, leveled similar charges at Haynsworth, arguing that he, a wealthy man, had participated as a judge in cases in which he had some financial interest, however small. In November 1969 the Senate refused to confirm Haynsworth. *(Details, p. 35)*

Determined to find a Southern conservative to place on the court, Nixon then submitted the name of G. Harrold Carswell, a Floridian who had served as a federal district

---

Deaths of Recent Supreme Court Justices

Eight former Supreme Court justices died during the dozen years from 1970 to 1982.

Two — Hugo L. Black and John Marshall Harlan — retired in failing health and died within a short time of leaving the bench. Two others — Earl Warren and William O. Douglas — lived several years after their retirement from the court.

The other four — Abe Fortas, Tom Clark, Charles Whittaker and Stanley Reed — left the court at least a decade before their death.

Fortas, after resigning in May 1969, practiced law in Washington. In March 1982 he made his first appearance before the court since his resignation, arguing a case for Puerto Rico's Popular Democratic Party. Within two weeks, he was dead, the victim of a heart attack.

Tom Clark, who made his name as Truman's staunchly anti-communist attorney general, was Truman's third appointee to the Supreme Court. He served there from 1949 until 1967, when he resigned to avoid any conflict of interest. His son, Ramsey Clark, had become Lyndon Johnson's attorney general. Clark was active until his death in June 1977, serving as the first director of the Federal Judicial Center, an organization that studies ways to improve the administration of the courts. Clark also accepted temporary assignments to sit as a judge on various U.S. appellate courts across the country to ease the courts' workload. He died June 13, 1977, at age 77.

Charles Whittaker, placed on the court by President Eisenhower in 1957, served only five years. He resigned in 1962, exhausted from overwork. He lived 11 years after his resignation, dying on Nov. 26, 1973, at the age of 72.

Stanley Reed, the man whom Whittaker succeeded on the court, outlived Whittaker. Reed, who served as solicitor general in the Roosevelt administration, was placed on the court by Roosevelt in 1938. He served for 19 years, retiring in 1957 at age 73. He died April 2, 1980, at age 95.

---

judge and, for a few years, as an appeals court judge.

Carswell lacked the distinguished legal and judicial record that Haynsworth brought to the nomination. Carswell also had made staunchly segregationist speeches earlier in his career. These factors, plus his general lack of intellectual distinction as a judge, provided ample basis for the Senate's decision in April 1970 to reject his nomination.

Bitter at these two defeats, Nixon moved to the Midwest, choosing Minnesotan Harry A. Blackmun, a quiet man who had served for a number of years on the U.S. court of appeals, 8th circuit, and a longtime friend of Burger's.

Blackmun, whose record was that of a moderate, and whose qualifications were impeccable, was easily confirmed.

Nixon had two more court vacancies to fill, and he filled them with conservatives. But having learned a lesson from the Haynsworth-Carswell debacle, he chose more carefully and tested the political waters before casting his nominations upon them.

In September 1971 two veteran justices, Hugo L. Black, Roosevelt's first court nominee, and John Marshall Harlan, placed on the court by Eisenhower, retired.

In October 1971, after several trial balloons promoting other names had been shot down by public or congressional opposition, Nixon named Lewis F. Powell Jr. to Black's seat and William H. Rehnquist to Harlan's.

Powell, a wealthy and distinguished Virginia lawyer with a strong record of community service, had served both as a member of Lyndon B. Johnson's Commission on Law Enforcement and the Administration of Justice and as president of the American Bar Association. He had made no secret of his view that the Warren court had moved too far in some cases toward protecting the suspect at the cost of protecting society. There was virtually unanimous acclaim for his nomination, and he was easily confirmed in December.

Rehnquist was little known outside of Washington, where he had served as an assistant attorney general in the Nixon administration, and Phoenix, where he had practiced law before coming to Washington in 1969.

Neither Rehnquist's intellectual capability nor his conservative views were seriously questioned during the confirmation process. The only real opposition to his nomination came from civil rights and civil liberties groups, who disagreed philosophically with his views. He also was confirmed that December.

By late 1971, within three years of taking office, Nixon had placed four "strict constructionists" on the court, more than any first-term president in half a century.

But the result was not quite what Nixon expected. At least one of his nominees — Blackmun — turned out to be more of a moderate than a conservative. Blackmun in fact was the author of the court's most controversial ruling of the decade. Speaking for the majority in a 1973 decision, Blackmun wrote that the Constitution protects a woman's decision to have an abortion.

And in 1974 it was this court, with the concurrence of three of Nixon's own nominees, that told the president that he, like any citizen, must comply with a prosecutor's subpoena for evidence. That July ruling led directly to Nixon's resignation from the presidency. *(Watergate tapes issue, p. 26)*

Ford, Douglas and Stevens

In 1971, as the Senate was confirming Rehnquist and Powell, House Minority Leader Gerald R. Ford, R-Mich., little dreamed that he would be the one choosing the next Supreme Court nominee.

Chosen first to replace Spiro T. Agnew as vice president in 1973, Ford succeeded to the presidency when Nixon resigned in August 1974.

Thus Ford was president when Justice William O. Douglas retired in 1975, after establishing a new record for longevity on the court. Douglas had suffered a stroke earlier that year, and in November he announced his retirement. He had served 36 and one-half years, many of them

characterized by controversy and criticism directed not only at his judicial performance but also at his independent and inconoclastic lifestyle. *(Biography, p. 173)*

It was highly ironic that Rep. Gerald R. Ford would choose Douglas' successor. In the wake of the rejection of Haynsworth and Carswell in 1969 and 1970, it was Ford who had spearheaded an attempt to begin an impeachment inquiry against Douglas. But the inquiry came to nothing.

There was no controversy surrounding Ford's choice to succeed Douglas: John Paul Stevens. Ford acted within three weeks of Douglas' announcement. Ford considered some two dozen men and women for the seat; both the American Bar Association and the FBI scrutinized the names.

One factor working for Stevens' selection was the backing of Ford's attorney general, Edward H. Levi, who came to the Cabinet from the University of Chicago, where Stevens had done some lecturing. Stevens, since 1970 a member of the U.S. court of appeals, 7th circuit, had practiced law in Chicago before being named to the bench by Nixon.

In announcing his selection, Ford emphasized that Stevens was the best qualified person he could find to succeed Douglas.

The ABA committee that had checked the list of possible nominees gave Stevens its highest rating, concluding that he met high standards of professional competence, integrity and judicial temperament.

Ford did not meet Stevens until the week he announced the selection. The judge had been a guest at a White House dinner for the judiciary the Monday night preceding the Friday on which his nomination was announced.

After informing Stevens of his selection, he notified key members of Congress before announcing it to the nation. Ford's press secretary said that Ford did not know what religion or party Stevens belonged to and that neither was considered in making the choice.

Stevens was easily confirmed in December and took his seat on the court before the holidays.

Reagan and O'Connor

The selection of a man to succeed Douglas disappointed those who had hoped Ford would appoint the first woman justice. Among those who were disappointed was First Lady Betty Ford, who had actively promoted a woman for the job.

President Jimmy Carter made it clear he would give strong consideration to putting a woman on the court. But during Carter's term there were no resignations or retirements from the court.

During the 1980 presidential campaign, the Carter record on appointing women to federal judgeships, plus the increasing political punch of women voters, persuaded Ronald Reagan to promise that he would appoint a woman to the court if given the opportunity.

Within six months of taking office, Reagan made good on that pledge. In June 1981 Justice Potter Stewart announced he would retire at the end of the current court term — early in July. Reagan wasted no time. Stewart retired on July 3. On July 7 Reagan proudly announced the selection of Arizona Judge Sandra Day O'Connor as Stewart's successor.

O'Connor had met Reagan only once before the president chose her. She was little-known outside her home

Changes in the Federal Judiciary...

Besides the power to nominate persons to the Supreme Court, the president is able to fill the lower federal courts — the district courts and the courts of appeals — with men and women of his choice.

The president's power to name persons to these well-paid, prestigious, lifetime posts is perhaps his strongest patronage lever. Federal judgeships traditionally go to persons of the president's political party.

In apparent contradiction of the American ideal of an independent, nonpartisan judiciary, the process of selecting federal judges is pure politics. No constitutional guidelines exist; only custom dictates that the president nominate and the Senate confirm federal judges below the Supreme Court level. Only tradition requires that federal judges reside in their districts or that they be attorneys.

Senatorial Courtesy

Under a tradition going back to 1840, senators of the president's party are awarded the prerogative of selecting persons for vacant or newly created federal judgeships that develop within their states. If there are no senators of his party from the state, the president usually looks to the party organization in the state for suggested nominees.

Senatorial recommendations carry less weight in the choice of persons for seats on the courts of appeals, each of which has jurisdiction over cases from a number of states. On most circuit courts of appeals, however, it is customary for each state to have some representation on the court at all times.

Once the nomination is made, it is sent from the White House to the Senate, where it is referred to the Senate Judiciary Committee. Hearings are held on virtually every nomination, but they are rarely more than perfunctory proceedings of brief length. Usually, the panel routinely recommends that the Senate confirm the nominee, which often occurs by voice vote and without debate.

Before the confirmation vote, a senator can object to a nominee for specific reasons or by using the stock, but rare, objection that the nominee is "personally obnoxious" to him. In this case, other senators usually join in blocking confirmation out of courtesy to their colleague.

An Era of Change: 1969-82

The federal judiciary in 1982, though the smallest of the three branches of government, was larger and quite different from what it had been in 1969, the year Warren E. Burger became chief justice. The expansion was due in large part to congressional recognition of the need for additional judges. The biggest change came in 1978, when Congress handed President Jimmy Carter a large patronage plum, enacting legislation expanding the size of the federal judicial branch by one-third, creating 152 new judgeships for Carter to fill. And the president filled those posts with liberal and moderate men and women, naming more women, more blacks and more Hispanics to federal judgeships than had any other president.

The importance of these judicial appointments, although often overlooked, is difficult to overestimate. These men and women preside over all federal trials and civil cases; it is their actions and decisions that determine federal law in many instances. Only a handful are ever reviewed by the Supreme Court.

These people are the federal judicial branch in their community; how they perform their duties has an immeasurable impact upon the confidence and respect their fellow citizens have for the system as a whole. And every federal judge is a potential candidate for a Supreme Court seat. Four current justices served first as federal appeals court judges.

The Nixon-Ford Legacy

Early in his second term, Richard Nixon surpassed Franklin Roosevelt's record for the most federal judges appointed by a president. In his five and a half years in office, Nixon named 213 federal district and appeals court judges, all but 15 of whom were Republicans. Nixon and his successor, Gerald Ford, between 1969 and 1976 chose five of the nine Supreme Court justices, 57 of the 97 judges on the U.S. courts of appeals, and 221 of 400 federal district judges.

Most of these appointees were men who had good Republican connections and shared Nixon and Ford's belief in judicial restraint, shunning the activism and concern for individual rights that had characterized the federal judiciary during the tenure of Chief Justice Earl Warren.

One of these men — William Webster — became director of the FBI in 1978. Appointed a federal district judge by Nixon in 1970, Webster moved to the U.S. court of appeals for the 8th circuit in 1973, again under Nixon. President Jimmy Carter chose him for the FBI post, in which he compiled a notable record for his management of that agency and his political skills in dealing with Congress.

Another Nixon nominee — John Paul Stevens — whom Nixon in 1970 placed on the U.S. court of appeals, 7th circuit, was Ford's choice for the Supreme Court five years later.

Another Nixon selection — Cornelia G. Kennedy — placed on the federal bench in 1970, was fre-

...Since the Nixon Presidency

quently mentioned as a potential nominee to the high court. Carter promoted her to the court of appeals, 6th circuit, in 1979.

Carter's Judges

Nixon's record did not stand long. Aided by the act of Congress that created 152 new federal judgeships, Carter dramatically changed the face of the federal judiciary during his administration.

During the 1976 presidential campaign, Ford and Carter each pledged to reduce the politics involved in picking judges and to appoint more women and minorities to the bench. After his election, Carter instituted a merit selection process, using panels to supply him with the names of persons best qualified for the courts of appeals vacancies that arose. The 1978 judgeships bill also required the issuance of "standards" for selecting judicial nominees. In line with this provision, senators in 30 states set up some mechanism for merit selection of judges.

Carter appointed 262 federal judges — 206 to district court posts and 56 to appeals court seats. Among those there were more women, more blacks and more Hispanics than ever before.

Of Carter's 56 appeals court appointees, 11 were women, nine were blacks and two were Hispanics. One of the nine blacks was a woman. Of the 206 district court appointees, 29 were women, 29 were blacks and 14 were Hispanics. Six of the 29 blacks were women, and one of the Hispanic appointees was a woman.

The diversity Carter achieved in his judicial appointments is dramatically demonstrated when his record is compared with those of other recent presidents. On the district court, 14.1 percent of Carter's appointees were women and 14.1 percent were blacks. By comparison, 1.6 percent of President Johnson's appointees were women and 3.3 percent were blacks. Of Nixon's appointments, 0.6 percent were women and 2.8 percent were blacks.

The comparison of Carter's appeals court appointees with those of previous presidents is even more striking. Almost one-fifth (19.6 percent) of Carter's appointments were women, while 16.1 percent were blacks; 2.5 percent of Johnson's appointees were women and 5 percent were blacks. Neither Nixon nor Ford appointed any women or blacks to appellate court seats.

The Reagan Record

The appointment of federal judges was again an issue in the 1980 campaign. Republicans emphasized the importance of judicial nominees' legal philosophy.

The Republican Party platform called for appointing judges who believed in "the decentralization of the federal government and efforts to return decision-making power to state and local elected officials." In reference to the abortion issue, the platform pledged that Republicans would "work for the appointment of judges at all levels of the judiciary who respect the traditional family values and the sanctity of innocent human life."

During the campaign, however, candidate Reagan emphasized that he would not decide on a potential nominee solely on one or two issues. "The whole philosophical viewpoint of the individual would be considered," he said.

In his first two years in office, Reagan not only nominated one member to the Supreme Court, Sandra Day O'Connor, the court's first woman justice, but also 88 persons to federal district and appeals courts seats.

Reagan discarded the guidelines set up during the Carter administration to ensure merit selection of nominees. A memorandum made public March 6, 1981, by Attorney General William French Smith suggested that each senator submit three to five candidates for district court seats and "encouraged" senators to screen those nominees to ensure that "highly qualified candidates are identified and recommended." Two months later, without fanfare, Reagan abolished the commissions Carter had set up to screen candidates for appeals court seats, returning to the less formal process of selecting these persons with input from Republicans in Congress, party officials, interest groups and sitting federal judges.

Most of Reagan's nominees were white males. Of the 88 federal district and appeals court nominations in his first two years in office, only one went to a black, three to women and two to Hispanics.

Most of Reagan's nominees were conservatives. One Justice Department official closely involved in the judicial selection process explained that Reagan had come into office realizing that Carter had appointed many judges of a philosophy quite different from Reagan's. "By and large," continued the official, "Carter tended to appoint people who have a very activist role in mind for the judiciary, who believe that judicial intervention can solve all manner of problems that might better be left to political intervention. The number of appointments was so massive that we would have been derelict in our responsibility if we did not pay some attention to our obligation to produce some semblance of balance."

Sheldon Goldman, a University of Massachusetts political science professor who has studied judicial selection closely, has said: "I think the Reagan administration has taken full advantage of the prerogatives of the presidency. They put on the bench those kind of people who are compatible with their ideology and political commitment. That was true of the Carter administration as well."

state, but she had the strong backing of two major political figures: Arizona Republican Sen. Barry Goldwater and Justice William H. Rehnquist, a Stanford Law School classmate of O'Connor's and a fellow Arizonan.

Reagan's selection clearly was a political coup. Although O'Connor appeared to share many of Reagan's conservative views, it was virtually impossible for any women's group to oppose the selection. In fact, the only opposition that arose came from the very conservative groups who targeted their concern on the issue of abortion. Merely by placing Reagan in opposition to those groups, the choice of O'Connor won the president some political points with moderate and liberal voters. *(Confirmation details, p. 37)*

THE COURT AND
THE ELECTION RETURNS

"No matter whether th' constitution follows th' flag or not," wrote Finley Peter Dunne, a turn-of-the-century commentator and humorist, "th' Supreme Court follows th' iliction returns." He was referring to the court's apparent concern about which way the political winds in the country were blowing and its tendency to mold its decisions to fit them.

In the 1970s the court seemed determined to refute this adage, particularly during the first years of that decade when President Richard M. Nixon proposed a number of policies that were quickly challenged before the court. Even the fact that four of its members were his appointees by 1972 was not enough to swing the court's decisions on most of these issues in Nixon's favor.

Early in the 1980s, another president — Ronald Reagan — proposed major shifts in national policy on a number of controversial issues, from abortion and civil rights to taxes. These, too, found their way quickly to the high court, and the nation watched closely to see what the justices' response would be.

The Nixon Experience

National security was a paramount concern of the Nixon administration. Mired in an unpopular war in Vietnam and fending off increasingly powerful waves of antiwar protest at home, Nixon and his aides were intent upon enforcing the Selective Service Act, curtailing the activities of domestic groups they viewed as subversive, and maintaining control over the release of official information about the Vietnam conflict.

The Supreme Court, on the other hand, tended to be receptive to those who protested certain Selective Service regulations, ruling in 1970 that the Selective Service System could not revoke deferments or accelerate the induction of persons who turned in their draft cards as a protest against the war.

The court that year also broadened the basis for conscientious objector status, holding that persons objecting to war because of deeply held moral or ethical beliefs were entitled to such status, even if they disavowed any religious basis for that belief.

The following year, the court overturned the conviction of the well-known black boxer Cassius Clay, who later changed his name to Mohammed Ali, for refusing induction. Clay had been denied conscientious objector status. The court held that the appeals board that issued the denial had failed to specify the reasons for its decision, thus its action was invalid.

In 1972 the court rebuffed the Nixon administration's claim that it had an inherent power to use wiretaps to keep track of the activities of persons or domestic groups that were suspected of subversive activities. The administration argued that it did not have to get a federal judge to approve each instance of such surveillance. The court said it did.

Justice Lewis F. Powell Jr., only six months into his term on the court, wrote the opinion, stating that "the price of lawful public dissent must not be a dread of subjection to an unchecked surveillance power. Nor must the fear of unauthorized official eavesdropping deter vigorous citizen dissent and discussion of government action in private conversations. For private dissent, no less than open public discourse, is essential to our free society." *(United States v. U.S. District Court, Eastern Michigan)*

William H. Rehnquist, another Nixon nominee, did not participate in the decision; Chief Justice Burger dissented.

The administration clashed with two of the nation's major newspapers in 1971, in the most dramatic First Amendment confrontation of the decade. In June *The Washington Post* and *The New York Times* published a series of articles based on a classified, government-produced account of U.S. involvement in Vietnam, the so-called Pentagon Papers. The documents had been copied by Daniel Ellsberg, a former Defense Department analyst, who then supplied the newspapers with copies of the papers.

The administration went to federal court seeking injunctions to halt the Post and the Times from publishing the articles. Attorney General John N. Mitchell argued that publication would threaten the national security and U.S. war efforts in Vietnam. Such an order was granted in the Times case, and denied in the Post case, by different lower courts in different cities.

Both cases moved quickly to the Supreme Court, which heard arguments immediately and just as quickly denied the administration's request for the injunctions. The vote was 6-3; each justice wrote a separate opinion expressing his views, but the point on which the majority agreed was that the government had to show much more danger to U.S. national security before it could win such an extraordinary order curtailing the freedom of the press to publish. *(New York Times v. United States, United States v. The Washington Post)*

To permit such a curtailment of freedom of the press, wrote Justices Hugo L. Black and William O. Douglas, "would make a shambles of the First Amendment.... The press was to serve the governed, not the governors. The government's power to censor the press was abolished so that the press would remain forever free to censure the government."

Chief Justice Burger and Justice Harry A. Blackmun, the only two Nixon appointees on the court at that time, dissented, as did Justice John Marshall Harlan. Burger wrote that the newspapers that received the Pentagon Papers shared "one of the basic and simple duties of every citizen with respect to the discovery ... of stolen property or secret government documents ... to report forthwith, to responsible public officers. This duty rests on taxi drivers, Justices and *The New York Times.*"

Domestic Issues

Nixon fared no better from the court when he sought major changes in domestic policy. The administration opposed the use of busing to desegregate public schools. But the court in 1971 unanimously approved the use of busing as a permissible interim means of ending state-imposed racial segregation of public schools. Burger wrote the court's opinion, in the case of *Swann v. Charlotte-Mecklenburg County Board of Education.*

Nixon favored increased aid by the states and the federal government to private and parochial schools. Four times during his term — in 1971 and in a set of 1973 cases — the court refused to approve various forms of state aid to such schools, holding that it violated the First Amendment ban on state action establishing an official religion.

During the 1968 campaign for the presidency, one of the primary themes sounded by Nixon when he spoke about the Warren court was his charge that through its rulings the court was hamstringing police efforts to curtail crime.

No decision of the Warren court drew more criticism on this point than its 1966 ruling in *Miranda v. Arizona,* which required police, before questioning a suspect in custody, to inform him that he had a constitutional right to remain silent in the face of incriminatory questions and to have the aid of an attorney during all critical stages of the investigation. If police failed to issue these warnings, any confession they obtained could not be used in court.

In 1971 the court appeared ready to modify *Miranda,* ruling in a case entitled *Harris v. New York* that statements from suspects who were not fully advised of their rights could be used if they conflicted with the suspect's in-court testimony. This ruling came by a narrow 5-4 margin, however, and within three years it had become clear that no further modification of *Miranda* would be forthcoming. In 1974 the court, by an 8-1 vote, reaffirmed *Miranda,* applying it to prevent the use of statements taken from a suspect not fully advised of his rights even though his arrest preceded the *Miranda* ruling. His trial followed that ruling, thus the rule applied in his case, wrote Nixon nominee William H. Rehnquist for the court. *(Michigan v. Tucker,* 1974)

Part of the Nixon administration's law-and-order policy was a firm belief in the efficacy of the death penalty as a deterrent to crime. But in 1972 the court effectively invalidated all existing capital punishment laws, ruling in *Furman v. Georgia, Jackson v. Georgia* and *Branch v. Texas* that such laws permitted the death penalty to be imposed in such a haphazard way as to be unconstitutional. All four Nixon nominees — Burger, Blackmun, Powell and Rehnquist — dissented.

Four years later, the court approved certain revised state death penalty laws by a vote of 7-2. The Nixon nominees were in the majority in those rulings.

On another issue, however, the court dealt the Nixon administration an unexpected blow early in 1973, the same week that Nixon was inaugurated for his second term after his landslide election victory the previous November.

By a 7-2 vote, the court ruled that the Constitution protected a woman's right to have an abortion early in pregnancy. With Justice Blackmun — one of Nixon's supposedly conservative court appointees — writing the opinion, the court with one stroke denied states the power to ban abortion as a criminal act under all circumstances. This ruling, in *Roe v. Wade* and *Doe v. Bolton,* was strongly criticized by Nixon himself; it set off a decade of increasingly vigorous efforts by groups opposed to abortion to win reversal of the court's ruling.

Several times during his presidency, Nixon claimed the power to impound — that is, to refuse to spend — money Congress specifically had provided for certain programs. Congress generally protested that the president lacked such power. Only one case involving this issue found its way to the Supreme Court, and this one was decided a year after Nixon left office. Once again, however, Nixon lost.

The court was unanimous in a February 1975 decision, *Train v. New York, Train v. Campaign Clean Water,* denying the president the power to impound funds authorized by Congress in the Water Pollution Control Act of 1972. Tying its ruling very closely to the language of that particular law, the court held that Congress left the president no leeway to withhold the funds it had authorized to be spent. The ruling resulted in the release of $9 billion provided in the authorization law and withheld by Nixon.

All of Nixon's other losses at the hands of the court paled in comparison to the final one — a personal humiliation as well as a policy defeat. When the Watergate special prosecutor insisted on his subpoena of White House tape recordings for use as evidence at the trial of former White House aides accused of trying to cover up their involvement in the June 1972 break-in at the headquarters of the Democratic National Committee, Nixon did not hesitate to take the matter to the high court.

After all, he had appointed four of its nine members, and surely he could count on winning one more vote, especially when he couched his argument in terms of executive privilege — the need of all presidents to preserve the confidentiality of their conversations in the Oval Office. But Nixon overlooked the fact that he came to the court in the posture of a suspect arguing against a prosecutor, and he had handpicked his court appointees for their sympathy with prosecutorial arguments. In that respect, he had chosen well.

Rehnquist did not take part in the court's consideration of the case of *United States v. Nixon.* He had come to Washington to work with Attorney General John Mitchell, who now was one of the coverup trial defendants.

The remaining eight justices voted unanimously against Nixon. Chief Justice Burger spoke for the court as it ordered him to surrender the tapes, a decision that compelled Nixon to surrender his office.

Reagan Referendum

Once again in the early 1980s, the court's decisions would demonstrate whether it was indeed responsive to public opinion as evidenced by the election returns.

After his landslide victory in 1980, President Ronald Reagan entered the White House confident of his mandate to make major changes in national policy in a number of areas.

Reagan took a conservative approach to the issues of civil and individual rights. He espoused an end to school busing, supported federal tuition tax credits for parents who sent their children to private and parochial schools, called for limits on the use of affirmative action to compensate for past discrimination, and advocated giving states more leeway to regulate abortions.

In the area of criminal law, Reagan proposed that the controversial exclusionary rule be modified to permit some use of illegally obtained evidence. For 70 years a major courtroom tool to protect the rights of criminal suspects, this rule generally barred use of evidence taken in violation of the defendant's rights.

And Reagan moved to lighten the load that, according to the president, government regulation placed on American business.

By January 1983, midway into his first term, all these proposed changes were under review by the Supreme Court. How the court ruled on them in all likelihood would determine their fate. A negative ruling declaring them unconstitutional would doom the administration's efforts.

In January the court acted on one of these issues, which the administration lost. The court rejected a request that it review a school busing case from Nashville, Tenn., and upheld a federal district judge's decision that it was more important for young students to attend their neighborhood school than it was for them to be bused to a more distant and more desegregated school.

Still awaiting the court's decision were cases in which:

● A Minnesota law giving state taxpayers a tax credit for certain school expenses was challenged as violating the First Amendment ban on establishment of religion. Both private and public school parents were able to take advantage of this credit, but the lion's share of the benefit went to those private school parents who paid tuition. A ruling that the Minnesota plan was unconstitutional would almost certainly doom Reagan's related nationwide proposal. The case was named *Mueller v. Allen.*

● Bob Jones University and the Goldsboro Christian Schools challenged the refusal of the Internal Revenue Service (IRS) to grant them tax-exempt status. The IRS refusal — which was not supported by the Reagan administration — was grounded in the schools' anti-black policies. The schools argued that those policies were religiously based and that the IRS action violated their First Amendment freedom of religion.

● White firefighters and policemen in Boston protested a federal judge's use of the affirmative action policy to override the usual employment rule — "last hired, first fired" — for determining who would be laid off when budget cuts dictated staff reductions. The Reagan administration joined this case on the side of the whites, urging a limit to the use of this remedial policy. These cases were *Boston Firefighters Union v. Boston Chapter, National Association for the Advancement of Colored People (NAACP), Boston Police Patrolmen's Association Inc. v. Castro, Beecher v. Boston Chapter, NAACP.*

● The city of Akron, Ohio, and the state of Missouri sought to impose a number of requirements upon women seeking, and on doctors who provided, abortions. These included mandatory hospitalization for all abortions after the first three months, discussion of particular aspects of abortion by the doctor with the patient before the operation was performed, and parental or judicial consent for unmarried minors. Some of these requirements were imposed even on abortions that took place in the first three months of pregnancy, the period in which the Supreme Court said in 1973 that the abortion decision was one strictly between a woman and her doctor. The administration, entering the Akron case, urged the court to permit

such regulation by states and cities unless it could be shown that such rules impermissibly burdened a woman's decision to have an abortion. The cases were *Akron v. Akron Center for Reproductive Health, Akron Center for Reproductive Health v. Akron, Planned Parenthood Association of Kansas City v. Ashcroft, Ashcroft v. Planned Parenthood of Kansas City.*

● Illinois, the Reagan administration and 31 other states and a number of law enforcement groups asked the court to modify the rule barring use of illegally obtained evidence and to permit its use when police, in acquiring it, acted in good faith and within constitutional limits. This case, *Illinois v. Gates,* involved the seizure of 350 pounds of marijuana from a car owned by a couple who were accused by an anonymous informant of drug dealing. The police who seized the drugs had a search warrant, but it later was held invalid because the warrant was based on the anonymous tip. The Reagan administration, which already had asked Congress to pass a law creating this type of "good-faith exception" to the exclusionary rule, filed a friend-of-the-court brief urging the justices to approve this exception.

● The auto industry and the Reagan administration asked the court to permit the rescission of a federal rule requiring all cars made in the United States to have air bags or automatic seat belts. The administration rescinded the rule in 1981, but an appeals court in 1982 declared that action arbitrary and capricious and reinstated the rule. The cases were *Motor Vehicle Manufacturers Association of the United States v. State Farm Mutual Automobile Insurance Co., Consumer Alert v. State Farm, Department of Transportation v. State Farm.*

● The nuclear power industry and the administration asked the court to reverse two federal court rulings requiring the federal agency regulating nuclear energy — the Nuclear Regulatory Commission (NRC) — to step up, rather than decrease, its regulation of the industry. In one case, the industry protested a court ruling requiring federal evaluation of the stresses that changes in the operation of a nuclear power plant can place on nearby communities. In the second case, the NRC appealed a decision requiring it to deal with the problem of nuclear waste disposal anew each time it licensed a nuclear power plant. The cases were *Metropolitan Edison Co. v. People Against Nuclear Energy, Nuclear Regulatory Commission v. People Against Nuclear Energy, Baltimore Gas and Electric Co. v. Natural Resources Defense Council (NRDC), Nuclear Regulatory Commission v. NRDC, Commonwealth Edison Company v. NRDC.*

JUSTICES AND POLITICS: THE MYTH AND THE REALITY

"When a priest enters a monastery, he must leave . . . all sorts of worldly desires behind him," wrote Justice Felix Frankfurter in 1943. "And this court has no excuse for being unless it's a monastery."

The tradition to which Frankfurter referred holds that justices, once they don their robes of office, should avoid involvement in political affairs. But a closer look at the reality of judicial life throughout the court's history — including Frankfurter's own career — shows that this tradition is, in the words of Bruce Alan Murphy, "more myth than history."

In 1982 Murphy published *The Brandeis/Frankfurter Connection*, a fascinating history of the secret political activities of Louis D. Brandeis, whose Supreme Court career spanned 22 years (1916-38), and Frankfurter, a member of the court from 1939 to 1962. Brandeis and Frankfurter are among the most brilliant and most respected justices of the 20th century.

Despite Frankfurter's metaphor of the monastery, with which Murphy prefaces his book, Murphy makes clear that these justices did not inherit a tradition in which Supreme Court justices divorced themselves from politics. To the contrary, he says, "fully two-thirds of all those who have sat on the court have engaged in some sort of off-the-bench political activity."

Nothing in the Constitution — except perhaps some of the language concerning the separation of powers — forbids justices to try to influence what goes on in the halls of Congress or in the offices of the executive branch, including the White House itself. Generally, however, it has been felt that such activities impair the functioning of the court by lessening public respect for the justices and their work. In 1948 Justice Owen J. Roberts declared that "every justice . . . who was bitten by political ambition and . . . actively promoted his own candidacy for office has hurt his own career as a judge and has hurt the court."

Candidacies and Campaigning

Blatant political ambitions have not been evident on the present court, nor on the Warren court, but earlier in the nation's history they were practically a constant factor in the court's work.

The first chief justice, John Jay, ran unsuccessfully for governor of New York from his seat on the court. A few years later, he accepted President George Washington's appointment as a special ambassador to England while still holding the post of chief justice, which he eventually relinquished after being elected governor of New York in 1795.

Jay's successor, Oliver Ellsworth, served as chief justice for three years and then, in 1799, also without relinquishing the chief justiceship, accepted the post of ambassador to France. From France, he finally resigned his court post the following year. This extrajudicial work of the first two chief justices was criticized during the presidential campaign of 1800.

Early justices did not hesitate to campaign openly for their party's candidates. Justices Samuel Chase (1796-1811) and Bushrod Washington (1798-1829) campaigned actively in 1800 for presidential candidates John Adams and Charles Pinckney, respectively. Chase's campaigning was denounced by the anti-Federalist press, which complained, somewhat disingenuously, that the justice was neglecting his court duties.

Other politically minded 19th century justices included Smith Thompson (1823-43), John McLean (1829-61), Salmon P. Chase, the chief justice (1864-73), who presided over the Senate impeachment trial of President Andrew Johnson, David Davis (1862-77) and Stephen J. Field (1863-97). Like Chief Justice Jay before him, Justice Thompson, a Democrat, ran for governor of New York in 1828 but, unlike Jay, conducted an all-out campaign — and lost.

28 Court Members Also Served in Congress

Of the 102 justices, 27 served in the Senate, the House or both chambers before they served on the court. One other justice, David Davis, left the court to serve in Congress. In 1877 the Illinois legislature elected Davis to the U.S. Senate.

A list of the justices with congressional service follows:

Justice	Congressional Service	Court Service
Senate		
William Paterson	1789-Nov. 13, 1790	1793-1806
Oliver Ellsworth	1789-March 8, 1796	1796-1799
Levi Woodbury	1825-31; 1841-1845	1845-1851
David Davis	1877-1883	1862-1877
Salmon P. Chase*	1849-1855; March 4-6, 1861	1864-1873
Stanley Matthews	March 21, 1877-1879	1881-1889
Howell E. Jackson	1881-April 4, 1886	1894-1895
Edward D. White*	1891-March 12, 1894	1894-1921
Hugo L. Black	1927-Aug. 19, 1937	1937-1971
Harold H. Burton	1941-Sept. 30, 1945	1945-1958
Sherman Minton	1935-1941	1949-1956
House		
John Marshall*	1799-June 7, 1800	1801-1835
Joseph Story	May 23, 1808-1809	1811-1845
Gabriel Duvall	Nov. 11, 1794-March 28, 1796	1812-1835
John McLean	1813-1816	1829-1861
Henry Baldwin	1817-May 8, 1822	1830-1844
James M. Wayne	1829-Jan. 13, 1835	1835-1867
Philip B. Barbour	Sept. 19, 1814-1825	1836-1841
Nathan Clifford	1839-1843	1858-1881
William Strong	1847-1851	1870-1880
Joseph McKenna	1885-1892	1898-1925
William H. Moody	Nov. 5, 1895-May 1, 1902	1906-1910
Mahlon Pitney	1895-Jan. 10, 1899	1912-1922
Fred M. Vinson*	Jan. 12, 1924-1929; 1931-May 12, 1938	1946-1953
Both Chambers		
John McKinley	S: Nov. 27, 1826-1831; March 4-April 22, 1837 H: 1833-1835	1837-1852
Lucius Q. C. Lamar	H: 1857-1860; 1873-1877 S: 1877-March 6, 1885	1888-1893
George Sutherland	H: 1901-1903 S: 1905-1917	1922-1938
James F. Byrnes	H: 1911-1925 S: 1931-July 8, 1941	1941-1942

Denotes chief justice.

Justice McLean, who had served in the Cabinets of Presidents James Monroe and John Quincy Adams before coming to the court in 1829, sought and failed to receive his party's presidential nomination in 1836, 1848, 1852 and 1856. Referring to McLean specifically and to the tendency of justices generally during that period to become involved in politics, Alexander Bickel wrote in his book, *Politics and the Warren Court*, "that the recurrence of justices with manifest political aspirations would in time destroy an institution whose strength derives from consent based on confidence." The conduct of justices acting upon their "manifest political aspirations," Bickel added, "is awkward, unseemly and may give occasion for dire suspicions."

Before his appointment as chief justice in 1864, Salmon P. Chase had been a U.S. senator, a governor, a Cabinet member and a presidential candidate. His political activities did not cease once he came to the Supreme Court. From the bench in 1868 he sought the presidential nomination of both major parties, but was unsuccessful.

Justice David Davis accepted nomination as a minor party candidate for president in 1872 before resigning from the court in 1877 to serve in the Senate. Justice Stephen J. Field periodically made known his availability for the Democratic presidential nomination.

Far fewer justices have sought elective office in the 20th century. Charles Evans Hughes resigned his seat on the court to run for president in 1916. Justice Robert H. Jackson was approached to run for governor of New York.

Presidents Roosevelt in 1944 and Truman in 1948 considered Justice William O. Douglas as a running mate. After President Eisenhower suffered a heart attack, Chief Justice Earl Warren was widely considered a possible Republican presidential nominee in 1956. In neither of these cases, however, did the justices actively seek elective office.

'Public Service' Justices

One ostensibly public-spirited activity on the part of five justices ended up involving the court in one of its most serious political controversies when Justices Nathan Clifford (1858-81), Samuel F. Miller (1862-90), Stephen J. Field (1863-97), William Strong (1870-80) and Joseph P. Bradley (1870-92) were appointed to serve on the electoral commission set up to resolve the disputed presidential election of 1876 between Democrat Samuel J. Tilden and Republican Rutherford B. Hayes.

1876 Electoral Commission

Congress set up the electoral commission in January 1877 and specified that it be composed of 15 members: three Republicans and two Democrats from the Senate, two Republicans and three Democrats from the House and two Democrats and two Republicans from the Supreme Court. The court itself was to choose a fifth justice.

The court eventually selected Bradley, a Republican. According to some historians, Bradley yielded to Republican pressure and cast the critical vote for Hayes. The commission's vote, announced Feb. 10, 1877, backed Hayes, and Congress acquiesced on March 2, 1877.

Historian Charles Warren wrote in his major work, *The Supreme Court in United States History*, that the justices' service on this commission did not enhance the court's prestige. "The partisan excitement caused by this election and by the inauguration of Hayes led some newspapers to assert that public confidence in the judges had been weakened, and that the country would be the less willing to accept the doctrines laid down by the Court."

A few 20th century justices have ignored the lessons of the Hayes-Tilden Electoral Commission and agreed to participate on officially non-partisan commissions or investigative bodies, despite the risk of involving the court in political controversy. Among these instances were the participation of Justice Joseph R. Lamar (1910-16) in international arbitration cases; Justice Owen J. Roberts' role on the German-American Mixed Claims Commission and on the Pearl Harbor Review Commission, Justice Robert H. Jackson's prosecution of Nazi war criminals at the Nuremberg trials, and Chief Justice Warren's role as head of the seven-member commission that investigated the assassination of President John F. Kennedy in 1963.

Jackson at Nuremberg Trials

Several justices were troubled by Jackson's one-year absence from the court because of his war-trial duties in Germany. Chief Justice Harlan Fiske Stone had opposed Jackson's acceptance of the assignment, and some of the other justices were angry about the extra work that Jackson's absence imposed on them. The situation became even worse after Stone's death in April 1946.

In his book, *Marble Palace*, John P. Frank wrote: "Taking a justice away from his primary duty can be done only at the expense of that duty. Stone's acute bitterness over the burdens placed upon the court by the absence of Jackson (who, Stone sputtered, was off running a lynching bee at Nuremberg) is understandable. Such extra-judicial work may also involve justices in controversies that lower the prestige so valuable to the court."

But the fact that the court did suffer some loss of prestige because of Jackson's role at Nuremberg had less to do with the workload burdens placed on the other justices than with Jackson's assault on Justice Hugo L. Black, issued from Germany at the time of Chief Justice Vinson's appointment in 1946. According to Frank, "Jackson . . . who had deeply desired the [chief justiceship] . . . himself, apparently felt that Black was in some way responsible for the appointment of Vinson. He issued a vitriolic public statement denouncing Black for having participated in a certain case in which Jackson felt that Black should have disqualified himself." Amidst the publicity that the statement received, Black "maintained a complete silence."

Somewhat surprisingly at the time, although now perhaps more explicable in light of Murphy's revelations about the justice's own activities, Felix Frankfurter did not share his colleagues' resentment of Jackson's role at the Nuremberg trials. However, before his appointment to the Supreme Court in 1939, as well as after his retirement in 1962, Frankfurter opposed the participation of justices in any public activities that were not strictly relevant to their judicial responsibilities.

In 1929, for example, Frankfurter wrote: "In suggesting that judges engage in public activities off the bench, we are in danger of forgetting that it is the business of judges to be judges. . . . It is necessary for judges to be less worldly than others in order to be more judicial." After his retirement in 1962, Frankfurter criticized Chief Justice Warren's decision to head the Kennedy assassination investigation.

Although Frankfurter had resigned immediately from the American Civil Liberties Union, the National Association for the Advancement of Colored People and even the Harvard Club when named to the court, he nevertheless served on several presidential and national commissions during his years as a justice.

The Warren Commission

One week after President John F. Kennedy was assassinated Nov. 22, 1963, President Lyndon B. Johnson created a seven-man commission to ascertain all the facts and circumstances relating to Kennedy's death. Warren agreed to head the commission, which also included Sens. Richard B. Russell, D-Ga. (1933-71), and John Sherman Cooper, R-Ky. (1946-49; 1952-55; 1956-73); Reps. Hale Boggs, D-La. (1941-43; 1947-73), and Gerald R. Ford Jr., R-Mich. (1949-73); Allen W. Dulles, former director of the CIA; and John J. McCloy, former disarmament adviser to President Kennedy.

The Warren Commission released its findings on Sept. 27, 1964, concluding that Lee Harvey Oswald, "acting alone and without advice or assistance," had shot the president. Before the report was released, critics of Warren's performance on the Supreme Court denounced the chief justice for neglecting his judicial duties and for participating in such a "political" undertaking. After the findings were released, those convinced that there had been a "conspiracy" joined in the criticism.

Continuing public concern about the thoroughness of the Warren Commission's investigation led in 1976 to creation of a select House Committee on Assassinations to reinvestigate the Kennedy assassination and also the 1968 killing of the Rev. Martin Luther King Jr.

When it filed its final report in 1979, the select committee said the Warren Commission had conducted its inquiry in good faith, but that the commission's final report was not in all respects "an accurate presentation of all the evidence available to the commission ... particularly on the issue of possible conspiracy in the assassination."

White House Advisers

Even before Murphy's disclosure of Frankfurter's extra-judicial political activities, it was well known that Frankfurter continued from the court to serve as an unofficial adviser to President Franklin D. Roosevelt, as he had done before his appointment. In 1939, for example, Frankfurter sent almost 300 notes to the president warning of the threat that Hitler posed and advising the president of actions he should take to counter the Nazi danger. Such actions led some to describe Frankfurter as "the outside insider" in the Roosevelt administration.

Frankfurter had a clear model for such a role in Justice Louis D. Brandeis, appointed to the court in 1916 by President Woodrow Wilson. Brandeis came to the court after a long and successful career as an advocate for reform in virtually all areas of life; he had argued and won a number of the first so-called "public interest" cases ever brought against American business on behalf of the consumer. His confirmation had not been easy, in part because he was a Jew — the first to sit on the court — and also because of his liberal and activist record.

Brandeis did not renounce all outside political involvement when he became a justice; such activity simply took another form. Murphy's book recounts that Felix Frankfurter, as a member of the faculty of Harvard Law School and a close friend of Brandeis', became the justice's alter ego, doing outside the court what Brandeis would have done himself. Brandeis financed this relationship through a "joint endeavors for the public good" fund at a Boston bank. Brandeis used to contribute $3,500 annually to this fund.

Frankfurter's activities on Brandeis' behalf were varied. They included arguing in print the case for the Italian immigrants Nicola Sacco and Bartolomeo Vanzetti, who had been convicted and sentenced to death for killing a paymaster and guard in South Braintree, Mass. It was widely thought that resentment against foreigners was responsible for their conviction rather than any solid evidence linking the men to the murder. When lawyers for the two men sought a stay of execution from Justice Brandeis, he refused to hear their arguments, aware that he already was too involved in the case to act impartially. The men were executed.

Brandeis and Frankfurter worked together to further the interests of the New Deal, placing a number of Frankfurter's former students in various important agency positions in the Roosevelt administration and making direct suggestions to Roosevelt's Cabinet members and other key advisers as to the manner in which particular economic problems might best be dealt with. When it appeared on one occasion that the administration was not going to accept Brandeis' suggestion in this area, Brandeis sent key administration officials a message that "he was declaring war" on the New Deal, meaning he would vote to hold unconstitutional New Deal measures with which he disagreed.

Frankfurter came to the court in 1939, the year Brandeis left it. Despite his public statements concerning the impropriety of justices' engaging in extra-judicial political activity, he remained extraordinarily involved in the Roosevelt administration. When FDR ran for re-election in 1940, Murphy writes that Frankfurter was "virtually an informal campaign manager, playing a central role in every aspect of the campaign, from drafting speeches to plotting election strategy."

As astonishing as these revelations are to observers in 1983, Supreme Court justices in fact have been advising presidents and other elected officials since the earliest days of the Republic. Chief Justice John Jay frequently consulted President Washington, and even advised him on the writing of his State of the Union messages.

Yet disclosure of this sort of relationship between the nation's highest judicial and executive officers has always brought public criticism.

When President Roosevelt indicated at a press conference in September 1939 that he had discussed the situation in Europe with Justices Stone and Frankfurter, there was a storm of protest over the involvement of justices in the foreign policy deliberations and decisions of the executive branch. Stone thereafter refused all invitations to confer with the president. Frankfurter, however, continued advising Roosevelt as well as his successors.

Extrajudicial Role Criticized

In the 1960s and succeeding decades, there was heightened sensitivity to such interplay between the branches of government. This initially was evident in the criticism of Justice Fortas, who continued to advise President Johnson on a variety of matters after he was appointed to the court in 1965. This sort of extrajudicial role became a key factor in the rejection of Fortas' nomination as chief justice in 1968.

Many Justices Held Federal Posts Before Their Appointment to the Court

Thirty-two justices of the Supreme Court — including nine chief justices — served as executive branch officials before or after their appointment to the court. Eighteen held Cabinet-level posts — nine of them were attorneys general — and eight served in other posts in the Justice Department.

Four men — Roger B. Taney, Levi Woodbury, William H. Moody and William Howard Taft — held more than one Cabinet post. Taft held more high executive branch posts than any other justice. He is the only man to serve both as president and chief justice of the United States.

The following table lists the 32 justices, the major executive branch positions they held and their years of service. The table does not include justices who served in Congress, as governors or in other state or local offices. *(Justices with congressional service, box p. 21)*

Justice	Position	Court Service
John Jay*	Secretary for Foreign Affairs under the Articles of Confederation, 1784-1789; U.S. Diplomat, 1794-1795	1789-1795
John Marshall*	Envoy to France, 1797-1798; Secretary of State, 1800-1801	1801-1835
Smith Thompson	Secretary of the Navy, 1818-1823	1823-1843
Gabriel Duvall	Comptroller of the Treasury, 1802-1811	1812-1835
John McLean	Postmaster General, 1823-1829	1829-1861
Roger B. Taney*	Attorney General, 1831-1833; Secretary of the Treasury, 1833-1834	1836-1864
Levi Woodbury	Secretary of the Navy, 1831-1834; Secretary of the Treasury, 1834-1841	1845-1851
Nathan Clifford	Attorney General, 1846-1848	1858-1881
Salmon P. Chase*	Secretary of the Treasury, 1861-1864	1864-1873
Lucius Q. C. Lamar	Secretary of the Interior, 1885-1888	1888-1893
Joseph McKenna	Attorney General, 1897-1898	1898-1925
William H. Moody	Secretary of the Navy, 1902-1904; Attorney General, 1904-1906	1906-1910
Charles E. Hughes*	Secretary of State, 1921-1925	1910-1916; 1930-1941
Willis Van Devanter	Counsel, Interior Department, 1897-1903	1910-1937
James McReynolds	Attorney General, 1913-1914	1914-1941
William H. Taft*	U.S. Solicitor General, 1890-1892; Secretary of War, 1904-1908; President, 1908-1912	1921-1930
Edward T. Sanford	Assistant Attorney General, 1907-1908	1923-1930
Harlan F. Stone*	Attorney General, 1924-1925	1925-1946
Owen J. Roberts	Prosecuting Attorney, Teapot Dome Scandal, 1924	1930-1945
Stanley Reed	Solicitor General, 1935-1938	1938-1957
William O. Douglas	Chairman, Securities and Exchange Commission, 1937-1939	1939-1975
Frank Murphy	Attorney General, 1938-1940	1940-1949
James F. Byrnes	Secretary of State, 1945-1947	1941-1942
Robert H. Jackson	Solicitor General, 1938-1939; Attorney General, 1940-1941	1941-1954
Fred M. Vinson*	Secretary of the Treasury, 1945-1946	1946-1953
Tom C. Clark	Attorney General, 1945-1949	1949-1967
Byron R. White	Deputy Attorney General, 1961-1962	1962-
Arthur J. Goldberg	Secretary of Labor, 1961-1962; Ambassador to the U.N., 1965-1968	1962-1965
Abe Fortas	Under Secretary of Interior, 1942-1946	1965-1969
Thurgood Marshall	Solicitor General, 1964-1967	1967-
Warren E. Burger*	Assistant Attorney General, 1953-1955	1969-
William H. Rehnquist	Assistant Attorney General, 1969-1971	1971-

Denotes Chief Justice

Sources: Leon Friedman Fred L. Israel, eds., *The Justices of the United States Supreme Court 1789-1969, Their Lives and Major Opinions*, 5 vols. (New York and London: Chelsea House, 1969, 1978); *Members of Congress Since 1789* (Washington D.C.: Congressional Quarterly, 1977); William F. Swindler, *Court and Constitution in the Twentieth Century*, 2 vols. (Indianapolis and New York: The Bobbs-Merrill Co., 1969, 1970).

In his book on that period, *In His Own Image: The Supreme Court in Richard Nixon's America*, James F. Simon described the events leading up to Johnson's withdrawal of Fortas' nomination. In the summer of 1968, after Warren had announced his plan to retire, "President Johnson named Associate Justice Abe Fortas to succeed Chief Justice Warren. At first, anti-Fortas forces, led by Republican Senator Robert P. Griffin of Michigan, opposed the nomination primarily because it had been made by a 'lame-duck' president. At the Senate's confirmation hearings, however, Fortas ran into deeper trouble. The chief justice-designate, it was learned, had counseled the president on national policy and had even done some behind-the-scenes lobbying on the president's behalf while sitting on the Supreme Court. Later, when Fortas admitted that he had received $15,000 for conducting a series of seminars at American University, his ethics as well as his policies were brought into question. As a result, his nomination as chief justice languished and was finally withdrawn by President Johnson." Fortas resigned from the court the following year.

Chief Justice Burger, who consistently has expressed his views on proposed legislation affecting the judiciary, and on related matters concerning judicial administration, also has come under fire. Yet his actions were no different than those of Chief Justice William Howard Taft, who successfully lobbied the White House and Congress on a variety of matters affecting the court from filling vacancies and constructing a new court building to redrawing the court's jurisdiction. *(Taft, box, p. 10; judicial lobbying, box, pp. 62-63)*

THE SUPREME COURT AND PRESIDENTIAL POWER

On July 24, 1974, the Supreme Court ruled that President Richard M. Nixon must turn over to the Watergate special prosecutor tape recordings subpoenaed for use in the criminal trial of several of his former aides. Nixon complied with the unanimous court decision and, politically disarmed by the revelations on those tapes, then resigned the presidency on Aug. 9.

No court decision in American history has been more dramatic in its effect. The court's ruling, in *United States v. Nixon*, was extraordinary in many respects. Only infrequently has the court had occasion to rule on the powers of the presidency. And even more infrequently have the justices ruled that presidential actions exceeded constitutional bounds.

Indeed, from the founding of the nation until the New Deal, there were virtually no direct confrontations between the court and the chief executive on the question of presidential power.

Not until the unprecedented expansion of the federal government in the 20th century did the court move to curb presidential power. This was particularly true of its rulings in several New Deal cases in the 1930s. Others included the steel seizure case of 1952 and the 1974 Watergate tapes ruling.

Deference to Presidential Role

The presidency has been insulated from frequent constitutional challenges by certain intangible factors. One of these is the generality with which the Constitution describes the powers of the chief executive.

The Constitution vests the president with broad executive power; it declares him commander-in-chief; it directs him to take care that the laws are faithfully executed. Such generalities provide an uncertain basis for constitutional litigation.

In addition, the office of the presidency holds a special position in American public opinion. More than any other branch of government, the presidency captures public attention and political support. "Executive power," wrote Justice Robert H. Jackson in 1952, "has the advantage of concentration in a single head in whose choice the whole Nation has a part, making him the focus of public hopes and expectations. . . . No other personality in public life can begin to compete with him in access to the public mind through modern methods of communications."

These factors have contributed to a particularly cautious attitude on the part of the court when it has considered challenges to presidential authority. Generally, Supreme Court justices have been careful to avoid locking constitutional horns with the chief executive on matters that clearly set their authority and prestige against the president's will.

The Congressional Factor

When such confrontations do occur, a key consideration by the court is the position of the third branch — Congress. Presidents acting with the support or acquiescence of the national legislature come to the court in a position of considerable strength. Joint action by the two political branches almost invariably is approved by the court.

When presidents have come to the court supported only by a claim of inherent power, they run a higher risk of defeat. The steel seizure case and the Watergate tapes matter provide ample evidence of this fact.

Inherent Foreign Policy Powers

Without exception, the Supreme Court has upheld presidential actions in matters of military policy and foreign affairs. The 1981 decision in the case of *Dames & Moore v. Regan*, the Iran agreements case, is the most recent example of this form of judicial deference.

Even more notable because of the sweep of the court's language, however, was the Supreme Court's ruling in a 1936 case, *United States v. Curtiss-Wright Export Corp.* At the beginning of the Roosevelt administration, the court stood adamantly opposed to the sweeping power claimed by the president in dealing with the deep-seated internal economic problems of the Great Depression. Time and again, the justices struck down major New Deal legislation, finding that Congress and the executive had overreached the limits of their constitutional powers. *(Details, p. 65)*

Nevertheless, in the midst of these rulings, the court affirmed a virtually unlimited inherent power for the president to act in foreign affairs, a "very delicate, plenary and exclusive power . . . as the sole organ of the federal government in the field of international relations — a power which does not require as a basis for its exercise an act of Congress, but which ... must be exercised in subordination to the applicable provisions of the Constitution."

Congress by joint resolution had authorized Roosevelt to embargo arms shipments to certain South American countries at war with each other. After he exercised this authority, one of the companies selling arms challenged it.

The Curtiss-Wright Export Corporation contended that Congress had given Roosevelt too much discretion in deciding when to impose such an embargo, an argument that had proven successful in invalidating some key New Deal domestic laws. But the argument did not persuade the justices in this case.

Speaking for the court, Justice George Sutherland, one of the conservatives opposed to the expansion of presidential power as it applied in the New Deal programs, declared: "[T]he President alone has the power to speak as a representative of the nation. He makes treaties with the advice and consent of the Senate; but he alone negotiates. ..."

Limits on Domestic Power

On the other hand, the court has been quite willing on occasion to deny the president such inherent power to deal with domestic problems. When President Truman seized the steel mills during the Korean War to prevent an interruption of steel production and supplies that were threatened by a labor strike, the court held his action invalid.

Notwithstanding Truman's role as commander in chief — on which he based his action — the court held that it was up to Congress — not the military — to take possession of private property in order to continue production in the face of a labor dispute.

The six-man majority ruling against Truman, in the case of *Youngstown Sheet and Tube Co. v. Sawyer,* relied in part upon the fact that Congress had, several years earlier, specifically decided not to grant the president the power to make such seizures.

Executive Privilege/Watergate

The impeachment proceedings against President Nixon in the Watergate scandal were the backdrop for the court's decision denying the president's claim of an executive privilege to withhold White House tape recordings sought as evidence in the case.

In the historic court decision resolving the tapes issue, however, the justices for the first time formally recognized the need for a limited executive privilege for the president to protect certain types of information from being disclosed.

The case of *United States v. Nixon* would never have arisen had it not been for a burglary and a congressional hearing. On June 17, 1972, five men were apprehended by District of Columbia police in the course of a break-in at the Democratic National Committee's headquarters in the Watergate Office Building in Washington, D.C. Subsequent investigations by the police and *The Washington Post* linked the burglars to the Committee for the Re-Election of the President and to presidential aides in the White House itself.

Thirteen months later, while a special Senate committee was investigating the break-in and surrounding events, former White House aide Alexander P. Butterfield astounded the nation by revealing that Nixon had taped all conversations in his White House and Executive Office Building offices since 1971.

A week after Butterfield's disclosure, the first of several subpoenas for those tapes was issued to the White House. This subpoena was initiated by Watergate Special Prosecutor Archibald Cox and was upheld by Federal District Judge John J. Sirica and the U.S. Circuit Court of Appeals for the District of Columbia in the fall of 1973. It provoked the so-called "Saturday night massacre" and cost Cox his job, but in the aftermath of that episode Nixon surrendered the tapes to Sirica for inspection and selective disclosure of their contents.

The subpoena that started the chain of events leading up to the historic July 24 Supreme Court decision was issued on April 18, 1974, by Judge Sirica at the request of the next Watergate special prosecutor, Leon Jaworski. Jaworski sought the tapes of 64 White House conversations for use as evidence against former Attorney General John N. Mitchell and former White House aides H. R. Haldeman and John Ehrlichman, all of whom had been indicted in March of that year for conspiracy and obstruction of justice as a result of their roles in the Watergate coverup.

In February the House of Representatives began an inquiry to determine "whether sufficient grounds exist for the House ... to impeach Richard M. Nixon, President of the United States of America."

In late April Nixon released the edited transcripts of a number of the subpoenaed tapes, but he refused to provide the tapes themselves. Early in May Nixon invoked executive privilege to shield himself from the subpoena. Three weeks later, Sirica rejected that claim. Special Prosecutor Jaworski asked the Supreme Court to review the case immediately; the White House opposed that request. On May 31 the court agreed to hear the case, which was argued July 8, 1974.

Three weeks later, as the House Judiciary Committee was entering its final stage of work on the impeachment inquiry — the public hearings on its findings — the court announced its decision.

The court ruled 8-0 against the president's claim of privilege.

Justice Rehnquist, who had served as an assistant attorney general to Mitchell in the first Nixon term, disqualified himself.

Chief Justice Burger, selected by Nixon for that post because of his hard-line views on criminal matters, wrote the opinion. The court upheld Sirica's order requiring Nixon to comply with the subpoena. The president was directed to submit the tapes to Sirica for private examination, excision of irrelevant portions and transfer of relevant admissible portions to Jaworski.

Ruling on Privilege Claim

The court did have the power to review the president's claim of privilege, Burger made clear: "Notwithstanding the deference each branch must accord the others, the 'judicial power of the United States' ... can no more be shared with the Executive Branch than the Chief Executive, for example, can share with the Judiciary the veto power, or the Congress share with the Judiciary the power to override a presidential veto. Any other conclusion would be contrary to the basic concept of the separation of powers and the checks and balances. ... We therefore reaffirm that it is 'emphatically the province and duty' of this court 'to say what the law is' with respect to the claim of privilege presented in this case."

The opinion made no mention of the ongoing impeachment proceedings in the House.

The court acknowledged that there was a constitutional basis for an executive privilege that would protect some material from disclosure under other circumstances. But "neither the doctrine of separation of powers, nor the need for confidentiality of high-level communications, without more, can sustain an absolute, unqualified, presidential privilege of immunity from judicial process under all circumstances," wrote Burger.

"The President's need for complete candor and objectivity from advisers calls for great deference from the courts. However, when the privilege depends solely on the broad undifferentiated claim of public interest in the confidentiality of such conversations, a confrontation with other values arises. Absent a claim of need to protect military, diplomatic or sensitive national security secrets, we find it difficult to accept the argument that even the very important interest in confidentiality ... is significantly diminished by production of such material for *in camera* inspection. . . .

"To read the Article II powers of the President as providing an absolute privilege as against a subpoena essential to enforcement of criminal statutes on no more than a generalized claim of the public interest in confidentiality of nonmilitary and nondiplomatic discussions would upset the constitutional balance of 'a workable government' and gravely impair the role of the courts" under the Constitution, the court declared.

"When the ground for asserting privilege as to subpoenaed materials sought for use in a criminal trial is based only on the generalized interest in confidentiality, it cannot prevail over the fundamental demands of due process of law in the fair administration of criminal justice. The generalized assertion of privilege must yield to the demonstrated specific need for evidence in a pending criminal trial," the court concluded. *(Excerpts of decision, p. 144)*

James D. St. Clair, the attorney who had argued the president's case, was with Nixon at the president's residence in San Clemente, Calif., when the decision was announced. A few hours after the news reached California, St. Clair issued a statement from Nixon, which said in part: "While I am, of course, disappointed ... I respect and accept the court's decision. . . . I was gratified ... to note that the court reaffirmed both the validity and the importance of the principle of executive privilege, the principle I had sought to maintain. By complying fully with the court's ruling in this case, I hope and trust that I will contribute to strengthening rather than weakening this principle for the future. . . ."

That evening the House Judiciary Committee began debating articles of impeachment. Within the week it approved articles calling for Nixon's impeachment for obstructing justice, misusing his presidential powers and contempt of Congress.

Then, at the beginning of the second week after the court's ruling, Nixon turned over to Judge Sirica three more transcripts of White House tape recordings. They clearly revealed his participation in the coverup, so long denied.

Nixon's already small band of defenders in Congress was completely disarmed by the new revelations.

Faced with certain impeachment by the House and probable conviction and removal from office by the Senate, Nixon resigned Aug. 9, 1974.

1981 Iran Agreements

An "international break-in" set off the chain of events leading to the Supreme Court's next major ruling on presidential power: *Dames & Moore v. Regan*, announced July 2, 1981.

Rather than a key event in the dramatic chain of circumstances surrounding the return of the 52 U.S. citizens held hostage by Iran for 14 months, the Supreme Court decision in this case was a legal postscript.

When the Iranian agreements concluded by President Carter to win the release of the hostages were challenged before the Supreme Court, the legal precedents clearly indicated that the president stood on firm ground. The traditional deference of the court to the president's actions in the field of foreign affairs was underscored in this case by the fact that Carter could cite several acts of Congress giving him authority to take such actions whenever he found it necessary.

Events Preceding Accord

On Nov. 4, 1979, Iranian militants, angered by the former shah's admission to the United States a few weeks earlier for medical treatment, seized the U.S. Embassy in Tehran. Sixty-six U.S. diplomatic personnel and visitors were taken hostage. Thirteen were released quickly and another in July 1980, but 52 Americans were held by the militants for more than 14 months, until Jan. 20, 1981.

These months were a difficult time for the Carter administration and the American people, humiliated by this international kidnapping yet not willing to set off a war to free the hostages. The national mood was further strained when eight U.S. servicemen were killed in an accident in the Iranian desert during an aborted rescue mission in April 1980. In protest of the mission, Secretary of State Cyrus R. Vance resigned; he was replaced by Sen. Edmund S. Muskie, D-Maine (1959-80).

Carter's Negotiations

After his election defeat to Ronald Reagan in November 1980, Carter continued his efforts to win release of the hostages, efforts that finally resulted in freedom for the 52 Americans just after noon on Inauguration Day, Jan. 20, minutes after the end of Carter's term.

The agreements that won the hostages freedom included several points. The United States pledged not to interfere in Iranian affairs. It also pledged to freeze all property and assets in the United States that were within the control of the former shah's estate or his close relatives. (The former shah had died in Cairo on July 27, 1980.)

In addition, Carter pledged that the Iranian assets in U.S. banks and otherwise under the jurisdiction of the United States, which the president had frozen in November 1979, would be transferred to Iran. Any judicial orders affecting them were nullified. These assets were estimated at $12 billion. And Carter agreed to "suspend" all claims by Americans against Iran, and to transfer them for resolution from U.S. courts to an Iran-United States Claims Tribunal set up to resolve such matters.

In his formal announcement of these accords, Carter

Court Rules Presidents
Immune From Civil Damage Suits

President Richard M. Nixon lost his bid for executive privilege in 1974, but he won a major victory for himself and all other presidents eight years later when the Supreme Court held that presidents enjoy absolute immunity from civil damage suits.

The court's ruling came in the case of *Nixon v. Fitzgerald*, announced June 24, 1982. The vote was 5-4, with Nixon appointees Chief Justice Warren E. Burger, Justices Lewis F. Powell Jr. and William H. Rehnquist in the majority, and Justice Harry A. Blackmun, Nixon's other appointee, dissenting.

Americans may impeach a president whom they feel has violated their constitutional rights, or they may simply refuse to re-elect him, wrote Powell for the court, but they may not sue him for damages for injuries they allege to have resulted from his official actions. This ruling did not affect the fact that presidents are subject to criminal prosecution for their actions.

The decision effectively terminated a long-running dispute between Nixon and former Air Force cost analyst A. Ernest Fitzgerald. The dispute began when Fitzgerald lost his job in 1969 and sued the Defense Department and the president. He contended that this was the result of a White House conspiracy to punish him for testifying on Capitol Hill in 1968 about massive cost overruns on the C-5A military transport plane project.

The court's ruling cut the legal ground out from under Fitzgerald's suit against Nixon for damages to compensate him for the loss of his job. However, Fitzgerald had been reinstated in his Pentagon job by the Civil Service Commission, and Nixon in 1980 had paid Fitzgerald $142,000. (Nixon at the time also had promised to pay an additional $28,000 to Fitzgerald if the Supreme Court ruling went against the president.)

The court majority based its finding of absolute immunity upon its view that such blanket protection was "a constitutionally mandated incident of the president's unique office, rooted in the constitutional tradition of the separation of powers and supported by . . . history."

The dissenters, Justices Blackmun, Byron R. White, William J. Brennan Jr. and Thurgood Marshall, responded angrily that "attaching absolute immunity to the office of the president, rather than to particular activities that the president might perform, places the president above the law. It is a reversion to the idea that the king can do no wrong."

Presidents are unique, declared the majority. "Because of the singular importance of the President's duties, diversion of his energies by concern with private lawsuits would raise unique risks to the effective functioning of government." Thus this immunity must extend even to "acts within the 'outer perimeter' of his official responsibility." Fitzgerald's claim of a conspiracy against him had not been proved in the course of the litigation.

Powell responded to the dissenters by describing their warning as "rhetorically chilling but wholly unjustified. . . . It is simply error to characterize an official as 'above the law' because a particular remedy is not available against him." He then pointed out that a president faces the remedies — or deterrents — of impeachment, denial of re-election, press scrutiny, congressional oversight, loss of prestige or an unfavorable assessment by history.

Powell left open the possibility that Congress might pass a law subjecting the president to liability in such damage suits, but Chief Justice Burger disassociated himself from such a suggestion, leaving only four justices supporting it.

In a related case decided the same day, the court held that presidential aides are not similarly shielded from damage suits. They enjoy only a qualified immunity, which they can claim if they are able to show that their challenged actions were taken in good faith.

The court set out in this case, *Harlow v. Fitzgerald*, a new standard to govern such suits. Officials would be protected from such claims, held the court, if they could prove that "their conduct does not violate clearly established statutory or constitutional rights of which a reasonable person would have known."

cited as authority for his actions the International Emergency Economic Powers Act of 1977. Carter had invoked the law soon after the seizure of the hostages, declaring on Nov. 14, 1979, that such an emergency existed. All Iranian assets in the United States were frozen, blocking their removal or transfer out of the country. Carter had acted after Iran announced it was withdrawing billions of dollars deposited in U.S. banks.

Agreements Challenged

In December 1979 Dames & Moore, a Los Angeles engineering firm, filed suit in federal court against the government of Iran, its Atomic Energy Organization and a number of Iranian banks, arguing that it was owed $3.5 million for services performed under a contract with the Iranian Atomic Energy Organization to conduct site studies in Iran for a proposed nuclear plant. The court hearing the case issued orders attaching the assets of certain Iranian banks and the Iranian government to protect Dames & Moore's claims in the event the judgment went against Iran.

After the hostages were returned, Dames & Moore asked the court to award it the money owed by Iran. The court did so, but then stayed the execution of that award in light of the agreements Carter had made, which 1) transferred Iranian assets in the United States to Iran, 2) nullified all existing attachments on those assets, and 3) suspended all pending claims against Iran by Americans.

In April 1981 Dames & Moore filed another lawsuit, this time suing the United States and the secretary of the Treasury, Donald T. Regan, to prevent enforcement of the agreements with Iran. The company argued that Carter had exceeded his constitutional power in entering into these agreements. The federal district court in which the case was filed dismissed it.

Dames & Moore asked the Supreme Court to take the unusual step of hearing the case before an appeals court had ruled on it and to act quickly. This request for expedited consideration was backed by the Justice Department, which pointed out that if the matter were not quickly resolved Iran could consider the United States to be in breach of the agreements.

Court Decision

The court agreed June 11 to hear the case, setting arguments for June 24, a full two months after the end of the regular oral argument schedule for that court term. On July 2, less than two weeks after argument, the court, in *Dames & Moore v. Regan*, upheld in all respects the Iran agreements Carter had concluded.

"The questions presented by this case touch fundamentally upon the manner in which our Republic is to be governed," wrote Justice Rehnquist for the court. This case is "only one more episode in the never-ending tension between the President exercising the executive authority in a world that presents each day some new challenge with which he must deal and the Constitution under which we all live. . . ."

A president's action in any particular instance usually falls "at some point along a spectrum running from explicit congressional authorization to explicit constitutional prohibition," Rehnquist continued. "This is particularly true as respects cases such as the one before us, involving responses to international crises the nature of which Congress can hardly have been expected to anticipate in any detail."

The court held that the International Emergency Economic Powers Act clearly authorized Carter to freeze the assets of Iran in the United States, to end the freeze and to nullify all court orders claiming part of those assets for Americans.

The purpose of giving the president this authority was to enable him to control foreign assets as a "bargaining chip" to be used in negotiating the resolution of an international emergency. To deny the president the authority to nullify the court orders attaching these assets would give individual claimants across the country the power to take this "bargaining chip" away through court orders reducing it piece by piece.

"Because the President's action in nullifying the attachments and ordering the transfer of the assets was taken pursuant to specific congressional authorization, it is 'supported by the strongest of presumptions and the widest latitude of judicial interpretation. . . .'" declared Rehnquist.

The court found no law that specifically authorized the president to suspend all American claims against Iran. But it refused to deny him that power, citing the broad authority given the president in several acts of Congress that enabled him to take action with regard to foreign property during national emergencies. And the court cited the modern tradition — in which Congress has acquiesced — permitting the president to settle international claims through executive agreements when settlement of the claims is necessary to resolve international disputes.

3

The Court and Congress

The U.S. Capitol is right across the street from the Supreme Court building. Without placing undue emphasis on geography, the proximity of the court to Congress is indicative of the continuous and complex relationship between these two institutions.

The U.S. Constitution traced out the rudimentary lines of the relationship between Congress and the court. It gave the Senate power to confirm Supreme Court nominees. It granted the Senate and the House of Representatives, acting in sequence, the power to impeach and remove justices. Congress was given the authority to define the court's appellate jurisdiction: its power to review decisions of lower state and federal courts. And the Constitution left entirely to Congress the organization and structure of all federal courts below the Supreme Court.

The street that separates, or connects, the court and Congress is a two-way street. The Constitution does not explicitly authorize the court to review acts passed by Congress or to nullify them if they do not meet constitutional standards. Since early in its history, however, the court has exercised that power of judicial review.

When Congress disagrees with a Supreme Court decision, it can do more than complain. If the ruling is based on the justices' reading of a federal law, Congress can amend the law. If the offending decision is the result of the court's reading of the Constitution, reversal is more difficult, requiring a constitutional amendment. Only four times in 194 years has that route to reversal succeeded.

And there are other means by which each of these institutions can influence the other. The court defines the limits of the immunity the Constitution grants to members of Congress. The court applies the constitutional guarantees of individual rights to congressional proceedings.

Congress sets the court's annual session, establishing its opening day by law. It approves salary increases for the justices and their staff, and it shapes the benefits available to justices, and their spouses, upon retirement.

Beyond its power over the court's appellate jurisdiction, Congress has an immeasurable influence on the workload of the court. The more federal laws there are, the more federal lawsuits find their way to the court. The more broadly Congress opens the doors for individuals to take their disputes to the federal court system, the more numerous are the cases that are taken all the way to the Supreme Court.

In late 1982 several justices spoke bluntly in urging Congress to act to reduce the burden of its ever-growing workload. Although such unusual public remarks by the justices were certain to spark debate in the 98th Congress, history provides little encouragement that Congress will act swiftly to find a remedy. In the court's first term in 1790, the justices complained repeatedly to Congress about the difficulty of acting as circuit judges — a duty imposed on them by the Judiciary Act of 1789 — as well as Supreme Court justices. It took a full century for Congress to respond and remove this obligation from the justices.

Judicial System

Article III, Section 1, of the Constitution declares: "The judicial Power of the United States shall be vested in one supreme Court, and in such inferior Courts as the Congress may from time to time ordain and establish." Thus, aside from the required Supreme Court, the structure of the lower federal judicial system was left entirely to the discretion of Congress.

In one of its first major acts, Congress passed the Judiciary Act of 1789. It provided for a Supreme Court composed of six members, who were to meet in February and August of each year. The law also created 13 district courts, each with a single judge; and above the district courts, three circuit courts were authorized, each presided over by one district and two Supreme Court judges. Thereafter, as the nation grew and the federal judiciary's workload increased, Congress established additional circuit and district courts. In 1982 there were 12 circuit courts of appeals, 89 district courts and three territorial courts (Guam, Virgin Islands and Northern Mariana Islands).

The influence of Congress over the federal judiciary goes beyond the creation of courts. Although the power to appoint federal judges resides with the president, by and with the Senate's advice and consent, the power to create judgeships to which appointments are made resides with Congress. It is in this area that politics historically plays its most important role. For example, in 1801 the Federalist-dominated Congress created additional circuit court judgeships to be filled by a Federalist president. However, in 1802, when the Jeffersonians came to power, the new posts were abolished.

Because federal judges are appointed to serve during

good behavior, the power of Congress to abolish judgeships is limited to providing, in the legislation creating a judgeship, that when it becomes vacant it cannot be filled. The history of the Supreme Court's size provides the best illustration of the earlier habit of creating and abolishing judgeships. The court originally was composed of six justices. But Congress altered the membership on several occasions in the 19th century. The court had five members between 1801-07; seven from 1807 to 1837; nine from 1837 to 1863; 10 between 1863-66; seven during 1866-69; and nine since 1869.

Jurisdiction of Federal Courts

Article III, Section 2, of the Constitution vests in the Supreme Court original jurisdiction — the power to hear a case argued that has not been argued first before a lower court — over only a few kinds of cases. The most important of these are suits between two states, which may concern such issues as water rights, offshore lands or other disputes. Article III, Section 2, also extends to the court "judicial power" over all cases arising under the Constitution, federal laws and treaties. This jurisdiction, however, is appellate, that is, limited to review of decisions from lower courts, and is subject to "such exceptions and . . . regulations as Congress shall make."

Most of the high court's present jurisdiction is defined by the Judiciary Act of 1925, largely drafted by the court itself under Chief Justice William Howard Taft. The 1925 act made the exercise of the court's appellate jurisdiction largely discretionary, giving the justices more leeway to refuse to review cases.

Except for certain limited types of cases in which the court is still "obligated" to take appeals, the court is allowed to decide whether the decisions of the lower courts present questions or conflicts important enough or of such a constitutional nature as to warrant the court's consideration on review. But only in this way is the court able to control the issues with which it deals. Its power is limited by the fact that it cannot reach out to bring issues before it, but must wait until they are properly presented in a case that has made its way through the lower courts.

In the relationship between the federal and state judicial systems, federal courts have jurisdiction (usually where $10,000 or more is involved) over cases relating to federal rights or actions in which the parties are citizens of different states. The state courts, on the other hand, usually deal with cases involving citizens of that state and their own state laws.

There is some overlap of jurisdiction. The state courts are empowered to hear litigation concerning some federal rights, and federal constitutional rights often form the basis of decisions in state court cases.

In the federal courts, where jurisdiction is based on a "diversity of citizenship," that is, the litigants are from different states, the court is obliged to find and apply the pertinent law of the state in which the court is sitting. In state court cases, similarly, in those few instances where a "federal question" might be resolved, the court is obliged to disregard its own precedents and apply appropriate federal law.

Judicial Review

The Supreme Court exerts a strong restraining influence upon Congress through its power to declare certain legislative acts unconstitutional and, hence, invalid. Although the Constitution did not expressly authorize the court to strike down acts it deems unconstitutional, the court assumed that important authority in 1803 through its own broad interpretation of its vested powers. Without this process, known as judicial review, there would be no assurance — not even the president's veto power — against domination of the entire government by runaway congressional majorities.

Surprisingly, the incidence of court rulings overturning

acts of Congress is not high; only a few more than 100 acts or parts of acts have been declared unconstitutional in 194 years of the Republic. Of those invalidated, many were unimportant and others, such as the measures prohibiting the spread of slavery and those carrying out parts of Franklin D. Roosevelt's New Deal program, were replaced by similar legislation that was fashioned in a way that could pass muster with the Supreme Court.

Most constitutional scholars agree that the significance of judicial review lies primarily in the deterrent effect on Congress of a possible Supreme Court veto. *(List of acts declared unconstitutional, p. 159)*

With few exceptions, the court has interpreted Congress' power to draft and approve legislation as broadly as it has its own authority to sit in review of the statutes.

The court's approach to its duties was defined in 1827, when Justice Bushrod Washington observed that "it is but a decent respect due to the wisdom, the integrity and the patriotism of the legislative body, by which any law is passed, to presume in favor of its validity until its violation of the Constitution is proved beyond all reasonable doubt." Justices on almost every court since Justice Washington's day have reaffirmed that attitude.

Changes in Court's Philosophy

Because Supreme Court justices are appointed for life terms, changes in the court's philosophy come about with less regularity than in the other two branches of the federal government. For its first 150 years, the court served primarily as a bulwark against encroachment on property rights. This concept was maintained even in the 1930s, when the need was evident for precedent-shattering legislation to grapple with the country's economic crisis. In 1935 and 1936 the court struck down 11 New Deal statutes — the heart of the Roosevelt administration's recovery program. But after President Roosevelt's overwhelming victory in the 1936 presidential election, and his threat to "pack" the court with additional justices who presumably would favor his program, the court relented, and revised versions of the New Deal legislation were upheld.

Since the mid-1930s, the philosophy reflected by a majority of the justices has inclined toward a flexible reading of the Constitution, permitting the achievement of national social goals. This represented a significant departure from the traditional practice of giving priority to protection of property. This shift was completed during the term of Chief Justice Earl Warren (1953-69) as the court promulgated a series of sweeping decisions in support of individual rights.

But with Warren's retirement, the pendulum began to swing back. The membership of the court changed. By 1982 only three Warren court justices remained. The court's rulings in the 1970s and 1980s have tended to interpret individual rights more narrowly, making clear that they are rarely absolute.

Moreover, in 1976, the court struck down economic legislation, enacted under the commerce clause, that applied federal wage and hour laws to state and local government employees. That action was reminiscent of the court's actions 40 years earlier overturning laws that affected the private sector of the economy; it raised questions about whether the court in the future would place additional limits on the power of Congress to control the actions of state and local governments.

Whatever its prevailing philosophy at any given time,

the court always has had its share of congressional critics, who are quick to accuse it of usurping the powers of the states or of the other branches of the federal government. The early Anti-Federalists (the Jeffersonians, later known as Democratic-Republicans and finally as Democrats) charged that the court had nullified the Constitution by a series of rulings strengthening federal power at the expense of individuals and the states. In the New Deal era, Democrats thought the court was attempting to seize the preeminent role in government by voiding much of their legislative program. In the 1950s and 1960s, Republicans and Southern Democrats were driven virtually to despair by the Warren court's decisions on school desegregation, criminal law and voter representation.

In the 1970s, as the court became more conservative, criticism came again from liberal observers who worried that the court unduly favored the state at the expense of the individual.

In each of these periods, representatives and senators tried to persuade their colleagues to use the power of Congress to curtail the authority of the court to issue decisions on certain matters. Proposals have included a requirement that the court command more than a simple majority vote to hold a law unconstitutional, that a less cumbersome means than impeachment be devised to remove justices from the court and that the court's appellate jurisdiction be redefined to exclude certain types of cases. Some of these proposals have attracted substantial support, but none has ever been enacted.

THE POWER TO CONFIRM: FROM BURGER TO O'CONNOR

On Sept. 21, 1981, the Senate voted 99-0 to confirm Sandra Day O'Connor as the first woman member of the U.S. Supreme Court.

O'Connor's confirmation came one month and two days after her nomination formally was submitted to the Senate. President Ronald Reagan had announced the appointment on July 7, but the formal papers naming her did not move to the Senate until mid-August.

The confirmation process ran smoothly for O'Connor. After the usual courtesy calls to particular senators, she underwent three days of questioning by the Senate Judiciary Committee, which then approved her nomination by a vote of 17-0, with one member abstaining. Confirmation by the full Senate came the following week. O'Connor was sworn in Sept. 25, just in time to begin the 1981 term that October.

For three out of four Supreme Court nominees, confirmation has been a mere formality. Most have been approved by voice vote of the Senate soon after their selection by the president. Only 11 nominees have been rejected outright; 16 others have been withdrawn or permitted to expire because Senate rejection appeared certain. *(Box, p. 34)*

Most of the rejections came in the 19th century. From 1894 until 1968, only one of 45 court nominees failed to win Senate approval: John J. Parker of North Carolina, who was rejected by the Senate in 1930 by a vote of 39-41.

Supreme Court Nominations Not Confirmed by the Senate

From 1789 through 1982, 27 Supreme Court nominations did not receive Senate confirmation. Of these, 11 were rejected outright and the remainder were withdrawn or allowed to lapse when Senate rejection appeared imminent. Following is the list of nominees who were not confirmed.

Nominee	President	Date of Nomination	Senate Action	Date of Senate Action
William Paterson	Washington	Feb. 27, 1733	Withdrawn**	
John Rutledge (for Chief Justice)	Washington	July 1, 1795	Rejected (10-14)	Dec. 15, 1795
Alexander Wolcott	Madison	Feb. 4, 1811	Rejected (9-24)	Feb. 13, 1811
John J. Crittenden	John Quincy Adams	Dec. 17, 1828	Postponed	Feb. 12, 1829
Roger Brooke Taney	Jackson	Jan. 15, 1835	Postponed (24-21)*	March 3, 1835
John C. Spencer	Tyler	Jan. 9, 1844	Rejected (21-26)	Jan. 31, 1844
Reuben H. Walworth	Tyler	March 13, 1844	Withdrawn	
Edward King	Tyler	June 5, 1844	Postponed	June 15, 1844
Edward King	Tyler	Dec. 4, 1844	Withdrawn	
John M. Read	Tyler	Feb. 7, 1845	Not Acted Upon	
George W. Woodward	Polk	Dec. 23, 1845	Rejected (20-29)	Jan. 22, 1846
Edward A. Bradford	Fillmore	Aug. 16, 1852	Not Acted Upon	
George E. Badger	Fillmore	Jan. 10, 1853	Postponed	Feb. 11, 1853
William C. Micou	Fillmore	Feb. 24, 1853	Not Acted Upon	
Jeremiah S. Black	Buchanan	Feb. 5, 1861	Rejected (25-26)	Feb. 21, 1861
Henry Stanbery	Andrew Johnson	April 16, 1866	Not Acted Upon	
Ebenezer R. Hoar	Grant	Dec. 15, 1869	Rejected (24-33)	Feb. 3, 1870
George H. Williams (for Chief Justice)	Grant	Dec. 1, 1873	Withdrawn	
Caleb Cushing (for Chief Justice)	Grant	Jan. 9, 1874	Withdrawn	
Stanley Matthews	Hayes	Jan. 26, 1881	Not Acted Upon**	
William B. Hornblower	Cleveland	Sept. 19, 1893	Rejected (24-30)	Jan. 15, 1894
Wheeler H. Peckham	Cleveland	Jan. 22, 1894	Rejected (32-41)	Feb. 16, 1894
John J. Parker	Hoover	March 21, 1930	Rejected (39-41)	May 7, 1930
Abe Fortas (for Chief Justice	Lyndon Johnson	June 26, 1968	Withdrawn	
Homer Thornberry	Lyndon Johnson	June 26, 1968	Not Acted Upon	
Clement F. Haynsworth Jr.	Nixon	Aug. 18, 1969	Rejected (45-55)	Nov. 21, 1969
G. Harrold Carswell	Nixon	Jan. 19, 1970	Rejected (45-51)	April 8, 1970

* Later nominated for chief justice and confirmed.
** Later nominated and confirmed.

Source: Library of Congress, Congressional Research Service

Confirmation Battles: 1968-70

In 1968, a turbulent year in American history, the first of several fierce confrontations over Supreme Court nominations erupted.

This sudden turmoil was set off by Chief Justice Earl Warren's announcement that he would retire as soon as his successor was chosen and confirmed by the Senate.

By the time Warren made his plans known, President Lyndon B. Johnson already had announced he would not run for re-election. Republicans, with Richard M. Nixon as their candidate, had high hopes of taking over the White House.

Although the Senate must vote to confirm, Congress has little say in a president's choice of a justice. Presidents generally have been permitted to chose almost anyone they please. But the Constitution does require that the Senate approve all court nominees. Politics always has played a major role in the confirmation process, and historically it has been difficult for a lame-duck president in an election year to win Senate approval of his choice for a seat on the court.

Disregarding that history, Johnson named Associate Justice Abe Fortas, whom he had placed on the court in 1965, to be the new chief justice. He chose federal Judge Homer Thornberry of Texas to fill the seat Fortas would vacate.

The Senate refused to confirm Fortas as chief justice, and thus did not act on the Thornberry nomination. Republican senators, hoping to reserve for Nixon the coveted opportunity of naming a chief justice, joined with conservative Democrats, who objected to Fortas' liberal views and to his close ties to Johnson, to filibuster the nomination. In October, a month before the general election, Johnson conceded defeat and withdrew the Fortas nomination.

A New Chief Justice

It fell to President Nixon in 1969 to name the successor to Chief Justice Warren. On May 21 the new president announced his choice: Warren E. Burger, 61, a conservative judge on the U.S. court of appeals, District of Columbia circuit.

Burger was confirmed June 9 by a vote of 74-3. He assumed his new office on June 23, 1969, in a brief ceremony marking Warren's retirement. In an unusual appearance for a president, Nixon attended the Supreme Court ceremony at which Burger was sworn in.

Fortas Resignation

The bitterness left by the unsuccessful fight to confirm Fortas as chief justice was exacerbated by Fortas' unexpected departure from the court in mid-May, just before the announcement of Burger's selection.

Fortas resigned his seat in the face of charges that he had acted improperly by receiving a $20,000 fee in 1966 from the family foundation of a convicted stock manipulator. Fortas, at that time an associate justice, returned the fee later the same year. He denied he had done anything wrong, but resigned on May 14 with the threat of impeachment hanging over him.

In his letter of resignation, Fortas said he was resigning in order to enable the court to "proceed with its work without the harassment of debate concerning one of its members."

The seat he vacated remained unoccupied for 13 months — until June 1970. The legacy of resentment the Fortas fight left among the justice's liberal supporters in the Senate created a difficult political atmosphere for any person nominated to succeed him.

Rejection of Haynsworth

President Nixon, who had promised during his presidential campaign to appoint men to the court who would turn that body in a more conservative direction, looked for a Southern conservative to replace Fortas.

Clement F. Haynsworth Jr., 56, was Nixon's first choice. Haynsworth, a well-to-do South Carolinian, was then serving as chief judge on the U.S. court of appeals, 4th circuit.

Nixon announced his selection on Aug. 18, 1969. Confirmation hearings before the Senate Judiciary Committee began in September. Still smarting from what they considered the unfounded criticism with which conservatives had forced Fortas to resign, liberal senators questioned Haynsworth closely about his participation in various cases in which he had some potential financial interest, however small or remote. They raised questions about his sensitivity to the appearance of ethical impropriety. Labor and civil rights groups also criticized him for rulings they viewed as counter to their interests.

After these concerns were fully aired, the Senate Judiciary Committee in October approved the nomination by a vote of 10-7. In the committee's report, filed a month later, the majority declared Haynsworth "extraordinarily well qualified" for a seat on the court.

The White House mounted a campaign of increasing intensity to generate support for Haynsworth among Republicans and conservative Democrats. But on Nov. 21 the Senate, by a vote of 45-55, withheld its confirmation of Haynsworth. The key to the White House defeat was the defection of moderate Republicans, including the Senate Republican leadership.

It was the first rejection of a Supreme Court nominee in 39 years. Within the year, it would happen again.

Clement Haynsworth returned to his post on the court of appeals. His work there in subsequent years won increasing praise from judicial scholars. It was generally conceded that he would have been confirmed had it not been for the particularly hostile political atmosphere of 1969.

Rejection of Carswell

Nixon reiterated his determination to place a Southern conservative on the court. On Jan. 19, 1970, he named G. Harrold Carswell of Florida, 50, as his next choice for the Fortas seat. Carswell, who at one time had been the youngest federal judge in the country, was at the time a judge on the U.S. court of appeals, 5th circuit.

The Senate responded cautiously to news of the nomination. Neither Democrats nor Republicans were anxious for another bruising confirmation battle. But opposition to Carswell gradually surfaced, sparked initially by civil rights groups, who pointed to speeches by Carswell early in his career endorsing segregation. They argued that his later votes and actions reflected no change in those views. Labor backed its traditional allies, calling the nomination "a slap in the face to the nation's black citizens."

Senate opponents began to mobilize, led by Edward W. Brooke, R-Mass. (1967-79), the only black member of that body, and Birch Bayh, D-Ind. (1963-81), who had led the opposition to Haynsworth.

Their efforts were given a critical boost by the opposition to Carswell that arose from within the legal profession itself. The American Bar Association labeled him qualified for the Supreme Court, but law school deans and professors across the country questioned that judgment, calling him mediocre and undistinguished in his career, as well as clearly hostile to civil rights causes.

Roman L. Hruska, R-Neb. (1954-76), the Senate leader of the pro-Carswell forces, drew much sarcasm when he attempted to respond to such criticism of the nominee's abilities, perhaps in jest, by saying that "there are a lot of mediocre judges and people and lawyers. They are entitled to a little representation, aren't they?"

In mid-February, the Judiciary Committee declared Carswell "thoroughly qualified" for the court, voting 13-4 to approve his nomination. But the vote of the full Senate on confirmation was delayed by the determination of the Senate Democratic leadership to finish work on a major civil rights bill before considering the Carswell nomination. Delay worked to the advantage of the opposition, which continued to gain strength.

On April 8, by a vote of 45-51, the Senate rejected Carswell. Thirteen Republicans voted against confirmation. Not since 1894 had a president had two Supreme Court nominations formally rejected by the Senate.

Soon after his rejection, Carswell resigned his seat on the court of appeals and ran unsuccessfully for the Senate from Florida.

Political Peace: 1970-71

After Senate rejection of the Carswell nomination, Nixon declared it was clear to him that, as "presently constituted," the Senate would not approve a Southern conservative for the court.

Blackmun

Looking West, Nixon next chose Harry A. Blackmun, a federal appeals court judge who was a longtime friend of Warren Burger, as his nominee for the court vacancy.

Blackmun, 61, was a member of the U.S. court of appeals, 8th circuit. Nixon announced his selection just a week after the vote denying Carswell the seat. The Senate Judiciary Committee held one day of hearings on Blackmun's selection and declared him "thoroughly qualified" for the Supreme Court. He was confirmed by the Senate May 12, 1970, by a vote of 94-0. He took his seat June 9, 1970.

Powell, Rehnquist

After his inauspicious start with the Haynsworth and Carswell episodes, Nixon went on to place more men on the Supreme Court in his first term than any other president since Warren G. Harding in the early 1920s. By December 1971 he had named four of the court's nine members.

In September 1971 two veteran justices retired from the court: Hugo L. Black, 85, named to the court in 1937 by Franklin D. Roosevelt, and John Marshall Harlan, 72, whom Eisenhower had placed on the court in 1955. Both were in failing health and died within the year. *(Biographies, pp. 172, 174)*

On Oct. 21, 1971, Nixon named Lewis F. Powell Jr. and William H. Rehnquist to replace them.

Powell, 64, was a nationally recognized attorney who

had served as president of the American Bar Association. His career had been spent in the private practice of law and community service in Richmond, Va.

Rehnquist, 47, was an Arizona attorney who had come to Washington in 1969 with the Nixon administration, assuming the post of assistant attorney general, office of legal counsel. In that position, he advised the attorney general, who advised the president, on the legal background and validity of proposed actions by the administration.

Neither Powell nor Rehnquist had judicial experience. No question about either man's ability was raised during the confirmation process, however.

The only significant issue raised during the Senate's consideration of Powell's nomination involved the manner in which he would deal with potential conflicts of interest arising from his considerable wealth and investments. Powell assured the committee he would not participate in court cases that had any relationship to businesses in which he had a financial interest.

Rehnquist drew considerably more criticism, particularly from civil rights and civil liberties groups, who objected to the conservative views he had voiced on Capitol Hill as an official of the Nixon administration.

The Judiciary Committee quickly approved the nominations, declaring both men "thoroughly qualified" for the court. Powell won unanimous approval of the panel. The vote on Rehnquist was 12-4.

The Senate then confirmed Powell Dec. 6 by a vote of 89-1. Rehnquist was approved four days later, 68-26.

Stability: 1971-81

From December 1971, when Powell and Rehnquist joined the court, until July 1981 there was only one change on the court.

In October 1973 William O. Douglas became the longest serving justice in the court's history. Roosevelt had named Douglas to the court in 1939 at the age of 40. Early in 1975 — at the age of 76 — Douglas suffered a stroke. Despite his valiant efforts to continue work, the pain and disability that remained in the wake of the stroke forced him to retire that November at age 77. He had served on the court 36 and one-half years. *(Biography, p. 173)*

Two weeks after his retirement, President Gerald R. Ford, who as a member of the House had once led an attempt to impeach Douglas, named John Paul Stevens as Douglas' successor. Stevens, 55, was a judge on the U.S. court of appeals, 7th circuit.

The nomination was favorably received and quickly approved. The Senate confirmed Stevens, 98-0, on Dec. 17. He took his seat two days later.

From that date until July 3, 1981, the membership of the court did not change — an unusually long period of stability for the court. During its history, it has welcomed a new member on the average every two years.

Between 1976 and 1981 there was recurring speculation about impending changes in the court's makeup. However, no changes occurred during the presidency of President Jimmy Carter. Carter thus became the first full-term president in history to be denied the opportunity to name at least one member to the court.

During the 1980 presidential campaign, Carter's and Reagan's record in choosing judges was scrutinized. As a result of pressure from women's groups, Reagan promised

O'Connor Appointment

Four days after Justice Stewart's resignation, President Reagan nominated Sandra Day O'Connor, a 51-year-old state appeals court judge from Arizona, to succeed him.

O'Connor, a graduate of Stanford Law School, had practiced law for a number of years before "retiring" to raise her three sons. After they were in school, she resumed her career, first as an assistant state attorney general. She then was elected to the state Senate, of which she became majority leader. Later, she became a state judge. *(Biography, p. 167)*

O'Connor responded to Reagan's announcement with a brief news conference in Phoenix at which she said she was honored, but declined to answer any questions of substance out of deference to the Senate confirmation process she was about to undergo.

Conservative Opposition

Despite her conservative record, and the enthusiastic support of Republican Sen. Barry Goldwater, R-Ariz., O'Connor immediately ran into opposition from radical conservative groups such as Moral Majority. They charged her with favoring abortion and criticized her for supporting ratification of the then-pending (later-defeated) Equal Rights Amendment.

Sen. Jesse Helms, R-N.C., a leading conservative spokesman in the Senate, said he was "skeptical" about the choice of O'Connor. The Rev. Jerry Falwell, the head of Moral Majority, declared the nomination a "disaster." The National Right to Life Committee, a major anti-abortion group, pledged an all-out fight against her confirmation. "O'Connor's appointment represents a repudiation of the Republican platform pledge" to appoint judges "who respect traditional family values and the sanctity of innocent human life," said Dr. J. C. Willkie, the committee's president.

But the chorus of praise from liberals and moderates was a loud one. "If we're going to have Reagan appointees to the court, you couldn't do much better" than O'Connor, said Rep. Morris K. Udall, D-Ariz. O'Connor, Udall said, "is about as moderate a Republican as you'll ever find being appointed by Reagan." Sen. Edward M. Kennedy, D-Mass., praised Reagan's choice, and Eleanor Smeal, president of the National Organization for Women, called the nomination "a major victory for women's rights."

While the FBI began its check into O'Connor's background, and the American Bar Association committee on the federal judiciary began its probe of her qualifications, O'Connor visited Washington. She had met privately with Reagan on July 1 before her selection was announced. This time, it was a public meeting, complete with photo opportunities in the Rose Garden. O'Connor met with White House staff members and Justice Department attorneys to plan the preparation and strategy for her confirmation hearing. She also spent several days paying courtesy calls to key senators, especially the members of the Senate Judiciary Committee.

Nomination Submitted

After the FBI check was completed, Reagan formally sent O'Connor's nomination to the Senate on Aug. 19, 1981.

Early in September, O'Connor returned for her confirmation hearing. She had spent the intervening weeks studying up on Supreme Court history and constitutional

Sandra Day O'Connor became the first woman justice of the Supreme Court Sept. 21, 1981, winning Senate confirmation by a 99-0 vote.

that "one of the first Supreme Court vacancies in my administration will be filled by the most qualified woman I can find...."

Six months after Reagan took office in January 1981, a surprise retirement gave him the opportunity to fulfill his pledge.

Stewart Retirement

On June 18, 1981, Justice Potter Stewart announced that he would retire — after 23 years on the court — when the court adjourned for the summer.

Despite his long tenure, Stewart, at 66, was one of the court's younger members. Amid the speculation of recent years about retirements, his name hardly was menioned.

Stewart explained that he simply wished to retire while he was still in good health and could enjoy time with his family.

"I've always believed that it is better to go too soon than to stay too long, said the justice, who was second in seniority only to Justice Brennan.

His retirement took effect July 3, 1981. *(Biography, p. 171)* law. After her arrival, she rehearsed possible questions and answers with Justice Department attorneys.

O'Connor filed a financial statement with the Senate Judiciary Committee that reported the net worth of O'Connor and her husband at more than $1.1 million, more than any sitting justice except Lewis F. Powell Jr. and Warren E. Burger. The bulk of the O'Connors' assets were their home near Phoenix, Mr. O'Connor's share in his law partnership and Mrs. O'Connor's share of her family's cattle and sheep ranch in southern Arizona.

Before the hearings began, the American Bar Association committee reported that it found O'Connor "qualified" for a seat on the court.

All three days of hearings (Sept. 9-11) were broadcast live. The opening proceedings resembled a wedding. Judiciary staffers ushered honored guests into a large reserved area behind the witness table. O'Connor came down the aisle of the packed hearing room on the arm of Chairman Strom Thurmond, R-S.C., and both smiled to friends they recognized. As O'Connor reached the witness table, committee members, like proud relatives, rushed to shake her hand and offer their congratulations.

The senators' opening remarks did nothing to dispel the atmosphere. Each praised the judge warmly and commented on the historic significance of the occasion.

Joseph R. Biden Jr., Del., the ranking Democrat on the committee, outlined the questions the committee hoped to answer during the hearings:

"First, does the nominee have the intellectual capacity, competence and temperament to be a Supreme Court justice?

"Second, is the nominee of good moral character and free of conflict of interest that would compromise her ability to faithfully and objectively perform her role as a member of the U.S. Supreme Court?

"Third, will the nominee faithfully uphold the laws and Constitution of the United States of America?"

Biden also pointed out that the committee was "not attempting to determine whether or not the nominee agrees with all of us on each and every pressing social or legal issue of the day. Indeed, if that were the test no one would ever pass by this committee, much less the full Senate."

However, Sen. Jeremiah Denton, R-Ala., speaking later in the day, made clear that O'Connor's views on one issue would affect his vote. He told the nominee that his decision to vote for or against her confirmation would be affected by his belief that "legalized abortion" was "a denial of the most fundamental ... national principle of this Nation."

O'Connor's Views

In her own brief opening statement, O'Connor emphasized that her experience in all three branches of state government had given her an appreciation of the role the states filled in the federal system and the importance of the separate functions of the three branches.

She made clear that she saw definite limits on her ability to answer questions from the committee: "I hope to be as helpful to you as possible in responding to your questions," she told members. But she added, "I do not believe that ... I can tell you how I might vote on a particular issue which may come before the court, or endorse or criticize specific Supreme Court decisions presenting issues which may well come before the Court again. To

do so would mean that I have prejudged the matter or have morally committed myself to a certain position. Such a statement ... might make it necessary for me to disqualify myself on the matter. This would result in my inability to do my sworn duty: namely, to decide cases that come before the Court. Finally, neither you nor I know today the precise way in which an issue will present itself in the future, or what the facts or arguments may be at that time, or how the statute being interpreted may read. Until those crucial factors become known, I suggest that none of us really know how we would resolve any particular issue."

Going out of her way to demonstrate her personal commitment to family values, O'Connor introduced her three sons, her husband, her sister and her brother-in-law. She prefaced those introductions with remarks she had used as a state judge in performing marriage ceremonies. In those, she stated: "Marriage is far more than an exchange of vows. It is the foundation of mankind's basic unit of society, the hope of the world and the strength of our country. It is the relationship between ourselves and the generations which follow."

Abortion. O'Connor's position on the question of legalized abortions was the primary focus of the committee hearing.

Chairman Thurmond began the questioning by giving O'Connor the chance to explain some of her votes as a state senator on this issue. The pertinent exchange follows (from the transcript of the hearings):

The CHAIRMAN. Judge O'Connor, there has been much discussion regarding your views on the subject of abortion. Would you discuss your philosophy on abortion, both personal and judicial, and explain your actions as a State senator in Arizona on certain specific matters: First, your 1970 committee vote in favor of House bill No. 20, which would have repealed Arizona's felony statutes on abortion....

O'CONNOR. Very well. May I preface my response by saying that the personal views and philosophies, in my view, of a Supreme Court Justice and indeed any judge should be set aside insofar as it is possible to do that in resolving matters that come before the Court.

Issues that come before the Court should be resolved based on the facts of that particular case or matter and on the law applicable to those facts, and any constitutional principles applicable to those facts. They should not be based on the personal views and ideology of the judge with regard to that particular matter or issue.

Now, having explained that, I would like to say that my own view in the area of abortion is that I am opposed to it as a matter of birth control or otherwise. The subject of abortion is a valid one, in my view, for legislative action subject to any constitutional restraints or limitations.

I think a great deal has been written about my vote in [the Arizona] Senate Judiciary Committee in 1970 on a bill called House bill No. 20, which would have repealed Arizona's abortion statutes.... The bill did not go to the floor of the Senate for a vote; it was held in the Senate Caucus and the committee vote was a vote which would have taken it out of that committee with a recommendation to the full Senate.

The bill is one which concerned a repeal of Arizona's then statutes which made it a felony, punishable

Justice Stewart Often Was Supreme Court's Swing Vote

"Whatever we may think as citizens, our single duty as judges is to determine whether the legislation before us was within the constitutional power of Congress to enact," wrote Justice Potter Stewart in 1970.

"A casual reader could easily get the impression that what we are being asked in these cases is whether or not we think allowing people 18 years old to vote is a good idea. Nothing could be wider of the mark."

This carefully defined view of judicial power, which sometimes produced "liberal" opinions and sometimes "conservative" ones, was the hallmark of Justice Stewart's philosophy. For 23 years Stewart was the court's "man in the middle" — during the Warren court era of liberal rulings as well as the Burger court era of more conservative decisions.

Named to the court in 1958 by President Dwight D. Eisenhower, Stewart found himself in disagreement with some of the Warren court's most controversial rulings. When the court in 1962 held unconstitutional New York's use of a prescribed daily prayer in public schools, Stewart was the only justice who dissented. He also dissented from the court's controversial 1966 decision in the case of *Miranda v. Arizona*, which forbade prosecutors in court to use statements by suspects who had not been warned in advance of their constitutional rights.

Stewart, nevertheless, joined the court in a number of other major rulings and was responsible for its innovative use of an 1866 civil rights law to ban discrimination in the private sale or rental of housing and in private schools.

His most quoted judicial statement came in a concurring opinion in a 1964 case in which the court wrestled in vain with the problem of obscenity. Stewart wrote that he would not attempt to define obscenity, "but I know it when I see it. . . ."

Stewart's middle-of-the-road position on women's rights was characteristic of his judicial stance. In 1973 he refused to join four of his colleagues to make sex-based classifications as difficult for a state to defend as race-based ones. But in 1974 he wrote the court's opinion striking down school board rules requiring teachers to take long maternity leaves. He joined the court's landmark 1973 ruling legalizing abortion. But in 1980 he wrote the majority opinion upholding the power of Congress to restrict public funding of abortions.

After Chief Justice Warren E. Burger succeeded Earl Warren, Stewart found himself both more powerful and more comfortable. He cast the deciding vote in a dozen major rulings in the 1970s and early 1980s on issues ranging from the death penalty to affirmative action.

When the court in 1972 held that all existing death penalty laws were unconstitutional, each justice wrote a separate opinion explaining his vote. It is Stewart's, however, that most often is quoted. Because those laws left so much discretion to the judge or jury in deciding when to impose a death sentence, he said, the "death sentences are cruel and unusual in the same way that being struck down by lightning is cruel and unusual." And the death sentence was being "wantonly" and "freakishly" imposed, he said.

But Stewart refused to go so far as to find that the death penalty always was unconstitutionally severe, and he took issue with the suggestion that retribution was a constitutionally impermissible ingredient in punishment. "The instinct for retribution is part of the nature of man, and channeling that instinct in the administration of criminal justice serves an important purpose in promoting the stability of a society governed by law. When people begin to believe that organized society is unwilling or unable to impose upon criminal offenders the punishment they 'deserve,' then there are sown the seeds of anarchy — of self-help, vigilante justice, and lynch law."

Four years later, the court reviewed the new death penalty laws enacted in the wake of the 1972 decision. Stewart explained why the court found mandatory death sentences unconstitutional but upheld other capital punishment laws that permitted consideration of the individual offense and the offender before a sentence was imposed. "[I]n capital cases," he wrote, "the fundamental respect for humanity underlying the Eighth Amendment [which bans cruel and unusual punishment] . . . requires consideration of the character and record of the individual offender and the circumstances of the particular offense as a constitutionally indispensable part of the process of inflicting the penalty of death."

Stewart's talent for picking a path between two extremes was apparent in later cases involving such questions as affirmative action and press freedom. In 1978 he was one of five justices who voted to hold illegal the minority quota system used by the medical school admissions committee for the University of California at Davis. A year later, he was one of five justices who voted to permit private employers voluntarily to adopt affirmative action plans.

Often considered a champion of a free press, Stewart in 1979 wrote the court's opinion when it voted 5-4 to uphold a trial judge's order excluding the press and public from a pretrial hearing. A year later, however, he joined the majority in holding that the First Amendment guarantees the press and public a right to attend criminal trials.

by from 2 to 5 years in prison, for anyone providing any substance or means to procure a miscarriage unless it was necessary to save the life of the mother. It would have, for example, subjected anyone who assisted a young woman who, for instance, was a rape victim in securing a D. & C. procedure within hours or even days of that rape.

At that time I believed that some change in Arizona statutes was appropriate, and had a bill been presented to me that was less sweeping than House bill No. 20, I would have supported that. It was not, and the news accounts reflect that I supported the committee action in putting the bill out of committee, where it then died in the caucus.

I would say that my own knowledge and awareness of the issues and concerns that many people have about the question of abortion has increased since those days. It was not the subject of a great deal of public attention or concern at the time it came before the committee in 1970. I would not have voted, I think, Mr. Chairman, for a simple repealer thereafter.

The CHAIRMAN. Now the second instance was your cosponsorship in 1973 of Senate bill No. 1190, which would have provided family planning services, including surgical procedures, even for minors without parental consent.

O'CONNOR... I viewed the bill as a bill which did not deal with abortion but which would have established as a State policy in Arizona, a policy of encouraging the availability of contraceptive information to people generally. The bill at the time, I think, was rather loosely drafted, and I can understand why some might read it and say, "What does this mean?"

That did not particularly concern me at the time because I knew that the bill would go through the committee process and be amended substantially before we would see it again....

It did not provide for any surgical procedure for an abortion, as has been reported inaccurately by some....

Mr. Chairman, I supported the availability of contraceptive information to the public generally. Arizona had a statute or statues on the books at that time, in 1973, which did restrict rather dramatically the availability of information about contraception to the public generally. It seemed to me that perhaps the best way to avoid having people who were seeking abortions was to enable people not to become pregnant unwittingly or without the intention of doing so.

The CHAIRMAN. The third instance, your 1974 vote against House Concurrent Memorial No. 2002, which urged Congress to pass a constitutional amendment against abortion.

O'CONNOR. Mr. Chairman, as you perhaps recall, the *Roe* v. *Wade* decision was handed down in 1973. I would like to mention that in that year following that decision, when concerns began to be expressed, I requested the preparation in 1973 of Senate bill No. 1333, which gave hospitals and physicians and employees the right not to participate in or contribute to any abortion proceeding if they chose not to do so and objected, notwithstanding their employment. That bill did pass the State Senate and became law.

The following year, in 1974, less than a year following the *Roe* v. *Wade* decision, a House Memorial was introduced in the Arizona House of Representa-

tives. It would have urged Congress to amend the Constitution to provide that the word person in the 5th and 14th amendments applies to the unborn at every stage of development, except in an emergency when there is a reasonable medical certainty that continuation of the pregnancy would cause the death of the mother. The amendment was further amended in the Senate Judiciary Committee.

I did not support the memorial at that time, either in committee or in the caucus.... I voted against it, Mr. Chairman, because I was not sure at that time that we had given the proper amount of reflection or consideration to what action, if any, was appropriate by way of a constitutional amendment in connection with the *Roe* v. *Wade* decision.

It seems to me, at least, that amendments to the Constitution are very serious matters and should be undertaken after a great deal of study and thought, and not hastily. I think a tremendous amount of work needs to go into the text and the concept being expressed in any proposed amendment. I did not feel at that time that that kind of consideration had been given to the measure.....

The CHAIRMAN. Now the last instance is concerning a vote in 1974 against a successful amendment to a stadium construction bill which limited the availability of abortions.

O'CONNOR. Also in 1974, which was an active year in the Arizona Legislature with regard to the issue of abortion, the Senate had originated a bill that allowed the University of Arizona to issue bonds to expand its football stadium. That bill passed the State Senate and went to the House of Representatives.

In the House it was amended to add a nongermane rider which would have prohibited the performance of abortions in any facility under the jurisdiction of the Arizona Board of Regents. When the measure returned to the Senate, at that time I was the Senate majority leader and I was very concerned because the subject had become one that was controversial within our own membership.

I was concerned as majority leader that we not encourage a practice of the addition of nongermane riders to Senate bills which we had passed without that kind of a provision.... I did oppose the addition by the House of the nongermane rider when it came back.

It might be of interest, though, to know, Mr. Chairman, that also in 1974 there was another Senate bill which would have provided for a medical assistance program for the medically needy. That was Senate bill No. 1165. It contained a provision that no benefits would be provided for abortions except when deemed medically necessary to save the life of the mother, or where the pregnancy had resulted from rape, incest, or criminal action. I supported that bill together with that provision, and the measure did pass and become law.

The abortion issue recurred throughout the three days of hearings. O'Connor was consistent in stating her personal opposition to abortion but also in emphasizing that her "personal views and beliefs in this area and in other areas have no place in the resolution of any legal issues that will come before the court. I think these are matters that of necessity a judge must attempt to set aside in resolving the

cases that come before the court."

In a later exchange with Sen. Dennis DeConcini, D-Ariz., O'Connor spoke of "my own abhorrence of abortion as a remedy. It is a practice in which I would not have engaged, and I am not trying to criticize others in that process. There are many who have very different feelings on this issue. . . ."

O'Connor's care in responding to these questions frustrated some committee members. On the last day of the hearings, Sen. Jeremiah Denton, R-Ala., said, after questioning O'Connor further on abortion, "I do not feel I have made any progress personally in determining where you stand on the issue of abortion. I believe when you say 'and there may be other matters,' or issues, or however you stated [it], that makes it totally vague and therefore I find myself at a loss. . . ."

Sen. John P. East, R-N.C., expressed a similar frustration with regard to O'Connor's caution in expressing an opinion on recent court decisions and on issues that might come before the court:

"If in our fulfilling that obligation which the framers gave to us we are forbidden to get real substantive comment on issues of consequence — for example, previous doctrines and cases — I dare say we set a precedent — potentially, do we not? — whereby we cannot really fulfill any meaningful constitutional obligation; hence, we might suspense [sic] with it.

"It is frustrating, as a Senator, because the Senate and the Congress are trying, I feel, in so many ways to reassert their policy-making function which many feel has been eclipsed by the bureaucracy under the direction of the executive branch or frequently by the Supreme Court and the judiciary.

"We are given a few tools in the Constitution to try to assert our check and balance in [the] separation of power. One of those is to be a part of the confirmation process. We have clearly that check or balance under the Constitution, but if we are forbidden by our own practices or those insisted upon by nominees, I query whether that formal and fundamental check and balance — and probably the most fundamental one we have in the appointment process — is not negated and eliminated simply because questions cannot be asked in a fairly thorough and substantive way.

"I can appreciate you cannot promise anything; I can appreciate you could not comment upon pending cases; but when we are told that there cannot be comment upon previous cases and previous doctrines of substance, I query as one lowly freshman Senator whether we are able really to get out teeth into anything."

Judicial Activism. In answer to a question from Sen. Biden, O'Connor distinguished between "judicial activism" and landmark Supreme Court decisions overturning settled practices, such as the 1954 decision in *Brown v. Board of Education* holding state-imposed public school segregation to be unconstitutional. O'Connor said:

"[W]ith all due respect I do not believe that it is the function of the judiciary to step in and change the law because the times have changed or the social mores have changed. . . . I believe that on occasion [as in *Brown*] the court has reached changed results interpreting a given provision of the Constitution based on its research of what the true meaning of that provision is — based on the intent of the framers, its research on the history of that particular provision. . . ."

Sex Discrimination. Sen. Edward M. Kennedy, D-Mass., and O'Connor discussed her views on sex discrimination (from the transcript of the hearing):

KENNEDY. You were active in several efforts in Arizona in the State senate to revise employment, domestic relations, and property laws which discriminated against women. I think at that time you pointed out the sharp discrepancies between the pay which men and women often received for similar work.

As you may have seen, recently there was a report by the EEOC [Equal Employment Opportunity Commission] about the continued aspects of job discrimination on the basis of sex, and the pay discrepancy is still widespread. Do you find that it is still widespread? Is this a matter of concern to you?

O'CONNOR. It has always been a matter of concern to me. I have spoken about it in the past and have addressed the fact that there does seem to be a wide disparity in the earnings of women compared to that of men.

We know that perhaps a portion of that is attributed to the fact that women have traditionally at least accepted jobs in lower paying positions than has been true for men, and that may be a factor.

When I went to the legislature in Arizona we still had on the books a number of statutes that in my view did discriminate against women. Arizona is a community property State, and the management of the community personal property was placed with the husband, for example. These were things that had been in place for some years. I did take an active role in the legislature in seeking to remove those barriers and to correct these provisions.

KENNEDY. From your own knowledge and perception, how would you characterize the level of discrimination on the basis of sex today?

O'CONNOR. Presently?

KENNEDY. Yes.

O'CONNOR. I suppose that we still have areas from State to State where there remain some types of problems. We know that statistically the earnings are still less than for men. I am sure that in some cases and some instances attitudes still have not followed along with some of the changes in legal provisions.

However, it is greatly improved. It has been very heartening to me as a woman in the legal profession to see the large numbers of women who now are enrolled in the Nation's law schools, who are coming out and beginning to practice law, and who are serving on the bench. We are making enormous changes. I think these changes are very welcome.

Excluding Evidence. Since 1914 the Supreme Court has held that evidence obtained in violation of a defendant's constitutional rights may not be admitted in federal court to be used against him. Since 1961 the court has applied this exclusionary rule to state courts. O'Connor discussed the rule, its impact and arguments for making some modifications several times during the hearings. Reflecting on her experience in this area as a state trial judge, she said:

"There are times when perfectly relevant evidence and, indeed, sometimes the only evidence in the case has been excluded by application of a rule which, if different standards were to be applied, maybe would not have applied in that situation, for instance to good faith conduct on the part of police [that is, where police have acted in the belief that they were behaving in a legal and constitutional fashion].

"I am not suggesting and do not want to be interpreted as suggesting that I think it is inappropriate where force or trickery or some other reprehensible conduct has been used, but I have seen examples of the application of the rule which I thought were unfortunate, on the trial court."

Importance of Precedent. With regard to the doctrine of *stare decisis* — deciding new cases similar to old ones in keeping with the decisions already announced by the court — O'Connor again demonstrated her ability to state an opinion without tying herself to a rigid standard (from the transcript of the hearing):

Stare decisis of course is a crucial question with respect to any decision of the Supreme Court and its work. I think most people would agree that stability of the law and predictability of the law are vitally important concepts.

Justice Cardozo pointed out the chaos that would result if we decided every case on a case-by-case basis

without regard to precedent. It would make administration of justice virtually impossible. Therefore, it plays a very significant role in our legal system.

We are guided, indeed, at the Supreme Court level and in other courts by the concept that we will follow previously decided cases which are in point. Now at the level of the Supreme Court, where we are dealing with a matter of constitutional law as opposed to a matter of interpretation of a congressional statute, there has been some suggestion made that the role of stare decisis is a little bit different in the sense that if the Court is deciding a case concerning the interpretation, for example, of a congressional act and the Court renders a decision, and if Congress feels that decision was wrong, then Congress itself can enact further amendments to make adjustments. Therefore, we are not without remedies in that situation.

Whereas, if what the Court decided is a matter of constitutional interpretation and that is the last word, then the only remedy, as you have already indicated, is either for an amendment to the Constitution to be offered or for the Court itself to either distinguish its holdings or somehow change them.

We have seen this process occur throughout the Court's history. There are instances in which the Justices of the Supreme Court have decided after examining a problem or a given situation that their previous decision or the previous decisions of the Court in that particular matter were based on faulty reasoning or faulty analysis or otherwise a flawed interpretation of the law. In that instance they have the power, and indeed the obligation if they so believe, to overturn that previous decision and issue a decision that they feel correctly reflects the appropriate constitutional interpretation.

What I am saying in effect is, it is not cast in stone but it is very important.

Sen. [PAUL] LAXALT, [R-Nev.]. It is still a highly persuasive consideration as a matter of principle.

O'CONNOR. Very.

Busing. Drawing on her own experience, O'Connor expressed strong reservations about the usefulness of busing children for the purpose of desegregating public schools. She noted that as a state legislator she voted in favor of legislation that requested action by the federal government to terminate the use of forced busing in desegregation cases.

"This is a matter of concern, I think, to many people. The transportation of students over long distances and in a time-consuming process in an effort to get them to school can be a very disruptive part of any child's educational program.

"In that perhaps I am influenced a little bit by my own experience. I grew up in a very remote part of Arizona and we were not near any school. It bothered me to be away from home to attend school, which I had been from kindergarten on. In the eighth grade I attempted to live at home on the ranch and ride a schoolbus to get to school. It involved a 75-mile trip each day, round trip, that is, and I found that I had to leave home before daylight and get home after dark.

"I found that very disturbing to me as a child, and I am sure that other children who have had to ride long distances on buses have shared that experience. I just think that it is not a system that often is terribly beneficial to the child."

State Prerogatives. In an exchange with Sen. Howell Heflin, D-Ala., O'Connor discussed the 10th Amendment — which reserves to the states and the people all powers the Constitution does not give to the federal government or deny to the states. Asked about her view of the judiciary's role in preserving federalism, O'Connor responded:

"I am sure that we have not seen the last of the inquiries that the Court will make, by any stretch, into the application of the 10th Amendment, but it sets forth a very vital pronouncement of the role of the states in the federal system. . . . I have some concerns about seeing that State governments and local governments are maintained in their abilities to deal with the problems affecting the people. The reason for that philosophically is because I think I would agree with those who think that the government closest to the people is best able to handle those problems."

Women in Combat. O'Connor said it was her personal opinion that it was not appropriate for women to engage in combat, "if that term is restricted in its meaning to a battlefield situation." But she indicated that she would be less opposed to women "pushing a button someplace in a missile silo."

Capital Punishment. On the question of the death penalty, O'Connor noted that she had participated "rather extensively" in drafting a new death penalty law for Arizona after the U.S. Supreme Court in 1972 struck down all existing death penalty statutes as unconstitutional. The court had ruled that the state laws gave juries too much discretion in deciding when to sentence a defendant to death.

Equal Rights Amendment. In one of the more unusual episodes of the confirmation hearing, Sen. Biden urged O'Connor to become an active spokesperson for women's issues.

That exchange went as follows (from the transcript of the hearing):

BIDEN. My time is running out, but let me ask you one other question, if I may, about the appropriateness to be involved in promotion of social issues. Would it be, in your opinion, inappropriate for you as the first and only woman at this point on the Supreme Court — if you are confirmed, as I believe you will and should be — to for example be involved in national efforts to promote the ERA?

O'CONNOR. Mr. Chairman, Senator Biden; I believe that it would be inappropriate.

BIDEN. Why would it be inappropriate for you to do that while it is appropriate for Justice Burger to be traveling around the country telling us and everyone else what State and Federal jurisdictions should do about prison construction and what attorneys should do about law schools and how they should be maintained, and whether or not we should have barristers and solicitors. I mean, what is the distinction? Is it a personal one or is there a real one?

O'CONNOR. Mr. Chairman——

BIDEN. I do not suggest he should not do that; I want to know what your distinction is. [Laughter.]

O'CONNOR. It seems to me that it is appropriate for judges to be concerned and, indeed, to express themselves in matters relating to the administration of justice in the courts, and as to matters which would improve that administration of justice in some fashion. Certainly the court system is very heavily involved in the criminal justice system.

BIDEN. However, doesn't he also speak not just about administration of justice? Hasn't he spoken — correct me if I am wrong — but hasn't he spoken about procedural changes in the law, not just for the administration of justice, in the broad sense of whether there are prisons or whether there are backlogs in the courts, but actually what should be the law relating to criminal matters and other matters? I mean, he has gone beyond and suggested legislation.

O'CONNOR. Mr. Chairman, Senator Biden, yes, I think that the canons of judicial ethics do say that a judge may engage in activities to improve the law and the legal system and the administration of justice. I am sure that those statements which have been made are made in——

BIDEN. I just do not want you to wall yourself off, Judge. You are a tremendous asset. You are a woman and the first one on the Court; don't let these folks, me included, run you out of being that. You are a woman; you do stand for something that this country needs very badly. We need spokespersons in positions of high authority. Don't lock yourself in, in this hearing or any other hearing, to do things that you are not proscribed from doing in the canons of ethics.

It is your right, if it were your desire, to go out and campaign very strongly for the ERA. It is your right to go out and make speeches across the country about inequality for women, if you believed it. Don't wall yourself off. Your male brethren have not done it. Don't you do it.

You are a singular asset, and you are looked at by many of us not merely because you are a bright, competent lawyer but also because you are a woman. That is something that should be advertised by you. You have an obligation, it seems to me, to women in this country to speak out on those issues that you are allowed to under the canons of ethics. Don't let us intimidate you into not doing it.

[Applause.]

The CHAIRMAN. I will warn the audience there will be no clapping, and the police will remove anyone who attempts it again.

BIDEN. Will they remove the person who causes it, Mr. Chairman? [Laughter.]

Other Committee Witnesses

In addition to O'Connor, Attorney General William French Smith, Sen. Barry Goldwater, R-Ariz., and various other members of Congress and Arizona legislators testified, as did the following individuals and groups.

Frank Brown, chairman of the National Association for Personal Rights in Education; Bruce Babbitt, governor of Arizona; Margaret Nancy, mayor of Phoenix, Ariz.; James McNulty, member of the Arizona Board of Regents; Brooksley Landau, chairperson of the American Bar Association Committee on the Federal Judiciary; Kathy Wilson of the National Women's Political Caucus; Dr. Carolyn F. Gerster of the National Right to Life Committee, Inc.; Joan Dempsey Klein, president of the National Association of Women Judges; Dr. Carl McIntire, president of the International Council of Christian Churches; Arnette R. Hubbard, president of the National Bar Association; Dick C. P.

Lantz, president-elect, American Judges Association; Father Charles Fiore, chairman of the National Pro-Life Political Action Committee; Eileen Camillo Cochran, president-elect, California Women Lawyers; Gordon S. Jones, executive director, United Families of America; Anne Neamon, national coordinator, Citizens for God and Country, and trustee, Truth In Press, Inc.; Stephen Gillers, co-chairman, Committee for Public Justice; Eleanor Smeal, president, National Organization for Women; Lynn Hecht Schafran, national director, Federation of Women Lawyers' Judicial Screening Panel; and Rita Warren, a private citizen.

Committee Vote

Four days after the hearings ended, the Senate Judiciary Committee Sept. 15 voted 17-0 to approve O'Connor's nomination, sending it to the full Senate. Sen. Denton abstained from the vote, saying that he had not been satisfied with O'Connor's responses to his questions on abortion.

Senate Floor Action

The Senate voted 99-0 Sept. 21 to confirm O'Connor. Four hours had been set aside for debate on the confirmation, but no real debate occurred. The Senate chamber was nearly deserted for much of that time.

Sen. Denton voted for confirmation; Sen. Max Baucus, D-Mont., who supported the nomination, was in Montana that day and did not vote.

After the vote, O'Connor appeared on the steps of the Capitol with Vice President George Bush. She thanked the Senate for its vote of approval and said she was "absolutely overjoyed."

She took her seat on the court on Sept. 25, 1981.

THE COURT'S POWER OF JUDICIAL REVIEW

Judicial review — the right of the Supreme Court to review acts of Congress to determine whether they are consonant with the Constitution and to strike down those that it finds in conflict — was not expressly provided for by the Constitution. The implicit justification for this authority lies in the supremacy clause (Article VI, Section 2), which states:

> This Constitution, and the Laws of the United States which shall be made in Pursuance thereof; and all Treaties made, or which shall be made, under the Authority of the United States, shall be the supreme Law of the Land; and the Judges in every State shall be bound thereby, any Thing in the Constitution or Laws of any State to the Contrary notwithstanding.

Most scholars of constitutional history are of the opinion that the framers did not intend to deny the court review power by omitting an express grant from the Constitution. The concept of judicial review was relatively well-recognized in the colonies at the time the Constitution was drafted. The Privy Council in London had reviewed the acts of the colonies for compliance with English law before the American Revolution. Several state courts had voided state laws considered inconsistent with their state constitutions.

During the Constitutional Convention, it was proposed on several occasions that the Supreme Court share the veto power over acts of Congress with the president. These suggestions were voted down, largely on the ground that the court should not be involved in enacting a law it might later be required to enforce. The decision was not made because the framers were opposed to judicial review, most historians agree.

According to the records of the Constitutional Convention compiled by Max Farrand, only two framers expressed reservations about judicial review, although other scholars have placed the number somewhat higher. During the ratification period, James Madison, who would later qualify his endorsement of judicial review, and Alexander Hamilton supported the concept in *The Federalist Papers*. Future Supreme Court Chief Justices Oliver Ellsworth and John Marshall endorsed the principle at their state ratification conventions. *(Box, p. 45)*

The first Congress, in Section 25 of the Judiciary Act of 1789, specifically granted the Supreme Court the right of judicial review over decisions of state courts holding invalid U.S. treaties, laws or claims under federal law or upholding a state constitution or law that was challenged as unconstitutional or in conflict with federal law.

No major constitutional clashes occurred during the Republic's first decade. Congress and the executive branch were firmly in the hands of the Federalists, who were united in their determination to stifle the political opposition: the states rights-minded Anti-Federalists. When Congress passed the far-reaching Sedition Act of 1798, which led to the imprisonment of several Anti-Federalist editors for criticizing the government, the court refused to strike down the act, despite Anti-Federalist assertions of its probable unconstitutionality.

Most of the early Supreme Court justices seemed to believe they were given the power of judicial review over federal statutes. Several of the justices, sitting as circuit court judges, refused to administer a 1792 federal pension law, arguing that the administrative duties it required of them were not judicial and thus were in conflict with the constitutional separation of powers.

Sitting as the Supreme Court in 1796, the justices assumed the power of judicial review by holding valid a federal tax on carriages. The ruling, since it upheld the law rather than nullified it, occasioned little comment. A few days later, the court ruled for the first time that a state law was invalid because it was in conflict with a federal treaty.

Thus, by the time John Marshall was appointed chief justice in 1801, the court already had exercised the power of judicial review, although it had not had occasion to test the extent of its power by declaring an act of Congress unconstitutional. When it did find the opportunity, the occasion arose as much from the politics of the day as from a clear-cut reading of the law.

Marbury: **The Power Asserted**

The decision considered by many legal scholars to be the most important in the court's history had its genesis in the aftermath of the bitter presidential election of 1800. In that year Democratic-Republican candidate Thomas Jef-

Interpretation of the Laws:
'Proper and Peculiar Province' of the Courts

Writing in No. 78 of *The Federalist Papers*, Alexander Hamilton made a strong case for the principle of judicial review in the new government. Reminding his readers that the Constitution placed limits on legislative authority, Hamilton wrote:

"Limitations ... can be preserved in no other way than through the medium of courts of justice, whose duty it must be to declare all acts contrary to the manifest tenor of the Constitution void. Without this, all the reservations of particular rights or privileges would amount to nothing....

"...There is no position which depends on clearer principles than that every act of a delegated authority, contrary to the tenor of the commission under which it is exercised, is void. No legislative act, therefore, contrary to the Constitution, can be valid. To deny this would be to affirm that the deputy is greater than his principal; that the servant is above his master; that the representatives of the people are superior to the people themselves; that men acting by virtue of powers may do not only what their powers do not authorize, but what they forbid.

"If it be said that the legislative body are themselves the constitutional judges of their own powers and that the construction they put upon them is conclusive upon the other departments it may be answered that this cannot be the natural presumption where it is not to be collected from any particular provisions in the Constitution. It is not otherwise to be supposed that the Constitution could intend to enable the representatives of the people to substitute their *will* to that of their constituents. It is far more rational to suppose that the courts were designed to be an intermediate body between the people and the legislature in order, among other things, to keep the latter within the limits assigned to their authority. The interpretation of the laws is the proper and peculiar province of the courts. A constitution is, in fact, and must be regarded by the judges as, a fundamental law. It therefore belongs to them to ascertain its meaning as well as the meaning of any particular act proceeding from the legislative body. If there should happen to be an irreconcilable variance between the two, that which has the superior obligation and validity ought, of course, to be preferred; or, in other words, the Constitution ought to be preferred to the statute, the intention of the people to the intention of their agents.

"Nor does this conclusion by any means suppose a superiority of the judicial to the legislative power. It only supposes that the power of the people is superior to both, and that where the will of the legislature, declared in its statutes, stands in opposition to that of the people, declared in the Constitution, the judges ought to be governed by the latter rather than the former."

Source: *The Federalist Papers*, with an Introduction by Clinton Rossiter (New York: Mentor, 1961), pp. 466-468.

ferson defeated the Federalist President John Adams. Unwilling to relinquish the power they had held since the beginning of the Republic, the Federalists sought to entrench themselves in the only branch of government still open to them — the judiciary. One of Adams' first acts after the election was to appoint his secretary of state, the committed Federalist John Marshall, to replace Oliver Ellsworth as chief justice.

The lame duck Congress speedily confirmed Marshall, who also continued for six weeks to serve as Adams' secretary of state until Adams left office on March 4, 1801. Congress, at Adams' behest, also approved measures creating 16 new circuit court judgeships, authorizing Adams to appoint as many justices of the peace for the newly created District of Columbia as he deemed necessary and reducing the number of Supreme Court justices from six to five at the next vacancy. This last bill was intended to deprive Jefferson of a quick appointment to the bench.

Adams named, and Congress confirmed, the 16 new circuit court judges as well as 42 justices of the peace. On March 3, Adams' last night in office, he signed the commissions for the new justices of the peace and had them taken to Marshall, who was to attach the Great Seal of the United States and have the commissions delivered to the appointees. Marshall did affix the seal but somehow failed to see that all the commissions actually were delivered.

William Marbury, an aide to the secretary of the Navy, was one of the appointees who did not receive his commission. After Jefferson took office, Marbury and three other men in the same position asked the president's secretary of state, James Madison, to give them their commissions.

When Madison, at Jefferson's direction, refused, Marbury asked the Supreme Court to issue a writ of *mandamus* ordering Madison to give the four men their commissions. In December 1801, Chief Justice Marshall asked Madison to show cause at the next session of the court why he should not comply with the order.

At about the same time, the Jeffersonians were talking of repealing the 1801 act that created the new circuit court judgeships. Congress did repeal the act in March 1802, and to forestall a court challenge on the ground that the repeal was invalid — since the Constitution stipulates that federal judges are appointed for life or good behavior — Congress also delayed the next meeting of the Supreme Court until

February 1803 — almost a year later.

In addition to the antagonism between the two political parties, Marshall and Jefferson shared a mutual dislike, and Marshall did not relish the thought that Jefferson would best him in this contest. Marshall, whose oversight had led to Marbury's suit in the first place, probably would have had to disqualify himself under modern ethical standards. And there also would be some question today whether the case was moot by the time the court heard it. But neither factor deterred Marshall from taking it up.

His insistence created an apparent dilemma. If the court ordered delivery of the commission, Madison might refuse to obey the order and the court would have no means to enforce compliance. It seemed likely that Madison would refuse; the government did not even argue its viewpoint before the court. And if the court did not issue the writ, it would be surrendering to Jefferson's point of view. Either way, the court would be conceding its lack of power.

Marshall resolved his dilemma with a remarkable decision, which one modern constitutional scholar — Robert G. McCloskey — has called a "masterwork of indirection, a brilliant example of Marshall's capacity to sidestep danger while seeming to court it, to advance in one direction while his opponents are looking in another."

Initially ignoring the question of jurisdiction, Marshall ruled that once the president had signed the commissions and the secretary of state had recorded them, the appointments were complete. He also ruled that a writ of *mandamus* was the proper tool to use to require the secretary of state to deliver the commissions.

Having thus rebuked Madison, and, more importantly, by implication Jefferson, Marshall turned to the question of whether the Supreme Court had the authority to issue the writ; he concluded it did not. Congress, Marshall said, had added unconstitutionally to the court's original jurisdiction when, under the Judiciary Act of 1789, it authorized the court to issue such writs to officers of the federal government.

To justify striking down a section of a federal statute, Marshall drew heavily on Hamilton's reasoning in No. 78 of *The Federalist Papers*. The chief justice wrote:

> [T]he powers of the legislature are defined and limited; and that those limits may not be mistaken or forgotten, the constitution is written. To what purpose are powers limited, and to what purpose is that limitation committed to writing, if these limits may, at any time, be passed by those intended to be restrained? The distinction between a government with limited and unlimited powers is abolished, if those limits do not confine the persons on whom they are imposed, and if acts prohibited and acts allowed, are of equal obligation. It is a proposition too plain to be contested, that the constitution controls any legislative act repugnant to it.

Having established the Constitution's supremacy over legislative enactments, Marshall turned to the question of whether the judiciary had the authority to determine when acts of Congress conflicted with the Constitution:

> It is, emphatically, the province and duty of the judicial department to say what the law is. Those who apply the rule to particular cases, must of necessity expound and interpret that rule. If two laws conflict with each other, the courts must decide on the operations of each. So, if a law be in opposition to the constitution; if both the law and the constitution apply to a particular case, so that the court must either decide that case, conformable to the law, disregarding the constitution; or conformable to the constitution, disregarding the law; the court must determine which of these conflicting rules governs the case: this is of the very essence of judicial duty. If then the courts are to regard the constitution, and the constitution is superior to any ordinary act of the legislature, the constitution, and not such ordinary act, must govern the case to which they both apply. . . .
>
> . . . The judicial power of the United States is extended to all cases arising under the constitution. Could it be the intention of those who gave this power, to say, that in using it, the constitution should not be looked into? That a case arising under the constitution should be decided, without examining the instrument under which it arises? This is too extravagant to be maintained.

Thus, while denying the court the power to issue writs of *mandamus* in such cases, Marshall asserted for the court the far more significant power of judicial review.

Marshall's claim of authority for the court was not generally viewed by his contemporaries with the same import given by future historians and political leaders. In fact, Jefferson, who believed that the legislature was the only branch capable of determining the validity of its actions, apparently did not find Marshall's claim of power particularly significant. According to Charles Warren, one of the premier historians of this period, "Jefferson's antagonism to Marshall and the Court at that time was due more to his resentment at the alleged invasion of his Executive prerogative than to any so-called 'judicial usurpation' of the field of Congressional authority."

The Power Exercised

Half a century passed before the court again struck down an act of Congress as unconstitutional. In those intervening decades, the court reviewed several acts of Congress and upheld each of them. Each time it did so, it reinforced the power Marshall had claimed in *Marbury*. And each time that the government appeared in court to defend the validity of the federal law, it again conceded the court's right of review.

The second and third times that the court held a law unconstitutional, it did so with decidedly negative consequences for itself and public confidence in it. Both its 1857 ruling in the case of *Dred Scott v. Sandford*, in which it said that Congress lacked the power to ban slavery in the territories, and in the 1870 case of *Hepburn v. Griswold*, in which it denied Congress the power to make paper money legal tender, are considered "self-inflicted wounds," undermining public respect for the court and its rulings. Both decisions subsequently were reversed: the *Dred Scott* ruling by the 14th Amendment and the *Hepburn* decision by the court itself in 1871.

The Dred Scott Case

Dred Scott, a slave, had been taken by his former master from the slave state of Missouri into territory made free by an act of Congress popularly known as the Missouri

Compromise. After returning to Missouri, Scott sued to establish his freedom on the ground that his sojourn in free territory had made him a free man. The Missouri Supreme Court held that he had indeed gained his freedom through being on free soil, but that he had lost it when he returned to the slave state of Missouri.

Since Scott's present master (Sanford) was a citizen of New York, the case was next considered by a federal court because it now was a controversy between citizens of different states, provided that Scott was a citizen of Missouri. When the case reached the U.S. Supreme Court, a majority of the justices decided initially that the case should have been dismissed in lower federal court for lack of jurisdiction because no Negro could be a citizen under the provisions of the Constitution. But the court did not stop there despite the finding that it did not have jurisdiction.

Chief Justice Roger Brooke Taney, who wrote what is considered the majority decision in the case (although nine separate opinions were filed by the justices), asserted that Scott was a slave because the Missouri Compromise — which had been repealed three years earlier by the Kansas-Nebraska Act — was unconstitutional. Congress, Taney declared, had no authority to limit the extension of slavery. The court's decision subsequently was voided by the 13th Amendment outlawing slavery.

The *Dred Scott* decision aroused tremendous resentment in the North, especially among members of the newly organized Republican Party, whose cardinal tenet was that Congress should abolish slavery in all the territories. The *New York Tribune* asserted editorially that the decision was "entitled to just so much moral weight as would be the judgment of a majority of those congregated in any Washington barroom.... Until that remote period when different judges sitting in this same court shall reverse this wicked and false judgment, the Constitution of the United States is nothing better than the bulwark of inhumanity and repression."

The Civil War and the 13th Amendment abolishing slavery put an end to the question of congressional power over slavery in the territories. And the 14th Amendment's first section, adopted in 1868, made clear that blacks as well as anyone else "born or naturalized in the United States" were citizens. (*Reversals, p. 61*)

The Legal Tender Case

There was no national currency in the United States until the Civil War, when Congress in 1862 and 1863 authorized the printing of paper money, or "greenbacks," and provided that this could be used as legal tender to pay all debts. In the case of *Bronson v. Rodes*, decided in 1869, the Supreme Court held that these greenbacks could not be used as payment in cases where a contract specifically stipulated that the debt would be paid in gold, the preferred medium of exchange.

The case of *Hepburn v. Griswold* already was before the court in 1869. In fact, it had already been argued twice, once in 1867 and again in 1868. Historian Charles Warren has written that the court's expected ruling on the validity of the greenbacks "had been the subject of long and excited debate in the community." Banks, mortgagees and creditors were lined up on one side, hoping for a ruling that paper money was not valid as payment of debts, while the railroads, municipal corporations, mortgagors and other debtors hoped for a ruling that paper money was valid.

On Feb. 7, 1870, the court delivered its opinion. At that time there were only seven sitting justices; there were two vacancies on the court.

By a 4-3 vote the court held that Congress lacked the power to make paper money legal tender for the payment of debts contracted prior to passage of the 1862 and 1863 acts. In the court's opinion, Chief Justice Salmon P. Chase, who as President Abraham Lincoln's secretary of the Treasury had advocated passage of the legal tender laws, declared those laws an improper use of congressional power. His reasoning called into question virtually all use of paper money.

Even while Chase was announcing the court's decision, President Ulysses S. Grant was sending to the Senate the names of his nominees for the two vacant seats on the court. This coincidence of timing led to charges that Grant specifically had picked his nominees — William Strong and Joseph P. Bradley — for their views favoring the validity of paper money.

Strong and Bradley were quickly confirmed. Less than two months after the decision in *Hepburn*, the court, with Strong and Bradley participating, granted review in two more legal tender cases and said it would reconsider its *Hepburn* decision.

A year later, on May 1, 1871, the court overruled *Hepburn v. Griswold*. The vote to do so, cast in the cases of *Knox v. Lee* and *Parker v. Davis*, was 5-4. Both Strong and Bradley voted with the majority. Strong wrote the court's opinion setting out the new majority's view that Congress acted properly in making greenbacks legal tender for payment of all debts.

There were many critics of the court's quick reversal, including Chief Justice Chase. The decision in *Hepburn* had been valid for only 15 months, and for most of that time the court had been reconsidering it. Chase and other critics of the 1871 ruling accused Grant of "packing" the court to win the reversal.

It was Charles Evans Hughes, who served as chief justice in the 1930s, who described this set of rulings and the *Dred Scott* decision as the court's "self-inflicted wounds." In his opinion, "[t]he reopening of the [*Hepburn*] case was a serious mistake and the overruling in such a short time, and by one vote, of the previous decision, shook popular confidence in the Court." Hughes concluded: "The argument for reopening was strongly presented in view of the great importance of the question but the effect of such a sudden reversal of judgment might easily have been foreseen. Stability in judicial opinions is of no little importance in maintaining respect for the Court's work."

The Income Tax Case

Until the Civil War, there was neither the need nor demand for a federal income tax. The federal government's revenue needs were modest and easily met by the excise taxes and duties on imported goods it traditionally had imposed. During the Civil War an income tax was imposed, but it expired in 1872. For the next 20 years, the nation went without a federal income tax.

Then in 1893 a depression reduced federal revenues, and the next year Congress levied a 2 percent tax on personal incomes of more than $4,000. Under this standard, only about 2 percent of the population was taxed.

The tax immediately was challenged as unconstitutional, a violation of the Constitution's requirement that all direct taxes be apportioned among the states on the basis of their population. It had never been defined precisely what "direct taxes" were, but for most of the nation's

Legislative Immunity: Broad Interpretation
Of the Constitution's 'Speech or Debate' Clause

The Constitution gives members of Congress immunity from arrest "in all cases, except Treason, Felony and Breach of the Peace ... during their attendance at the session of their respective Houses, and in going to and returning from the same." But the far more important constitutional provision — in modern times — provides that "for any Speech or Debate in either House, they shall not be questioned in any other Place."

The practical protection these provisions afford members of Congress has been determined by a series of recent Supreme Court decisions. Though these and various lower court rulings have made the "privilege from arrest" clause practically obsolete for U.S. legislators, the court has issued several major rulings since 1966 interpreting broadly the protection provided by the "speech or debate" clause.

In 1966 the court held that members of Congress are immune from prosecution for their words and legislative deeds on the floor of either house of Congress, with the slender exception that they may be prosecuted under a narrowly drawn law enacted by Congress itself to regulate its members' conduct. In the 1966 ruling, in the case of *United States v. Johnson*, the court forbade the executive branch to inquire into a member's motives for making a speech in Congress, even though the speech allegedly was made as the result of a bribe.

The court held that the "speech or debate" clause was intended to protect the independence of Congress from pressure from an unfriendly executive or a hostile judiciary.

Two years after the decision was handed down in his case, Rep. Thomas F. Johnson, D-Md. (1959-63), was convicted on conflict-of-interest charges. Those charges arose after he made a 1960 speech on the House floor defending savings and loan institutions. The speech allegedly was made in return for a "campaign contribution" of more than $20,000 to Johnson from a Maryland savings and loan company then under indictment.

In 1972 the Supreme Court narrowed the category of actions protected by legislative immunity. In the case of *United States v. Brewster*, the court permitted the government to prosecute former Sen. Daniel B. Brewster, D-Md. (House 1959-63; Senate 1963-69), on charges that he took a bribe from Spiegel Inc., a Chicago mail-order firm, to influence his actions and votes on postal rate legislation.

"Taking a bribe is, obviously, no part of the legislative process or function," held the Supreme Court. The indictment was valid, it explained, because it was not necessary for the government to inquire into Brewster's acts or votes or motives in order to prove that he had taken a bribe. Brewster stood trial and was convicted of a lesser bribery charge. His conviction was reversed; he was scheduled for a new trial but pleaded no contest to a felony charge of accepting an illegal gratuity, making a new trial unnecessary.

Also in 1972, the court listed certain legislative activities of a senator and his aides that are protected by the Constitution's immunity clause. This enumeration came in the case of *Gravel v. United States*, which arose after Sen. Mike Gravel, D-Alaska (1969-81), convened a hearing of his Public Works Subcommittee on Public Buildings in mid-1970 and read into the record classified documents from the so-called Pentagon Papers history of U.S. military involvement in Southeast Asia in the 1960s and early 1970s. He also arranged for the publication of the papers.

The court held that a grand jury could question Gravel and his aides about some of their actions in relation to the acquisition and release of the documents, but only those actions not directly related to their legislative responsibilities.

"While the Speech or Debate Clause recognizes speech, voting and other legislative acts as exempt from liability that might attach," stated the court, "it does not privilege either senator or aide to violate an otherwise valid criminal law in preparing for or implementing legislative acts."

The court concluded that a senatorial aide had immunity — the same as that of the senator himself — that protects him from prosecutions that "directly impinge upon or threaten the legislative process."

In 1979 the court issued two rulings on the subject of congressional immunity.

● In *United States v. Helstoski*, the court reiterated its earlier holding that federal prosecutors may not use evidence of past legislative actions in prosecuting members of Congress for bribery.

● In *Hutchinson v. Proxmire*, however, the court held that senators were not entirely protected from libel suits based on remarks made in Congress if those remarks later were published. Only remarks made in Congress are protected, held the court. It gave the green light to a libel suit based on the reprinting in a newsletter and press release of a Senate floor speech by Sen. William Proxmire, D-Wis. in 1975 in which the senator gave the National Aeronautics and Space Administration and the Office of Naval Research his so-called Golden Fleece Award. Those agencies had awarded a scientist $500,000 for research into how monkeys exhibit aggression. Proxmire had ridiculed the work of the scientist, Ronald Hutchinson, who later sued the senator. Proxmire eventually reached an out-of-court settlement with Hutchinson.

history up to that time, it was generally accepted that the only direct taxes were so-called "head" taxes and taxes on land.

But in the case of *Pollock v. Farmers' Loan and Trust Co.*, it was argued that the federal income tax was a direct tax and therefore invalid because it was not apportioned on the basis of state population. After two rounds of arguments in the spring of 1895, the court ruled by a 5-4 vote that the tax was unconstitutional.

Eighteen years later, Congress and the states overrode that ruling by ratifying the 16th Amendment, which empowered Congress to levy income taxes without concern for apportioning them among the states.

Protecting Property

During the 1920 and 1930s, the court vigorously wielded its power of judicial review to invalidate acts of Congress that it viewed as unconstitutional. While the court between 1790 and 1865 struck down only two laws passed by Congress, it struck down 32 in the period from 1920 to 1936.

Among the laws the court held invalid during the 1920s — primarily because it found that Congress was encroaching too far on the rights of the states or on the rights of property owners and businessmen — were two laws barring child labor and another setting a minimum wage for women and children working in the District of Columbia.

The climax of the court's activity in overturning congressional legislation, however, came in the mid-1930s, when the new economic legislation passed by Congress at the behest of the Roosevelt administration came before the court. One after another, the depression-born statutes were struck down by the Supreme Court in 1935 and 1936.

Among the laws the justices found Congress lacked the power to enact were:

● Railroad Retirement Pension Act of 1934, in which the court found that Congress, in establishing the pension system, had exceeded its power under the commerce clause of the Constitution and also that the act was in violation of the due process guarantee, which protects private property from being taken for public use without just compensation.

● National Industrial Recovery Act of 1933, in which the court held that Congress had delegated too much legislative power to the executive branch without setting standards to be followed in carrying out the delegated duties.

● Agricultural Adjustment Act of 1933, in which the court held that Congress had overstepped the bounds of its taxing power and infringed upon the powers left to the states.

● Bituminous Coal Conservation Act of 1935, in which the court held that Congress had exceeded the power granted it by the Constitution to regulate interstate commerce.

● Frazier-Lemke Farm Mortgage Act of 1934, which the court found to be unconstitutional because it violated the property rights of creditors.

● Home Owners' Loan Act of 1933, which the court found that it encroached too far on the reserved powers of the states.

● Municipal Bankruptcy Act of 1934, which was held to be an invalid interference in state sovereignty.

This extraordinary wielding of the power of judicial review to wipe out an entire national economic recovery program, proposed by a popular president and approved by Congress, soon moved the Roosevelt administration to threaten drastic action.

After winning re-election in 1936, President Roosevelt took note of the advancing age of a number of the court's members and proposed legislation to allow the president, when any federal judge or Supreme Court justice had served more than 10 years and chose not to retire within six months of becoming 70, to appoint an additional judge to the court in question.

Passage of the law would have enabled Roosevelt immediately to appoint six additional justices to the Supreme Court, bringing that court to the unprecedented size of 15 members, and thus presumably assuring the administration of court rulings favorable to the New Deal.

Despite the heavy criticism in Congress and the country of the court's rulings striking down the New Deal measures, Roosevelt's plan was not popular. Chief Justice Charles Evans Hughes presented an able defense of the court before the Senate Judiciary Committee in the spring of 1937, and the committee in June reported the administration proposal adversely.

But by that time, the Supreme Court had abandoned its stubborn opposition to the New Deal, and Roosevelt's court plan no longer was necessary. Late in March 1937 the court signaled this shift, which matched the shift away from its staunch protection of property rights and the so-called freedom of workers to contract for their wages, by upholding a state minimum wage law similar to the District of Columbia law that had been held unconstitutional only a year earlier.

Two weeks later, the court upheld the constitutionality of the National Labor Relations Act of 1935, another key element in the New Deal program. Even more important than the fact that the court upheld the law was that the majority based its decision on a broad view of Congress' power to regulate interstate commerce, a view totally at odds with that espoused by the court in its earlier rulings striking down the New Deal measures.

Civil, Individual Rights

In the 1950s the Supreme Court, now led by Chief Justice Earl Warren, struck down a number of laws Congress had passed during the "Cold War" period when concern about subversive activities grew rapidly.

In 1956 the court curbed the power of the federal government to dismiss government employees considered to be security risks, holding that an employee could be dismissed for this reason only if he held a "sensitive" position. The following year, the court held that a person could be prosecuted for advocating the forcible overthrow of the government only if he advocated that doctrine with the intent of inciting action. The court also interpreted the meaning of the word "organize" as it was used in the Smith Act of 1940 so narrowly that it permitted prosecution only of a person who had been involved in the initial organization of groups advocating violent revolution, not persons who had engaged in subsequent supporting activities, such as recruiting members. Five years later, Congress passed legislation broadening the meaning of the word "organize" in the Smith Act to include such continuing organizational activities.

In 1964 the court held unconstitutional a portion of the Subversive Activities Control Act of 1950 that deprived all members of the U.S. Communist Party of their U.S. passports. In other decisions during this period the court held unconstitutional laws that had denied citizenship to: persons who left the country to escape military service in wartime, persons who voted in foreign elections, and naturalized citizens who spent extended periods in the country of their birth or in a country where they formerly were citizens.

In addition, the court held that Congress had overstepped the Constitution's boundaries when it prohibited communists from serving as officers or employees of labor unions and when it required compulsory registration of Communist Party members.

These cases continued to come to the court throughout Chief Justice Warren's 16-year tenure. As late as 1967, the court held that a provision of the 1950 Subversive Activities Control Act that denied members of communist-front organizations the opportunity to work in a defense plant was unconstitutional because it violated the First Amendment's protection of freedom of association.

The Modern Power

After Earl Warren was succeeded in 1969 by Warren E. Burger as chief justice, the court continued to find acts of Congress unconstitutional primarily because of their adverse effect on individual rights.

A particularly notable group of rulings invalidated various federal laws because they unfairly treated men and women differently. These included a 1973 decision in *Frontiero v. Richardson* striking down a law that assumed that the wives of men in the military were dependent and eligible for certain benefits, but which required proof of dependence before extending those benefits to the husbands of women in the military.

In 1975 the court held that Congress acted unconstitutionally in drafting a provision of the Social Security Act that granted survivor's benefits to widows with young children, but not to widowers with young children. That ruling, in *Weinberger v. Wiesenfeld*, was followed by several others in 1977 in which Social Security provisions requiring widowers but not widows to prove actual dependence in order to qualify for survivor's benefits were held unconstitutional.

In December 1970 the court struck down an act of Congress that lowered to 18 the voting age in all federal, state and local elections. The Nixon administration, dubious about the power of Congress to lower the voting age in non-federal elections, had sought Supreme Court review of the law.

The justices held that Congress lacked the power to lower the voting age for state and local elections. Their decision spurred Congress to approve, and the states to quickly ratify, the 26th Amendment to the Constitution, which lowered the voting age for all elections to 18. *(Reversals, p. 61)*

Campaign Financing

One of the major examples of the court's use of judicial review in this period came early in 1976, when the court issued its decision on the constitutionality of key provisions of the Federal Elections Campaign Act Amendments of 1974. The court found that some of those provisions infringed too far on the freedom of political action and expression guaranteed by the First Amendment. And another key portion of the law was held unconstitutional because it violated the separation of powers principle of the Constitution.

The multi-part opinion in this case, *Buckley v. Valeo*, provides an excellent example of the way in which the court selectively exercises its power to strike down some portions of an act of Congress while upholding others, and of the way in which each member of the court individually formulates and expresses his or her position. *(Excerpts from decision, p. 148)*

The 1974 law was a major legacy of the Watergate scandal, which, among other problems, had revealed substantial misuse of campaign funds during the 1972 presidential campaign. This law for the first time limited the amount of money candidates for president could spend, and it provided public financing of presidential election campaigns. The 1974 law also set up the Federal Election Commission (FEC) to enforce federal election laws. The FEC was established through amendments to the Federal Election Campaign Act of 1971, which limited spending by federal candidates on media advertising and also required full disclosure of campaign contributions and expenditures.

The campaign financing law took effect Jan. 1, 1975. The controversy that had arisen even before its enactment virtually assured a Supreme Court test of the law's validity; in fact, a constitutional challenge was filed Jan. 2, 1975. The case was brought by a heterogeneous group of plaintiffs including Sen. James L. Buckley, Cons-R N.Y. (1971-77), former Sen. Eugene J. McCarthy, D-Minn. (1959-71), who ran as an independent presidential candidate in 1976; the Libertarian Party, the Mississippi Republican Party and the New York Civil Liberties Union.

They challenged the law's limitations on campaign contributions and expenditures, contending they violated the First Amendment's guarantee of freedom of political expression. They also argued that the public financing provisions discriminated against minor parties and candidates in favor of the two major parties and their candidates.

In August 1975 the U.S. Court of Appeals, District of Columbia Circuit, upheld all of the major provisions under attack. The Supreme Court moved with unusual speed, hearing arguments on the case that fall and issuing its decision on Jan. 30, 1976.

The court's ruling in *Buckley v. Valeo* was long and complex. It was not signed by any single justice. John Paul Stevens, who had only recently joined the court, did not take part in the ruling. Only three justices — William J. Brennan Jr., Potter Stewart and Lewis F. Powell Jr. — agreed with the decision in its entirety. The other five wrote separate opinions signaling the points on which each agreed and disagreed with the majority.

The court upheld the limits the law placed on contributions by individuals and political committees to candidates, the system of public financing of presidential campaigns, and the public disclosure requirements for large campaign contributions and campaign expenditures. The court also upheld spending limits on candidates for the presidency who accepted public financing of their campaigns.

The court struck down spending limits on all candidates for federal office other than the presidency, finding them to be a violation of the First Amendment guarantee of freedom of expression. It also struck down the law's limits on the amount a candidate could spend of his own money. And it held that the manner in which the FEC was set up was an unconstitutional violation of the separation of powers because its members were appointed by Congress and the president, but the commission had executive powers. Only if it were exclusively presidentially appointed, could it carry out the executive functions of administering and enforcing the federal campaign law, held the court.

Congress immediately began work on revising the FEC structure, but it was May 1976 before revised legislation reached the White House. As enacted, the Federal Election Campaign Act Amendments of 1976 reconstituted the FEC as a panel appointed by the president and confirmed by the Senate.

State Powers: Wage and Hours

Less than six months after the *Buckley v. Valeo* ruling, the court struck down another major act of Congress. By a 5-4 vote, the court held that Congress intruded too far upon the powers of the states when it required them to observe federal minimum wage and maximum working hours requirements for their own state and local government employees. This ruling, in the case of *National League of Cities v. Usery*, marked the first time since 1936 that the court had held Congress to have exceeded the bounds of the broad constitutional grant of power to regulate interstate commerce. *(Excerpts of decision, p. 152)*

Early in the 20th century, the Supreme Court was notably inhospitable to progressive state laws setting minimum wage and maximum hours requirements for workers. In 1941, however, after its turnabout on such questions in the late 1930s, the court upheld the first federal minimum wage and maximum hours law. Over the next 35 years, Congress steadily extended the reach of that law to more and more of the nation's workers.

Until 1974, employees of state and local governments remained outside the reach of this law. In 1961 Congress had extended the law to cover the wages and hours of state hospital employees as well as persons employed by state institutions and schools. That extension had been challenged by the states as interfering too deeply in their affairs, but the court in a 1968 ruling in *Maryland v. Wirtz* upheld the 1961 law.

In 1974 Congress once again amended the Fair Labor Standards Act, this time to require states and cities to comply with federal minimum wage/maximum hours regulations in dealing with their own employees.

This law immediately was challenged by the National League of Cities, the National Governors Conference and a number of states and cities. They argued that Congress had ignored the limits the 10th Amendment placed on its powers and had intruded too far into their domain. The 10th Amendment reserves to the people and the states all powers not granted by the Constitution to the federal government or denied to the states.

The three-judge panel that heard this case acknowledged the substance of the states' argument, but pointed to *Maryland v. Wirtz* as a precedent for rejecting their challenge.

But when the case was argued before the Supreme Court, the cities and states persuaded a five-justice majority of the court to overrule *Maryland v. Wirtz* and hold the 1974 extension of the wage and hours law unconstitutional. It was the first time in 40 years that the court had curtailed Congress in its exercise of the power to regulate commerce by invoking the 10th Amendment.

The decision in *National League of Cities v. Usery* was announced in June 1976. Justice William H. Rehnquist wrote the opinion, explaining that Congress was forbidden by the 10th Amendment "to force directly upon the states its choices as to how essential decisions regarding the conduct of integral governmental functions are to be made."

"We have repeatedly recognized," wrote Rehnquist, "that there are attributes of sovereignty attaching to every state government which may not be impaired by Congress.... One undoubted attribute of state sovereignty is the states' power to determine the wages which shall be paid to those whom they employ in order to carry out their governmental functions, what hours those persons will work, and what compensation will be provided where these employees may be called upon to work overtime.... If Congress may withdraw from the states the authority to make those fundamental employment decisions upon which their systems for performance of these functions rest, we think there would be little left of the states' 'separate and independent existence.'"

Safety and Searches

In 1970 Congress enacted the Occupational Safety and Health Act (OSHA), which set up federal health and safety standards that American businesses and industry had to observe and provided a federal inspection program to enforce those standards.

One provision of that law authorized federal inspectors to search the work area of any business that came within the scope of the law. There was no requirement that such inspections had to be authorized by a warrant if the owner of the business objected to the search.

There was widespread criticism of OSHA, as the law was called. Persistent efforts were made to amend its provisions in order to relax what many businessmen felt were unnecessarily burdensome regulations and requirements dealing with worker health and safety.

In 1978 the court, in *Marshall v. Barlow's Inc.* struck down as unconstitutional a portion of the law permitting warrantless inspections by OSHA personnel.

The case arose after Bill Barlow, an electrical and plumbing contractor in Pocatello, Idaho, objected to an inspection of his business by an OSHA agent. The OSHA inspector acknowledged that there had been no complaint about conditions at his business and that the inspection simply was the result of a random selection of businesses in that area to be checked out. Barlow asked the OSHA inspector if he had a search warrant. The inspector did not. Barlow then refused to admit the inspector to the nonpublic portions of his place of business, invoking his right under the Fourth Amendment to be secure from unreasonable searches by government inspectors.

A three-judge federal court backed Barlow's position, as did the Supreme Court on a 5-3 vote three years later. Justice William J. Brennan Jr. took no part in the decision. Justice Byron R. White wrote the court's opinion.

The Fourth Amendment's requirement of a warrant to authorize a search "protects commercial buildings as well as private homes," wrote White. He added:

"To hold otherwise would belie the origin of that Amendment, and the American colonial experience.... The general warrant was a recurring point of contention in the colonies immediately preceding the Revolution. The particular offensiveness it engendered was acutely felt by the merchants and businessmen whose premises and products were inspected for compliance with the several Parliamentary revenue measures that most irritated the colonists.... Against this background, it is untenable that the ban on warrantless searches was not intended to shield

Legislative Veto:
The Constitutional Questions

The constitutional issues raised by the increasing use by Congress of the legislative veto were before the Supreme Court in 1983. The veto is a device Congress has inserted in a variety of laws to give members a chance to review, and to veto if necessary, the orders and regulations issued by the executive to implement particular laws.

In three different cases involving three different acts passed by Congress, the veto was held by lower courts to be unconstitutional. These rulings held that the veto constituted a trespass by Congress on the domains reserved under the Constitution to the executive and the courts.

Congress drafts the laws; the executive carries them out; and the courts decide when the laws, or the manner in which they are executed, is improper. The legislative veto, its critics maintain, permits Congress to participate in executing the laws and reviewing the manner in which they are executed.

In defense of the veto, attorneys for Congress argue that it simply is a means whereby Congress is able to delegate authority to the executive to deal with a complex modern problem while retaining some control over the manner in which that delegated power is exercised.

The Challenge

The case of *Immigration and Naturalization Service v. Chadha* was argued twice before the Supreme Court in 1982; a decision was expected in 1983. That case involved a provision of federal immigration law that permitted the House or the Senate to override the attorney general's decision not to deport a particular individual.

The court was considering whether or not to grant full review in the other two cases. One focused on a provision of the Natural Gas Policy Act of 1978 that permitted either house to veto certain pricing regulations adopted by the Federal Energy Regulatory Commission (FERC). The other concerned provisions of the Federal Trade Commission Improvements Act of 1980 that allowed the House and the Senate, acting in concert, to veto FTC regulations dealing with the sale of used cars.

The legislative veto came into use in the late 1930s after the Supreme Court declared several key New Deal measures unconstitutional because they delegated too much legislative power to the executive.

Continued use of the legislative veto, argued the Reagan administration in the Immigration and Naturalization Service case, could spell the end of executive power in the federal system.

If the veto provision is upheld as constitutional, the government brief in the *Chadha* case warned, "it would appear that Congress could pass legislation authorizing one of its Houses to veto virtually every decision or order of the President or other office of the United States in the execution of a law passed by Congress."

The threat the veto posed to judicial power was cited by Alan Morrison, the public interest attorney representing the young man (Chadha) whose deportation was the original issue in this case. "While Congress can certainly provide for review of executive actions to determine if there has been an abuse of discretion, such review is a judicial, not a legislative function.... Under our Constitution it is the judiciary, not the legislature, which is responsible for determining questions of whether the law has been followed.... Congress cannot both make and judge the law."

Opponents of the legislative veto also argue that it contravenes the constitutional procedures for enacting legislation. By permitting one house to act without the other, as in the immigration and natural gas laws, the veto violates the constitutional requirement that legislation be approved by both chambers. And in cases where the two chambers must cast such a veto, as in the FTC measure, the veto still conflicts with those procedures because the veto is not sent to the president for his approval or disapproval.

The Defense

The legislative veto is a creative modern response — within constitutional bounds — to complex contemporary problems, respond the attorneys for the House and the Senate.

These "legislative review" provisions are but the "necessary and proper" means of carrying out the particular powers granted Congress by the Constitution, according to the House and Senate briefs. This type of "legislative review ... has not served as a means for enactment of new legislation ... [but] has allowed Congress to delegate extraordinary authority sought by the President and agencies to respond to problems of the Depression, World War II, and the 1970s, while providing a mechanism for assuring democratic accountability for the exercise of that broad authority. When these checks and balances on the exercise of extraordinary governmental power are examined in particular statutes and cases, they will be seen to serve rather than to evade the objectives of separation of powers," they maintain.

The use of this veto to ensure legislative review is "not ... a device to impair the system of checks and balances," concludes the Senate argument, but "a means for making that system work in the face of modern problems."

places of business as well as of residence."

Abortion, Mining and the Military

Exercising its power of judicial review to uphold certain challenged laws passed by Congress, the court in 1980 and 1981 reviewed arguments that Congress acted unconstitutionally in curtailing public funding of abortions under the Medicaid program, imposing strict environmental requirements on strip mine operations, and excluding women from the military draft.

In each of these cases, the court upheld the legislation.

In *Harris v. McRae*, decided in June 1980 by a 5-4 vote, the court held that Congress acted within constitutional bounds when it denied federal funding for abortions under the Medicaid program unless the abortion was required to save the pregnant woman's life, or to terminate a pregnancy caused by a promptly reported rape or incest.

A year later, the court unanimously rebuffed a challenge by strip mine operators and several affected states to the Surface Mining Control and Reclamation Act of 1977. The court held that on its face the law, which imposed severe land use restrictions and strict reclamation requirements on strip miners, was not unconstitutional as a violation of states' rights or of the strip mine operators' rights. The cases in which the court ruled were *Hodel v. Virginia Surface Mining and Reclamation Assn., Virginia Surface Mining and Reclamation Association v. Hodel, Hodel v. Indiana.*

On June 25, 1981, the court, by a 6-3 vote, upheld the power of Congress to exclude women from the military draft. Signaling particular deference to decisions made by Congress in the exercise of its constitutional power to raise armies, the court, in the case of *Rostker v. Goldberg,* found ample justification for a male-only draft in the fact that women were forbidden by law and policy from holding combat positions. *(Harris, Rostker decisions, p. 153, 156)*

Bankruptcy

In 1982 the court struck down two acts of Congress, both of which dealt with the relatively noncontroversial topic of bankruptcy. In March, the court held unanimously that the Rock Island Transition and Employee Assistance Act of 1980 was unconstitutional because it applied only to the affairs of one bankrupt railroad.

Congress is authorized by the Constitution to "establish ... uniform laws on the subject of Bankruptcies throughout the United States," the court noted, finding such a special bankruptcy law in violation of that requirement of uniformity. That decision, in *Railway Labor Executives' Assn. v. Gibbons,* marked the first time in history that the court had applied that particular section of the Constitution to hold an act of Congress unconstitutional.

In 1978 Congress had approved a major overhaul of the nation's bankruptcy laws, the first in nearly 40 years. Central to the modernized bankruptcy system was a new corps of bankruptcy judges, appointed by the president for 14-year terms and equipped with far more authority than the bankruptcy "referees" they replaced.

The most controversial issue during congressional consideration of the measure had been the status of these new judges: whether or not they would be appointed for life, as are all other federal judges. Chief Justice Warren E. Burger was one of the most active opponents of a life term for these judges, drawing some criticism for the vigor with which he made his views known. *(Box, pp. 70-71)*

When Congress completed work on the legislation, the new bankruptcy judges did not have life tenure, but they did have broad power to resolve virtually all civil matters relating to the affairs of a bankrupt individual or corporation.

This combination of limited tenure and broad power was unconstitutional, the Supreme Court held late in June 1982. Ruling in the case of *Northern Pipeline Co. v. Marathon Pipe Line,* the court explained that this arrangement threatened the independence of the federal judiciary because it opened the door to possible congressional pressure upon its members.

The court gave Congress until Oct. 4 to reconstitute the corps of bankruptcy judges. But Congress failed to act by that date. In response to a request from the Reagan administration, the court extended the deadline to Dec. 24.

Congress failed to meet that deadline as well, leaving the bankruptcy system in legal limbo as the new year began and placing the issue of bankruptcy reform high on the agenda of the 98th Congress.

CONGRESS' POWER TO CURB THE COURT

Throughout U.S. history, congressional critics of various Supreme Court rulings have sought to use the power of Congress to curb the court. They have proposed a variety of solutions: impeaching justices whose decisions they did not agree with, requiring more than a simple majority vote of the court to strike down acts of Congress, or actually removing the court's jurisdiction over certain categories of cases.

Few of these proposals have ever won the approval of either chamber, but the most serious of the congressional challenges to the court's independence — and the one most recently in vogue — is the effort to deny the court the authority to hear certain categories of cases. Lawmakers have this power under the Constitution's grant to Congress of the authority "to make exceptions" to the court's appellate jurisdiction — its power to hear cases that already have been ruled on by lower state or federal courts. The limits of this power are hotly debated today and have not been tested in modern times. *(Court curbing proposals, box, p. 58)*

The first attempt to remove some of the Supreme Court's jurisdiction came in the 1820s and 1830s when Congress sought unsuccessfully to repeal a section of a 1789 act that gave the court the power to overturn state laws in certain circumstances.

Only once has Congress repealed the court's jurisdiction to stop the court from issuing a decision. This occurred in 1868 when Congress repealed the Supreme Court's power to review federal court denials of writs of *habeas corpus.* The repeal was aimed at preventing the court from hearing a *habeas corpus* appeal that called into question the constitutionality of the Reconstruction Acts of 1867.

In the last 35 years Congress has considered legislation to repeal the court's authority to review specific subjects, such as international security programs, certain criminal procedures, local education problems such as desegregation

The Power to Impeach, Remove Justices...

Congress is empowered by the Constitution to impeach and remove Supreme Court justices from office if it finds them to be guilty of treason, bribery or other high crimes and misdemeanors.

Only once has a justice stood trial before the Senate on such charges, and on that occasion he was acquitted. Yet even in disuse, this power remains a formidable threat. In May 1969 Justice Abe Fortas resigned his seat after the House threatened to begin an impeachment inquiry into charges that Fortas had acted improperly in maintaining a business relationship with the family foundation of an industrialist later convicted of securities law violations. Fortas' resignation terminated talk of impeachment.

Only one other justice, William O. Douglas, has faced a serious threat of impeachment, and he faced it twice: in 1953, after he stayed the execution of convicted atomic spies Julius and Ethel Rosenberg, and in 1970, after the Senate had refused to confirm President Richard M. Nixon's first two nominees to succeed Fortas. The latter move was engineered by critics of Douglas' controversial writings and other allegedly inappropriate extrajudicial behavior.

The Chase Impeachment

In 1804 the House, controlled by the Democratic-Republicans and unhappy with the decisions of the Federalist-dominated judiciary, impeached Justice Samuel Chase for misconduct.

The Democratic-Republicans' plan, had Chase been convicted and removed from the bench, was to proceed in similar fashion against the other Federalist justices, particularly Chief Justice John Marshall.

But the Senate acquitted Chase, and the Democratic-Republicans abandoned their plan. Marshall and his Federalist philosophy continued to dominate the court for the next 30 years, until his death in 1835.

Chase was impeached for allegedly partisan, harsh and unfair judicial behavior while acting as a circuit judge, a duty that all Supreme Court justices performed in the 19th century. The real basis for the House action against him, however, was the Democratic-Republican Party's desire to rid the federal judiciary of Federalist influence. With Jefferson's election in 1800, and the election of a Democratic-Republican controlled Congress that year, the federal courts were the last Federalist stronghold in the national government.

In that political atmosphere, Marshall's sharp rebuke to President Thomas Jefferson in *Marbury v. Madison* for the president's refusal to deliver William Marbury's commission, and his assertion for the court of the power of judicial review, were viewed with both alarm and irritation by the Democratic-Republicans (the Jeffersonian party). *(Judicial review, p. 44)*

The *Marbury* ruling convinced the Jeffersonians to move against the court. Other contemporary events made the idea of impeachment attractive. In January 1803 the Pennsylvania legislature had impeached and convicted a state judge of "high crimes and misdemeanors" even though it was evident that his only "crime" was being an active Federalist. In early February that year, Jefferson sent to the U.S. House documents complaining of the behavior of U.S. District Judge John Pickering of New Hampshire. As one commentator described it, Pickering "was making a daily spectacle of himself on the bench because of intoxication aggravated by copious and blasphemous profanity." The House responded immediately, passing a resolution March 2, 1803, impeaching Pickering. He subsequently was convicted and removed from office.

Then in May 1803 Justice Chase provided the Democratic-Republicans with the excuse they needed to move against a member of the Supreme Court.

The Charges. An active patriot during the Revolutionary War, Chase was a signer of the Declaration of Independence and chief justice of Maryland before his appointment to the Supreme Court by President George Washington in 1796. Chase's legal ability and integrity were unquestioned. But his personality made him unpopular with contemporaries, who found him arrogant, arbitrary and guilty of using his position as a judge to advance his Federalist beliefs. As an associate justice, Chase openly approved passage of the hated Alien and Sedition Acts and actively campaigned for the re-election of President John Adams in 1800.

The justice was severely condemned for his arbitrary and intemperate treatment of the sedition trial of Democratic-Republican printer James T. Callender. The justice also was sharply criticized for his conduct of the trial of John Fries, the Pennsylvania farmer who had organized the Whiskey Rebellion against payment of the 1798 "war taxes." Although Fries and his men were armed, little violence occurred. Chase nonetheless insisted that the grand jury indict Fries for treason; he then found Fries guilty and sentenced him to death. To avoid public outrage, Adams subsequently pardoned the farmer.

On yet another occasion, Chase refused to dismiss a Delaware grand jury that had ignored his hints that it should indict a Wilmington publisher Chase thought guilty of publishing seditious statements. Finally, in May 1803, Chase delivered what was described as a political harangue to a Baltimore grand jury in which he denounced the Jeffersonian administration and its policies.

Enraged at this behavior, Jefferson on May 13, 1803, wrote to Rep. Joseph R. Nicholson of Maryland: "You must have heard of the extraordinary charge of Chace [sic] to the Grand Jury at Balti-

...The Samuel Chase Affair of 1804-05

more? Ought this seditious and official attack on the principles of our Constitution, and on the proceedings of a state, to go unpunished? ..."

House Impeachment

Jeffersonians in the House took the president's broad hint. In January 1804, just as the Senate was beginning Judge Pickering's impeachment trial, Rep. John Randolph of Virginia proposed an impeachment resolution against Chase. Randolph made eight charges against him. Six of them dealt with his conduct of the Callender and Fries trials, the seventh with his conduct before the Delaware grand jury and the eighth with his diatribe to the Baltimore grand jury.

Just an hour after the Senate voted March 12 to remove Pickering from office, the House voted to impeach Chase. The vote was 73-32, split along strictly partisan lines.

Senate Trial

The Senate chamber was filled with spectators, including Chief Justice Marshall and the associate justices, as Chase's trial began Jan. 2, 1805. Vice President Aaron Burr, who recently had killed Alexander Hamilton in a duel, presided over the trial. Rep. Randolph led the team of House managers who prosecuted Chase. Defending Chase was a battery of able lawyers, including a celebrated orator, Maryland Attorney General Luther Martin, and former U.S. Attorney General Charles Lee.

Chase himself appeared before the Senate on the opening day of the trial to read a statement in which he maintained he had not engaged in impeachable conduct:

"To these articles ... I say that I have committed no crime or misdemeanor whatsoever for which I am subject to impeachment according to the Constitution.... I deny, with a few exceptions, the acts with which I am charged; I shall contend, that all acts admitted to have been done by me were *legal*, and I deny, in every instance, the *improper* intentions with which the acts charged are alleged to have been done, and in which their supposed criminality altogether consists."

Chase asked for a delay in the trial so that he could prepare his defense and was granted a month. When the proceedings resumed in February, 52 witnesses, including Marshall, testified before the Senate. Marshall's principal biographer, Albert J. Beveridge, wrote that the chief justice's performance was marked by trepidation and that his responses were not favorable to Chase's cause. Marshall's demeanor may have been caused by his worry that should Chase be convicted, Marshall was sure to be the next target.

Once testimony was completed, a major debate commenced over whether a justice must have committed an indictable crime to be impeached and convicted. While Chase might have comported himself in a highly questionable manner, he had done nothing in violation of any federal law.

The House managers argued that offensive conduct was sufficient for impeachment. Rep. George W. Campbell of Tennessee said: "Impeachment ... according to the meaning of the Constitution, may fairly be considered a kind of inquest into the conduct of an officer [of the United States] merely as it regards his office; the manner in which he performs the duties thereof; and the effects that his conduct therein may have on society. It is more in the nature of a civil investigation than of a criminal prosecution."

In Chase's behalf, attorney Joseph Hopkinson argued that "no judge can be impeached and removed from office for any act or offense for which he could not be indicted.... I maintain as a most important and indispensable principle, that no man should be criminally accused, no man can be criminally condemned, but for the violation of some known law by which he was bound to govern himself. Nothing is so necessary to justice and to safety as that the criminal code should be certain and known. Let the judge, as well as the citizen, precisely know the path he has to walk in, and what he may or may not do."

On March 1, 1805, the Senate was ready to vote. Of the 34 senators present, 25 were Democratic-Republicans, nine were Federalists. Since 23 votes (a two-thirds majority) were needed for conviction, the Jeffersonians could have carried the day had they voted together. But at least six of them sided with the Federalists on each vote, and Chase was acquitted of all eight charges.

The closest vote came on the complaint that triggered the impeachment — Chase's political harangue to the grand jury. Eighteen senators found Chase guilty; 16, not guilty.

Randolph's response to the acquittal was immediate. He strode to the House floor and offered a constitutional amendment to provide for the removal of Supreme Court justices by the president at the request of a majority of both houses of Congress. The House approved the amendment by a 68-33 vote, but the proposal never emerged from the Senate.

The outcome of the trial forced the Jeffersonians to give up their plans for further impeachments; Federalist judges on both the Supreme Court and inferior federal courts were secure for the first time since Jefferson's election. The exercise probably proved that impeachment and conviction of a judge could not succeed if it were motivated primarily by partisanship. But the episode did not resolve the fundamental constitutional question whether only indictable offenses are impeachable.

and school prayer, and state laws forbidding abortions. Although the court's decisions in all these areas were controversial and generated an outpouring of opposition from the public and members of Congress, none of the jurisdictional repeal attempts were successful.

Attempts to Repeal 1789 Act

The first congressional attempts to repeal the Supreme Court's jurisdiction were occasioned by the court's early decisions overturning state laws. Section 25 of the Judiciary Act of 1789 authorized the court to review, and to uphold or declare invalid, decisions of the states' highest courts upholding state laws challenged on the ground that they conflicted with the U.S. Constitution, federal statutes or treaties. With each successive ruling striking down a state law, opposition to Section 25 grew among states' rights proponents. After the Supreme Court emphatically upheld its review power under Section 25 in the case of *Cohens v. Virginia* (1821), several states appealed to their congressional delegations to remove this review power from the court.

The first of these proposals was introduced in the Senate in 1821. Sen. Richard M. Johnson of Kentucky proposed a constitutional amendment to give the Senate appellate jurisdiction in cases raising a federal question where a state was a party. This suggestion received little support, primarily because small states held the balance of power in the Senate and were considered likely to prefer a strong national government.

The following year, legislation to repeal the court's Section 25 review power was introduced, but it received little attention then or in the immediate future. However, the court's rulings against state sovereignty in *Craig v. Missouri* (1830) and *Cherokee Nation v. Georgia* (1831), coupled with Georgia's outright defiance of the court, generated a major clash over the proper balance of power between the states and the federal government.

As part of that confrontation the House ordered its Judiciary Committee to report a measure repealing Section 25. The committee reported the measure on Jan. 24, 1831. Repeal of Section 25 was viewed as a grave threat by members of the court. Chief Justice John Marshall wrote that the "crisis of our Constitution is now upon us," while Justice Joseph Story lamented that "if the Twenty-Fifth Section is repealed, the Constitution is practically gone."

The measure was never fully debated in the House. Using parliamentary tactics, court supporters were able to repulse the repeal movement by a wide margin. Moves to repeal that section were made in later years, but none came any closer to passage.

Reconstruction Acts Controversy

Only once in the nation's history has Congress prevented the Supreme Court from deciding a pending case by repealing its appellate jurisdiction over the subject matter at issue.

Such extraordinary action was taken by a Congress dominated by the Radical Republicans, who wanted to prohibit the court from reviewing the constitutionality of the Reconstruction Acts of 1867. Those acts substituted military rule for civilian government in the 10 Southern states that initially refused to rejoin the Union after the Civil War. They also established procedures for those states to follow to gain readmittance and representation in the federal government.

The court twice avoided taking a stand on the constitutionality of the Reconstruction Acts. In April 1867, just before the acts were scheduled to take effect, the state of Mississippi asked the court for permission to seek an injunction to stop the president from implementing them. The court unanimously rejected the request in *Mississippi v. Johnson*, holding that the president's duties under the acts were political, and therefore the court was without jurisdiction to order the injunction.

The court in May that year dismissed a similar request by Georgia and Mississippi officials seeking to bar the secretary of war and the commanders of the five military districts from enforcing the Reconstruction Acts. The court again held that the suit raised political questions over which it had no jurisdiction.

It was not until November 1867, several months after military rule was established in the Southern states, that the events that would touch off the confrontation between the court and Congress began. William H. McCardle, the editor of the *Vicksburg* (Miss.) *Times*, was not loath to express editorially his distaste for Reconstruction and his views that blacks should be excluded from participation in government and from the protections of the 14th Amendment.

McCardle reserved his bitterest criticisms for Major General Edward O. C. Ord, the commanding general of the Fourth Military District, which included Mississippi and Arkansas. Ord finally had McCardle arrested and held for trial by a military tribunal, charging him with disturbing the peace, inciting insurrection, slowing the pace of reconstruction and printing libelous statements.

A protection against illegal imprisonment, a writ of *habeas corpus* orders a person holding a prisoner to explain why the prisoner is being held. Seeking to protect blacks and federal officials in the South from harassment by white Southerners, Congress in February 1867 passed legislation expanding the Supreme Court's jurisdiction to review denials of writs of *habeas corpus*.

Before passage of the 1867 law, the court had no appellate jurisdiction over lower court denials of *habeas corpus* relief. The new statute permitted appeals from federal circuit courts to the Supreme Court in "all cases where any person may be restrained of his or her liberty in violation of the Constitution or of any treaty or law in the United States," and provided for his or her release through a writ of *habeas corpus*.

The statute was not intended to protect Southern whites, but McCardle sought a writ of *habeas corpus* in a federal circuit court, charging that the Reconstruction Acts, which sanctioned his arrest and trial by military tribunal, were unconstitutional. When the circuit court denied the writ, he appealed directly to the Supreme Court.

Rumors abounded that the court would use McCardle's case to declare the Reconstruction Acts unconstitutional. The Radical Republicans could not afford to have the Reconstruction Acts declared unconstitutional until they had solidified their political power in the South and forced the Southern states to ratify the 14th Amendment as the price for readmittance to the Union.

Thus when McCardle's attorney, Jeremiah S. Black, appealed to the Supreme Court in December 1867 to act quickly on the case, Republicans in the House moved just as quickly to stave off an adverse ruling. In January 1868 the House Judiciary Committee reported, and the House passed, a bill to require two-thirds of the justices to concur in decisions finding federal laws unconstitutional.

According to historian Charles Warren, the Republicans' measure had little public support, and the Senate postponed action on it indefinitely. Moreover, it was widely believed that the measure would have failed to accomplish its purpose; of the eight justices then on the court, at least five were thought to believe the Reconstruction Acts invalid.

Meanwhile, the Supreme Court agreed to Black's request and set arguments for the first week in March.

Arguments in the case, *Ex parte McCardle*, concluded March 9. On March 12 the Radical Republicans in Congress made their move. Pending in the House was an insignificant Senate-passed bill to expand the Supreme Court's appellate jurisdiction to cases concerning customs and revenue officers. Rep. James F. Wilson, R-Iowa, chairman of the House Judiciary Committee, offered an amendment to repeal the 1867 grant of appellate jurisdiction over *habeas corpus* cases and to prohibit the court from acting on any appeals then pending. Democrats and moderate Republicans who might have opposed Wilson's measure apparently did not understand what was happening, and the amendment was passed without debate or objection. The bill as amended was then returned to the Senate, which approved it later the same day by a 32-6 vote.

President Andrew Johnson waited as long as possible before vetoing the bill in the hope that the Supreme Court would defy Congress and decide the *McCardle* case. Although the court met in conference March 21, it did not announce a decision in the case, taking note instead of the repeal bill and saying it would postpone a decision in the case until action on the legislation was concluded.

Johnson vetoed the bill March 25, declaring that the repeal "establishes a precedent which, if followed, may eventually sweep away every check on arbitrary and unconstitutional legislation." Congress two days later overrode the veto.

March 30 was the court's next opinion day. When it became obvious that the justices would say nothing about the *McCardle* case, attorney Black asked that the effect of the repeal legislation on the case be argued formally before the court. The court agreed but at the same time decided on a postponement until the December 1868 term to give government attorneys more time to prepare their arguments.

Gideon Welles, who had been Lincoln's secretary of the Navy and close ally and a noted diarist, wrote that the "Judges of the Supreme Court have caved in, fallen through, failed in the *McCardle* case." Former Justice Benjamin R. Curtis, who defended President Johnson at his impeachment trial, said that "Congress with the acquiescence of the country, has subdued the Supreme Court, as well as the President."

Final arguments in the *McCardle* case were anticlimactic. On April 12, 1869, the court issued a unanimous decision upholding the repeal measure and dismissing the case for lack of jurisdiction. Chief Justice Salmon P. Chase wrote that the Constitution gave Congress authority to make exceptions to the court's appellate jurisdiction and that Congress had expressly exercised that authority when it repealed the court's right to review denials of writs of *habeas corpus*:

> We are not at liberty to inquire into the motive of the legislature. We can only examine into its power under the Constitution, and the power to make exceptions to the appellate jurisdiction of this Court is given by express words. What, then, is the effect of the repealing act upon the case before us? We cannot doubt as to this. Without jurisdiction the Court cannot proceed at all in any cause. Jurisdiction is power to declare the law, and when it ceases to exist, the only function remaining to the Court is that of announcing the fact and dismissing the cause....

Modern Repeal Efforts

Almost a century elapsed between the *McCardle* case and the next serious attempt by Congress to trim the court's jurisdiction.

The 1954 appointment of former California Gov. Earl Warren as chief justice of the United States initiated a period unique in the nation's history, one in which the court led the other governmental institutions in protecting individual rights from various forms of discrimination.

The Warren court decisions inspired a series of anti-court efforts by many members of Congress. Perhaps the most serious of these occurred in 1957-58 when Southerners opposed to desegregation joined forces with other conservative lawmakers who believed the court's decisions protecting persons alleged to have participated in communist activities threatened to undermine the nation's security.

In addition to trying to reverse the court's decisions, these groups launched two major attacks on the court's power to review certain classes of cases. But despite the conservative alliance and widespread opposition to the court's decisions, Congress ultimately refused to adopt any court-curbing proposals.

Jenner-Butler Bill. The broader of the two assaults on the jurisdiction of the court was initiated in the Senate by William E. Jenner, R-Ind. (1944-45, 1947-59). His bill (S 2646), introduced in July 1957, would have barred the Supreme Court from accepting appeals in five categories:

● Cases involving the powers of congressional investigating committees and contempt of Congress proceedings. This was aimed at *Watkins v. United States* (354 U.S. 178, 1957). The court in this case had ruled that a witness before the House Un-American Activities Committee was not guilty of contempt of Congress for refusing to answer certain questions. The court declared that the scope of the committee's inquiry had not been clearly defined by Congress and that the committee had failed to show the pertinency of its questions to its investigation.

● Cases involving federal laws and regulations governing hiring and firing of government employees on loyalty grounds. This provision was directed at the court's ruling in *Cole v. Young* (351 U.S. 536, 1956), which held that loyalty-security procedures under the Summary Suspension Act of 1950 applied only to "sensitive" jobs and not to all federal employment.

● Cases involving school regulations dealing with alleged subversive activities of teachers. This was directed at the court's jurisdiction over cases like *Slochower v. Board of Higher Education of the City of New York* (350 U.S. 551, 1956), in which the court ruled that New York City could not dismiss a City College professor from his job merely because he refused to cooperate with a congressional committee investigating subversive activities, but had to grant him all the procedural rights due him under state and city laws regulating employment of teachers suspected of engaging in forbidden activities.

● Cases involving state laws and regulations prohibiting

Congress Has a Myriad of Ways
To Influence the Work of the Court

In addition to the powers of confirmation, impeachment and control of the court's appellate jurisdiction, Congress has a variety of more mundane channels through which it affects the operations of the Supreme Court.

Congress determines the size of the court; it can increase or reduce the number of justices. In the 19th century, Congress tended to reduce the number of seats on the court when it wished to deny an unpopular president the opportunity to place someone of his choice on that bench. And Congress usually has increased the number of seats on the court when it wished to influence the court's philosophical balance.

On four occasions Congress has enlarged the court: from six to seven members in 1807, to nine in 1837, to 10 in 1863 and to nine (after an intervening reduction) in 1869. There have been no changes since 1869. This last enlargement of the court enabled President Ulysses S. Grant in 1870 to name William Strong and Joseph Bradley to the court, nominations that were crucial in the court's quick reversal of its decision that paper money could not be used as legal tender.

From time to time, members of Congress have proposed that the justices be required to submit to periodic reconfirmation, but legislation to that effect never has received more than passing interest.

More serious consideration has been given to proposals that the court be required to muster an extraordinary majority, perhaps even unanimity, in order to hold an act of Congress or a state law unconstitutional. A similar proposal offered early in this century suggested that Congress be authorized to override such Supreme Court decisions by repassing the contested law by a two-thirds majority vote of each house. None of these measures ever won congressional approval.

Congress by law sets the date for the beginning of the court's term. Since 1917 the term has begun on the first Monday in October. That term ends the following summer, usually in June or July. Once Congress even postponed a court term — in 1802 — until the following year.

Congress sets the justices' salaries. It cannot reduce them, but it must pass legislation to raise them. Traditionally, it has been slow to respond to suggestions from the justices that they are underpaid. In recent years, particularly during the Warren court era of the 1960s, Congress actually gave the justices a smaller raise than other top officials, in large measure as an expression of congressional pique over the court's rulings on such issues as internal security, school prayer and school desegregation.

In the 1970s Congress granted, and then attempted to rescind, cost-of-living increases for the justices and other top federal officials. This led to litigation, which ended with a decision by the court itself in December 1980 giving the justices two of the four cost-of-living increases they sought and spelling out for Congress the way in which it had to act if it wished to rescind such pay adjustments in a constitutional fashion.

Congress also is responsible for whatever retirement plan exists for the justices. Until 1937 there was no adequate retirement system, which was a major reason, some have speculated, that so many aging justices did not retire. But in 1937, spurred by Roosevelt's court-packing proposal, Congress passed a retirement law that permitted justices 70 or older with 10 years of service, or 65 or older with 15 years of service, to retire at full salary.

Almost immediately, one of the court's older members announced he would retire, giving Roosevelt his long-awaited first chance to name a new member to the court.

In addition to its control over the appellate jurisdiction of the court, Congress exerts considerable influence over the workload of the court through the laws it passes.

In 1982 many justices were free with their advice to Congress on ways in which the legislature might act to curtail the increasingly heavy flow of cases into the federal system and to the Supreme Court in particular.

Some of the proposals under consideration by Congress included measures to 1) abolish diversity jurisdiction (which permits cases to be heard in federal court not because they involve any federal matter or federal law but simply because the opposing parties live in different states), 2) abolish the existing system under which the court is obliged to give certain types of cases preference in granting review, and 3) revise certain criminal and civil rights laws to limit the access of individuals to the federal courts, channeling their cases instead to state courts.

subversive activities directed against the federal government. This provision was aimed at the ruling in *Pennsylvania v. Nelson* (350 U.S. 497, 1956), in which the court held that provisions of the Pennsylvania Sedition Act punishing persons who engaged in subversive activities directed against the federal government were invalid because Congress had pre-empted this field of legislation when it passed the 1940 Smith Act.

● Cases involving state regulation of admissions to the bar, aimed at cases like *Konigsberg v. State Bar of California* (366 U.S. 36, 1957), in which the court ruled that an applicant could not be denied admission to a state bar solely because he refused to answer questions about past or present Communist Party membership.

The "extreme liberal wing of the court" has "become a majority," Jenner said on Aug. 7, 1957, the opening day of hearings on his bill, "and we witness today the spectacle of a court constantly changing the law, and even changing the meaning of the Constitution, in an apparent determination to make the law of the land what the court thinks it should be."

But solving the problem by removing the court's jurisdiction proved too strong a medicine for many witnesses, who perceived this threat to the independence of the judiciary to be a graver danger to national security than that posed by communists.

At the suggestion of Sen. John Marshall Butler, R-Md. (1951-63), Jenner's bill was substantially amended by the Senate Judiciary Committee. As reported by the committee in May 1958, only one section of the original Jenner proposal — the provision barring the Supreme Court from reviewing state bar admissions rules — was retained. Instead of repealing the court's jurisdiction over the other categories of cases, the committee recommended language to overturn the offending decisions.

The bill did not come to the Senate floor until Aug. 20, 1958, in the final days of the session. Senate Majority Leader Lyndon B. Johnson, D-Texas (House, 1937-49; Senate 1949-61), apparently hoped he could avoid bringing up the bill altogether, but under pressure from Southern colleagues, and knowing he had the votes to defeat the measure, he allowed it to be offered as an amendment to a minor House-passed bill dealing with appeals from rulings of federal administrative agencies. After lengthy supporting speeches by Jenner and Butler, and rebuttals by opponents Thomas C. Hennings Jr., D-Mo. (House 1935-48; Senate 1951-60), and Alexander Wiley, R-Wis. (1939-63), Hennings offered a motion to table the Jenner-Butler bill. The motion was adopted by a 49-41 vote, and the bill was killed. Measures similar to various sections of the Jenner-Butler bill subsequently were considered in the House and Senate, but none was ever enacted.

Implied Pre-emption. The second attempt during this period to repeal Supreme Court jurisdiction was more limited in scope but came closer to winning congressional approval. Under the pre-emption doctrine, based on Article IV, Section 2, of the Constitution, which states that federal laws are the "supreme law of the land," courts have invalidated state laws in the following circumstances: when Congress declared an intention to pre-empt a given field of legislation; when there was a conflict between federal and state laws; and when the court inferred an intention by Congress to pre-empt the field.

It was to prohibit this "pre-emption by implication" that the most important of several anti-pre-emption proposals (HR 3) was offered. Its key provision said: "No act of Congress shall be construed as indicating an intent on the part of Congress to occupy the field in which such act operates, to the exclusion of all state laws on the same subject matter, unless such act contains an express provision to that effect or unless there is a direct and positive conflict between such act and a state law so that the two cannot be reconciled or consistently stand together."

HR 3 was introduced in the House in 1955 by Rules Committee Chairman Howard W. Smith, D-Va. (1931-67), after the Pennsylvania Supreme Court held in 1954 that the 1940 Smith Act pre-empted provisions of state anti-sedition laws that punished persons found guilty of subversive activities directed against the federal government. The ruling, when affirmed by the U.S. Supreme Court in *Pennsylvania v. Nelson* (1956), affected anti-subversive laws of 43 states.

The House Judiciary Committee reported HR 3 in July 1956 after narrowing it so it applied only to the *Nelson* decision. The Senate Judiciary Committee reported bills similar to the original Smith proposal and the narrower HR 3 version, but neither chamber acted on the legislation.

Smith reintroduced HR 3 in 1957. Spurred by opposition to the Supreme Court's ruling in *Nelson*, the House Judiciary Committee reported a broader version of HR 3 as well as the version merely overturning the *Nelson* decision. The full House passed HR 3 on July 17, 1958, by a 241-155 vote after merging it with the narrower bill.

Similar bills were reported in the Senate. One was considered in August 1958, but intense lobbying by opponents led to adoption, by a 41-40 vote, of a motion to recommit the bill, thus killing it and ending consideration of the issue in the 85th Congress. In 1959 the House again approved HR 3, but with diminished support. Smith continued to introduce the measure in subsequent years, but it was never again considered by the House or the Senate.

Reapportionment Disputes

After the Supreme Court, in the landmark *Baker v. Carr* ruling of 1962, gave federal courts the go-ahead to consider cases challenging malapportionment of state legislatures, efforts began in virtually every state to redraw the states' legislative districts.

Many members of Congress considered this to be unwarranted federal intervention in matters that belonged to the states, arguing that within limits a state should be able to apportion its legislature as it wished. Members came under heavy pressure from state legislators to help preserve the existing apportionment arrangements.

Numerous measures were proposed to curtail or undo the impact of the court's ruling. One recommendation, a constitutional amendment, would have declared that a state could apportion one house of a bicameral legislature on some basis other than population. But the slow process of approving and ratifying a constitutional amendment was an inadequate response to the problem, critics of the ruling felt. Attention turned instead to a proposal denying the Supreme Court and other federal courts the jurisdiction to hear state apportionment cases.

While this measure, proposed by Rep. William M. Tuck, D-Va. (1953-69), a one-time governor of Virginia, was pending, the court added fuel to the apportionment fire. On June 15, 1964, it ruled in *Reynolds v. Sims* that the seats of both houses of every state legislature must be apportioned among districts of substantially equal population. Two months later, on Aug. 19, 1964, the House approved Tuck's bill by a vote of 218-175. The Senate however, refused to go along with the House, and the bill died at the end of the 88th Congress.

Criminal Confessions

Congressional critics of the court barely had time to assess their reapportionment defeat when the Warren court ignited another storm of complaints with its decision in 1966 in *Miranda v. Arizona*. In that ruling the court spelled out procedures to protect the constitutional rights of criminal defendants and held that confessions or incriminating statements obtained from suspects who had not been warned of their rights could not be used in court.

Several members of the Senate Judiciary Committee succeeded in amending a major crime bill to include language preventing the Supreme Court from reviewing any trial judge's ruling on the admissibility of a confession. But this provision was eliminated during Senate debate on the measure. Nevertheless, as enacted that bill contained language permitting the use of a "voluntary" confession, even if the suspect giving it had not been warned of his rights in line with the *Miranda* ruling. *(Reversals of court rulings, p. 67)*

Abortion, Busing and Prayer

Early in the 1980s a group of conservative senators and representatives, angered by years of Supreme Court rulings contrary to their positions on controversial issues, introduced legislation to remove the court's authority over the issues of abortion, school desegregation and school prayer. Enactment of such measures would permit each of the 50 states to enact their own laws on these matters.

There was intense disagreement within Congress and within the academic community over the wisdom and validity of these measures, and the 97th Congress adjourned without enacting any changes in the court's authority.

"The Supreme Court brought this on itself," said Sen. John P. East, R-N.C., cosponsor of a bill to eliminate federal court jurisdiction over abortion cases. "It's the abuse of power of judicial review.... The court has been eroding the deliberative process of Congress. They've precipitated the crisis."

But Rep. Robert W. Kastenmeier, D-Wis., an adamant opponent of the efforts to remove the court's jurisdiction on these subjects, charged that the "bills are merely a form of chastisement. If we do it in one case, we could do it in many cases....

"If Congress can decide willy-nilly that the Supreme Court and the federal appellate courts have no appellate jurisdiction by a simple majority vote," Kastenmeier said, "then we have arrogated to ourselves considerable power."

Sen. Orrin G. Hatch, R-Utah, chairman of the Senate Judiciary Committee's Subcommittee on the Constitution and a leading proponent of the court-curbing approach, said in a May 3, 1981, article in *The Washington Post*: "The federal judiciary has been courting constitutional disaster by reading its own predilections into the nation's foundational document.

"The Supreme Court is the body charged with policing the bounds drawn by the Constitution. When the policeman violates the law, a higher authority must undertake to protect freedom. The Constitution is that higher authority and has outlined the means to prevent overreaching."

However, three veteran Republican members of the House Judiciary Committee, including Rep. Henry J. Hyde of Illinois, a leader of the congressional anti-abortion drive, expressed reservations about such bills.

"I believe in the principle of judicial review," said Hyde, the ranking minority member of the Civil and Constitutional Rights Subcommittee, in 1981. "I personally am not convinced we can deny to the Supreme Court the right of review concerning a question of constitutionality, and I

rather doubt it." Tom Railsback, R-Ill. (1967-83), and M. Caldwell Butler, R-Va. (1972-83), also expressed doubts about whether Congress could or should take away the Supreme Court's authority to hear cases.

"I think it's very dangerous. We run the risk of setting a dangerous precedent," Railsback said. Depriving the high court of the right to pass on the constitutionality of laws, he added, would be "depriving the Supreme Court, which is the ultimate reviewing tribunal, of its constitutional mandate and prerogative."

Butler called the court-curbing bills unwise as a matter of policy. He said Congress ought to address controversial issues "more directly," adding that he believed there was "running room" on some of the controversial issues for "congressional action that does not take jurisdiction away from the courts."

These court jurisdiction bills of 1981-82 were a long time in the making. The starting point was the Supreme Court's landmark decision in *Brown v. Board of Education of Topeka*, the 1954 ruling that repudiated the "separate but equal" doctrine and said that school segregation deprived blacks of equal protection under the law.

A second *Brown* opinion in 1955 ordered public schools to desegregate with "all deliberate speed."

Just how to desegregate was another matter. The court directly addressed that issue in the 1971 case of *Swann v. Charlotte-Mecklenburg (N.C.) County Board of Education*. The unanimous decision in this case said busing, racial balance quotas and gerrymandered school districts were appropriate interim methods of eliminating the vestiges of school segregation.

In 1973, two years after the *Swann* decision, the court took on the abortion controversy and, in *Roe v. Wade*, struck down state anti-abortion laws.

The court said the Constitution implicitly guarantees a right of personal privacy that is "broad enough to encompass a woman's decision whether or not to terminate her pregnancy." In the first trimester of pregnancy, the court said, the decision on whether to have an abortion rests exclusively with a woman and her doctor.

The third controversial issue, school prayer, erupted much earlier, in 1962, when the court ruled in *Engel v. Vitale* that the use of a non-denominational school prayer was "wholly inconsistent" with a clause in the First Amendment prohibiting the establishment of religion. A year later, in two other cases, *School District of Abington Township v. Schempp* and *Murray v. Curlett*, the court declared that daily Bible readings in public school classrooms likewise were unconstitutional.

For years, members of Congress upset by these decisions tried unsuccessfully to overturn the rulings through legislation or by proposing constitutional amendments. As of the start of the 98th Congress, all attempts had failed, although the lawmakers occasionally managed to narrow the scope of certain court rulings.

Busing. The Senate Judiciary Committee in 1977 reported a bill that would have allowed a court to order busing for desegregation purposes only after determining that "a discriminatory purpose in education was a principal motivating factor" in the segregation that busing was supposed to correct. The bill was not considered by the Senate.

Sen. Joseph R. Biden Jr., D-Del., who sponsored the 1977 bill, tried to attach a similar provision to an education authorization bill but failed by two votes.

The House in 1979 considered a constitutional amendment to prohibit school busing, but it was defeated by a 209-216 vote.

At the end of the 96th Congress, senators, led by Strom Thurmond, R-S.C., and Jesse Helms, R-N.C., added a rider (nongermane amendment) to an appropriations bill that was intended to prevent the Justice Department from bringing desegregation lawsuits that could lead to busing. The House also had adopted the provision. But it was dropped in a House-Senate conference committee after President Jimmy Carter threatened to veto the bill.

In March 1982 the Senate approved language that would have stripped the federal courts of their authority to order busing for racial balance in the public schools. That measure, however, died in the House Judiciary Committee at the end of the 97th Congress.

School Prayer. In a 1979 compromise on legislation creating the Department of Education, Sen. Helms won Senate approval of a separate bill that included a provision prohibiting the Supreme Court from handling school prayer cases. That bill, however, died in Rep. Kastenmeier's House subcommittee.

In 1982 the Senate spent six weeks debating a proposal that would have barred the federal courts from hearing cases in which "voluntary" school prayer was challenged as unconstitutional. Helms had tried to add this proposal as an amendment to a measure increasing the ceiling on the public debt.

The Senate ultimately killed the proposal. It voted 79-16 to direct the Senate Finance Committee to strip the prayer amendment from the debt measure.

Abortion. Since the mid-1970s Congress has approved language, on an annual basis, severely limiting the use of public funds to carry out abortions, but moves to ban abortion altogether have failed.

After lengthy debate in September 1982, the Senate agreed by a one-vote margin, 47-46, to table a Helms-backed anti-abortion amendment to the public debt ceiling bill. That amendment did not deny the court power to hear abortion cases, but it declared that the court's 1973 decision had erred by failing to recognize the humanity of the unborn and to protect them. It would have permitted a direct appeal to the court for challenges to any state law banning abortions.

CONGRESS' POWER
TO REVERSE COURT RULINGS

Congress has been conspicuously unsuccessful in the use of its many powers — the confirmation power, the impeachment power, its power to increase justices' pay and its control of the court's appellate jurisdiction — to influence the the court's rulings. Nevertheless, Congress on numerous occasions has overruled the court on particular issues.

Congress can reverse the court's ruling on a question of federal law simply by amending the law, or passing a new one. It is more difficult to reverse the court's holding on a constitutional question. That requires a constitutional amendment, but four times in U.S. history Congress and the states have taken that route to remedy what they

considered an error by the court.

The two most recent examples are the 16th Amendment providing the authority for the federal income tax and the 26th Amendment giving 18-year-olds the right to vote in state, local and federal elections.

Recent statutes that resulted from congressional reversals of earlier court decisions include a 1978 law requiring employers to extend additional disability insurance coverage to pregnant workers and a 1980 law giving news organizations special protection from police searches.

Constitutional Amendments

There have been only four occasions in which Supreme Court decisions have been overturned by means of constitutional amendments. Several other proposed amendments to nullify unpopular high court rulings have been offered over the years, but these either did not receive the requisite two-thirds majority of both the House and Senate or did not win approval from three-fourths of the states.

States' Rights

The 11th Amendment, ratified in 1795, was the first amendment adopted to negate a Supreme Court decision; it is the only constitutional amendment that actually removed part of the jurisdiction of the federal courts. The other three overturned specific rulings of the court.

Article III, Section 2, of the Constitution gave the Supreme Court jurisdiction over cases arising between a state and citizens of another state or of a foreign country.

A South Carolinian named Chisholm, acting as executor for a British creditor, sued the state of Georgia for property confiscated from an Englishman. The court's decision in the case of *Chisholm v. Georgia*, Feb. 18, 1793, upheld the right of citizens of one state to sue another state in federal court.

The decision, according to Supreme Court historian Charles Warren, "fell upon the country with a profound shock." Anti-Federalists argued that the decision compromised the sovereignty of the states and made them nothing more than corporations. But the real fear was that the decision would lead to a proliferation of citizen suits against the states that would further jeopardize the states' already precarious financial conditions.

The day after the *Chisholm* decision was announced, a resolution proposing a constitutional amendment to bar citizen suits against states was offered in the House. The Senate approved it Jan. 14, 1794, by a 23-2 vote. The House approved it March 4, 1794, by an 81-9 vote.

Three-fourths of the states approved the amendment in less than a year, but almost four years passed before its ratification was officially recognized. President John Adams sent a message to Congress Jan. 8, 1798, stating that three-fourths of the states having acted, the amendment "may now be deemed to be a part of the Constitution."

The Supreme Court acquiesced in the amendment, stating in 1798 that ratification of the 11th Amendment had removed its jurisdiction "in any case, past or future, in which a State was sued by citizens of another State, or by citizens or subjects of any foreign States."

Citizenship

In one of the most devastating rulings in its history,

Lobbying by Federal Judges...

When it comes to money and organization, federal judges can't hold a candle to the oil industry. But when judges lobby Congress, members usually listen.

While lobbying is an integral thread in the fabric of congressional life, such activity raises eyebrows — particularly among academics — when the federal judiciary is involved.

Many federal judges and legislators, on the other hand, think judicial lobbying can be entirely appropriate.

A cornerstone of the argument against judicial lobbying is the constitutional doctrine of separation of powers, which gives each branch of the government specific and separate duties.

"The judiciary in this country prides itself on being independent. Getting involved in legislation subtly chips away at that independence," says Arthur S. Miller, a constitutional law specialist and professor emeritus of George Washington University's law school.

"I am personally of the opinion that judges have no business, either individually or collectively, to volunteer their opinions on legislation, either pending or legislation that might be thought about," Miller adds.

Members of Congress most directly involved in legislation affecting judges and the courts, and several prominent federal judges, disagree.

They argue that the central issue is developing good legislation, and those affected by the laws — judges included — should have a role in their creation. To these members and judges, the separation of powers concept need not be rigidly construed.

"There is nothing wrong with legislators visiting with judges. As a matter of fact, there should be more of it done," said Tom Railsback, R-Ill. (1967-83), at the time the senior Republican on the House Judiciary Committee's Courts, Civil Liberties and Administration of Justice Subcommittee.

To Sen. Howell Heflin, D-Ala., a former state Supreme Court chief justice, judicial participation in legislating is a must.

"Judges have a right as well as a requirement to improve the administration of justice," Heflin said. "If they didn't participate, I think you'd have a void."

'Absolute Obligation'

Many prominent judges, including Chief Justice Warren E. Burger, share Heflin's view. In a 1978 speech, the chief justice conceded that judges must be insulated "from political activities generally," but he added that "participation in legislative and executive decisions that affect the judicial system is an absolute obligation of judges just as it is of lawyers."

"It is not only appropriate for judges to comment upon issues which affect the courts, but absolutely necessary," Burger said.

Burger regularly has suggested that Congress be required to make "judicial impact statements" for any proposed legislation. These studies would assess how much litigation a new law might generate.

One of the more active appellate judges, James R. Browning, chief judge of the 9th U.S. Circuit Court of Appeals, described his views on judicial lobbying this way: "I have not hesitated to write or call whether they [members of Congress] inquired or not, if legislation affects the operation of the courts in this circuit.... I cannot believe the public interest is served by saying 'Do not speak until spoken to about legislation that directly affects the administration of the courts'."

"No one questions Congress' ultimate authority to make decisions," Browning says, "but surely they want to make them with the facts."

The judiciary's participation in the legislative process is not a recent phenomenon. Perhaps its heyday was during the tenure of Chief Justice William Howard Taft, a former president.

In a 1973 book, "The Politics of Federal Judicial Administration," Duke University political science Professor Peter G. Fish noted that "personally intervening in the congressional process was a role both important and congenial to Chief Justice Taft."

"No question of propriety gnawed at Taft's conscience, for he considered it part of his 'duty,' as head of the federal judicial system, to suggest needed reform...," Fish observed.

Fish wrote that Taft used to meet frequently in private with members of the Judiciary and Appropriations committees to discuss legislation. In one instance, Fish said, Taft initiated a newspaper campaign in an effort to block a bill altering the federal courts' jurisdiction.

Taft had written the editor of a St. Louis newspaper, who then wrote two editorials criticizing the bill. Taft also contacted his brother, a prominent New York lawyer, and suggested that his brother contact *The New York Times*. Within days, two editorials espousing the chief justice's position appeared.

The Judicial Conference

The creation of the Judicial Conference in 1922, and its refinement over the years as a policy-making arm of the federal courts, has virtually eliminated the lobbying tactics Taft used.

Over the last 30 years, in particular, Congress regularly has solicited testimony from spokesmen for the 25-member group on a variety of court-related bills. In a 1978 speech, Burger noted that the confer-

...Little Publicized, But Effective

ence received between 50 and 100 congressional requests for testimony each year.

The conference consists of the chief judges of the 12 federal circuits, a district judge from every circuit, and the chief judge of the U.S. Court of Appeals for the Federal Circuit.

Starting in the 1940s, the conference began to take a larger role in the legislative process. In addition to offering testimony on request, the conference took positions on a number of bills, whether its views were sought or not.

In 1968, after some members criticized the conference for commenting on wiretap legislation, the panel adopted a resolution asserting its right to comment.

The resolution stated the view "that it is appropriate for the conference to study legislation affecting the judiciary and that the views of the conference should be given in advance of consideration of such legislation even though its views have not specifically been sought."

Personal Lobbying

Although the Judicial Conference is considered the official representative of the judiciary, its existence has not meant the end of personal lobbying by judges. Opinions vary, however, on the extent of the contacts between judges and members of Congress.

Sen. Heflin said he had "very few" contacts with judges. Republican Sen. Thad Cochran of Mississippi and Rep. M. Caldwell Butler, R-Va. (1972-83), characterized their contacts with judges as "occasional."

Rep. Robert W. Kastenmeier, D-Wis., who heads the Judiciary Committee's Courts subcommittee, said that while judges sometimes call him, "I really wouldn't term them aggressive at all. They are very diplomatic, very discreet."

Some judges and legislators try to draw distinctions among the kinds of bills that spur judicial lobbying. Their thesis is that judges generally contact members about bills affecting court operations rather than substantive laws, that is, issues the judges may have to resolve in a lawsuit.

Examples of judicial lobbying over the last few years illustrate that point. Federal judges lobbied on the Omnibus Judgeship Act, creating 152 new federal judgeships (PL 95-486); the judicial discipline act (PL 96-458); and legislation creating two circuits out of the old Fifth Circuit Court of Appeals (PL 96-452).

Burger's Activist Role

Despite legislators' generally sanguine approach to judicial lobbying, Chief Justice Burger in 1978 incurred the wrath of Sen. Dennis DeConcini, D-Ariz., at the time the chairman of the Judiciary Committee's Improvements in Judicial Machinery Subcommittee, when he personally called the senator about a bill to overhaul bankruptcy laws.

DeConcini contended the chief justice had been "very, very irate and rude." Spokesmen for Burger disputed that charge. Since that incident, the chief justice has been careful in his direct contacts with Congress — particularly with DeConcini.

Well before the bankruptcy incident, Burger had been considered an activist chief justice, one who lobbied in the public forum through speeches.

Early in his tenure, Burger started speaking out on what was to become a constant theme: steadily growing caseloads and too little congressional concern about the impact new laws might have on the judiciary.

In a 1978 speech to state chief justices, he asserted that "the burdens imposed upon the present federal judicial structure are so great that had it not been for the service above and beyond the call of duty of approximately 130 senior federal judges, the federal system would have foundered in many districts."

In the same speech, Burger urged his state court colleagues to tell Congress that state courts are "able and willing" to handle cases currently in federal court.

Burger has been concerned about maintaining a workable relationship with Congress, and toward that end he worked with the Brookings Institution in 1978 to set up informal meetings once a year with selected members, judges and lawyers to discuss judicial issues.

Burger clearly wishes to keep control over any lobbying by federal judges. In 1981 he was blunt in telling fellow federal judges that he disapproved of their organizing to lobby Congress for higher pay. *(Pay raise controversy, box, p. 68)*

In a letter to a federal district court judge, who was spearheading the organization effort, Burger said he feared that "in the long run, an organization such as you propose will obstruct, rather than advance, accomplishment of those things needed by the judiciary."

In his letter, Burger said that while he understood "the frustrations of all federal judges, and indeed share them," he disapproved of the action because it could "undercut" efforts of the U.S. Judicial Conference, which is authorized to speak for the judiciary.

"I urge all judges to channel these well-intended efforts through that body," Burger concluded.

Source: Adapted from Nadine Cohodas, "When Federal Judges Lobby, Congressmen Usually Listen," *Congressional Quarterly Weekly Report,* Oct. 18, 1980, pp. 3167-3171.

the Supreme Court in 1857 declared that Congress lacked the authority to prohibit slavery in the territories and that blacks could never be U.S. citizens. This decision, *Dred Scott v. Sandford*, contributed to the divisions between North and South over the slavery issue and accelerated the momentum in the country toward civil war.

Within a decade, soon after the Civil War had ended, Congress approved, and the states ratified, the 14th Amendment to the Constitution. The first section of this amendment specifically overruled the citizenship portion of the *Dred Scott* decision. It declared that all persons born or naturalized in the United States and subject to its jurisdiction are citizens of the United States and the state in which they live. It extended constitutional protections to all citizens, and to other persons, against state action denying them due process, equal protection or their rightful privileges and immunities.

The amendment was approved by the House and Senate in 1866, and ratification by three-fourths of the states was completed in 1868. It contains the only definition of citizenship to appear in the Constitution.

Income Taxes

In 1895 the court struck down a general federal income tax law, finding it unconstitutional because it was a "direct tax," which the Constitution required to be apportioned among the states on the basis of their relative populations. When the court announced its decision, the chief justice, Melville W. Fuller, invited Congress to overturn it. "If it be true that the Constitution should have been so framed that a tax of this kind could be laid, the instrument defines the way for its amendment," he wrote in *Pollock v. Farmers' Loan & Trust Co.* (1895).

The decision was very unpopular with many groups, which gradually elected more and more members of Congress who favored enactment of an income tax. Finally, in 1909, Congress approved a constitutional amendment that permitted a federal income tax to be established without being apportioned. In less than four years, by February 1913, it was ratified by three-fourths of the states and became part of the Constitution, clearing the way for a federal income tax.

The Right to Vote

Adoption of the fourth constitutional amendment, the last to date that overturned a Supreme Court decision, occurred with the apparent cooperation of the court itself.

In 1970 Congress approved an amendment to the Voting Rights Act of 1965 that lowered the voting age to 18 for federal, state and local elections. President Nixon objected to the provision even though he signed it into law in June 1970. He said he favored lowering the voting age but felt — "along with most of the Nation's leading constitutional scholars — that Congress has no power to enact it by simple statute, but rather it requires a constitutional amendment."

The Nixon administration quickly brought suit to test the validity of the legislative measure, and the Supreme Court cooperated by deciding the case just six months after the measure was signed into law. By a 5-4 vote, the court ruled in December 1970 that Congress had the authority to pass legislation lowering the voting age for federal elections but not for state and local elections.

This decision created immense administrative difficulties for the 47 states that did not allow 18-year-olds to vote.

State election officials and legislators said the task of producing dual registration books, ballots and voting machines could not be completed in time for the 1972 elections. Amendments to state constitutions changing voting age requirements would have been difficult if not impossible for some states to approve before 1972.

To assist the states, an amendment to the Constitution lowering the voting age to 18 years in all elections was introduced in both houses of Congress early in 1971. The Senate approved the amendment unanimously March 10, 1971. The House adopted it by a 401-19 vote March 23. The states also acted in record time, ratifying the amendment July 1, 1971, just three months and seven days after it was submitted to them.

Unsuccessful Amendments

In 1916 Congress passed a law outlawing child labor. That law was declared unconstitutional by the Supreme Court two years later. In 1919 Congress responded by passing a new law that sought to ban child labor by imposing a stiff tax on products made by young laborers. In 1922 the court again declared this law unconstitutional, reiterating its view that child labor was a matter for state, not federal regulation.

In 1924 Congress tried to overrule those decisions, approving a constitutional amendment that specifically authorized Congress to regulate child labor. In 14 years, however, only 28 states approved it, well short of the three-fourths required for ratification. In 1938 Congress enacted a law that banned child labor. Times had changed, and so had the court, which in 1941 reversed itself and upheld the 1938 law. This made action on the constitutional amendment unnecessary.

There have been many other unsuccessful efforts in modern times to use the constitutional amendment route to overturn, or blunt the effect of, a Supreme Court decision. In the 1960s and 1970s, members of Congress proposed constitutional amendments as a way to discard the "one person, one vote" rule for reapportionment, permit prayer in public schools, ban the use of busing for school desegregation and outlaw abortion.

Apportionment. The court in 1962 discarded its long-held view that the federal courts should not become involved in questions of legislative apportionment. In subsequent decisions the high court ruled that reapportionment must be based on the "one person, one vote" principle. Opponents of this ruling introduced legislation to blunt its impact, but when that failed, Sen. Everett McKinley Dirksen, R-Ill. (House 1933-49; Senate 1951-69), led an effort in 1965-66 to win approval of a constitutional amendment permitting states to apportion one chamber of their legislature on some basis other than population. A majority of the Senate twice approved the amendment, but on each occasion the proponents fell short of the two-thirds vote needed to approve a proposed constitutional amendment. *(Other proposals on this issue, p. 59)*

Discouraged, advocates of the Dirksen amendment tried a third route permitted by the Constitution: the calling of a constitutional convention. By 1969, 33 states had submitted petitions to Congress calling for the convocation of a convention to propose the drafting of a constitutional amendment directed at the court's reapportionment ruling. But this number was one short of the two-thirds necessary to convene a convention, and no other states between 1969 and 1982 joined the call.

School Prayer. At about the same time it was causing havoc with the state legislatures through its reapportionment decisions, the Supreme Court created another controversy by ruling in 1962 and again in 1963 that the First Amendment's prohibition against the establishment of religion barred officially prescribed or supported religious observances in public schools.

Although most major religious organizations were opposed to a constitutional amendment as a means of overriding these decisions, mail advocating such an amendment flooded congressional offices. The House Judiciary Committee reluctantly held hearings on proposed amendments in 1964 but took no further action. In the Senate, Minority Leader Dirksen proposed a constitutional amendment in 1966, but the Senate failed by nine votes to approve it by the necessary two-thirds majority.

Little else happened on the issue until 1971, when an intense two-year grass-roots campaign succeeded in dislodging a school prayer amendment from the House Judiciary Committee. But this effort, too, was unsuccessful when fewer than two-thirds of House members voted for the amendment.

Abortion and Busing. In 1969 the Supreme Court held that busing schoolchildren to certain schools was a permissible way to remedy school segregation. The use of busing became a hotly debated national issue, and many communities throughout the country found themselves embroiled in controversy over this method of desegregating their schools. Hundreds of legislative proposals to restrict or ban the use of busing were considered in Congress in the 1970s, but not until 1979 did supporters of a constitutional amendment banning school busing succeed in getting a bill to the House floor. The House, however, rejected it, 209-216. Opponents of school busing then returned to regular legislative means to try to end this practice.

After the court in 1973 held that states could not make abortion a crime, pressure to reverse that ruling increased steadily on Congress for the rest of the decade. In the late 1970s Congress approved language that severely curtailed federal funding of abortions, but despite efforts by certain senators and representatives to win approval of a constitutional amendment overturning the 1973 ruling, no such amendment had been approved by either chamber as of January 1983, the 10th anniversary of the court's decision.

Reversals by Legislation

A speedier and frequently more successful means than the constitutional amendment for reversing Supreme Court decisions is by passage of a new law or modification of an existing law.

The court generally acquiesces in such legislative overrides. Its opinions often actually suggest that Congress re-enact the measure in question after tailoring it to remove the court's objections to its validity.

The justices, however, do not always bow to congressional efforts to void court decisions by legislation. After the court declared unconstitutional the 1916 child labor law, which barred shipment in interstate commerce of goods made by children, Congress passed a second measure placing a prohibitively high tax on profits from such goods. The court declared this law invalid, too. Congress then took the constitutional amendment route, discussed above.

According to historian Charles Warren, Congress first reversed the Supreme Court by legislation in 1852. In *Pennsylvania v. Wheeling and Belmont Bridge Co.*, the court ruled that because a bridge built across the Ohio River obstructed interstate commerce and violated a congressionally sanctioned compact between Kentucky and Virginia, it either had to be raised so ships could pass under it or taken down.

Congress immediately passed a law reversing the decision by declaring that the bridge did not obstruct interstate commerce and requiring instead that ships be refitted so they could pass under the bridge. In 1856 the court sustained this legislative reversal.

Civil Rights

Congress does not always act with such dispatch to counter the court. In the area of civil rights, more than 80 years passed between a Supreme Court decision and its reversal by legislation. In 1883 the court held unconstitutional the Civil Rights Act of 1875, which made it a misdemeanor for any individual to discriminate against another individual on account of race in the use of public accommodations, transportation or public entertainment. The court specifically ruled that Congress had exceeded its power under the 13th and 14th Amendments when it approved that statute.

Not until passage of the 1964 Civil Rights Act did Congress reverse the 1883 ruling. In the 1964 law Congress used its authority to regulate interstate commerce to bar racial discrimination in public accommodations that serve interstate travelers or sell goods or provide entertainment, a substantial portion of which moves in interstate commerce.

Six months after this measure was signed into law, the court unanimously sustained its constitutionality.

New Deal Legislation

The New Deal period saw Congress overturn the court on more important measures than in any other period in the nation's history. At President Franklin D. Roosevelt's instigation, Congress in the early and mid-1930s enacted several laws aimed at ending the Great Depression and restoring the nation's economic well-being. Of eight major statutes, the Supreme Court upheld only two — acts establishing the Tennessee Valley Authority and abolishing gold clauses in public and private contracts.

At first frustrated by the economically conservative court majority's unwillingness to sustain most of the New Deal programs and then encouraged by the court's apparent philosophical about-face on economic issues by 1937, Congress revised five of the six laws the court had declared invalid. The court subsequently sustained all of these laws as modified by Congress. In lieu of the sixth law originally overturned by the court, the National Industrial Recovery Act, Congress enacted the National Labor Relations Act, which the court also sustained.

The six original statutes, the cases striking them down, the revised laws and the cases sustaining the revised laws' validity were:

● National Industrial Recovery Act of 1933, struck down in *Panama Refining Co. v. Ryan* (1935) and *Schechter Poultry Co. v. United States* (1935), replaced by the National Labor Relations Act of 1935, upheld in *National Labor Relations Board v. Jones & Laughlin Steel Corp.* (1937).

● Railroad Retirement Pension Act of 1934, struck down

in *Railroad Retirement Board v. Alton* (1935), replaced by railroad retirement acts adopted in 1935, 1937 and 1938, which were never challenged before the Supreme Court.

● Frazier-Lemke Farm Mortgage Act of 1934, struck down in *Louisville Joint Stock Land Bank v. Radford* (1935), modified by Frazier-Lemke Act of 1935, upheld in *Wright v. Vinson Branch* (1937).

● Agricultural Adjustment Act of 1933, struck down in *United States v. Butler* (1936), modified in Agricultural Adjustment Act of 1937, upheld in *Mulford v. Smith* (1939).

● Bituminous Coal Conservation Act of 1935, struck down by *Carter v. Carter Coal Co.* (1936), modified in Bituminous Coal Act of 1937, upheld in *Sunshine Anthracite Coal Co. v. Adkins* (1940).

● Municipal Bankruptcy Act of 1934, struck down in *Ashton v. Cameron County District* (1936), modified in Municipal Bankruptcy Act of 1937, upheld in *United States v. Bekins* (1938).

Tidelands Oil

Congress in one instance successfully overruled both the Supreme Court and a president. In the 1947 case of *United States v. California*, the court ruled that the federal government, not the states, owned the three-mile strip of oil-rich submerged land adjacent to the ocean shores. Legislation to reverse this ruling was introduced in 1948, 1949 and 1950 but was not approved by Congress. After the court reaffirmed its 1947 ruling in two 1950 cases affecting Louisiana and Texas, Congress a year later passed a bill giving ownership of the tidelands to the states. President Harry S Truman, whose administration had brought the 1947 suit claiming federal ownership, vetoed it.

No attempt was made to override the veto, but the question of who controlled the submerged lands became a major campaign issue in the 1952 presidential elections, with Republicans promising to restore the lands and their oil deposits to the states. The Republicans won the election, and Congress in 1953 approved, and President Dwight D. Eisenhower signed into law, the Submerged Lands Act ceding to the states the mineral rights to lands lying offshore between the low tide mark and the states' historic boundaries. The Supreme Court upheld this cession in 1954.

Internal Security

Distressed by many of the Supreme Court's rulings on internal security cases in the 1940s and 1950s, Congress tried between 1957 and 1959 to remove the court's jurisdiction to review such cases and also to reverse the objectionable rulings. Only one of these attempts — modification of a ruling in *Jencks v. United States* (1957) — was successful. The other proposals failed, primarily because the Senate refused to approve them. *(Court-curbing proposals, p. 57)*

The Jencks Case. The Supreme Court in June 1957 reversed the conviction of labor leader Clinton E. Jencks, who had been charged with perjury for swearing he was not a communist. The five-justice majority held that reports filed by FBI-paid informants alleging Jencks' participation in Communist Party activities should have been made available to Jencks' defense attorneys when requested. The court ruled that the prosecution either had to turn over to the defense directly any portion of statements previously made by government witnesses that related to the trial testimony or drop the case.

Justice Tom C. Clark, a former U.S. attorney general, dissented in *Jencks*, along with Justices Harold H. Burton and John Marshall Harlan. Clark said that unless Congress nullified the decision through new legislation, "those intelligence agencies of our government engaged in law enforcement may as well close up shop." He added that the decision would result in a "Roman holiday" for criminals to "rummage" through secret files.

Clark's dissent was seized upon by those in Congress who opposed the court's decision. They drew encouragement from the fact that the court majority had not specified that the prosecution might withhold from the defense any irrelevant portions of testimony requested by the defense. One result of that vagueness was that lower courts were left to their own interpretations of the ruling, and the government was ordered in a number of subsequent trials to produce entire files in a case, regardless of relevancy. Several important prosecutions were dismissed because the government refused to produce the requested files.

At the behest of the White House, the Justice Department and the FBI, the House and Senate Judiciary committees moved quickly to report bills to narrow the impact of the *Jencks* decision. The Senate passed its version by voice vote Aug. 26, 1957; the House passed a related measure a day later with only 17 dissenting votes. Both chambers agreed overwhelmingly Aug. 30 to a compromise version, and President Eisenhower signed the bill into law Sept. 2.

The law did not reverse the *Jencks* decision but, rather, restricted it. Following testimony by a government witness, a defendant in a criminal case could request relevant pretrial statements made by that witness so long as the statement was written and signed by the witness or was a transcription made at the time the statements were given. The statute also authorized the trial judge to screen requested statements for relevance.

The House in 1958 and 1959 approved measures to reverse a portion of the court's ruling in *Yates v. United States* (1957) that defined the word "organize," as defined in the Smith Act of 1940, to mean only the act of initially bringing together a group of people. This greatly narrowed the effect of the law on the existing members of the American Communist Party, initially organized in 1945. The 1958-59 legislation would have redefined the word to make it a crime not only to bring into being such a group seeking to overthrow the government by force but also to conduct continuing organizational activities. The Senate took no action on the House-passed bill.

In 1961, however, the House again approved a measure broadening the definition of the word "organize" as used in this portion of the Smith Act. The Senate approved the bill in 1962 by voice vote, and President Kennedy signed it into law June 19, 1962.

Unsuccessful Legislative Attempts. Reversal of another court decision came within a hairsbreadth of congressional approval. In the 1956 case of *Cole v. Young*, the court held that federal employee security procedures applied only to sensitive jobs and that government employees in non-sensitive positions could not be summarily dismissed for suspected disloyalty.

The Senate in August 1957 approved a bill to permit government supervisors to transfer suspected security risks from sensitive to non-sensitive jobs instead of suspending such personnel. In July 1958 the House approved an amended version of that bill that extended federal employee security procedures to all government employees so that anyone suspected of subversive activities could be summarily dismissed.

A compromise version, which was identical to the House bill except that it was limited to one year, was never taken up by the Senate, and it died at adjournment.

After the court held in *Kent v. Dulles* (1958) that Congress had not authorized the State Department to deny passports to American citizens affiliated with the Communist Party, the department proposed legislation to overturn the decision. The House passed an amended version of the proposal by voice vote, but a threatened filibuster in the Senate blocked consideration there. The House passed similar legislation in 1959, but although three Senate subcommittees held hearings on the issue no bill was reported in the Senate.

Criminals and Confessions

Congressional efforts to limit the effects of several court decisions of the 1950s and 1960s dealing with the use of confessions of suspected criminals had little direct effect. These rulings protected the rights of suspected criminals and were strongly criticized, especially by law enforcement officers, who said they coddled the criminal at the expense of the public.

Responding to this outcry, Congress tried unsuccessfully for 10 years to reverse one of the earliest of these rulings. Then, in 1968, rising crime rates, urban riots and the assassinations of civil rights leader Martin Luther King Jr. and presidential candidate Robert F. Kennedy supplied the added impetus that was needed. Congress, over the objections of the president, enacted legislation modifying some of these decisions. The legislation, however, affected only federal courts, in which only about 7 percent of all criminal cases are heard; the vast majority come to state courts.

The Mallory Decision. In 1943 the court in *McNabb v. United States* ruled that a confession obtained by police during an "unnecessary delay" in a suspect's arraignment could not be used as evidence in federal court, even if the confession had been given voluntarily.

In 1957 the Supreme Court reaffirmed the *McNabb* decision in its ruling overturning the rape conviction of Andrew Mallory. District of Columbia police had arrested Mallory and questioned him for several hours before he confessed. No attempt was made to bring official charges against him during this period, although arraigning magistrates were available in the same building throughout the time Mallory was being questioned. The court held that because police had not complied with the *McNabb* doctrine and with federal rules that require prompt arraignment, Mallory had been detained illegally, and his confession therefore was not admissible as evidence.

Reaction to the decision in *Mallory v. United States* was immediate and widespread. Less than a month after it was handed down, a House Judiciary subcommittee created specifically to examine controversial decisions of the Warren court began hearings on proposals to reverse the *Mallory* decision. The House in July 1958 passed "corrective" legislation by an overwhelming vote of 294-79. The House measure barred federal courts from disqualifying confessions otherwise admissible as evidence in criminal cases solely because of delay in arraigning the suspect.

The Senate passed the bill after amending it to permit federal courts to throw out confessions obtained during unreasonable delays in arraignment. The House-Senate conference committee struck a compromise, which stated that a reasonable delay in arraignment would not disqualify a confession "provided that such delay is to be considered as an element in determining the voluntary or involuntary nature of such confessions and statements."

The House approved the compromise language easily, but in the Senate an opponent of the bill raised a point of order on a technicality dealing with Senate rules. Vice President Richard M. Nixon, who was presiding, sustained the point of order, and the legislation was killed.

In 1959 the House again passed its version of the *Mallory* reversal legislation, but the Senate took no action and the issue cooled during the 1960s.

Miranda, Wade Decisions. The court in the 1960s handed down two more decisions that prompted Congress to act. In the 1966 case of *Miranda v. Arizona* the court set out a new rule for police to follow in interrogating suspects. Under the so-called "Miranda rights" rule, confessions were inadmissible as evidence in state or federal criminal trials if the accused had not been informed of his right to remain silent, if he had not been warned that any statement he made might be used against him and if he had not been informed of his right to have an attorney present during the police interrogation.

The following year in *United States v. Wade*, the court held that identification of a defendant based solely on a police lineup staged when the defendant's attorney was not present was inadmissible. The majority said such a procedure violated the defendant's Sixth Amendment right to counsel.

These decisions brought an outpouring of public criticism of the court. In 1967 President Lyndon B. Johnson proposed a crime control act providing federal financial assistance to local law enforcement agencies. The House passed an amended version and sent it to the Senate, where a Judiciary subcommittee added several provisions to modify the controversial Supreme Court decisions and limit the court's jurisdiction to review such cases.

The Johnson administration opposed the subcommittee amendments, and when the bill reached the full Senate in May 1968 liberals succeeded in deleting the language limiting the court's jurisdiction. But they were unable to defeat the amendments designed to modify the *Miranda*, *Mallory* and *Wade* decisions. As passed by the Senate these sections:

● Modified the *Miranda* decision by making confessions admissible in evidence in federal courts if voluntarily given. The trial judge was to rule on any question of voluntariness by taking into consideration the circumstances surrounding the act of confessing. No single factor had to be conclusive on the issue of voluntariness.

● Modified the *Mallory* decision to provide that a confession made by a person in the custody of law officers was not inadmissible in evidence in federal court solely because of a delay in arraigning the defendant if 1) the confession were found to be voluntary, 2) the weight to be given the confession were left to jury determination and 3) the confession were given within six hours immediately following the arrest.

● Modified the *Wade* decision to provide that the testimony of an eyewitness that he saw the accused commit the crime for which he was being tried was admissible in evidence in any federal criminal trial.

The amended Senate bill reached the House floor in June 1968, just hours after an assassin shot Robert F.

Court Overrules Congress On Pay Raises for Judges

When Congress decided to play Indian-giver with the pay of federal judges, it soon found itself involved in a lawsuit, which eventually produced a Supreme Court decision slapping the hand of the legislative body.

In 1975 Congress agreed that Supreme Court justices and other federal judges, along with other top federal officials, should receive annual cost-of-living adjustments in their salaries.

But second thoughts about the wisdom of this move led Congress in 1976, 1977, 1978 and 1979 to rescind the increases for fiscal years 1977, 1978, 1979 and 1980. Those rescissions, which also denied raises to members of Congress and top executive branch officials, were contained in riders (non-germane amendments) added to various appropriations bills.

One group of federal judges decided to sue, calling Congress' actions unconstitutional. By withholding the increases, they contended, Congress violated the Constitution's promise that the salaries of federal judges "shall not be diminished during their Continuance in Office." They argued that once Congress included judges under the cost-of-living pay system, those annual increases became part of each judge's compensation, protected by the Constitution.

On Dec. 15, 1980, the Supreme Court, in *United States v. Will*, rejected the judges' basic argument, ruling that the cost-of-living increases did not become part of the judges' compensation until the first day of each new fiscal year, Oct. 1. But the judges won a partial victory, nevertheless. The court held that Congress cannot rescind a cost-of-living increase once the fiscal year in which they take effect has begun. The court held that Congress had failed to meet that deadline for two of those years — fiscal 1977 and 1980 — and thus the judges won half of the pay raise they had sought. Because Congress had acted before Oct. 1 in rescinding the 1978 and 1979 increases, those rescissions were valid, the court held.

Recent Reversals

Between 1978 and 1982, Congress on four occasions has successfully reversed the court's holdings on a particular legal issue, acting quickly and without much controversy.

On the other hand, Congress, despite repeated efforts, has done little to reverse the court's controversial and much-criticized rulings on school busing and abortion. *(pp. 60, 65)*

Pregnancy Disability. In December 1976 the Supreme Court held that the 1964 Civil Rights Act did not require employers who provided their employees with disability insurance if they were temporarily incapacitated to also provide benefits under that plan to women temporarily unable to work because of pregnancy-related disabilities. The decision came in the case of *General Electric v. Gilbert.*

In 1978, however, Congress overruled that decision by amending the 1964 act to ban discrimination against pregnant women. That law also specifically required employers who offered health insurance and temporary disability plans to provide women employees coverage for pregnancy, childbirth and related medical conditions.

Endangered Species. Even before the Supreme Court ruled that the Tennessee Valley Authority could not put into operation a new $119 million dam because it would destroy the home of an endangered species of fish known as the snail darter, the Senate was moving to write into the law procedures for resolving such conflicts. The court's ruling, based on the Endangered Species Act of 1973, came in June 1978 in the case of *Tennessee Valley Authority v. Hill.*

Within four months, Congress had reversed the court, amending the 1973 act to set up a Cabinet-level board to resolve these controversies. This measure was given final approval in October 1978. Sentiment for such a modification in the law was so strong that even members allied with environmental groups gave up fighting the idea early in the process and simply concentrated on minimizing the impact of the changes.

Newsroom Searches. A few weeks before the snail darter decision, the court decided the case of *Zurcher v. Stanford Daily,* which set off another effort at legislative reversal. In the Stanford case, the court held that the First Amendment's guarantee of freedom of the press did not prohibit police, with valid search warrants, from searching the offices of a news organization, even if neither the organization nor its employees were suspected of a crime. Attorneys for the media had argued that the police should be required to obtain subpoenas, rather than search warrants, to get such information. Such searches, they contended, were very likely to result in serious infringement of the First Amendment guarantee of a free press.

The Senate held hearings on the ruling soon after it was announced, but it was two years before Congress passed the 1980 Privacy Protection Act. That law prohibited law enforcement officers from conducting searches of news organizations or other groups engaged in First Amendment activities. The two exceptions to this ban permitted searches with warrants when the person thought to possess the sought-after information was suspected of a crime involving that material or when there was reason to believe that death or serious injury to another person would result if the materials were not immediately seized.

The bill was signed into law Oct. 13, 1980.

Military Pensions. In June 1981 the court held, in

Kennedy in a Los Angeles hotel. Although opponents of the Senate amendments moved to send the bill to a House-Senate conference where they hoped the provisions would be deleted, the House was anxious to approve the crime-control legislation and the motion was rejected on a 60-318 vote. The House then approved the Senate version without further change.

Although he opposed the criminal procedures modifications provisions, Johnson signed the bill.

McCarty v. McCarty, that state courts, in dividing a divorcing couple's assets, could not consider the retirement pay of a retired military officer as community property subject to division.

In August 1982 Congress approved a defense authorization bill that included, as an amendment, the Uniformed Services Former Spouses' Protection Act, which permitted state courts, under certain circumstances, to treat military pensions as property subject to division in divorce settlements. Women's groups hailed this congressional reversal as a notable victory, recognizing the contribution that a military man's spouse made to his career.

COURT-RELATED LEGISLATION: 1969-82

During the years from 1969 to 1982, Congress approved numerous legislative measures that had a direct impact on the functioning of the federal judiciary. Laws were enacted increasing the number of judges, setting standards for judicial disqualification, giving judges new powers, requiring speedy trials for criminal defendants and revising the rules of criminal procedure for the courts.

Most laws approved by Congress have some effect on the judicial system, but the following is a brief description of legislation enacted during the period that was designed to improve the nation's judicial machinery.

Personnel

In 1970 Congress approved an additional 58 permanent federal district judgeships and three temporary judgeships (PL 91-272). In large part as a result of this legislation — which gave the president 61 new judicial posts to fill — President Nixon in 1973 broke President Roosevelt's record for the most federal judges appointed by a president. (This record later was eclipsed by President Carter.)

The Judicial Conference of the United States, which acts as the "board of directors" of the federal judiciary, in 1972 asked Congress to create 10 new posts on the courts of appeals and 51 new federal district judgeships. Two years later, Congress still had not acted, and the Judicial Conference increased to 15 its request for appeals court positions. In keeping with the traditional reluctance of a Democratic Congress to give a Republican president a whole set of new judgeships to fill, the 92nd, 93rd and 94th Congresses took no action on the requests.

The impasse finally was broken in the 95th Congress, after the Carter administration took office. In 1978 Congress approved the Omnibus Judgeships Act (PL 95-486), authorizing the creation of 152 new judgeships, the largest one-time expansion of the federal judiciary in the nation's history. Of that number, 117 were district judgeships and 35 were additional appeals court seats. The legislation allowed President Carter to appoint more new federal judges than any other president. In doing so, he named more women, blacks and Hispanics to federal judgeships than any of his predecessors.

In approving the first major revision of the nation's bankruptcy laws in nearly 40 years, Congress in 1978 created a new corps of bankruptcy judges to assist creditors as well as consumer and business debtors. Though retaining the existing system under which bankruptcy courts operated as adjuncts to federal district courts, the law (PL 95-598) made a number of controversial changes upgrading the status and powers of bankruptcy judges. Subsequently, the Supreme Court in June 1982 ruled that those provisions were unconstitutional. Congress, according to the court, gave the bankruptcy judges too much power with too little independence. The decision did not invalidate previous actions of the bankruptcy courts, but Congress was directed to rewrite the 1978 law. The court gave lawmakers until Oct. 4, 1982, later extended to Dec. 24, to complete the revisions, but Congress was not able to agree on new bankruptcy provisions before the 1982 session ended. As a result, the nation's bankruptcy regulations were placed in legal limbo, forcing Congress to consider the issue again in the 98th Congress.

To facilitate the use of interpreters in federal cases in which the parties or witnesses have difficulty speaking or understanding English, Congress in 1978 approved the creation of a central list of certified interpreters for the federal judiciary.

PL 95-539 required the Administrative Office of the U.S. Courts to establish a procedure to certify interpreters as qualified to serve in federal courts and to maintain on file a list of certified interpreters. An interpreter was to be appointed whenever a judge determined that a party to a case before him or a witness in that case spoke only or primarily a language other than English, or suffered from a hearing impairment. In some cases, convictions of persons with poor English proficiency had been reversed on due process grounds because no interpreters had been appointed for their trials.

Congress in 1980 approved legislation (PL 96-439) providing for three additional judgeships for the U.S. Tax Court, increasing the number of court judges to 19. PL 96-439 also removed the age ceiling for judges serving on the tax court. The ceiling had been 65.

Judicial Salaries

Congress acquiesced in a judicial pay raise in February 1969. Not until 1977 did the judiciary receive another pay increase, although in 1975 Congress brought the federal judiciary under the law authorizing cost-of-living salary increases for federal workers.

The next judicial pay raise did not materialize until 1980 — despite the cost-of-living pay formula — and that occurred because of an action by the Supreme Court rather than by Congress. In every year from 1977 through 1980 Congress had rescinded the annual cost-of-living increase for judges as well as other top government officials and members of Congress. But in December 1980 the high court ruled, in a case brought by a group of federal judges, that in two of those years (1977 and 1980) Congress had acted too late to rescind the increase. As a result, judicial salaries were increased, retroactive to Oct. 1, 1980, to the following levels: chief justice of the United States — $92,400 (from $75,000); associate justices of the Supreme Court — $88,700 (from $72,000); appeals court judges — $70,900 (from $57,500); and district court judges — $67,100 (from $54,500).

In 1981 Congress once again denied federal judges a

Help for Overworked Justices:...

In the mid-1970s, and again in the early 1980s, concern about the heavy workload burdening the Supreme Court led to proposals for creating a new court that would have responsibilities and powers midway between those of the existing circuit courts of appeal and the Supreme Court.

Central to the proposal, which took various forms, was the idea that such a court could assist the high court by taking over some of its less important functions. However, disagreement over what functions properly might be delegated to another court — as well as differing views among the justices about the severity of the workload — stymied congressional action on the proposal.

In 1975 the first serious congressional discussions of the problem led to the drafting of legislation creating a national court of appeals. Under that measure, a new court, consisting of seven justices appointed by the president, would decide cases referred to it by the Supreme Court or transferred to it by federal courts of appeals. All cases it decided would be subject to final review by the Supreme Court. The legislation was introduced by Sen. Roman L. Hruska, R-Neb. (1954-76), who had headed the Commission on Revision of the Federal Court Appellate System, which was created by Congress to study the problem. The Hruska commission in 1974 had recommended a national appeals court.

Neither chamber acted on the proposal during the 94th Congress. Five of the sitting justices had

endorsed the idea of a new court: Chief Justice Warren E. Burger and Justices Byron R. White, Harry A. Blackmun, Lewis F. Powell Jr. and William H. Rehnquist. The other four — William J. Brennan Jr., Potter Stewart, Thurgood Marshall and William O. Douglas — did not feel at the time that such a court was needed.

By the early 1980s, however, some of them had changed their minds, particularly Brennan, the court's most senior member.

In an unusual round of public statements late in 1982, seven justices expressed dissatisfaction with the workload and with the way the court was dealing with it. Justice John Paul Stevens, who replaced Douglas in 1975, sparked this renewed campaign to lighten the court's heavy agenda. He criticized the court for doing a "poor job" of deciding which cases to review by full oral argument. He suggested that a new court be created to take over the function of screening the 4,000 to 5,000 cases that come before the court each year seeking full review. This idea was similar to a proposal submitted in 1972 by a special study committee set up at Burger's behest by the Federal Judicial Center.

Stevens' proposal was opposed by Justice White. Although he agreed that there was a problem, White said that Stevens' recommendation was merely "plastic surgery" and would not solve the problem.

Justice Powell added his voice, suggesting some minor legislative changes Congress could make: giv-

cost-of-living pay raise. And it used a fiscal 1982 emergency funding measure (PL 97-92) as a vehicle to remove federal judges and Supreme Court justices from the 1975 law providing for automatic cost-of-living adjustments. As a result, Congress now must take affirmative action to raise judicial salaries. Congress did that in 1982, raising annual salary scales to the following levels as of Dec. 17, 1982: chief justice — $100,700; associate justices — $96,700; appeals court judges — $77,300; district court judges — $73,100.

Justices' Annuities

Congress in 1972 increased to $10,000 from $5,000 the annuities paid to widows of Supreme Court justices and set up a contributory annuity system for retired and active justices (PL 92-397).

Court Executives

Congress in 1970 created (PL 91-647) the post of circuit court executive, allowing each of the judicial circuits to name to its staff a professional administrator to assist the circuit's chief judge with the day-to-day administrative responsibilities of the circuit. Two years later, Congress approved (PL 92-238) creation of a similar post for the Supreme Court, authorizing the appointment of an administrative assistant to the chief justice.

Magistrates

In 1968 Congress abolished the outmoded system of U.S. commissioners and replaced it with a federal magistrates system. Magistrates are officers of federal district courts; their functions include issuing warrants, fixing bail, holding preliminary hearings and conducting trials for minor offenses.

In 1972 Congress raised the ceiling on magistrates' salaries to $30,000 from $22,500 (PL 92-428) and approved the temporary assignment, in emergency situations, of magistrates to areas outside their regular jurisdictions (PL 92-239).

A significant expansion of the authority of magistrates was approved by Congress in 1979, enabling them to try civil cases and criminal misdemeanors if the parties agreed to have their case heard before a magistrate rather than a federal district judge. The new law (PL 96-82) allowed magistrates to try such cases with or without a jury. Appeals from the verdict generally were to go directly to the appropriate U.S. court of appeals.

PL 96-82 also created a merit selection process for magistrates, who are appointed by federal district judges.

Before enactment of PL 96-82, magistrates could try only non-jury misdemeanor cases in which the possible penalty did not exceed one year in prison and a $1,000 fine.

... A New, Almost Supreme, Court?

ing the court complete discretion to decide what cases to review, curtailing the flow of cases into the federal system by removing "diversity" jurisdiction (cases brought in federal court because they involve parties from different states rather than questions of federal law), limiting the use of laws that permit civil rights damage suits and curtailing access by state prisoners to federal courts for review of their cases.

Stevens' suggestion for a court to screen cases before they come to the justices also was criticized by Brennan, who described the screening function as "an indispensable and inseparable part of the entire process," which "cannot be withdrawn from the court without grave risk of impairing the very core of the court's unique and extraordinary functions." But Brennan for the first time acknowledged that the sheer volume of cases coming to the court was creating a problem. "There is a limit to human endurance," Brennan said, adding that "with the ever increasing complexity of many of the cases that the court is reviewing in this modern day" the current workload "takes that endurance to its limits."

Justice Marshall spoke out, too, expressing displeasure with the increasingly used practice of deciding certain cases summarily — without hearing full oral arguments or receiving complete written briefs. Such "cursory" treatment created substantial "potential for error and confusion," he warned.

Justice Rehnquist warned that by piling more and more work on judges at all levels of the system,

the nation was risking "a bureaucratization of the courts." Since it was Congress that defined the jurisdiction, and thus the workload, for most of the federal courts, Rehnquist noted, the solution was up to Congress.

Chief Justice Burger said in November 1982 that "if every case in the Supreme Court is to continue receiving close individual attention of justices, as had been the tradition, the caseload cannot continue at the present rate. . . . If some drastic changes are not made, we will not be able to maintain standards of quality the country has a right to expect from its highest court."

In a February 1983 address to the American Bar Association, Burger was more specific. "Only fundamental changes in structure and jurisdiction will provide a solution" to this problem, he said. He urged Congress to create an intermediate court of appeals, perhaps as part of the new Court of Appeals for the Federal Circuit, that would have the task of resolving legal conflicts between the existing circuit courts of appeals — one category of cases that the Supreme Court feels a particular urgency in resolving. This would remove between 35 and 50 cases a year from the arguments calendar of the Supreme Court, according to Burger.

To reach a long-term solution, Burger urged Congress to create another study commission to consider the situation and recommend a permanent remedy.

Jury Service

Congress in 1972 approved a bill lowering the minimum age for federal jury service to 18 from 21 (PL 92-269). This action was consistent with ratification in 1971 of the 26th Amendment to the Constitution lowering the voting age for all citizens to 18.

Judicial Conduct/Reform

In the wake of the controversies of the late 1960s involving the financial dealings of Supreme Court Justice Abe Fortas, who resigned in May 1969, and President Richard M. Nixon's first choice to replace Fortas, U.S. Appeals Court Judge Clement F. Haynsworth, the Judicial Conference in 1973 adopted a code of judicial conduct for all federal judges.

The new code incorporated specific guidelines governing judicial disqualification.

In 1974 Congress wrote into law certain standards defining the situations in which a federal judge, Supreme Court justice, magistrate or bankruptcy referee should disqualify himself from participating in a case. That law (PL 93-512) required disqualification in cases in which the judge's impartiality might reasonably be questioned. It specified a number of situations in which disqualification

was appropriate, including: 1) cases in which a judge had a previous relationship with one of the lawyers; 2) cases in which he had a personal prejudice; 3) cases in which he, as a government official, had served as counsel, adviser or material witness, or had expressed an opinion on the matter in controversy; 4) cases in which he was related to any party to the case; and 5) cases in which he had a financial interest, however small, that could be substantially affected by the outcome of the proceeding.

After debating the question for several years, Congress in 1980 approved legislation (PL 96-458) providing the federal judiciary with procedures for disciplining federal judges for misconduct, without taking the drastic step of impeaching them. Chief judges and the governing councils of each federal judicial circuit were given authority to investigate complaints against judges and to impose sanctions short of impeachment.

A disciplining action could be appealed to the U.S. Judicial Conference. The Judicial Conference also could take any case to the House of Representatives for possible impeachment proceedings.

Judicial Reorganization

Congress in 1972 set the stage for wide-ranging changes in the structure and operation of the federal appeals system by creating a Commission on Revision of the Federal Court Appellate System (PL 92-489). The commission was to study and recommend changes in the geographic boundaries of the judicial circuits and in the operations of the federal appeals courts.

The commission subsequently recommended that Congress split two existing judicial circuits — the Fifth Circuit in the Deep South and the Northwest Ninth Circuit — in two, creating two additional circuits. *(For action on Fifth Circuit, see below.)*

It also recommended creation of a national court of appeals that would be superior to the existing appeals courts but inferior to the Supreme Court. The national court would resolve cases from the appeals courts that were referred to it by the Supreme Court. Congress took no action on those recommendations in the 1970s or early 1980s. *(National court of appeals proposals, box, pp. 70-71)*

In 1980 Congress approved legislation (PL 96-452) creating a new circuit court of appeals — the 11th. The existing Fifth Circuit Court of Appeals was split in two. The new Fifth Circuit, having 14 judges, consisted of Louisiana, Mississippi, Texas and, until 1983, the Canal Zone. The 11th Circuit Court of Appeals had 12 judges and heard appeals from Alabama, Georgia and Florida.

Civil rights groups had opposed earlier attempts to divide the Fifth Circuit, fearing it would alter the old circuit's strong civil rights disposition. With a different mix of states proposed for the reorganization, these concerns were effectively allayed by 1980.

Direct Appeals

Responding to Chief Justice Warren E. Burger's plea to reduce the number of appeals that come by special routes to the Supreme Court — rather than through the circuit courts of appeals — Congress in the 1970s:

● Eliminated the special path by which civil antitrust cases had, since 1903, moved directly from the trial level to the Supreme Court. In 1974 Congress repealed the provision for such direct appeals as part of a larger antitrust measure (PL 93-528).

● Required cases appealing actions of the Interstate Commerce Commission to be reviewed first by a circuit court of appeals rather than by a three-judge panel, as was previously the case. With this change (PL 93-584), approved in 1974, the Supreme Court gained more discretion to refuse to review the lower court's decisions than it had when such matters came directly to it from the three-judge court.

● Did away with the authority under which persons who challenged a state or federal law as unconstitutional, and asked for an injunction against its enforcement, could request that a three-judge panel be convened to hear such cases. The decision of that panel could be appealed directly to the Supreme Court. In dropping that procedure in 1976 (PL 94-381), Congress did not affect the right to convene a three-judge panel in reapportionment cases or cases in which Congress specifically authorized the convening of such a panel.

Congress in 1970 also approved a measure (PL 91-271) modernizing the operations of the U.S. customs courts.

New Courts

Congress in 1982 created a new appellate court, the U.S. Court of Appeals for the Federal Circuit, that was intended primarily to handle patent cases. Although the new court was on the same footing as the 12 existing appeals courts, its jurisdiction differed. Whereas the other circuit courts heard cases by region, the Court of Appeals for the Federal Circuit took cases by subject matter from any region of the country. In establishing the new court (PL 97-164), Congress merged the appellate division of the U.S. Court of Claims with the U.S. Court of Customs and Patent Appeals.

The 1982 law also created a new trial-level court, the U.S. Claims Court, to handle the cases that had been heard by the trial division of the U.S. Court of Claims. The new court, unlike the existing claims court, was given authority to issue injunctions and temporary restraining orders in contract cases.

A new court was established by Congress in 1978 as part of a law, the Foreign Intelligence Surveillance Act (PL 95-511), requiring the federal government to obtain court orders before it conducted electronic surveillance in national security cases. The special court to hear such requests for warrants consisted of seven federal district judges, each from a different judicial district, selected by the chief justice of the United States. *(See also new court procedures for handling classified information under Rules of Procedure.)*

The U.S. Court of International Trade, established by Congress in 1980 (PL 96-417), was given exclusive jurisdiction in suits against the United States challenging duties the federal government placed on imports as well as suits against federal "anti-dumping" duties. The U.S. trade court also was given authority to hear lawsuits initiated by the United States concerning import transactions and to review decisions by the secretaries of commerce and labor certifying which workers, businesses and communities were eligible for assistance because of economic injury caused by import competition. The law abolished the U.S. Customs Court.

Rights and Powers

In 1974 Congress enacted the Speedy Trial Act (PL 93-619) to spur federal courts to deal with their overloaded dockets and sluggish trial schedules. PL 93-619 allowed a person charged with a crime to move to have the charges against him dropped if he were not brought to trial within 100 days of his arrest.

This deadline was intended to put muscle behind the Sixth Amendment's guarantee of a speedy trial. PL 93-619 did not become fully effective until 1980, but federal courts were required to meet progressively tighter deadlines beginning in 1976.

Congress in 1979 delayed for one year, until July 1, 1980, the requirement in PL 93-619 that persons charged with federal crimes be brought to trial within 100 days of arrest, or the case against them would be dismissed. The Justice Department as well as the Judicial Conference of the United States, the policy-making arm of the federal judiciary, had asked Congress for a two-year delay, but Congress granted only one year (PL 96-43).

Congress in 1980 approved legislation (PL 96-349) to enable the federal courts to deal more efficiently and quickly with complex antitrust cases. That law was the outgrowth of proposals made in 1979 by the National Commission for the Review of Antitrust Laws and Procedures. The authority of the Justice Department was expanded to allow it to analyze complicated business documents and to obtain information from investigative targets. The 1980 law also enlarged the authority of federal judges to discipline attorneys whose conduct unreasonably delayed antitrust litigation.

With support from both the intelligence and the law enforcement communities, Congress in 1980 established new procedures (PL 96-456) for courts to follow in handling criminal cases involving classified government information. (Classified information was defined as that material designated by law or executive order as requiring protection from unauthorized disclosure for national security reasons.) PL 96-456 allowed a judge to screen sensitive information before a trial began to determine whether it could be used during the proceedings. The law was aimed at a problem frequently dubbed "graymail" — a term that referred to a defendant's threat to disclose classified information as part of his defense against charges that he engaged in criminal activity.

Prosecutors saw the tactic as an effort to force the government to drop a case rather than risk disclosure of the information. But defense attorneys responded that the strategy was a legitimate maneuver and that disclosure of such information might be essential to an individual's defense.

Attorneys' Fees

The Supreme Court ruled in 1975 *(Alyeska Pipeline Service Co. v. Wilderness Society)* that federal judges did not have broad power to award attorneys' fees to a successful plaintiff in a public interested case unless Congress had specifically provided such authority in the law under which the case was brought.

Responding to that ruling, Congress in 1976 specifically amended the Civil Rights Acts of 1861, 1866, 1870 and 1871, as well as Title II of the 1964 Civil Rights Act and Title IX of the 1972 Education Act, to authorize such awards (PL 94-559).

Rules of Procedure

Since the early days of the Republic, the Supreme Court has been empowered by Congress to set out rules governing the procedures to be followed by the federal courts in dealing with various types of cases. Since 1934 Congress has required the court to submit proposed rules to it and to provide a certain amount of time to elapse before they become effective.

In 1973 Congress received a set of rules — rules of evidence — from the court. Concerned that the rules governing what could and could not be introduced as evidence in the federal courts were more substantive than procedural, Congress delayed (PL 93-12) their effective date from July 1, 1973, until such time as they were approved by Congress.

In 1974 Congress approved the first uniform code of evidence for the federal courts, a single set of rules to guide judges and lawyers in federal courts across the country in deciding what was admissible as evidence. As finally enacted, the code of evidence (PL 93-595) was substantially

different from the proposals submitted by the court, tending less toward innovation and more toward codification of the existing rules and procedures already in effect in many of the federal districts. For example, the code did not contain a recommended section codifying the law of privilege — which protects certain relationships from official demands for information. Instead, it simply stated that existing common law governed the use of privilege.

Jurisdiction of Federal Courts

Congress in 1980 eliminated a requirement that cases posing questions that arise under the U.S. Constitution, U.S. laws or treaties — so-called "federal questions" cases — had to have at least $10,000 in dispute before they could be considered by federal courts. The measure (PL 96-486) provided that any such "federal question" case could be considered by a federal court regardless of the amount at stake. The new law retained the $10,000 jurisdictional amount requirement for "diversity cases" brought in federal court because they involved parties from different states rather than because they raised questions of federal law.

Rules of Criminal Procedure

The court in April 1974 sent Congress a set of proposed changes in the rules of criminal procedure for federal courts. But Congress delayed the effective date of these changes for one year — from Aug. 1, 1974, to Aug. 1, 1975 (PL 93-361).

In the meantime, Congress in 1975 approved a measure (PL 94-64) incorporating some of those changes. The revised rules for the first time formally recognized the practice of plea bargaining, the process by which a defendant agrees to plead guilty to a lesser charge, thus avoiding the need for a full trial, in exchange for a reduction of the charges against him and, perhaps, some assurance of a lighter sentence than he might get if his case went to trial. The rules set up regulations to guide the process. They also set up guidelines for pretrial discovery, use of alibis as a defense, and summonses and arrest warrants.

Several changes in the Federal Rules of Criminal Procedure proposed by the Supreme Court in April 1979 went into effect on Dec. 1, 1980. A bill to block four of the proposed changes was rejected by the House in September 1980. The proposed changes that would have been blocked or altered by enactment of the House bill:

● Excluded from evidence statements made by a defendant during plea bargaining only if the statements were made to a government attorney. Statements made in that context to a law enforcement officer, on the other hand, were admissible. Under the previous rules, all such statements were inadmissible.

● Required the defense to give the prosecution copies of statements by defense witnesses. No such requirement existed until that change took effect.

● Required a judge to hold a hearing before modifying the terms of a person's probation.

● Empowered a judge to require a defendant to obtain his own lawyer rather than share a lawyer with a codefendant.

The Court at Work

The Supreme Court is not a bureaucracy. As one justice remarked several years ago, the justices do their own work, a fact that makes the court quite different from the other two branches of the national government. Here, the justices do their own thinking, their own internal negotiations, their own writing — and they sign their opinions.

Because the justices operate as individuals, even when they meet as a committee of nine, it is useful to know something of the background of each justice, to be familiar with the experiences and characteristics of the nine persons who comprise the highest court. It is of equal importance to see where today's justices fit philosophically in the context of the long history of the court, to see how its members resemble or differ from those of earlier courts.

At first glance, the 102 justices who have served on the court seem to be a fairly homogeneous group. All but one have been white. All but one have been men. All but 11 have been Protestants. Yet, a closer look reveals considerable diversity in their politics, cultural and geographical backgrounds and education.

There are no constitutional or statutory qualifications for Supreme Court justices. A president may choose whomever he wishes, subject only to Senate confirmation. Once confirmed, the justice has his job for life, so long as he behaves in a manner to avoid impeachment by Congress. Only one justice has been impeached — in 1804 — but he was acquitted by the Senate.

Unlike elective office in the executive and legislative branches, there is no minimum age requirement for service on the court; justices as young as 32 have been appointed. And there is no mandatory retirement age; justices have served well into their 80s, and Justice Oliver Wendell Holmes Jr. was 90 when he retired in 1932.

Further, there is no requirement that justices be native-born Americans; in fact, six of the 102 justices were born outside the United States. Justices are not required to be attorneys, yet all to date have been.

The court in its 1982-83 term was unique in one major respect. It was the first to have a woman justice: Sandra Day O'Connor, appointed in 1981 by President Ronald Reagan. There was one black justice — Thurgood Marshall, appointed in 1967 — and one Catholic justice — William J. Brennan Jr., at 76 the court's senior member. There was no Jewish member on the court.

Today's court is an aging one. Five of its members —

Chief Justice Warren E. Burger and Justices Brennan, Marshall, Harry A. Blackmun and Lewis F. Powell — are 74 or older. Justices Byron R. White and John Paul Stevens are in their 60s. Justices William H. Rehnquist and O'Connor are in their 50s.

Seven of today's nine justices were placed on the court by Republican presidents. Brennan was an Eisenhower nominee; Burger, Blackmun, Rehnquist and Powell were Nixon choices; Stevens was selected by Ford, and O'Connor by Reagan. Only White, selected by Kennedy, and Marshall, chosen by Johnson, owe their seats to Democrats.

Yet, historically, there has been little correlation between the party or philosophy of the appointing president and the performance of the appointed justice. Current examples of the vitality of that tradition are Justices Brennan and Blackmun, liberal justices appointed by conservative presidents, and Justice White, basically a conservative judge appointed by a liberal Democrat.

The importance of geography has diminished in the 20th century as a factor in presidential selection of justices, but it is interesting to note that as the population of the United States moved south and west, representation of these areas on the court has increased.

Today, a majority of the justices hail from the West or Midwest. Burger and Blackmun are from Minnesota; Rehnquist and O'Connor are from Arizona; White is from Colorado and Stevens is from Illinois. Brennan is from New Jersey, Marshall from Maryland and Powell from Virginia. In earlier times both New York and New England took it for granted that there always would be at least one justice from their regions on the court.

Five of today's justices came to the court after serving on other benches. Brennan and O'Connor were state judges; Burger, Blackmun and Stevens were federal appeals court judges.

Three of the others came to the court after practicing law and spending a relatively brief time at the Justice Department. Marshall, a noted civil rights lawyer, served as a federal appeals court judge and then solicitor general before being named to the court. White and Rehnquist also first served in subcabinet-level Justice Department posts.

Justice Powell was chosen for the court after a highly successful career in private practice.

Of the nine justices, only O'Connor previously had legislative experience.

NINE JURISTS: JUDICIAL PORTRAITS

With the opinions he or she writes for the court and in dissent, every justice of the Supreme Court gradually sketches a judicial self-portrait. The portrait changes during the years on the bench; it is dynamic and not definitive.

After the court hears arguments and votes on a case, the chief justice decides who will write the opinion. If the chief justice dissents, the senior justice in the majority assigns the task. All members of the majority must approve the majority opinion before it is announced, a requirement that results in majority opinions more carefully phrased and moderate in tone than many dissenting or concurring opinions, which set forth the views of one or a few justices.

The following self-portraits of each of the justices sitting on the Supreme Court in early 1983 are drawn from the opinions delivered during the court terms from October 1969 through June 1982. The portraits are not inclusive in every case — three of the justices served on the court for several years before this period began. But the opinions surveyed and the selections presented portray to some degree each justice's characteristic themes and concerns.

Brennan: Liberal Spokesman

"From its founding, the nation's basic commitment has been to foster the dignity and well-being of all persons within its borders," wrote Justice William J. Brennan Jr. in 1970.

At the time, he was writing about welfare rights, but this concern for individual dignity and this affirmative view of the role of federal power has characterized Brennan's position on many issues before the court. *(Biography, p. 168)*

When the court in 1982 struck down a Texas law that denied free public education to children who were illegal aliens *(Plyler v. Doe)*, Brennan spoke for the majority. Although the court has not held that there exists a constitutional right to a public education, Brennan left no doubt that the Constitution denies states the power to decide that they will educate some children but not others. "Illiteracy is an enduring disability," he wrote. "The inability to read and write will handicap the individual deprived of a basic education each and every day of his life. The inestimable toll of that deprivation on the social, economic, intellectual and psychological well-being of the individual, and the obstacles it poses to individual achievement, makes it most difficult to reconcile the cost or the principle of a status-based denial of basic education with the framework of equality embodied in the Equal Protection Clause."

During his first dozen years as a justice, Brennan often spoke for the liberal majority of the Warren court, sharing its belief that the courts were the guardians of the individual's rights, obligated to act when other parts of the government failed to do so. It was Brennan who in 1962 wrote the opinion asserting the court's jurisdiction over the "political" question of electoral districts, clearing the way for enunciation of the "one person, one vote" standard used in redistricting. *(Baker v. Carr)* Four years later, it was Brennan who wrote the court's opinion upholding the Voting Rights Act of 1965, enacted by Congress to remedy the racial discrimination that had disenfranchised thousands of blacks in the South. *(Katzenbach v. Morgan)*

But in the post-Warren era, Brennan found himself a member of a shrinking minority on the court. One by one his liberal colleagues departed, until he and Thurgood Marshall remained the only certain liberal votes. Together they dissented time and again, with particular vigor when the court acted to curtail the rights of defendants or to restrict access to the federal courts.

The individual's innate dignity, and the government's responsibility to respect that, were the keystones of Brennan's argument in 1972 that all capital punishment was unconstitutional. "The state, even as it punishes, must treat its citizens in a manner consistent with their intrinsic worth as human beings," he wrote in 1976, dissenting from the court's decision upholding certain new and carefully drawn state death penalty laws. "The fatal constitutional infirmity in the punishment of death is that it treats 'members of the human race as non-humans, as objects to be toyed with and discarded. [It is] thus inconsistent with the fundamental premise ... that even the vilest criminal remains a human being possessed of common human dignity.'" *(Gregg v. Georgia)*

Brennan sees the federal courts, the Supreme Court in particular, as responsible for protecting the individual against mistreatment by the government. When in 1976 the majority held that the Constitution provided no protection for a person's interest in his good reputation, Brennan dissented: "I had always thought that one of this court's most important roles is to provide a formidable bulwark against government violation of the constitutional safeguards securing in our free society the legitimate expectations of every person to innate human dignity and sense of worth." *(Paul v. Davis)*

William J. Brennan Jr.

As the court in the 1970s and early 1980s has tended to restrict access to the federal courts, Brennan has protested, characterizing the majority as "slam[ming] the courthouse door" in the face of individual citizens. In keeping with his view that the Constitution created a federal court system "to provide a hospitable forum" for those who feel that their constitutional rights have been violated, Brennan has written several opinions for the court expanding the right of persons to file federal suits against state or federal officials charged with denying them their rights under the Constitution or federal law. *(Carlson v. Green, 1980; Davis v. Passman, 1979; Monell v. Department of Social Services of New York, 1978; Maine v. Thiboutot, 1980)*

In keeping with his affirmative view of federal judicial power, Brennan wrote the court's pioneer rulings striking down sex-based classifications as unconstitutional. When in 1973 it struck down military regulations that treated servicewomen differently from servicemen, he wrote: "There can be no doubt that our nation has had a long and unfortunate history of sex discrimination ... rationalized by an attitude of 'romantic paternalism' which, in practical effect, put women not on a pedestal, but in a cage." (*Frontiero v. Richardson*)

In 1976 Brennan formulated the standard that the court uses today to test state laws that treat men and women differently. "To withstand constitutional challenge," he wrote, "classifications by gender must serve important government objectives and must be substantially related to achievement of those objectives." (*Craig v. Boren*)

Brennan also champions the individual's right to privacy in certain decisions and his freedom from government interference. The court's only Catholic, Brennan quietly sides with the pro-choice forces on the issue of abortion. He also has written several court opinions striking down state restrictions on access to contraceptives. "If the right of privacy means anything," he wrote in 1972, "it is the right of the individual, married or single, to be free from unwarranted governmental intrusion into matters so fundamentally affecting a person as the decision whether to bear or beget a child." (*Eisenstadt v. Baird*)

In matters of criminal law, Brennan is as concerned about the impact of improper law enforcement methods on society as about its effect on the individual suspect or defendant. When the court in 1970 held that charges against a juvenile, like those against an adult, must be proved "beyond a reasonable doubt," he explained: "It is critical that the moral force of the criminal law not be diluted by a standard of proof that leaves people in doubt whether innocent men are being condemned. It is also important in our free society that every individual going about his ordinary business have confidence that his government cannot adjudge him guilty of a criminal offense without convincing a proper fact-finder of his guilt with utmost certainty." (*In re Winship*)

Brennan sees the First Amendment guarantees of free speech, free press and freedom of association and religion as close to absolute. It was he who set out the high standards of proof for libel suits in the 1964 case of *New York Times Co. v. Sullivan*. And in 1971 he stated his firm belief in the Pentagon Papers case that "the First Amendment tolerates absolutely no prior judicial restraints of the press predicated upon surmise or conjecture."

Brennan wrote the court opinions holding that national political parties have a constitutional freedom of association in which state courts may not interfere, and that patronage hiring and firing are unconstitutional violations of that First Amendment freedom for individuals. (*Cousins v. Wigoda*, 1975; *Elrod v. Burns*, 1976)

Brennan is the court's most insistent exponent of separation of church and state, opposing virtually all state aid to church-related schools.

In 1982 Brennan spoke for the court in striking down a state law that burdened the Unification Church of the Rev. Sun Myung Moon, and other denominations that receive a substantial amount of financial support from non-members, with certain registration and reporting requirements, while exempting most established religious denominations from such obligations. This sort of denominational preference is forbidden by the First Amendment's ban on state action "establishing" religion, wrote Brennan. "Free exercise" of religious belief, he continued, "can be guaranteed only when legislators — and voters — are required to accord to their own religions the very same treatment given

to small, new or unpopular denominations." (*Larson v. Valente*)

White: Strict Constructionist

Oddly enough, the justice who comes closest to fitting President Richard M. Nixon's description of a "strict constructionist" is Byron R. White — the only justice appointed by President John F. Kennedy, Nixon's political protagonist.

White takes a literal approach to legal issues, leavened at times by his pragmatic assessment of circumstances. This approach usually lands him on the conservative side of an issue. Early in the 1970s, White was described by some observers as a "one-man Supreme Court." This label referred to the fact that when he voted with the four Nixon nominees, their position became the majority view on the court, as, for example, in the 1973 decision giving states more leeway to control obscenity. (*Biography, p. 168*)

Exemplifying White's adherence to the letter of the law was his opinion curtailing the president's power to impound congressionally authorized funds. The decision, announced in 1975, was long-awaited, but when it came it was neither broad nor dramatic. White took a hard look at the law in question — the 1972 Federal Water Pollution Control Act Amendments — and saw no leeway for the president to refuse to spend the funds it provided. Rejecting arguments that Congress intended to provide such discretion, White was blunt: "Legislative intention, without more, is not legislation." (*Train v. New York*, 1975)

Byron R. White

But White's literal approach does not always result in conservative decisions. In 1970 the court shattered tradition by holding that juries need not be made up of 12 persons, that they could have fewer members. White explained: "The fact that the jury at common law was composed of precisely twelve is a historical accident, unnecessary to effect the purposes of the jury system and wholly without significance 'except to mystics.'" (*Williams v. Florida*)

Characteristic of White's ability to draw careful lines distinguishing the permissible from the impermissible are several of his opinions concerning the Fourth Amendment guarantee of security from unreasonable search and seizure. It was White who stated in 1969 that this guarantee was "clearly invaded when the police enter and install a listening device as ... when the entry is made to undertake a warrantless search for tangible property...." (*Alderman v. United States*)

In 1978 White wrote the court opinion admonishing Congress for ignoring the Fourth Amendment guarantee by authorizing federal occupational safety and health inspectors to enter business premises without a warrant over the objection of the owner. (*Marshall v. Barlow's Inc.*) That same year, however, White wrote the opinion explaining why the court rejected the claim of newspapermen that police should be required to use subpoenas, rather than search warrants, to seek evidence that might be in the possession of a news organization. The men who drafted the Fourth Amendment, he wrote, were "aware of the long struggle between Crown and press," yet they "did not forbid [the use of] warrants where the press was involved...." (*Zurcher v. Stanford Daily*)

As the latter decision indicates, White tends to view the protection of the First Amendment — freedom of the press, expression and religion — somewhat narrowly. In 1979 he spoke for the court in the case of *Herbert v. Lando*, ruling that it was permissible for attorneys in a libel suit to inquire into the "editorial process" of producing the article or television program that allegedly libeled their client. Three years later, it was White who announced the court's ruling that pornographic depictions of children were outside the First Amendment's protection. (*New York v. Ferber*) Also during the 1981-82 term, White dissented when the majority cited the First Amendment to require state university officials to permit a student group to hold regular religious meetings in university buildings and when the majority struck down a city ordinance limiting the amount of money citizens could contribute to groups working for or against certain ballot issues. (*Widmar v. Vincent, Citizens Against Rent Control/Coalition for Fair Housing v. City of Berkeley*)

In the mid-1970s, the court began to emphasize that civil rights groups challenging official actions must show discriminatory intent as well as effect in order to obtain relief. White signaled this new direction in 1976: "We have not held that a law, neutral on its face and serving ends otherwise within the power of government to pursue, is invalid under the Equal Protection Clause simply because it may affect a greater proportion of one race than another. Disproportionate impact is not irrelevant, but it is not the sole touchstone of an invidious racial discrimination forbidden by the Constitution." (*Washington v. Davis*)

White has continued to sound this theme in various cases. During the 1981-82 term, for example, he referred to it in a case involving certain seniority systems that had been challenged as illegal under the 1964 Civil Rights Act and in a case in which certain election laws were attacked as unconstitutional. (*American Tobacco Co. v. Patterson, Rogers v. Lodge*)

White has a soft spot for young people and their concerns. In 1975 he was the spokesman for the court when it expanded the rights of students to procedural safeguards before they were suspended and to allow the filing of damage suits against school board members when disciplinary actions violated their constitutional rights. (*Goss v. Lopez, Wood v. Strickland*)

And when the court in 1977 refused to apply the ban on cruel and unusual punishment to corporal punishment in the nation's schools, White's dissent was vigorous: "I am ... not suggesting that spanking ... is in every instance prohibited by the Eighth Amendment. My own view is that it is not. I only take issue with the extreme view of the majority that corporal punishment in public schools, no matter how barbaric, inhumane or severe, is never limited by the Eighth Amendment. Where corporal punishment becomes so severe as to be unacceptable in a civilized society, I can see no reason that it should become any more

acceptable just because it is inflicted on children in the public schools." (*Ingraham v. Wright*)

When the court in 1973 struck down state laws banning abortion, White dissented, in part because the majority based its decision on an elusive constitutional right of privacy, which the literal White could not locate. He continued to dissent in subsequent abortion rulings in which the court invalidated state restrictions on this procedure.

When the court struck down a state law requiring that the husband consent to his wife's abortion, he wrote: "A father's interest in having a child ... may be unmatched by any other interest in his life.... These are matters which a state should be able to decide free from the suffocating power of the federal judge...." He also objected to the court's action striking down a requirement that parents must give their consent before a daughter, a minor, could have an abortion: "This is the traditional way by which States have sought to protect children from their own immature and improvident decisions; and there is absolutely no reason ... why the State may not utilize that method here." (*Planned Parenthood of Central Missouri v. Danforth*, 1976)

White's pragmatic philosophy was exemplified in several of his opinions on the subject of official immunity — the extent to which public officials are protected from liability for their actions that injure persons. In 1978 White wrote the court's opinion holding that Cabinet officials did not have absolute immunity from damage suits brought by individuals who felt they had suffered injury in such cases. (*Butz v. Economou*)

When the court in 1982 decided that former President Nixon — and all presidents — were immune from civil damage suits relating to actions taken while they were in office, White spoke for the four justices who vigorously dissented. Immunity should attach to particular functions of an official, not to particular offices, wrote White, arguing that that view had prevailed in the court's earlier rulings on this subject. "The Court casually, but candidly, abandons the functional approach to immunity" with this holding, he said. "Attaching absolute immunity to the office of the President, rather than to particular activities that the President might perform, places the President above the law. It is a reversion to the old notion that the King can do no wrong." (*Nixon v. Fitzgerald*)

Marshall: Social Conscience

In announcing his selection of Thurgood Marshall as the Supreme Court's first black member, President Lyndon B. Johnson said Marshall had "already earned his place in history." Marshall, then the nation's first black solicitor general, was unlikely to issue any decision during his court career that had the impact of the decision he had won, as an advocate for the civil rights movement, in the case of *Brown v. Board of Education of Topeka* (1954). (*Biography, p. 169*)

That decision began the Warren era; Marshall was appointed to the court at that era's end. As the court's membership grew increasingly conservative during the 1970s, Marshall often found himself in dissent and less and less frequently a majority spokesman.

In 1982, when the court voted 8-1 to uphold California's Proposition 1, which limited the power of state courts to order busing to desegregate schools, Marshall alone dissented. "Proposition 1 has placed an enormous barrier between minority children and the effective enjoyment of their constitutional rights, a barrier that is not placed in the path of those who seek to vindicate other rights granted by state law," he wrote. (*Crawford v. Board of Education of Los Angeles*)

By coincidence or design, Marshall has written few major civil rights rulings. He did, however, write the first decision interpreting the Equal Pay Act to require a company to equalize the salaries of men and women doing the same work, and he wrote the court's ruling giving white victims of job discrimination the same right to sue under federal law as black victims of such actions.

Thurgood Marshall

Marshall is an advocate of a strong role for the courts and, secondarily, the executive. His distrust for the more political branches of the government is easily understood in light of the long history of unconcern for blacks and other minorities by political leaders.

Such a view pervaded his dissent when the court in 1973 upheld state systems of financing public schools through property taxes. These systems had been challenged as resulting in unequal funding per pupil from district to district. The court's decision to uphold those systems, wrote Marshall, "can only be seen as a retreat from our historic commitment to equality of educational opportunity... I ... am unsatisfied with the hope of an ultimate 'political' solution sometime in the indefinite future while, in the meantime, countless children unjustifiably receive inferior educations that 'may affect their hearts and minds in a way unlikely ever to be undone,'" just as segregation did. (*San Antonio Independent School District v. Rodriguez*)

Marshall concluded his passionate dissent from a 1977 court decision in which the majority held that states were not required to fund abortions for indigent women, with the plea: "When elected leaders cower before public pressure, this court, more than ever, must not shirk its duty to enforce the Constitution for the benefit of the poor and powerless." (*Beal v. Doe*)

When the court in 1981 upheld Congress' decision to exclude women from having to register for the military draft, Marshall dissented, criticizing his colleagues for being too deferential to Congress. "It is as if the majority has lost sight of the fact that 'it is the responsibility of this Court to act as the ultimate interpreter of the Constitution.' ... Congressional enactments in the area of military affairs must, like all other laws, be *judged* by the standards of the Constitution. For the Constitution is the supreme law of the land and all legislation must conform to the principles it lay [sic] down." (*Rostker v. Goldberg*)

Of all the present justices, Marshall is the most familiar with the plight of the nation's poor, and his concern for them often has found expression in his dissenting opinions.

When the court in 1973 refused to waive the $50 filing fee for an indigent who wished to file for bankruptcy relief in federal court, and the majority suggested that the man might forego some small expenses and save that amount, Marshall wrote: "It is disgraceful for an interpretation of the Constitution to be premised upon unfounded assumptions about how people live.... It may be easy for some people to think that weekly savings of less than $2 are no burden ... but no one who has had close contact with poor people can fail to understand how close to the margin of survival many of them are.... A pack or two of cigarettes may be, for them, not a routine purchase, but a luxury indulged in only rarely.... They have more important things to do with what little money they have." (*United States v. Kras*)

Perhaps Marshall's most poignant dissenting opinion accompanied the court's ruling upholding a state's right to refuse to provide Medicaid abortions: "The enactments challenged here brutally coerce poor women to bear children whom society will scorn for every day of their lives. Many thousands of unwanted minority and mixed race children now spend blighted lives in foster homes, orphanages and 'reform' schools.... Many children of the poor will sadly attend second-rate segregated schools.... And opposition remains strong against increasing AFDC [Aid to Families with Dependent Children] benefits for impoverished mothers and children so that there is little chance for the children to grow up in a decent environment.... I am appalled at the ethical bankruptcy of those who preach a 'right to life' that means, under present social policies, a bare existence in utter misery for so many poor women and their children." (*Beal v. Doe*, 1977)

Three years later, Marshall described the court's ruling upholding Congress' decision to prohibit Medicaid-funded abortions for poor women as "a cruel blow to the most powerless members of society." The choices that this denial left to a poor pregnant woman seeking an abortion were "grotesque," he wrote. (*Harris v. McRae*, 1980)

Marshall's first major opinion for the court made plain his commitment to the First Amendment and the primacy of the rights it guaranteed. In that opinion, the court held that peaceful labor pickets have a First Amendment right to picket within a large suburban shopping center despite the objections of the center's owner. (*Amalgamated Food Employees v. Logan Valley Plaza*, 1968)

The First Amendment, Marshall wrote for the court in 1969, protected an individual's right to own and use obscene material in his own home. "The Constitution protects the right to receive information and ideas.... This right to receive information and ideas, regardless of their social worth ... is fundamental to our free society.... Whatever may be the justifications for other statutes regulating obscenity, we do not think they reach into the privacy of one's own home. If the First Amendment means anything, it means that a state has no business telling a man, sitting alone in his own house, what books he may read or what films he may watch." (*Stanley v. Georgia*)

Marshall finds capital punishment "morally unacceptable" and hence unconstitutional. On other criminal law issues he often sounds a dissenting note, warning against any relaxation of absolute fidelity to the letter of the Constitution's safeguards for the rights of the accused. "Good police work," he wrote in a concurring opinion in 1977, "is something far different from catching the criminal at any price." (*Brewer v. Williams*)

Burger: Conservative Chief

Chief Justice Warren E. Burger's most famous opinion brought to an end the political career of the president who named him to the nation's highest judicial post. On July 24, 1974, Burger announced the Supreme Court's unanimous decision that President Richard M. Nixon was required to turn over certain White House tape recordings to the Watergate special prosecutor for use as evidence in an upcoming trial of the Watergate cover-up defendants, among them some of Nixon's former close advisers.

Burger's opinion, siding with the special prosecutor over the president, displayed the very characteristics that had commended him to President Nixon in the 1960s: an abiding sympathy for law enforcement officials and a firm belief in the public interest in effective criminal proceedings. *(Biography, p. 165)*

Burger's position, however, was carefully phrased and contained the first official acknowledgement that there was a constitutionally based right of executive privilege to preserve the confidentiality of certain communications between the president and his advisers.

Warren E. Burger

To allow the president to assert this privilege "to withhold evidence that is demonstrably relevant in a criminal trial would cut deeply into the guarantee of due process of law and gravely impair the basic functions of the courts," wrote Burger.

"A president's acknowledged need for confidentiality in the communications of his office is general in nature, whereas the constitutional need for production of relevant evidence in a criminal proceeding is specific and central to the fair adjudication of a particular criminal case.... Without access to specific facts a criminal prosecution may be totally frustrated.... To read the [constitutional] ... powers of the president as providing an absolute privilege as against a subpoena essential to enforcement of criminal statutes on no more than a generalized claim of the public interest in confidentiality of nonmilitary and non-diplomatic discussions would upset the constitutional balance of 'a workable government' and gravely impair the [constitutional] role of the courts...." *(United States v. Nixon)*

Burger's concern about "the constitutional balance of 'a workable government' " is reflected in many of his opinions. He has a clear-cut, conservative view of the court's role. He explained his views in 1982 in dissenting from the court's decision invalidating a Texas law that denied a free public education to children who were illegal aliens. "Were it our business to set the Nation's social policy, I would agree without hesitation that it is senseless for an enlightened society to deprive any children — including illegal aliens — of an elementary education," Burger wrote. "However, the Constitution does not constitute us as 'Platonic Guardians' nor does it vest in this Court the authority to strike down laws because they do not meet our standards of desirable social policy, 'wisdom,' or 'common sense'.... We trespass on the assigned function of the political branches under our structure of limited and separate powers when we assume a policy making role, as the Court does today," he said. "The Constitution does not provide a cure for every social ill, nor does it vest judges with a mandate to try to remedy every social problem." *(Plyler v. Doe)*

Burger came to the post of chief justice with a conservative reputation on criminal matters. In 1971 he wrote the first ruling limiting the impact of the court's controversial decision (*Miranda v. Arizona*, 1966) requiring that evidence obtained from a suspect who was not fully warned of his rights be excluded from use at the trial. In the 1971 ruling, Burger wrote that if the defendant testified in his own defense, and contradicted statements he had made before being fully warned of his rights, those statements could be used to impeach his credibility. Said Burger: "Every criminal defendant is privileged to testify in his own defense.... But that privilege cannot be construed to include the right to commit perjury.... The shield provided by *Miranda* cannot be perverted into a license to use perjury by way of a defense, free from the risk of confrontation with prior inconsistent utterances." *(Harris v. N.Y.)*

Burger has found himself in dissent from some of the court's major criminal law rulings, particularly those excluding from use as evidence information that appears to be reliable. He argues that evidence should be excluded only when it is essential to safeguard the "integrity of the truth-seeking process." *(Brewer v. Williams, 1977)*

And Burger has dissented vigorously from the court's decisions striking down state capital punishment laws: "Our constitutional inquiry ... must be divorced from personal feelings as to the morality and efficacy of the death penalty and be confined to the meaning and applicability of the uncertain language of the Eighth Amendment.... It is essential to our role as a court that we not seize upon the enigmatic character of the guarantee as an invitation to enact our personal predilections into law." *(Furman v. Georgia, 1972)*

Burger is the court's chief spokesman in a campaign to reduce the flood of cases into the federal court system and to curtail the role that federal judges play in matters outside the traditional jurisdiction of the courts.

Writing in 1974 to reject a taxpayer's challenge to the secrecy of the Central Intelligence Agency's budget, Burger set forth his views of the proper forum for such a discussion: "It can be argued that if [the plaintiff] ... is not permitted to litigate this issue, no one can do so. In a very real sense the absence of any particular individual or class to litigate these claims gives support to the argument that the subject matter is committed to the surveillance of Congress, and, ultimately, to the political process. Any other conclusion would mean that the Founding Fathers intended to set up something in the nature of an Athenian democracy or a New England town meeting to oversee the conduct of the national government by means of lawsuits in the federal courts." *(United States v. Richardson, 1974)*

Burger's judicial image is not uniformly conservative. In 1979 he spoke for the court when it held for the first time that the guarantee of due process applies to the procedures for committing persons to mental institutions. *(Addington v. Texas)* The following year, Burger wrote the court's opinion that the First Amendment guarantees newsmen and citizens the right to attend criminal trials.

(*Richmond Newspapers Inc. v. Commonwealth of Virginia*)

And in 1981 Burger, who himself shuns television cameras, declared for the court that nothing in the Constitution denies states the power to experiment with televising trials and other courtroom proceedings. (*Chandler v. Florida*) When the court found that Congress had granted candidates for federal office a right of access to network time, Burger explained the majority's reasoning. (*CBS v. FCC*, 1981) And when the court decided that the First Amendment guarantees citizens the right to spend as much money as they wish to oppose or support ballot issues, Burger again was its spokesman. (*Citizens Against Rent Control/Coalition for Fair Housing v. City of Berkeley*, 1981)

Generally, when the individual and the governmental establishment collide before the court, Burger sides with the government. In recent cases, the court considered the claim of former CIA agent Philip Agee that the Department of State unconstitutionally revoked his U.S. passport and an Amish farmer's claim that to require him to pay Social Security taxes on his employees violated his freedom of religion. In both cases, the court ruled against the individual, and Burger wrote the majority opinions. The chief justice emphasized national security considerations in the Agee case and the need to preserve a functioning Social Security system in the Amish case. (*Haig v. Agee*, 1981; *United States v. Lee*, 1982)

Blackmun: Practical Pioneer

"Must our law be so rigid and our procedural concepts so inflexible that we render ourselves helpless when the existing methods and the traditional concepts do not quite fit and do not prove to be entirely adequate for new issues?" asked Justice Harry A. Blackmun not long after arriving on the high court. (*Biography, p. 169*)

Too quickly labeled a judicial twin to his friend and fellow Minnesotan, Chief Justice Warren E. Burger, Justice Blackmun by the mid-1970s had demonstrated an independence of mind and philosophy that often placed him squarely on the liberal side of an issue.

Blackmun's single most important judicial statement was also the court's most controversial ruling of the 1970s. When the court announced on Jan. 22, 1973, that the Constitution protected a woman's decision, early in pregnancy, to abort the child she had conceived, it was Blackmun who explained the court's reasons. His willingness to stretch some traditional legal concepts to make room for new issues and new concerns was clearly apparent, as he quickly dismissed the state's argument that the case was moot because the pregnant women bringing the case had already borne their children: "The normal ... gestation period is so short that the pregnancy will come to term before the usual appellate process is complete. If that termination makes a case moot, pregnancy litigation seldom will survive much beyond the trial stage and appellate review will be effectively denied. Our law should not be that rigid."

Blackmun — the court's medical law expert after his years of work with the Mayo Clinic — carefully balanced the medical facts, personal privacy and the state's interests at each stage of pregnancy, holding that different restrictions might be placed on abortion as a pregnancy progressed. In the first trimester, he wrote that "the right of privacy ... is broad enough to encompass a woman's decision whether or not to terminate her pregnancy." (*Roe v. Wade, Doe v. Bolton*, 1973)

When the court in 1977 rejected the argument that states should be required to provide Medicaid funding for abortions, Blackmun joined the court's liberals — Brennan and Marshall — in one of his strongest dissents: "Implicit in the court's holdings is the condescension that she [the poor pregnant woman] may go elsewhere for her abortion. I find that ... alarming, almost reminiscent of 'let them eat cake'.... The court's financial argument, of course, is specious. To be sure, welfare funds are limited ... but the cost of a nontherapeutic abortion ... holds no comparison whatsoever with the welfare costs that will burden the state for the new indigents and their support in the long years ahead. Neither is it an acceptable answer ... to say that the Congress and the states are free to authorize the use of funds

Harry A. Blackmun

for nontherapeutic abortions. Why should any politician incur the demonstrated wrath and noise of the abortion opponents when mere silence and nonactivity accomplish the results the opponents want?" (*Beal v. Doe*)

Three years later, he echoed these sentiments in dissent as the court upheld Congress' decision to deny the use of Medicaid funds for most abortions. (*Harris v. McRae*, 1980)

Blackmun's sympathy for the individual who finds himself at a disadvantage in dealing with the government is clear from his court writings. One of his first major opinions for the court held that it was unconstitutional for a state to deny welfare benefits to resident aliens. Setting in motion the legal rationale for striking down many other restrictions on the opportunities and benefits available to aliens, Blackmun stated that "classifications based on alienage, like those based on nationality or race, are inherently suspect and subject to a close judicial scrutiny." (*Graham v. Richardson*, 1971)

Blackmun's concern for society's less fortunate members has been restrained by his conservative views on the judge's role, which he elaborated upon when he dissented from the court's 1972 rulings finding existing death penalty laws unconstitutional. "Cases such as these," he said, "provide for me an excruciating agony of the spirit. I yield to no one in the depth of my distaste, antipathy and indeed, abhorrence, for the death penalty ... buttressed by a belief that capital punishment serves no useful purpose.... Were I a legislator I would vote against the death penalty for the policy reasons argued by counsel.... There — on the legislative branch of the state or federal government, and, secondarily on the executive branch — is where the authority and responsibility for this kind of action lies. The authority should not be taken over by the judiciary.... We should not allow our personal preferences ... to guide our judicial decisions...." (*Furman v. Georgia*, 1972)

As Blackmun's term on the court has lengthened, however, he has become more willing to see the need for judicial action. In 1982 he wrote the court's opinion holding unconstitutional the state of Washington's initiative directed specifically at forcing the Seattle school board to drop a school busing plan it had approved voluntarily.

Blackmun said the effect of the initiative was to make it more difficult for groups seeking to desegregate the schools to achieve that purpose. "And when the state's allocation of power places unusual burdens on the ability of racial groups to enact legislation specifically designed to overcome the 'special condition' of prejudice, the governmental action seriously 'curtail[s] the operation of those political processes ordinarily to be relied upon to protect minorities.' ... In a most direct sense, this implicates the judiciary's special role in safeguarding the interest of those groups that are 'relegated to such a position of political powerlessness as to command extraordinary protection from the majoritarian political process.' " (*Washington v. Seattle School District No. 1*)

Earlier in 1982, Blackmun spoke for a closely divided court when the majority imposed new constitutional standards upon states that acted, through child neglect laws, to terminate the rights of parents over children. In that opinion, Blackmun wrote: "The fundamental liberty interest of natural parents in the care, custody, and management of their child does not evaporate simply because they have not been model parents or have lost temporary custody of their child to the state. Even when blood relationships are strained, parents retain a vital interest in preventing the irretrievable destruction of their family life.... When the state moves to destroy weakened familial bonds, it must provide the parents with fundamentally fair procedures." (*Santosky v. Kramer*, 1981)

Blackmun has spoken for the court in still another developing area of law: the extension of the First Amendment protection to commercial speech. Blackmun wrote the first of these opinions in 1975. In it, he held that the First Amendment protected a newspaper editor from prosecution under state law for printing an advertisement about legal abortion services in another state. (*Bigelow v. Cole*) The following year, Blackmun again wrote the court's opinion striking down a state law forbidding the advertising of drug prices. (*Virginia State Board of Pharmacy v. Virginia Citizens Consumer Council*)

"Advertising, however tasteless ... is nonetheless dissemination of information as to who is producing and selling what product, for what reason and at what price. So long as we preserve a predominantly free enterprise economy, the allocation of our resources in large measure will be made through numerous private economic decisions. It is a matter of public interest that those decisions, in the aggregate, be intelligent and well informed. To this end, the free flow of commercial information is indispensable."

And in 1977 Blackmun spoke for the court when it held that states could not, without violating the First Amendment, forbid attorneys to advertise their services and fees. (*Bates v. Arizona State Bar*)

Rejecting the argument that advertising would erode the professional character of the practice of law, Blackmun wrote, somewhat tongue-in-cheek, that that argument "presumes that attorneys ... conceal from themselves and from their clients the real-life fact that lawyers earn their livelihood at the bar...."

Powell: Careful Conservative

"The ultimate solutions must come from the lawmakers and from the democratic pressures of those who select them," wrote Justice Lewis F. Powell Jr. in 1973, explaining the court's refusal to hold school financing systems based on property taxes unconstitutional. (*San Antonio Independent School District v. Rodriguez*)

"The irreplaceable value of the power" of judicial review, he wrote a year later, "lies in the protection it has afforded the constitutional rights and liberties of individual citizens and minority groups against oppressive or discriminatory government action ... not [in] some amorphous general supervision of the operations of government." (*United States v. Richardson*, 1974)

"Repeated and essentially head-on confrontations between the life-tenured branch and the representative branches of the government will not, in the long run, be beneficial to either," Powell added. "The public confidence essential to the former ... may well erode if we do not exercise self-restraint in the utilization of our power to negate the action of other branches."

These tenets — judicial restraint and an obligation to protect the individual's rights — are balanced against each other again and again in the opinions produced by Justice Powell during his years on the bench. (*Biography, p. 170*)

One of Powell's first opinions for the court struck down a state law that placed unacknowledged illegitimate children at a disadvantage in receiving workmen's compensation benefits of a deceased parent. "Courts are powerless to prevent the social opprobrium suffered by these hapless children," Powell wrote, "but the equal pro-

Lewis F. Powell Jr.

tection clause does enable us to strike down discriminatory laws relating to status of birth where — as in this case — the classification is justified by no legitimate state interest...." (*Weber v. Aetna Casualty and Surety*, 1972)

But the limited role of the courts was paramount in Powell's thinking when he wrote the court's controversial Medicaid abortion opinion in 1977. Powell, who had joined the pro-choice side in the court's earlier decisions, wrote that neither the Constitution nor the Social Security Act required states to fund Medicaid abortions: "We leave entirely free both the federal government and the states, through the normal processes of democracy, to provide the desired funding. The issues present policy decisions of the widest concern. They should be resolved by representatives of the people, not by this court." (*Beal v. Doe*)

By the time Powell celebrated his 10th anniversary on the court, however, he had become a bit less reluctant to step in when the political branches of government did not act. Concurring in the court's 1982 decision that states could not refuse to admit to their public schools children of illegal aliens, Powell made it clear that he felt the court must act because "Congress — vested by the Constitution with the responsibility of protecting our borders and legislating with respect to aliens — has not provided effective leadership in dealing with this problem. It therefore is certain that illegal aliens will continue to enter the United States. . . . I agree with the court that their children should not be left on the streets uneducated." (*Plyler v. Doe*)

Powell often is the spokesman for the majority on controversial issues before the court. In 1976 he spoke for the court in a decision limiting the application of the "exclusionary rule" — which bars at a trial the use of evidence by the prosecution if it has been obtained in violation of the defendant's rights. *(Stone v. Powell, Wolff v. Rice, 1976)*

Powell wrote the court opinion in 1976 when it upheld certain new death penalty laws while striking down others that were mandatory sentencing statutes.

And two years later, when the court for the first time gave full consideration to the difficult issue of affirmative action, it was Powell who announced the court's opinion in the landmark case of *Regents of the University of California v. Bakke.*

The other eight justices divided evenly on the issue of whether a school may properly set aside for minority applicants a quota of slots in an entering class. Powell cast the crucial vote against such a rigid preference system. The constitutional guarantee of equal protection, wrote Powell, "cannot mean one thing when applied to one individual and something else when applied to a person of another color. . . . Preferring members of any one group for no reason other than race or ethnic origin is discrimination for its own sake. This the Constitution forbids. . . ."

Powell also cast the deciding vote on a second issue in that case, agreeing with the court's more liberal members that race could be taken into account by admissions officers as a factor favoring the admission of a minority student over that of a non-minority student.

In line with his concern that the courts protect the individual against improper government actions, Powell wrote the court's opinion in 1972 rejecting the Nixon administration's claim that electronic surveillance of suspected domestic subversives need not be authorized by a court warrant: "The price of lawful public dissent must not be a dread of subjection to an unchecked surveillance power. Nor must the fear of unauthorized official eavesdropping deter vigorous citizen dissent and discussion of government actions in private conversations. For private dissent, no less than open public disclosure, is essential to our free society." *(United States v. U.S. District Court, Eastern Michigan)*

A decade later, however, Powell spoke for the court when it declared that Nixon and other chief executives enjoyed absolute immunity from civil damage suits brought by persons who claimed they had been injured by the president's actions in the course of his official duties.

In the case of *Nixon v. Fitzgerald*, Powell explained the practical basis for such a sweeping decision. "The President occupies a unique position in the constitutional scheme. . . . Because of the singular importance of the President's duties, diversion of his energies by concern with private lawsuits would raise unique risks to the effective functioning of government. . . . Cognizance of this personal vulnerability frequently could distract a President from his public duties, to the detriment not only of the President and his office but also the Nation that the Presidency was designed to serve. . . . In view of the special nature of the President's constitutional office and functions, we think it appropriate to recognize absolute Presidential immunity from damages liability for acts within the 'outer perimeter' of his official responsibility."

In the late 1970s and early 1980s, Powell also spoke for the court as it recognized for the first time a corporate right of free speech. In 1978 Powell wrote the court's decision holding that states could not ban corporate expenditures relative to a referendum issue. Two years later, Powell wrote a pair of decisions in which the court held that the First Amendment prevented states from denying utilities the right to send out statements of their views on public matters to their customers or to engage in promotional advertising. (*First National Bank of Boston v. Bellotti*, 1978; *Consolidated Edison of New York v. Public Service Commission of New York*, 1980; *Central Hudson Gas & Electric Co. v. Public Service Commission of New York*, 1980)

More than any other member of the present court, Powell has found himself in agreement with the majority on a wide range of issues. When he does dissent, it is usually on practical grounds. Criticizing the court for "unnecessarily open[ing] avenues for judicial intervention in the operation of our public schools," the former state and city school board member dissented from the 1975 rulings expanding the rights of school children to contest disciplinary measures. (He later wrote the court's decision refusing to apply the constitutional ban on cruel and unusual punishment to corporal punishment in the schools.)

And he criticized the court for holding patronage hiring and firing unconstitutional, saying the majority displayed "a disturbing insensitivity to the political realities. . . . Patronage hiring practices have contributed to American democracy by stimulating political activity. . . . The candidates for these [local] offices derive their support . . . and their modest funding . . . from cadres of friends and political associates who hope to benefit if their 'man' is elected. . . ." (*Elrod v. Burns*, 1976)

Rehnquist: Radical Conservative

Any thought that Justices Powell and William H. Rehnquist, nominated and confirmed at the same time, would be judicial look-alikes quickly was dispelled. It soon was apparent that Rehnquist was the court's most consistently conservative member. He took a literal, narrow approach to questions of individual rights and was unwavering in his belief that the court should exercise its power with great deference to the decisions of the other partners in the federal system — Congress, the president and the states. *(Rehnquist biography, p. 166)*

Rehnquist's literalism was evident in his very first term. When Powell held that it was unconstitutional for a state to discriminate against certain illegitimate children with respect to workmen's compensation benefits earned by their father, Rehnquist dissented. He criticized the majority's contention that there are "fundamental personal rights" that are protected — if not mentioned specifically by the Constitution. "That Constitution," he wrote, "contains numerous guarantees of individual liberty, but the right of illegitimate children to sue in state courts to recover workmen's compensation benefits is not among them." (*Weber v. Aetna Casualty and Surety Co.*, 1972)

In this, the first of many dissenting opinions critical of the majority's expansive interpretation of the guarantee of equal protection, Rehnquist said: "The equal protection clause ... requires neither that state enactments be 'logical' nor does it require that they be 'just'. ... It requires only that there be some conceivable set of facts which may justify the classification involved."

Rehnquist's inclination to defer to the other branches of government and his view of federal judicial power was spelled out in 1979 when he wrote the court's opinion rejecting the claim that certain practices at a federal detention center violated the constitutional rights of persons detained there awaiting trial. Rehnquist wrote that "under the Constitution, the first question to be answered is not whose plan [for running the prisons] is best, but in what branch of the Government is lodged the authority to initially devise the plan. This does not mean that constitutional rights are not to be scrupulously observed. It does mean, however, that the inquiry of federal courts into prison management must be limited to the issue of whether a particular system violates any prohibition of the Constitution, or in the case of a federal prison, a statute. The wide range of 'judgment calls' that meet constitutional and statutory requirements are confined to officials outside the Judicial Branch of Government." (*Bell v. Wolfish*)

William H. Rehnquist

In light of these beliefs, it is not surprising that Rehnquist spoke for the majority in two major 1981 decisions: the first upheld the decision of Congress to exclude women from the requirement to register for the military draft; the second reaffirmed the power of the president to enter into the agreements with the Iranian government that led to the release of the American hostages held in Iran for over 14 months.

In the draft case, Rehnquist wrote that "the scope of Congress' constitutional power in this area [is] broad" and "the lack of competence on the part of the courts [in this area] is marked." He added, "We of course do not abdicate our ultimate responsibility to decide the constitutional question, but simply recognize that the Constitution itself requires such deference to congressional choice." (*Rostker v. Goldberg*)

Prefacing the court's opinion in the Iran agreements case, Rehnquist said, "Our decision today will not dramatically alter this situation [the balance of power among the branches of government], for the Framers 'did not make the judiciary the overseer of our government.' " (*Dames & Moore v. Regan*)

Throughout his tenure on the court, Rehnquist has displayed an abiding sympathy for law enforcement officers and a related lack of concern for the arguments of suspects and prisoners. Pointing out that neither police efforts nor trials are required to be perfect, only fair, Rehnquist has backed police searches of motorists stopped for traffic violations, broad federal agent access to individual banking records and the congressional decision not to pro-

vide poor prisoners challenging their convictions free transcripts of their trial.

Rehnquist dissented when the court struck down state capital punishment laws. In a 1972 opinion he urged "rigorous attention to the limits of this court's authority ... because of the natural desire that beguiles judges along with other human beings into imposing their own views of goodness, truth and justice upon others. ..." (*Furman v. Georgia*)

Along with a growing number of justices on the court, Rehnquist feels that limits should be placed on federal court review of state criminal convictions. Writing a 1977 opinion for the court, he explained that a state trial should be "the 'main event' so to speak, [in a criminal prosecution] rather than a tryout on the road for what will later be the determinative federal ... hearing." (*Wainwright v. Sykes*)

Rehnquist has written the court's opinions in recent cases narrowing the circumstances in which persons can demand exclusion from the courts of illegally obtained evidence and upholding Texas' habitual offender law, which required a sentence of life in prison for a man convicted of three relatively petty, non-violent offenses.

In 1976 Rehnquist wrote two significant majority opinions curtailing federal intervention in local affairs. In the first, the court held that a federal court had no business ordering a local police department to improve its method of dealing with complaints of police brutality. The order in this case was "an unwarranted intrusion by the federal judiciary" into local affairs, wrote Rehnquist. (*Rizzo v. Goode*)

In the second case, the court struck down a 1974 law extending to employees of state and local governments the federal minimum wage and overtime laws. This legislation, wrote Rehnquist, represented impermissible federal meddling in the affairs of sovereign governments: "If Congress may withdraw from the states the authority to make those fundamental employment decisions upon which their systems for performance of these functions must rest, we think there would be little left of the states' 'separate and independent existence'. ... This exercise of congressional authority does not comport with the federal system of government embodied in the Constitution." (*National League of Cities v. Usery*)

In the civil rights field, Rehnquist has emphasized in colorful terms his disagreement with the court's rulings finding it unconstitutional for private schools to refuse to accept black students, expanding remedies for victims of job discrimination, striking down laws discriminating against women, aliens and illegitimate children, upholding the right to an abortion, granting students new rights, extending the First Amendment to protect advertising, and striking down state aid to parochial schools.

Rehnquist is one of the justices least receptive to arguments by both men and women claiming injury as a result of sex discrimination.

In a 1976 opinion, he came down on the side of private employers who refused to provide disability insurance for pregnant employees, a decision later overturned by Congress. Five years later, he rejected a young man's argument that California discriminated against men by enforcing a statutory rape law under which only men could be prosecuted, not women. Rehnquist found the state's reasons for punishing the men, and not their sometimes cooperative "victims," practical and convincing.

"Because virtually all of the significant harmful and inescapably identifiable consequences of teenage pregnancy fall on the young female," he wrote, "a legislature acts well within its authority when it elects to punish only the participant who, by nature, suffers few of the consequences of his conduct.... Moreover, the risk of pregnancy itself constitutes a substantial deterrence to young females. No similar natural sanctions deter males. A criminal sanction imposed solely on males thus serves to roughly 'equalize' the deterrent on the sexes." (*Michael M. v. Superior Court of Sonoma County*, 1981)

Stevens: Impatient Independent

With surprising speed, Justice John Paul Stevens hit his stride as a member of the Supreme Court fellowship. Although he did not take his seat until just before Christmas 1975, within six months he had delivered two of the court's long-awaited opinions in a complex of capital punishment cases. He shared with Justices Powell and Potter Stewart the task of explaining to the nation why mandatory death penalty statutes were unconstitutional, while less inflexible capital punishment laws were permissible. (*Biography, p. 166*)

Blunt, down-to-earth and possessing an open judicial mind —which makes him the least predictable member of the court — Stevens is a master at constitutional line-drawing. In his first two majority opinions, Stevens displayed this ability. In these decisions the court struck down the Civil Service Commission's regulation banning aliens from holding federal civil service jobs, and upheld a congressional decision that aliens were not eligible for supplemental Medicare benefits if they had not lived in the country for five years and were not permanent residents. (*Hampton v. Mow Sun Wong, Mathews v. Diaz*, 1976)

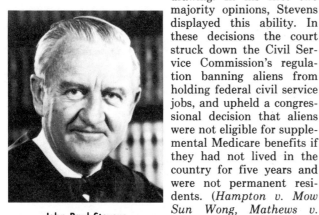

John Paul Stevens

"The federal sovereign ... must govern impartially," wrote Stevens in the civil service case. Although such a ban was a deprivation of liberty, it might still be within federal power to impose — but if it were imposed, due process required that it be done not by a mere executive agency, but rather by the president or Congress.

On the one hand, although aliens are protected by the Fifth and 14th Amendments from "deprivation of life, liberty or property without due process of law," it does not follow that "all aliens are entitled to enjoy the advantages of citizenship," Stevens wrote in the Medicare case. "Neither the overnight visitor, the unfriendly agent of a hostile foreign power, the resident diplomat, nor the illegal entrant, can advance even a colorable constitutional claim to a share in the bounty that a conscientious sovereign makes available to its own citizens and *some* of its guests...."

Stevens would allow the state more leeway than would his liberal colleagues on the bench in protecting the health and welfare of minors. He dissented in 1976 when the court held that a state could not require parental consent for an unmarried minor to have an abortion. "The state's interest in protecting a young person from harm justifies the imposition of restraints on his or her freedom even though comparable restraints on adults would be constitutionally impermissible," Stevens said. (*Planned Parenthood of Central Missouri v. Danforth*)

In another case affecting minors, Stevens concurred when the court in 1977 overturned a New York State law forbidding the distribution of contraceptives to minors. Although he agreed with the state's objective, Stevens found the means unconstitutional. To choose that means to discourage premarital sex, wrote Stevens, was "as though a state decided to dramatize its disapproval of motorcycles by forbidding the use of safety helmets." (*Carey v. Population Services International*)

Stevens reflected a similar concern for the nation's young in a dissenting opinion when the court upheld Social Security requirements allowing certain illegitimate children to receive survivor's benefits only if they could prove that the deceased was their father and had supported them, requirements not imposed on other children. "The reason why the United States government should not add to the burdens that illegitimate children inevitably acquire at birth is radiantly clear: we are committed to the proposition that all persons are created equal," Stevens wrote. (*Mathews v. Lucas*, 1976)

Like his conservative colleagues, Stevens leans toward reducing the role of the federal courts in resolving the problems of individuals. Early in his Supreme Court career, he wrote the court's opinion holding that a policeman discharged for allegedly false and defamatory reasons did not have a federal case against his employer: "The federal court is not the appropriate forum in which to review the multitude of personnel decisions that are made daily by public agencies. We must accept the harsh fact that numerous individual mistakes are inevitable in the day-to-day administration of our affairs. The United States Constitution cannot feasibly be construed to require federal judicial review for every such error." (*Bishop v. Wood*, 1976)

But Stevens sided with the liberals, in dissent, when the court refused to grant inmates the right to a hearing before they were transferred from one prison to another. The majority's rationale was more disturbing than its ruling, wrote Stevens, setting out his belief that the individual's liberty originates neither in the Constitution nor in the laws: "If man were a creature of the state, the analysis could be correct. But neither the Bill of Rights nor the laws of sovereign states create the liberty which the due process clause protects.... Of course, law is essential to the exercise and enjoyment of individual liberty in a complex society. But it is not the source of liberty, and surely not the exclusive source." (*Meachum v. Fano*, 1976)

Stevens' ability to express difficult concepts clearly was illustrated in 1982, when the court managed to clarify its hitherto ambiguous position on the question of police power to conduct warrantless searches of closed containers or packages found in cars that had been stopped because the occupants were suspected of illegal activity. Stevens explained that "when a legitimate search is under way ... nice distinctions between ... glove compartments, upholstered seats, trunks and wrapped packages ... must give way to the interest in the prompt and efficient completion of the task at hand. This rule applies equally to all containers.... For just as the most frail cottage in the kingdom is absolutely entitled to the same guarantees of privacy as the most majestic mansion, so also may a traveler who carries a toothbrush and a few articles of clothing in a paper bag or knotted scarf claim an equal right to conceal his possessions from official inspection as the sophisticated executive with the locked attaché case." *(United States v. Ross)*

Stevens occasionally has displayed impatience with his fellow justices' tendency to gloss over certain salient facts. When the court found no sex discrimination in disability plans that covered all ailments except pregnancy, he said: "The rule at issue places the risk of absence caused by pregnancy in a class by itself. By definition, such a rule discriminates on account of sex; for it is the capacity to become pregnant which primarily differentiates the female from the male." *(General Electric v. Gilbert, 1976)*

Several times in his first year on the court, Stevens explained his view that "the fact that speech is protected by the First Amendment does not mean that it is wholly immune from state regulation." In 1976 he wrote the court's opinion upholding a city's right to use its zoning power to disperse adult bookstores and adult theaters throughout the area, rather than concentrate them in a certain neighborhood. *(Young v. American Mini Theatres)*

And by 1977, his position on the issue of obscenity had aligned him firmly with the liberal wing of the court as he called for an end to the effort to control offensive materials through criminal prosecutions. "Criminal prosecutions are an unacceptable method of abating a public nuisance which is entitled to at least a modicum of First Amendment protection.... The line between communications which 'offend' and those which do not is too blurred to identify criminal conduct. It is also too blurred to delimit the protections of the First Amendment." *(Smith v. United States, 1977)*

Stevens spoke for the court in two other rulings that expanded the bounds of First Amendment protections. In 1980 he wrote the opinion forbidding the firing of government employees just because they belong to the "wrong" political party.

In 1982 Stevens wrote the landmark decision holding that a state cannot ban a non-violent civil rights boycott nor assess its participants damages for any economic losses they cause. "Through speech, assembly and petition — rather than through riot or revolution — petitioners [blacks in Port Gibson, Miss., led by the NAACP] sought to change a social order that had consistently treated them as second-class citizens," wrote Stevens. Such an exercise of First Amendment rights is protected from state interference, wrote Stevens.

While the First Amendment does not protect violence, he said, those who argued in the NAACP case that "fear rather than protected conduct was the dominant force in the movement" must prove that contention. "A court must be wary of a claim that the true color of a forest is better revealed by reptiles hidden in the weeds than by the foliage of countless free-standing trees," he warned. *(National Association for the Advancement of Colored People v. Claiborne Hardware Co.)*

O'Connor: Forthright Freshman

The first-term opinions of Justice Sandra Day O'Connor present no more than the initial sketch of her self-portrait, providing an incomplete outline of her judicial philosophy. In addition to a basic conservatism, her first pronouncements reflect a no-nonsense approach to the law, clarity of expression, concern for the practical and distaste for the ambiguous.

Despite the fact that she is the newest and youngest justice, O'Connor clearly did not feel intimidated during her first months on the court. She wrote several major opinions for the court, contributed some equally important dissenting views and did not hesitate to point out sloppy work on the part of her colleagues.

She holds strong, generally conservative, views. When the court upheld the 1978 national energy policy law, which was challenged as encroaching too far on states' rights, O'Connor spoke for the four dissenting justices. "The court's conclusion [that the 1978 law was constitutional] ... rests upon a fundamental misunderstanding of the role that state governments play in our federalist system," wrote O'Connor, the only member of the court with experience as a state assistant attorney general, state senator and state judge. *(Biography, p. 167)*

Sandra Day O'Connor

"State legislative and adminstrative bodies are not field offices of the national bureaucracy. Nor are they think tanks to which Congress may assign problems for extended study. Instead, each State is sovereign within its own domain, governing its citizens and providing for their general welfare...." With its decision today, O'Connor wrote, "the court ... permits Congress to kidnap state utility commissions into the national regulatory family." *(Federal Energy Regulatory Commission v. Mississippi, 1982)*

In the 1981-82 term, O'Connor wrote the court's opinions in three major cases concerning the procedure federal judges should use in dealing with requests from inmates in state prisons that they be set free because of some error in the way the state handled their cases. In the first of these, O'Connor succinctly summarized the court's view. She said that where prisoners are thinking of bringing such requests to the federal courts, the Supreme Court's ruling means that "before you bring any claims to federal court, be sure that you have first taken each one to state court." *(Rose v. Lundy, 1982)*

In the second case, O'Connor emphasized the "special costs" that federal review of state criminal proceedings imposes on the federal system: "Federal intrusions into state criminal trials frustrate both the States' sovereign power to punish offenders and their good faith attempts to honor constitutional rights." Thus, she wrote for the court, state prisoners must show a good reason why they failed to make their constitutional claim at the time of their trial, and that they actually were prejudiced by the alleged violation of their rights, before a federal court can order them set free. *(Engle v. Isaac, 1982)*

In the third case, she held that similar requirements applied to federal prisoners challenging their treatment and conviction. "Once the defendant's chance to appeal has been waived or exhausted ... we are entitled to presume he stands fairly and finally convicted," she wrote. "Our trial and appellate procedures are not so unreliable that we may not afford their completed operation any binding effect beyond the next in the series of endless post-conviction collateral attacks." (*United States v. Frady*, 1982)

One notable exception to the conservative complexion of O'Connor's judicial views involves questions of sex discrimination. She wrote the court's 1982 opinion holding impermissible the decision of a state-supported university in Mississippi to deny a man admission to its nursing program solely because of his sex. The state did not present sufficient justification for such a clear act of sex discrimination, O'Connor declared. Differential treatment of the sexes by states or state institutions will be upheld by this court only if there is "exceedingly persuasive justification" for such unequal treatment," she stated. (*Mississippi University for Women v. Hogan*, 1982)

But even her feelings on this point are tempered by a pragmatic reality. In a job bias case involving women who had been discriminated against, O'Connor wrote the court's opinion stating that the employer could terminate his li-ability for back pay to the employees he had discriminated against by offering them the job he previously had denied them. "The victims of job discrimination want jobs, not lawsuits," O'Connor wrote, explaining that this ruling would encourage employers to remedy their discrimination by hiring those they wrongly had refused to hire. A person who complains of job bias "cannot afford to stand aside while the wheels of justice grind slowly toward the ultimate resolution of the lawsuit," she added. That person "needs work that will feed a family and restore self-respect. A job is needed — now." (*Ford Motor Company v. Equal Employment Opportunity Commission*, 1982)

O'Connor demands high standards for her own performance — as well as for her colleagues. When she detected fuzzy thinking or unclear writing, she has not hesitated to say so. When Chief Justice Warren E. Burger wrote an opinion she considered unsatisfactory, she wrote a concurring opinion in which she said the majority contributed to "an uncertain jurisprudence" while her separate opinion reached "the same destination as the court, but along a course that more precisely identifies the evils of the challenged statute."

Key Court Decisions: 1969-82

Every Supreme Court decision begins with a dispute between persons. The court does not deal with the theoretical or the hypothetical case. In recent years it has refused to rule on several major cases of public interest, even after hearing oral arguments, because it found that the original dispute no longer existed: the case no longer was alive. For example, in 1974 the court refused to rule on the case of a man complaining that he was refused admission to law school because by the time it could have decided the matter he would have graduated from the school.

Persons who bring their cases to the court vary widely — from a poor black man charged with rape to the nation's most powerful corporations, from an elderly buyer of magazines to the president of the United States.

The subjects the cases encompass and the questions they pose are equally varied. The court decides each case on its particular merits. The immediate impact of the decision is simply to resolve that one factual situation. Sometimes the ruling has little further impact, particularly if the set of facts involved are unique. But more often, the decision has a "ripple" effect, nullifying or upholding laws or practices similar to those involved in the case actually decided.

For example, when the Supreme Court ruled on capital punishment in 1972, it dealt with challenges to the laws of two states — Georgia and Texas. It found that those laws allowed the death penalty to be imposed in such an arbitrary and unfair way that they were unconstitutional. Because all existing federal and state death penalty laws were similar to the ones in these two state laws, they were by implication also struck down, even though they were not directly involved in the cases before the court.

The following section of this book contains summaries of some of the court's major decisions announced between October 1968 and July 1982, from the last term of the court under Chief Justice Earl Warren through the first 13 terms led by Chief Justice Warren Burger.

Within this section, the summaries are arranged by subject categories, keyed to the major point of the court's ruling. The categories are broad — criminal law, First Amendment rights, civil rights, powers of Congress — and they sometimes overlap. Cases that arrive at the court heralded as major questions of criminal law or individual rights are sometimes decided on the basis of another issue entirely. In recent years, the justices frequently have held that the persons bringing the cases did not have the right to pose those questions in federal court.

Although cases move slowly to the Supreme Court through the state or federal judicial system, the body of issues before the court over a particular period does provide a reflection of the trends of public concern. Early in this period, civil rights cases primarily involved racial discrimination. Beginning in the early 1970s, those questions were joined by complaints of sex discrimination, and, toward the end of the period, cases of "reverse" discrimina-

Contents

tion — discrimination against a majority group. Early in the period, the nation's controversial involvement in Southeast Asia precipitated many cases challenging the power of the Selective Service System and challenging state and local laws that were used to penalize anti-war protestors. By the end of this period, such cases were almost non-existent.

The following are summaries of the major Supreme Court rulings in the 1969-82 period: the case name, the citation, which locates the decision in the U.S. Reports (an * indicates the citation was not yet available for a 1982 decision), the vote by which the case was decided, the date upon which the decision was announced, the name or names of the justices writing the court's opinion and of the dissenting justices, and a summary statement of the court's holding.

DECISIONS ON CRIMINAL LAW

The major court rulings on criminal law issues in the 1969-82 period may be grouped under the general categories of: 1) search-and-seizure issues arising under the Fourth Amendment, including wiretapping and the controversial exclusionary rule; 2) questions of double jeopardy and compelled self-incrimination under the Fifth Amendment guarantee against those risks; 3) issues of fair trial and the right to receive the aid of legal counsel guaranteed by the Sixth Amendment; 4) questions of cruel and unusual punishment, which is forbidden by the Eighth Amendment; and 5) decisions interpreting the 14th Amendment's guarantees of due process and equal protection as they apply to criminal trials, prison discipline and law enforcement.

Fourth Amendment

Search and Seizure

Davis v. Mississippi (394 U.S. 721), decided by a 6-2 vote, April 22, 1969. Brennan wrote the opinion; Fortas did not participate; Black and Stewart dissented.

John Davis, a black youth from Mississippi, was convicted of rape after his fingerprints — obtained by the police during his warrantless detention as part of a police dragnet — matched those found at the scene of the crime. The court reversed his conviction, finding that the police action taking Davis' fingerprints violated the Fourth Amendment guarantee against unreasonable search and seizure. The court held that the fingerprints so obtained could not be used as evidence against him, directing that henceforth such "investigatory arrests" must be authorized by warrants if such evidence is to be used in court.

"Nothing is more clear," stated the majority, "than that the Fourth Amendment was meant to prevent wholesale intrusions upon the personal security of our citizenry, whether these intrusions be termed 'arrests' or 'investigatory detentions.'" In dissent, Justice Black lamented the decision as "one more in an ever-expanding list of cases in which this court has been so widely blowing up the Fourth Amendment's scope that its original authors would be hard put to recognize their creation."

Chimel v. California (395 U.S. 752), decided by a 6-2 vote, June 23, 1969. Stewart wrote the opinion; Black and White dissented.

Over complaints from Justices Black and White that the court was imposing unreasonable restrictions upon police action, the court overruled a 20-year-old decision (*U.S. v. Rabinowitz*, 339 U.S. 56, 1950) to restrict the area that can be searched, without a warrant, incident to a lawful arrest. If police wish to search beyond the immediate area in which a person is arrested, in order to prevent the arrested person from obtaining a weapon or destroying evidence, they first must obtain a search warrant, the court held. The entire dwelling cannot be subjected to a warrantless search simply because a person is arrested there.

Vale v. Louisiana (399 U.S. 30), decided by a 6-2 vote, June 22, 1970. Stewart wrote the opinion; Blackmun did not participate; Burger and Black dissented.

Under the Constitution, police cannot search a suspect's house, incident to his arrest just outside, without a warrant.

Coolidge v. New Hampshire (403 U.S. 443), decided by a 5-4 vote, June 21, 1971. Stewart wrote the opinion; Burger, Black, Blackmun and White dissented in part.

The court held that evidence cannot be used at a trial if it is seized by officers acting under a search warrant issued by an official actively involved in prosecuting the case; warrants must be authorized by "neutral and detached magistrates" to be constitutionally valid.

Bivens v. Six Unknown Named Agents (403 U.S. 388), decided by a 6-3 vote, June 21, 1971. Brennan wrote the opinion; Burger, Black and Blackmun dissented.

A person whose dwelling was searched illegally by the federal agents who arrested him may sue those agents for damages for violating his constitutional right against unreasonable search and seizure. Chief Justice Burger dissented, arguing that Congress alone could create this remedy — a damage suit against the federal government.

U.S. v. Mara (410 U.S. 19), ***U.S. v. Dionisio*** (410 U.S. 1), decided by 6-3 votes, Jan. 22, 1973. Stewart wrote the opinion; Douglas, Brennan and Marshall dissented.

The Fourth Amendment guarantee against unreasonable search and seizure does not prohibit a grand jury from ordering a witness to furnish examples of his handwriting and his speaking voice. Physical characteristics that a person knowingly exposes to the public are not protected by the Fourth Amendment.

Schneckloth v. Bustamonte (412 U.S. 218), decided by a 6-3 vote, May 29, 1973. Stewart wrote the opinion; Marshall, Brennan and Douglas dissented.

A warrantless search is not unreasonable or a violation of the Fourth Amendment if consent is voluntarily given. In determining, in a particular case, whether consent is voluntarily given, the totality of the circumstances should be considered, not just the question whether the person giving his consent knew he had a right to withhold it, thus forcing the police to obtain a search warrant.

Cupp v. Murphy (412 U.S. 291), decided by a 7-2 vote, May 29, 1973. Stewart wrote the opinion; Brennan and Douglas dissented.

Police did not violate the Fourth Amendment rights of a murder suspect when they took evidence from under his fingernails without a search warrant, and over his protest, while he was detained at a police station. This seizure of evidence falls within the exception to the warrant requirement for searches incident to a valid arrest.

Almeida-Sanchez v. U.S. (413 U.S. 266), decided by a 5-4 vote, June 21, 1973. Stewart wrote the opinion; White, Burger, Blackmun and Rehnquist dissented.

The U.S. border patrol may not conduct, without probable cause, warrantless searches of any vehicle it wishes to search within a 100-mile zone of the border.

Gustafson v. Florida (414 U.S. 260), ***U.S. v. Robinson*** (414 U.S. 218), decided by 6-3 votes, Dec. 11, 1973. Rehnquist wrote the opinion; Marshall, Douglas and Brennan dissented.

Once a motorist is arrested by a policeman, the policeman has the authority to conduct a full warrantless search of the motorist. "It is well settled that a search incident to a lawful arrest is a traditional exception to the warrant requirement of the Fourth Amendment," wrote Rehnquist.

U.S. v. Brignoni-Ponce (422 U.S. 873), decided by a 9-0 vote, June 30, 1975. Powell wrote the opinion.

Roving representatives of the border patrol cannot, without probable cause, stop cars near the U.S.-Mexican border to question occupants about their citizenship and immigration status merely because they appear to be of Mexican ancestry.

U.S. v. Ortiz (422 U.S. 891), decided by a 9-0 vote, June 30, 1975. Powell wrote the opinion.

Border patrol officers cannot, without probable cause, search cars without the consent of the car's driver at traffic checkpoints away from the border.

U.S. v. Watson (423 U.S. 411), decided by a 6-2 vote, Jan. 26, 1976. White wrote the opinion; Stevens did not participate; Marshall and Brennan dissented.

In a public place, police can arrest without a warrant

persons suspected of having committed serious crimes.

U.S. v. Miller (425 U.S. 435), decided by a 7-2 vote, April 21, 1976. Powell wrote the opinion; Brennan and Marshall dissented.

A bank depositor has no Fourth Amendment right shielding his bank account records from a government subpoena, even if the records are to be used as evidence against him. These records are not private; they are the bank's business records.

U.S. v. Santana (427 U.S. 38), decided by a 7-2 vote, June 24, 1976. Rehnquist wrote the opinion; Marshall and Brennan dissented.

Under *U.S. v. Watson (left column)* and the rationale that allows law enforcement officers in hot pursuit of a suspect to make warrantless arrests in places where warrants otherwise would be required, police did not violate the Fourth Amendment by pursuing a woman into her home, after she was spotted in the doorway of her house, and arresting her, even though they did not have a warrant.

U.S. v. Martinez-Fuerte, Sifuentes v. U.S. (428 U.S. 543), decided by a 7-2 vote, July 6, 1976. Powell wrote the opinion; Brennan and Marshall dissented.

Border patrol officers at fixed traffic checkpoints away from the U.S.-Mexican border constitutionally may stop cars there for brief questioning of occupants without a warrant and without having to explain that they believed the car contained illegal aliens.

GM Leasing Corp. v. United States (429 U.S. 338), decided by a vote of 9-0, Jan. 12, 1977. Blackmun wrote the opinion.

Internal Revenue Service agents violated the Fourth Amendment guarantee against unreasonable search and seizure by entering an office-residence without a warrant and seizing assets of a corporation to satisfy the income tax liability of a taxpayer. A warrant was not required for agents to seize antique cars owned by the corporation from public parking places, but it was required for agents to enter the office-residence of the corporation. "One of the primary evils intended to be eliminated by the Fourth Amendment," wrote Blackmun, "was the massive intrusion on privacy undertaken in the collection of taxes. . . ."

United States v. Ramsey (431 U.S. 606), decided by a 6-3 vote, June 6, 1977. Rehnquist wrote the opinion; Stevens, Brennan and Marshall dissented.

The Fourth Amendment does not require customs officials to have probable cause or to obtain a search warrant before opening an envelope being brought into the United States that, they suspect, contains contraband. "Searches made at the border, pursuant to the longstanding right of the sovereign to protect itself by stopping and examining persons and property crossing into this country are reasonable simply by virtue of the fact that they occur at the border," wrote Rehnquist, noting that the same Congress that proposed the Bill of Rights (including the Fourth Amendment) also passed the first law allowing such customs inspections.

United States v. Chadwick (433 U.S. 1), decided by a 7-2 vote, June 21, 1977. Burger wrote the opinion; Blackmun and Rehnquist dissented.

Federal agents are required by the Fourth Amendment

Search and Seizure

The right of the people to be secure in their persons, houses, papers and effects, against unreasonable searches and seizures, shall not be violated, and no Warrants shall issue, but upon probable cause, supported by Oath or affirmation, and particularly describing the place to be searched, and the persons or things to be seized.

—Fourth Amendment to the U.S. Constitution

to obtain a search warrant before they open and search a locked trunk seized by them when they arrested its owner.

Michigan v. Tyler (436 U.S. 499), decided by votes of 7-1 and 6-2, May 31, 1978. Stewart wrote the opinion; Brennan did not participate; Rehnquist, White and Marshall dissented in part.

The Fourth Amendment guarantee against unreasonable search and seizure does not require fire officials to obtain a search warrant to search the location of a suspicious fire during the fire or immediately after the flames are extinguished. But the Fourth Amendment does require that subsequent searches of the site be authorized by a warrant; otherwise, any evidence then obtained is not usable in court.

Zurcher v. The Stanford Daily (436 U.S. 547), decided by a vote of 5-3, May 31, 1978. White wrote the opinion; Brennan did not participate; Stewart, Marshall and Stevens dissented.

The Fourth Amendment does not preclude or limit the use of search warrants for searches of places owned or occupied by innocent third parties not suspected of any crime. "Under existing law, valid warrants may be issued to search *any* property . . . at which there is probable cause to believe that fruits, instrumentalities, or evidence of a crime will be found. . . ."

The First Amendment guarantee of freedom of the press does not require police to use a subpoena rather than a search warrant to obtain information pertaining to a crime that a newspaper is thought to possess.

Mincey v. Arizona (437 U.S. 385), decided by votes of 9-0 and 8-1, June 21, 1978. Stewart wrote the opinion; Rehnquist dissented in part.

There is no "murder scene" exception to the warrant requirement of the Fourth Amendment. In general, it remains the rule that warrantless searches "are *per se* unreasonable under the Fourth Amendment — subject only to a few specifically established and well-delineated exceptions." Evidence obtained in a warrantless four-day search of the apartment where a murder had been committed was not admissible in court.

Interrogation of a wounded and hospitalized suspect by police, in disregard of his calls for an attorney, produced

involuntary statements that may not be used in any way against him because they have been obtained in violation of his constitutional rights.

Franks v. Delaware (438 U.S. 154), decided by a vote of 7-2, June 26, 1978. Blackmun wrote the opinion; Rehnquist and Burger dissented.

When a defendant makes a substantial showing to defend his charge that police used false statements to obtain a search warrant to seize evidence against him, the Fourth Amendment requires that he be given a pretrial hearing to examine that charge. If his charge is proved at the hearing, and the remaining information upon which the warrant was based is insufficient to justify its issuance, the evidence obtained by the search is inadmissible.

Delaware v. Prouse (440 U.S. 648), decided by a vote of 8-1, March 27, 1979. White wrote the opinion; Rehnquist dissented.

The Fourth Amendment forbids police to stop motorists at random merely to check licenses and auto registrations. Without cause to believe that a car is being driven in violation of the law, such a random check violates the guarantee against unreasonable search and seizure.

Dunaway v. New York (442 U.S. 200), decided by a vote of 6-2, June 5, 1979. Brennan wrote the opinion; Burger and Rehnquist dissented; Powell did not participate.

Police may not detain a person for questioning in custody if they lack probable cause for detaining him. Such a detention constitutes an unreasonable "seizure" of the person. Self-incriminating statements made by a person detained without probable cause may not be used as evidence against him, even if he makes them after being warned of his constitutional rights according to procedures set out in *Miranda v. Arizona* (384 U.S. 436, 1966).

Arkansas v. Sanders (442 U.S. 753), decided by a vote of 7-2, June 20, 1979. Powell wrote the opinion; Blackmun and Rehnquist dissented.

The Fourth Amendment requires the police, in the absence of exigent circumstances, to obtain a search warrant before they open and search luggage seized from a taxicab.

Brown v. Texas (443 U.S. 47), decided by a 9-0 vote, June 25, 1979. Burger wrote the opinion.

Police may not stop a person on the street without a reasonable suspicion to believe he is engaged in criminal conduct, or require him to identify himself and explain his presence. Such a "seizure" of his person violates the Fourth Amendment guarantee against unreasonable search and seizure. The court overturned the conviction of an individual who refused, under these circumstances, to identify himself.

Ybarra v. Illinois (444 U.S. 85), decided by a vote of 6-3, Nov. 28, 1979. Stewart wrote the opinion; Rehnquist, Blackmun and Burger dissented.

Without a search warrant naming or describing him, and without probable cause to suspect him of a crime, a bar patron's constitutional right to be secure against unreasonable searches was violated when state police searched him in the course of conducting a search of a bar with a warrant. The court reversed the narcotics conviction of Ventura

Ybarra because the conviction was based on heroin the police found on Ybarra when they searched the bar.

Payton v. New York, Riddick v. New York (445 U.S. 573), decided by a vote of 6-3, April 15, 1980. Stevens wrote the opinion; White, Burger and Rehnquist dissented.

Police may not enter a house to arrest an occupant without a warrant for his arrest or the consent of the occupant. The Fourth Amendment requires either a warrant or consent unless an immediate arrest is warranted by emergency circumstances.

The court struck down as unconstitutional a New York State law that authorized police to enter a residence without a warrant and by force, if necessary, to make a routine arrest of a person charged with a felony. (The New York law was similar to those in 23 other states.)

United States v. Mendenhall (446 U.S. 544), decided by a vote of 5-4, May 27, 1980. Stewart wrote an opinion announcing the court's decision, joined only by Rehnquist; Burger, Powell and Blackmun concurred in the decision; White, Marshall, Brennan and Stevens dissented.

The court upheld as proper under the Fourth Amendment the action of federal drug agents in stopping Sylvia Mendenhall at an airport and questioning and searching her because her behavior fit a "profile" of drug couriers, a description of conduct characteristic of persons carrying illegal narcotics.

United States v. Salvucci (448 U.S. 83), decided by a vote of 7-2, June 25, 1980. Rehnquist wrote the opinion; Marshall and Brennan dissented.

The court overruled *Jones v. United States* (362 U.S. 257, 1960) insofar as it allowed a person charged with a crime of possession to challenge the legality of the search that produced the item he was charged with possessing, regardless of whether he could assert a property or privacy interest in the place that was searched.

An individual may challenge a search and seizure on grounds that it is illegal and a violation of the Fourth Amendment guarantee only if he has either a property or a privacy interest in the place searched or the item seized.

Rawlings v. Kentucky (448 U.S. 98), decided by a vote of 7-2, June 25, 1980. Rehnquist wrote the opinion; Brennan and Marshall dissented.

Privacy, more than property, is the touchstone for the Fourth Amendment guarantee against unreasonable searches. The court refused to dismiss a man's conviction on drug charges, which he challenged because the drugs themselves were taken in an illegal search of his companion's pocketbook. He had neither a privacy nor a property interest in the purse, held the court, and thus had no standing to challenge the search or the use of the drugs as evidence.

United States v. Cortez (449 U.S. 411), decided by a 9-0 vote, Jan. 21, 1981. Burger wrote the opinion.

Facts that may seem insignificant to an untrained person may properly be used by law enforcement officers, border patrol officers in Arizona, in this case, to justify stopping a vehicle near the border and questioning its occupants.

Steagald v. United States (451 U.S. 204), decided by a 7-2 vote, April 21, 1981. Marshall wrote the opinion; Rehnquist and White dissented.

Police with a warrant for the arrest of a suspect may not enter and search the home of another person without obtaining a separate warrant for that search, even if the police believe the suspect may be at that home. "Warrantless searches of a home are impermissible absent consent or exigent circumstances," stated the majority.

Michigan v. Summers (452 U.S. 692), decided by a 6-3 vote, June 22, 1981. Stevens wrote the opinion; Stewart, Brennan and Marshall dissented.

Police acted properly when they detained a homeowner while searching his home for narcotics, even though they had a warrant only for the house search, not for his arrest. Such a detention is a limited intrusion on personal security justified by substantial law enforcement interests in preventing flight, minimizing risk to police and facilitating the orderly completion of the search of the home.

New York v. Belton (453 U.S. 454), decided by a 6-3 vote, July 1, 1981. Stewart wrote the opinion; Brennan, Marshall and White dissented.

When the occupant of an automobile is lawfully arrested, police may, incident to his arrest and without a warrant, search the passenger compartment of the auto in which he is riding. Any evidence uncovered in that search, even in the closed pockets of clothing found in the passenger compartment, is admissible in court.

Robbins v. California (453 U.S. 420), decided by a 6-3 vote, July 1, 1981. Stewart wrote the opinion, joined by three other justices; Powell and Burger concurred; Blackmun, Rehnquist and Stevens dissented.

Police may not, without a search warrant, open a closed piece of luggage or other container found in the lawful search of a car. If police open such a container without a warrant, its contents may not be used as evidence in court.

Washington v. Chrisman (*), decided by a 6-3 vote, Jan. 13, 1982. Burger wrote the opinion; White, Brennan and Marshall dissented.

A policeman who arrested a student and accompanied him to the student's room could properly search that room without a warrant and seize evidence for use in court against the student and his roommate. The "plain view" exception to the warrant requirement of the Fourth Amendment permits a law enforcement officer to seize clearly incriminating evidence when it is discovered in a place where the officer has the right to be. Once an officer places someone under arrest he has the right to remain at that person's elbow at all times.

United States v. Ross (*), decided by a 6-3 vote, June 1, 1982. Stevens wrote the opinion; White, Brennan and Marshall dissented.

Police officers who stop a vehicle and have probable cause to suspect that it contains drugs or other contraband may search the entire vehicle, as thoroughly as if they had a warrant; the search can include all containers and packages found in the vehicle that might contain the object of the search. The contrary holding in *Robbins v. California* (1981) *(see above)* — requiring police to obtain a warrant to search such containers — was rejected.

Taylor v. Alabama (*), decided by a 5-4 vote, June 23, 1982. Marshall wrote the opinion; O'Connor, Burger, Powell and Rehnquist dissented.

A confession obtained without physical coercion from a suspect who is arrested without probable cause or without an arrest warrant, and who is warned of his constitutional rights, is inadmissible in court because it is the product of an illegal arrest.

Exclusionary Rule

To enforce the Fourth Amendment guarantee that citizens cannot be subjected to unreasonable search and seizure by law enforcement officers, the Supreme Court in 1914 announced the "exclusionary rule." This rule forbids the use at trial of evidence obtained by unreasonable search and seizure against persons whose rights are so violated. The court applied this rule to all federal trials in 1921 and to all state trials in 1961. The rule, particularly during the 1960s and 1970s, was the subject of intense criticism from law enforcement personnel, who contended that it imposed an excessive penalty for what were often technical violations of the Fourth Amendment or violations by police acting in good faith.

U.S. v. Calandra (414 U.S. 338), decided by a 6-3 vote, Jan. 8, 1974. Powell wrote the opinion; Brennan, Marshall and Douglas dissented.

The exclusionary rule should not used to bar use of illegally obtained evidence in questioning grand jury witnesses. The deterrent effect of the rule is accomplished by forbidding the use of this evidence at trial; to extend the rule to grand jury investigations would impede the effective and expeditious discharge of the grand jury's duties for no good reason.

Stone v. Powell, Wolff v. Rice (428 U.S. 465), decided by a 6-3 vote, July 6, 1976. Powell wrote the opinion; Brennan, Marshall and White dissented.

Federal courts are not required to use the writ of *habeas corpus* to enforce the exclusionary rule. As long as the state has provided an opportunity for "full and fair litigation" of a defendant's Fourth Amendment claim, there is no constitutional obligation for federal courts to grant *habeas corpus* relief on the grounds that illegally seized evidence was used at trial.

Application of the exclusionary rule at such a late stage in the process is outweighed by the cost of such application to other values, wrote Powell. The issue on which the prisoners had sought federal review did not bear on the basic justice of their imprisonment, he said, and thus did not justify federal action ordering their release or a new trial. "Despite the broad deterrent purpose of the exclusionary rule, it has never been interpreted to proscribe the introduction of illegally seized evidence in all proceedings or against all persons.... The policies behind the exclusionary rule are not absolute. Rather, they must be evaluated in light of competing policies."

U.S. v. Janis (428 U.S. 433), decided by a 5-3 vote, July 6, 1976. Blackmun wrote the opinion; Stevens did not participate; Brennan, Marshall and Stewart dissented.

The exclusionary rule does not apply in civil proceedings to bar from use in federal court evidence improperly seized by state law enforcement officers acting in good faith.

Rakas v. Illinois (439 U.S. 128), decided by a 5-4 vote, Dec. 11, 1978. Rehnquist wrote the opinion; White, Brennan, Marshall and Stevens dissented.

Passengers in a car from which a gun is seized by police without a warrant have no basis on which to argue that their Fourth Amendment rights have been violated by that seizure and thus that the gun should not be used as evidence against them. The passengers claimed to own neither the car nor the gun and so lacked standing to ask for suppression of that evidence.

The Fourth Amendment right to be secure against unreasonable search and seizure is a personal right, wrote Rehnquist: "A person who is aggrieved by an illegal search and seizure only through the introduction of damaging evidence secured by a search of a third party's premises or property has not had any of his Fourth Amendment rights infringed."

United States v. Havens (446 U.S. 620), decided by a vote of 5-4, May 27, 1980. White wrote the opinion; Brennan, Marshall, Stewart and Stevens dissented.

Prosecutors may use illegally obtained evidence to impeach the credibility of a witness who responds to questions on cross-examination with answers that appear to be contradicted by the evidence in the government's possession.

United States v. Payner (447 U.S. 727), decided by a vote of 6-3, June 23, 1980. Powell wrote the opinion; Brennan, Marshall and Blackmun dissented.

The court reaffirmed its position that only a defendant whose Fourth Amendment rights have been denied can move to exclude illegally obtained evidence. The court held that a federal judge lacks the power to exclude from use as evidence items taken in violation of the Fourth Amendment guarantee when the defendant is not the person whose Fourth Amendment rights have been violated.

Wiretapping

Alderman v. U.S., Butenko v. U.S., Ivanov v. U.S. (394 U.S. 165), decided by a 5-3 vote, March 10, 1969. White wrote the opinion; Marshall did not participate; Black, Harlan and Fortas dissented.

The court, to the dismay of the Justice Department, ruled that the federal government must turn over for examination all material obtained by illegal electronic surveillance to a defendant whose rights were violated by the surveillance and against whom it might be used, even if the surveillance involved U.S. national security. The court also held that such material, although unusable as evidence against anyone whose constitutional rights against unreasonable search and seizure had been violated in the surveillance, might be usable as evidence against another defendant whose rights had not been so violated.

U.S. v. White (401 U.S. 745), decided by a 6-3 vote, April 5, 1971. White wrote the opinion; Douglas, Harlan and Marshall dissented.

Opening a loophole in its wall of disapproval of warrantless electronic surveillance, the court held that it was not unconstitutional for an electronic device to be voluntarily carried by an informer, without a warrant, to overhear conversations between the informer and another person. In his dissent, Douglas argued that such monitoring of conversations stifled free speech: "Free discourse . . .

may be frivolous or serious, humble or defiant, reactionary or revolutionary, profane or in good taste; but it is not free if there is surveillance.... Must everyone live in fear that every word he speaks may be transmitted or recorded and later repeated to the entire world? I can imagine nothing that has a more chilling effect on people speaking their minds and expressing their views on important matters."

U.S. v. U.S. District Court, Eastern Michigan (407 U.S. 297), decided by a 6-2 vote, June 19, 1972. Powell wrote the opinion; Rehnquist did not participate; Burger and White dissented.

The court rejected the Justice Department's claim that it did not have to get court approval for the use of electronic surveillance of persons or domestic groups suspected to be subversive. Powell wrote: "The price of lawful public dissent must not be a dread of subjection to an unchecked surveillance power. Nor must the fear of unauthorized official eavesdropping deter vigorous citizen dissent and discussion of government action in private conversation. For private dissent, no less than open public discourse, is essential to our free society."

"Unreviewed executive discretion," warned Powell, "may yield too readily to pressures to obtain incriminating evidence and overlook potential invasions of privacy and protected speech.... We cannot accept the government's argument that internal security matters are too subtle and complex for judicial evaluation.... If the threat is too subtle or complex for our senior law enforcement officers to convey its significance to a court, one may question whether there is probable cause for surveillance."

U.S. v. Giordano (416 U.S. 505), decided by votes of 9-0 and 5-4, May 13, 1974. White wrote the opinion; Powell, Burger, Blackmun and Rehnquist dissented in part.

Congress set up a critical precondition for any court-approved wiretap, requiring, as part of Title III of the Omnibus Crime Control and Safe Streets Act of 1968 that all applications for court orders allowing wiretaps be approved either by the attorney general or an assistant attorney general specially designated to sign such papers. Evidence obtained by wiretaps must be suppressed if the application for the court order authorizing the tap was not signed by one of the authorized officials. The court was unanimous on those points.

Information obtained from surveillance during any extension of the original wiretaps in this case also should be suppressed, the court held by a 5-4 vote.

U.S. v. Chavez (416 U.S. 562), decided by votes of 9-0 and 5-4, May 13, 1974. White wrote the opinion; Douglas, Brennan, Stewart and Marshall dissented in part.

The court once again unanimously held invalid evidence obtained from a wiretap, the application for which was signed by the attorney general's special assistant, not by the designated assistant attorney general whose purported signature was on it.

The court, however, by a 5-4 vote, approved as valid evidence obtained by surveillance for which the application actually had been signed by the attorney general, although he had signed the name of the assistant attorney general designated to share the approval power.

United States v. Donovan (429 U.S. 413), decided by a 6-3 vote, Jan. 18, 1977. Powell wrote the opinion; Brennan, Marshall and Stevens dissented.

Title II of the 1968 Omnibus Crime Control and Safe Streets Act requires the government, in applying to a federal judge for an order authorizing electronic surveillance, to identify all persons whom it suspects of the criminal activity under investigation and whom it expects to overhear. The government also is required, after the surveillance, to furnish the judge with a list of all persons overheard so that the judge can decide who should be informed of the surveillance. Failure to comply fully with these requirements, however, does not require suppression of evidence obtained by the surveillance involved; failure to comply does not make an otherwise lawful surveillance unlawful.

United States v. New York Telephone Co. (434 U.S. 159), decided by votes of 9-0, 6-3 and 5-4, Dec. 7, 1977. White wrote the opinion; Stewart, Stevens, Brennan and Marshall dissented in part.

Pen registers — devices that intercept numbers dialed from a particular telephone but not the conversations conducted on the phone — are not governed by Title III, the wiretapping section of the 1968 Crime Control and Safe Streets Act. A federal court has the inherent power to authorize installation of such devices and to order a third party — the telephone company in this case — to provide technical assistance to government agents in installing the pen registers.

Scott v. United States (436 U.S. 128), decided by a vote of 7-2, May 15, 1978. Rehnquist wrote the opinion; Brennan and Marshall dissented.

Apparent disregard by federal agents of the requirement in Title III of the 1968 Crime Control and Safe Streets Act that electronic surveillance be conducted in such a way as to minimize the interception of irrelevant conversations is not sufficient reason to exclude evidence obtained by a wiretap from use in court.

Dalia v. United States (441 U.S. 238), decided by votes of 9-0, 6-3 and 5-4, April 18, 1979. Powell wrote the opinion; Brennan, Marshall, Stevens and Stewart dissented in part.

Covert entry of a dwelling or office by federal agents for the purpose of planting electronic surveillance devices — "bugs" — need not be authorized specifically in the warrant authorizing the surveillance. Such entry is neither unconstitutional nor illegal.

"The Fourth Amendment does not prohibit *per se* a covert entry performed for the purpose of installing otherwise legal electronic bugging equipment," declared the court unanimously. But it was divided over whether Congress, in approving the provisions of the 1968 Crime Control and Safe Streets Act authorizing electronic surveillance, also authorized such covert entry. The court majority said Congress did authorize that procedure, and it approved such entry as necessary to install electronic "bugs."

Fifth Amendment

Double Jeopardy

Benton v. Maryland (395 U.S. 784), decided by a 6-2 vote, June 23, 1969. Marshall wrote the opinion; Harlan and Stewart dissented.

In the last decision announced by the Warren court, the court overruled its 32-year-old holding in *Palko v. Connecticut* (302 U.S. 319, 1937) and applied the constitutional guarantee against double jeopardy to the states.

In an earlier decision, the court majority had held that if a right guaranteed by the Bill of Rights is "fundamental to the American scheme of justice" it also must apply to the states. The double jeopardy clause certainly is fundamental, the court ruled.

North Carolina v. Pearce, Simpson v. Rice (395 U.S. 711), decided by a 6-2 vote, June 23, 1969. Stewart wrote the opinion; Black and Harlan dissented in part.

The double jeopardy clause requires that a judge credit punishment already exacted when resentencing a defendant who has been retried for an offense for which he has already been convicted and sentenced. If a more severe sentence is imposed after the retrial, the judge must place in the record affirmative reasons for the heavier penalty, based objectively on the conduct of the defendant since his original sentencing.

Ashe v. Swenson (397 U.S. 436), decided by a 7-1 vote, April 6, 1970. Stewart wrote the opinion; Burger dissented.

After a jury has acquitted a person on charges of robbing one victim of a multi-victim single robbery, that person cannot be retried on charges of robbing another of the victims of that robbery.

Waller v. Florida (397 U.S. 387), decided by an 8-0 vote, April 6, 1970. Burger wrote the opinion.

A state cannot try a person on charges arising from an action for which he already has been tried and convicted by a municipal court.

Price v. Georgia (398 U.S. 323), decided by an 8-0 vote, June 15, 1970. Burger wrote the opinion; Blackmun did not participate.

Once a man has been tried on murder charges but convicted only of manslaughter, and that conviction has been overturned, he cannot be retried by the state on any charge more serious than manslaughter. A guilty verdict on a lesser offense, such as manslaughter in this case, is an "implicit acquittal" on the greater charge of murder.

Chaffin v. Stynchcombe (412 U.S. 17), decided by a 5-4 vote, May 21, 1973. Powell wrote the opinion; Douglas, Marshall, Brennan and Stewart dissented.

A defendant who has challenged his original conviction and won a new trial is not protected by the double jeopardy clause from receiving a harsher sentence from the jury in the second trial than he received at the first trial, so long as the jury is not aware of the original sentence and demonstrates no vindictiveness toward the defendant.

The court refused to apply its ruling in *North Carolina v. Pearce* (1969) *(see above)* to resentencing by a jury, rather than by a judge.

Breed v. Jones (421 U.S. 519), decided by a 9-0 vote, May 27, 1975. Burger wrote the opinion.

A juvenile's constitutional protection against double jeopardy is violated by his trial as an adult after a juvenile court has already found that he violated the law.

U.S. v. Dinitz (424 U.S. 600), decided by a 6-2 vote, March 8, 1976. Stewart wrote the opinion; Stevens did not participate; Brennan and Marshall dissented.

The guarantee against double jeopardy does not protect a defendant from being retried on the original charges after he has requested and been granted a mistrial due to judicial error.

Jeffers v. United States (432 U.S. 137), decided by a 5-4 vote, June 16, 1977. Blackmun wrote the opinion; White concurred; Stevens, Stewart, Brennan and Marshall dissented.

A defendant normally is entitled to have charges against him on both greater and lesser offenses resolved in a single proceeding, but the double jeopardy clause is not violated when he chooses to have the two offenses tried separately.

Brown v. Ohio (432 U.S. 161), decided by a 6-3 vote, June 16, 1977. Powell wrote the opinion; Blackmun, Burger and Rehnquist dissented.

A state violates the guarantee against double jeopardy when it charges and convicts a man of auto theft after it has convicted him of operating the car without the owner's consent.

United States v. Wheeler (435 U.S. 313), decided by an 8-0 vote, March 22, 1978. Stewart wrote the opinion; Brennan did not participate.

The Fifth Amendment guarantee against double jeopardy does not bar prosecutions by separate sovereigns of the same person for the same action. An Indian defendant convicted in tribal court of certain crimes may be tried again by federal authorities for those same actions.

Burks v. United States, Greene v. Massey (437 U.S. 1), decided by votes of 8-0, June 14, 1978. Burger wrote the opinion; Blackmun did not participate.

The Fifth Amendment double jeopardy clause forbids a second trial of a person whose first conviction has been overturned because of insufficient evidence. The clause does not forbid a retrial of a person whose first conviction is overturned because of trial error.

Crist v. Bretz (437 U.S. 28), decided by a 6-3 vote, June 14, 1978. Stewart wrote the opinion; Burger, Powell and Rehnquist dissented.

State courts must use the same rules as federal courts to determine when jeopardy "attaches" during a trial — that is, when a defendant actually is placed in jeopardy within the meaning of the Fifth Amendment. Thus state courts must rule, as federal courts do, that jeopardy attaches once a jury is sworn in.

Sanabria v. United States (437 U.S. 54), decided by a 7-2 vote, June 14, 1978. Marshall wrote the opinion; Blackmun and Rehnquist dissented.

Once a person is acquitted of a crime, even if the acquittal results from an error, the double jeopardy clause bars his retrial on the same action. "[T]here is no exception permitting retrial once the defendant has been acquitted, no matter how 'egregiously erroneous'" the acquittal, the court majority wrote.

Busic v. United States, LaRocca v. United States (446 U.S. 348), decided by a 6-3 vote, May 19, 1980. Brennan wrote the opinion; Stewart, Stevens and Rehnquist dissented.

The constitutional guarantee against double jeopardy, which includes a guarantee that no one shall suffer multiple punishment for one action, forbids the imposition of a double sentence. The court held that a person convicted of a federal crime that necessarily involved the use of a firearm, such as assaulting a federal officer with a gun — may not be sentenced to consecutive prison terms, one for the crime of which he was convicted and a second under a law authorizing stiffer penalties for persons who carry firearms while committing a federal crime.

United States v. DiFrancesco (449 U.S. 117), decided by a 5-4 vote, Dec. 9, 1980. Blackmun wrote the opinion; Brennan, White, Marshall and Stevens dissented.

The Fifth Amendment guarantee against double jeopardy is not violated by the provisions of the 1970 Organized Crime Control Act that permit federal prosecutors to appeal sentences they consider too lenient for dangerous special offenders.

Hudson v. Louisiana (450 U.S. 40), decided by a 9-0 vote, Feb. 24, 1981. Powell wrote the opinion.

The double jeopardy clause forbids a state to retry a defendant for a crime if he already has been tried and convicted and the first verdict has been set aside on appeal for lack of evidence.

Albernaz v. United States (450 U.S. 333), decided by a 9-0 vote, March 9, 1981. Rehnquist wrote the opinion.

Congress did not violate the double jeopardy clause when it approved provisions of the Drug Abuse Prevention and Control Act of 1970 that allow the imposition of consecutive prison sentences on persons found guilty of conspiring to import and to distribute marijuana, even if there was only a single conspiracy for the two actions.

Bullington v. Missouri (451 U.S. 430), decided by a 5-4 vote, May 4, 1981. Blackmun wrote the opinion; Powell, Burger, White and Rehnquist dissented.

A state cannot be given a second chance to try to convince a jury to impose the death sentence on a defendant. Once a jury has decided that a particular defendant should not be sentenced to die for his crime, that defendant's right to be protected against double jeopardy forbids the state to seek the death penalty, even if a new trial is granted,.

Tibbs v. Florida (*), decided by a 5-4 vote, June 7, 1982. O'Connor wrote the opinion; White, Brennan, Marshall and Blackmun dissented.

When a defendant's conviction has been reversed by a state appeals court, which has found the guilty verdict contrary to the weight of the evidence presented at the trial, a retrial is not barred by the Fifth Amendment protection against double jeopardy. The reversal simply affords the defendant a second opportunity to seek an acquittal.

Self-Incrimination

Orozco v. Texas (394 U.S. 324), decided by a 6-2 vote, March 25, 1969. Black wrote the opinion; Fortas did not participate; White and Stewart dissented.

The court's landmark ruling in *Miranda v. Arizona* (384 U.S. 436, 1966) — that a suspect, before interrogation

---

Double Jeopardy, Incrimination

... Nor shall any person be subject for the same offence to be twice put in jeopardy of life or limb; nor shall be compelled in any Criminal Case to be a witness against himself; nor be deprived of life, liberty, or property, without due process of law....

—Fifth Amendment to the U.S. Constitution

---

by police, must be advised of his constitutional rights to remain silent and to have legal counsel — applies to questioning of a suspect in custody outside as well as inside a police station, even in bed in his own home.

Leary v. U.S. (395 U.S. 6), decided by an 8-0 vote, May 19, 1969. Harlan wrote the opinion.

Reversing the conviction of former Harvard psychologist Timothy F. Leary for failing to pay a federal tax on marijuana transfers, the court found the law imposing the tax unconstitutional as a violation of the right not to incriminate oneself. Anyone complying with the federal law would provide evidence that would incriminate him of violating state laws forbidding the possession of marijuana.

Minor v. U.S., Buie v. U.S. (396 U.S. 87), decided by a 6-2 vote, Dec. 8, 1969. White wrote the opinion; Douglas and Black dissented.

Refusing to reverse convictions of men for selling heroin and marijuana without certain federal order forms required by law, the court held that the law requiring use of those forms did not violate the privilege against self-incrimination. Drug dealers were not forced to incriminate themselves by selling without the required forms; they did have the alternative of not selling the drugs at all.

Turner v. U.S. (396 U.S. 398), decided by a 6-2 vote, Jan. 20, 1970. White wrote the opinion; Black and Douglas dissented.

The court upheld a federal law presuming that a person possessing heroin that is not stamped with the required federal tax stamps knows that it is illegally produced, purchased, possessed and distributed because heroin is not produced in the United States or imported legally. But the court invalidated a similar law concerning possession of unstamped cocaine because some cocaine is produced in the United States and some is imported legally.

Harris v. New York (401 U.S. 222), decided by a 5-4 vote, Feb. 24, 1971. Burger wrote the opinion; Black, Douglas, Brennan and Marshall dissented.

Modifying its ban imposed in *Miranda v. Arizona* (1966) on any in-court use of statements made by defendants not properly advised of their rights, the Supreme

Court held that these statements, so long as they were voluntary, could be used to impeach a defendant's credibility if he contradicted them in testifying in his own behalf.

Burger wrote that "every criminal defendant is privileged to testify in his own defense or to refuse to do so. But that privilege cannot be construed to include the right to commit perjury.... The shield provided by *Miranda* cannot be perverted into a license to use perjury by way of a defense, free from the risk of confrontation with prior inconsistent utterances."

U.S. v. Freed (401 U.S. 601), decided by a 9-0 vote, April 5, 1971. Douglas wrote the opinion.

As revised in 1968, the federal gun control law, which requires registration of firearms only by the transferor and forbids use of any information provided by registration for prosecution, does not violate the privilege against self-incrimination.

Kastigar v. U.S. (406 U.S. 441), decided by a 5-2 vote, May 22, 1972. Powell wrote the opinion; Rehnquist and Brennan did not participate; Douglas and Marshall dissented.

The court upheld the witness immunity provisions of the 1970 Organized Crime Control Act, ruling that a limited grant of immunity from prosecution to a witness compelled to testify fulfilled constitutional requirements. The court did specify, however, that in any subsequent prosecution of the witness, the prosecution must show that the evidence against the witness was derived from sources independent of his own testimony.

Couch v. U.S. (409 U.S. 322), decided by a 7-2 vote, Jan. 9, 1973. Powell wrote the opinion; Douglas and Marshall dissented.

When a taxpayer turns over records to a tax preparer for assistance in filing an income tax return, those records no longer are protected by the taxpayer's constitutional privilege against self-incrimination. This is a personal privilege that one cannot assert over records no longer in one's possession.

Bellis v. U.S. (417 U.S. 85), decided by an 8-1 vote, May 28, 1974. Marshall wrote the opinion; Douglas dissented.

The protection of the Fifth Amendment against compelled self-incrimination does not shield against a grand jury subpoena the records of a dissolved law partnership that were in the possession of one of the former partners. This constitutional privilege is a personal one, not a corporate one, "protecting only the natural individual from compulsory incrimination through his own testimony or personal records."

Maness v. Meyers (419 U.S. 449), decided by a 9-0 vote, Jan. 15, 1975. Burger wrote the opinion.

A lawyer cannot be held in contempt for advising his client to assert his Fifth Amendment privilege and to refuse to supply incriminating subpoenaed material.

U.S. v. Hale (422 U.S. 171), decided by a 9-0 vote, June 23, 1975. Marshall wrote the opinion.

A prosecutor cannot, as a rule, use as evidence against a defendant who testifies in his own defense the fact that the defendant remained silent when questioned by police.

Brown v. Illinois (422 U.S. 590), decided by a 9-0 vote, June 26, 1975. Blackmun wrote the opinion.

Statements made to police by a person illegally arrested, but warned of his constitutional rights before being questioned, cannot be used in court against him.

Michigan v. Mosley (423 U.S. 96), decided by a 6-2 vote, Dec. 9, 1975. Stewart wrote the opinion; Brennan and Marshall dissented.

The assertion by a suspect in custody of his constitutional right to remain silent and to refuse to answer questions about a crime does not foreclose later police efforts, after a second reminder to the suspect of his rights, to question him about another crime. If the suspect responds to the questions about a second crime, he is assumed to have done so voluntarily, waiving his right to remain silent.

Garner v. U.S. (424 U.S. 648), decided by an 8-0 vote, March 23, 1976. Powell wrote the opinion; Stevens did not participate.

A taxpayer must claim his Fifth Amendment privilege against self-incrimination at the time he files his income tax return, or forego the right to claim that privilege to bar use of tax return information against him in a nontax-related criminal proceeding.

U.S. v. Kasmir, Fisher v. U.S. (425 U.S. 391), decided by 9-0 votes, April 21, 1976. White wrote the opinions.

Neither a taxpayer nor his attorney can claim Fifth Amendment protection against a summons for working papers developed by the taxpayer's accountant in preparing the client's tax returns. These are business papers, not the client's private papers, and thus cannot be protected by a claim that producing them would be self-incrimination. White made clear that the court was not ruling on "whether the Fifth Amendment would shield the taxpayer from producing his own tax records in his possession."

Beckwith v. U.S. (425 U.S. 341), decided by an 8-1 vote, April 21, 1976. Burger wrote the opinion; Brennan dissented.

A taxpayer questioned by Internal Revenue Service (IRS) agents in a private home and not in custody need not be fully advised of his constitutional rights, as required by *Miranda v. Arizona* (1966) for persons in police custody.

U.S. v. Mandujano (425 U.S. 564), decided by an 8-0 vote, May 19, 1976. Burger wrote the opinion; Stevens did not participate.

Miranda v. Arizona (1966) does not require grand jury witnesses to be fully informed of their constitutional rights before testifying. The Fifth Amendment privilege against compulsory self-incrimination cannot be claimed by a grand jury witness who challenges the use of his admittedly false testimony against him in his trial for perjury. The Fifth Amendment privilege provides no protection for the commission of perjury. Burger cited an earlier statement by the court: "Our legal system provides methods for challenging the government's right to ask questions — lying is not one of them." *(Bryson v. U.S.,* 396 U.S. 64, 1969)

Andresen v. Maryland (427 U.S. 463), decided by a 7-2 vote, June 29, 1976. Blackmun wrote the opinion; Brennan and Marshall dissented.

An attorney's Fifth Amendment privilege is not violated by the use — as evidence against him — of business records that were taken from his office by police having a valid search warrant. The court majority reasoned that use of his materials was not self-incrimination because the attorney was not compelled to help the police find them or produce or authenticate them.

The dissenting justices cited an 1886 decision (*Boyd v. U.S.*, 116 U.S. 616, 633) in which the court said it was "unable to perceive that the seizure of a man's private books and papers to be used in evidence against him is substantially different from compelling him to be a witness against himself."

United States v. Washington (431 U.S. 181), decided by a 7-2 vote, May 23, 1977. Burger wrote the opinion; Brennan and Marshall dissented.

The Fifth Amendment privilege against compelled self-incrimination is not violated when prosecutors fail to inform a grand jury witness, before his testimony, that he is a potential defendant. The Fifth Amendment does not protect a person from all self-incrimination, only from officially coerced self-incrimination. Grand jury witnesses are equally protected by the Fifth Amendment whether or not they are potential defendants, so a warning of that status is irrelevant.

Lefkowitz v. Cunningham (431 U.S. 801), decided by a 7-1 vote, June 13, 1977. Burger wrote the opinion; Rehnquist did not participate; Stevens dissented.

A state cannot compel state political party officers to testify and incriminate themselves, in violation of the Fifth Amendment, by threatening them with loss of office if they claim protection under the Fifth Amendment.

Corbitt v. New Jersey (439 U.S. 212), decided by a 6-3 vote, Dec. 11, 1978. White wrote the opinion; Stevens, Brennan and Marshall dissented.

A state does not penalize the exercise of the Sixth Amendment right to a jury trial or the Fifth Amendment right to plead "not guilty" when it issues a mandatory life sentence to a person convicted of murder after a jury trial, while imposing lesser sentences on persons who plead "no contest" to the same crime and forgo a trial.

Fare v. Michael C. (442 U.S. 707), decided by a 5-4 vote, June 20, 1979. Blackmun wrote the opinion; Marshall, Brennan, Stevens and Powell dissented.

The Fifth Amendment privilege against compelled self-incrimination, as interpreted by the court in *Miranda v. Arizona* (1966) to require police to follow specific procedures when interrogating suspects in custody, does not require that police cease to question a juvenile after he requests the presence of his probation officer during the interrogation.

The request for a probation officer is not the same as the request for an attorney. *Miranda* therefore does not require suppression of self-incriminatory statements made in the absence of the probation officer.

United States v. Euge (444 U.S. 707), decided by a vote of 6-3, Feb. 20, 1980. Rehnquist wrote the opinion; Brennan, Marshall and Stevens dissented.

Congress has authorized the Internal Revenue Service (IRS) to compel a taxpayer to provide the IRS with examples of his handwriting. This demand does not violate the Fifth Amendment privilege against self-incrimination or

the Fourth Amendment protection against unreasonable search and seizure.

Jenkins v. Anderson (447 U.S. 231), decided by a vote of 7-2, June 10, 1980. Powell wrote the opinion; Brennan and Marshall dissented.

When a defendant charged with murder takes the witness stand and argues that he killed in self-defense, prosecutors do not infringe his constitutional privilege against self-incrimination when they point out to the jury that he remained silent for two weeks after the killing, neither reporting it nor turning himself in. The use of his pre-arrest silence to impeach the credibility of his testimony "advances the truth-finding function of the criminal trial" and does not violate his rights.

Carter v. Kentucky (450 U.S. 288), decided by an 8-1 vote, March 9, 1981. Stewart wrote the opinion; Rehnquist dissented.

Whenever a defendant does not wish to take the witness stand in his own defense, and requests the judge to instruct the jury that his failure to testify is not to be viewed as evidence of guilt, the judge is obligated under the Constitution to issue those instructions to protect the defendant's right to remain silent and to be protected from compelled self-incrimination.

Sixth Amendment

Fair Trial

Illinois v. Allen (397 U.S. 337), decided by an 8-0 vote, March 31, 1970. Black wrote the opinion.

The right to be present at one's own trial is not absolute, ruled the court. A defendant can lose his right to be present if, after being warned that he will be removed from the courtroom if he continues to disrupt the trial, he continues to act in such a way that the trial cannot continue while he is present. Black noted that it also would be permissible constitutionally, for a judge, if necessary, to have an obstreperous defendant bound and gagged.

Dickey v. Florida (398 U.S. 30), decided by an 8-0 vote, May 25, 1970. Burger wrote the opinion.

The right to a speedy trial is denied by a seven-year delay between arrest and trial, even if the defendant is, for that period, in federal prison in another state for another crime.

Williams v. Florida (399 U.S. 78), decided by a 7-1 vote, June 22, 1970. White wrote the opinion; Blackmun did not participate; Marshall dissented.

It is just as constitutional, in non-capital cases, for a six-member jury as for a 12-member panel to try a defendant. The number 12 as applied to jury composition was merely a "historical accident"; the jury can perform its role just as well with six as with 12 members.

Baldwin v. New York (399 U.S. 66), decided by a 5-3 vote, June 22, 1970. White wrote the opinion; Blackmun did not participate; Burger, Harlan and Stewart dissented.

States must provide trial by jury for all persons charged with offenses punishable by more than six months' imprisonment.

Mayberry v. Pennsylvania (400 U.S. 455), decided by a 9-0 vote, Jan. 20, 1971. Douglas wrote the opinion.

A criminal defendant charged with contempt for insulting the trial judge and disrupting trial proceedings is entitled to a public trial by another judge on the contempt charges.

McKeiver v. Pennsylvania (403 U.S. 528), decided by a 6-3 vote, and *In re Burrus* (403 U.S. 528), decided by a 5-4 vote, June 21, 1971. Blackmun wrote the opinion; Douglas, Black and Marshall dissented in both, joined by Brennan in the second case.

The Sixth Amendment does not establish a right to trial by jury for a juvenile delinquent.

U.S. v. Marion (404 U.S. 307), decided by a 7-0 vote, Dec. 20, 1971. White wrote the opinion.

The right to a speedy trial does not require dismissal of an indictment returned three years after the alleged crime became known to the government; that right concerns the interval between an arrest and the trial. The right to due process may bar excessive and unjustifiable delay in seeking the indictment, but harm from the delay must be shown before the indictment can be dismissed on that basis.

Johnson v. Louisiana, Apodaca v. Oregon (406 U.S. 356, 404), decided by a 5-4 vote, May 22, 1972. White wrote the opinion; Douglas, Brennan, Stewart and Marshall dissented.

The constitutional guarantee of a jury trial, as applied to the states, does not require the jury to be unanimous in its verdict. Lack of unanimity on the question of guilt does not itself indicate reasonable doubt of guilt.

Kirby v. Illinois (406 U.S. 682), decided by a 5-4 vote, June 7, 1972. Stewart wrote the opinion; Douglas, Brennan, Marshall and White dissented.

Before an indictment, the right to counsel at post-arrest investigatory confrontations, like lineups, does not apply.

Barker v. Wingo (407 U.S. 514), decided by a 9-0 vote, June 22, 1972. Powell wrote the opinion.

When defining the precise meaning of the constitutional right to a speedy trial, the court "cannot definitely say how long is too long in a system where justice is supposed to be swift but deliberate." No inflexible rule can be set, but a balancing test must be applied in which the conduct of both the prosecution and the defense are considered. Among the factors that should be considered are: length of delay, reason for delay, the defendant's assertion of his right to a speedy trial and the harm to the defendant resulting from the delay.

Strunk v. U.S. (412 U.S. 434), decided by a 9-0 vote, June 11, 1973. Burger wrote the opinion.

The only possible remedy for denial of a defendant's right to a speedy trial is dismissal of the charges against him. The court rejected a judge's attempt to remedy a 10-month delay in going to trial by reducing the eventual sentence imposed on the defendant by the length of the delay.

Murphy v. Florida (421 U.S. 794), decided by an 8-1 vote, June 16, 1975. Marshall wrote the opinion; Brennan dissented.

A defendant's right to a fair trial is not denied him simply because some jurors have been exposed to news accounts of his prior convictions or of the crime for which he is on trial.

Ballew v. Georgia (435 U.S. 223), decided by a 9-0 vote, March 21, 1978. Blackmun announced the court's decision, but no one opinion had the support of a majority of the court. White, Powell and Brennan wrote separate opinions.

In order to fulfill the constitutional guarantee of trial by jury, state juries must be composed of at least six members. *(See Williams v. Florida, p. 97)*

Duren v. Missouri (439 U.S. 357), decided by an 8-1 vote, Jan. 9, 1979. White wrote the opinion; Rehnquist dissented.

States violate the constitutional requirement that juries be drawn from a cross-section of the community when they provide a blanket exemption for all women, upon request, from jury duty.

Burch v. Louisiana (441 U.S. 130), decided by a unanimous vote, April 17, 1979. Rehnquist wrote the opinion.

A state may constitutionally use juries of as few as six persons, but if it does so the Constitution requires that the jury must reach its verdict unanimously. *(See Johnson v. Louisiana, left column)*

Chandler v. Florida (449 U.S. 560), decided by a 8-0 vote, Jan. 26, 1981. Burger wrote the decision; Stevens did not participate in the decision.

Nothing in the Constitution — neither the guarantee of due process nor the promise of a fair trial — forbids states to experiment with television coverage of criminal trials.

Rosales-Lopez v. United States (451 U.S. 182), decided by a 6-3 vote, April 21, 1981. White wrote an opinion joined by three justices; Rehnquist and Burger concurred in the result; Stevens, Brennan and Marshall dissented.

A Mexican-American defendant was not denied his right to trial by an impartial jury because the trial judge refused to question prospective jurors about possible prejudice against Mexicans, although he did question them about prejudice against aliens.

Smith v. Phillips (*), decided by a 6-3 vote, Jan. 25, 1982. Rehnquist wrote the opinion; Marshall, Brennan and Stevens dissented.

A defendant's due process right to a fair trial was not violated simply because a juror in the case had applied for a job with the prosecutor's office at the time the murder trial was in progress. The trial judge, in a hearing on the situation, found "beyond a reasonable doubt" that this situation did not result in any prejudice to the defendant.

"Due process does not require a new trial every time a juror has been placed in a potentially compromising situation. Were that the rule, few trials would be constitutionally acceptable.... Due process means a jury capable and willing to decide the case solely on the evidence before it, and a trial judge ever watchful to prevent prejudicial occurrences and to determine the effect of such occurrences when they happen," declared the court majority.

United States v. MacDonald (*), decided by a 6-3 vote, March 31, 1982. Burger wrote the opinion; Marshall, Brennan and Blackmun dissented.

The Sixth Amendment guarantee of the right to a speedy trial applies to the period between arrest and indictment, not to the period after military charges have been dismissed against a suspect and before a civilian indictment has been obtained.

An Army doctor, initially charged by the military with the murder of his wife and daughters, was not denied his speedy trial right by the delay of several years between dismissal of the military charges and institution of the civilian charges.

The Sixth Amendment right to a speedy trial is not intended primarily to prevent prejudice to the defense caused by passage of time. That interest is protected by the due process clause and statutes of limitations. The speedy trial guarantee is intended to limit the impairment of liberty of an accused before his trial and to shorten the disruption of life caused by unresolved criminal charges.

Public Trial

Gannett Co. Inc. v. DePasquale (443 U.S. 368), decided by a 5-4 vote, July 2, 1979. Stewart wrote the opinion; Blackmun, Brennan, White and Marshall dissented.

The court upheld the decision of a state judge to shut out the press and the public from a pretrial hearing concerning the efforts of defendants charged with murder to exclude from their trial use of certain evidence. The defendants requested that the hearing be closed.

The Sixth Amendment guarantee of a public trial assures that right to the defendant, not to the press or the public, held the court majority. Thus the press had no right to challenge the decision to close the hearing.

"To safeguard the due process rights of the accused, a trial judge has an affirmative constitutional duty to minimize the effects of prejudicial pretrial publicity," wrote Stewart. "Closure of pretrial proceedings is often one of the most effective methods that a trial judge can employ to attempt to insure that the fairness of a trial will not be jeopardized by the dissemination of such information

---

Fair Trial

In all criminal prosecutions, the accused shall enjoy the right to a speedy and public trial, by an impartial jury of the State and district wherein the crime shall have been committed . . . and to be informed of the nature and cause of the accusation; to be confronted with the witnesses against him; to have compulsory process for obtaining witnesses in his favor, and to have the Assistance of Counsel for his defense.

—Sixth Amendment to the U.S. Constitution

---

throughout the community before the trial itself has even begun."

The dissenters viewed the Sixth Amendment as incorporating a right of public access to trials and pretrial hearings: "Publicity is essential to the preservation of public confidence in the rule of law and in the operation of courts. Only in rare circumstances does this principle clash with the rights of the criminal defendant to a fair trial so as to justify exclusion." *(See Richmond Newspapers Inc. v. Commonwealth of Virginia, p. 125)*

Right to Counsel

Coleman v. Alabama (399 U.S. 1), decided by a 6-2 vote, June 22, 1970. Brennan wrote the opinion; Blackmun did not participate; Burger and Stewart dissented.

The right to counsel applies at a preliminary hearing, which is a critical stage in a state's criminal proceedings.

Argersinger v. Hamlin (407 U.S. 25), decided by a 9-0 vote, June 12, 1972. Douglas wrote the opinion.

The right to counsel applies to all offenses, state or federal, that involve potential incarceration.

Ross v. Moffitt (417 U.S. 600), decided by a 6-3 vote, June 17, 1974. Rehnquist wrote the opinion; Douglas, Brennan and Marshall dissented.

The state's constitutional obligation to provide appointed legal counsel for indigent defendants exercising their right to appeal their conviction does not extend beyond those appeals to which the defendant has a legal right and which the courts are bound to decide.

States are not obligated to provide counsel for those defendants appealing their convictions to courts that have the discretion to refuse to review their cases, such as the U.S. Supreme Court.

"The fact that a particular service might be of benefit to an indigent defendant does not mean that the service is constitutionally required," wrote Rehnquist.

Faretta v. California (422 U.S. 806), decided by a 6-3 vote, June 30, 1975. Stewart wrote the opinion; Blackmun, Burger and Rehnquist dissented.

Individual defendants have a constitutional right to conduct their own defense and to reject appointed counsel. "There can be no blinking the fact that the right of the accused to conduct his own defense seems to cut against the grain of this court's decisions holding that the Constitution requires that no accused can be convicted and imprisoned unless he has been accorded the right to the assistance of counsel," wrote Stewart. "But it is one thing to hold that every defendant, rich or poor, has the right to the assistance of counsel, and quite another to say that a state may compel a defendant to accept a lawyer he does not want."

Geders v. U.S. (425 U.S. 80), decided by an 8-0 vote, March 30, 1976. Burger wrote the opinion; Stevens did not participate.

The Sixth Amendment right to effective assistance by counsel was denied to a defendant when the judge prevented him from consulting with his attorney during an overnight recess in the trial, which came in the middle of the defendant's testimony.

Weatherford v. Bursey (429 U.S. 525), decided by a

7-2 vote, Feb. 22, 1977. White wrote the opinion; Brennan and Marshall dissented.

The court refused to adopt the rule that whenever the prosecution knowingly permits intrusion into the relationship between a defendant and his attorney, the constitutional right to counsel has been sufficiently violated to require a new trial.

In this particular case, although an undercover agent had been present at pretrial conferences between the defendant and his lawyer, and later had been used as a surprise prosecution witness, the agent had revealed nothing of defense strategy to the prosecution nor otherwise aided prosecution attorneys as a result of his attendance at the pretrial sessions with the defendant. There was no tainted evidence as a result. Thus, held the court, there was no violation of the right to counsel.

Brewer v. Williams (430 U.S. 387), decided by a 5-4 vote, March 23, 1977. Stewart wrote the opinion; Burger, White, Blackmun and Rehnquist dissented.

The right of a defendant in a murder case to have effective counsel was violated when police took the defendant on a long automobile ride and refused to permit the defendant's attorney to accompany them and, in the course of the ride, induced the defendant to lead them to the victim's body. "Whatever else it may mean," wrote Stewart, "the right to counsel . . . means at least that a person is entitled to the help of a lawyer at or after the time that judicial proceedings have been initiated against him."

Holloway v. Arkansas (435 U.S. 475), decided by a 6-3 vote, April 3, 1978. Burger wrote the opinion; Powell, Blackmun and Rehnquist dissented.

Effective assistance of counsel was denied to three defendants charged with and tried together for the same offense when the trial judge, over their objections, appointed the same public defender to represent all of them. Joint representation is not *per se* a denial of the right to counsel, but in this case it resulted in a conflict of interest that prevented effective representation of all three defendants.

Scott v. Illinois (440 U.S. 367), decided by a 5-4 vote, March 5, 1979. Rehnquist wrote the majority opinion; Brennan, Marshall, Blackmun and Stevens dissented.

The Sixth Amendment guarantee of the right to legal counsel requires the state to provide a lawyer at a trial of every criminal defendant who is sent to prison for his offense, but not to every defendant whose crime might, but in fact did not, result in a prison sentence. "Actual imprisonment" is the proper test for determining when the right to counsel applies in such cases.

Rhode Island v. Innis (446 U.S. 291), decided by votes of 9-0 and 6-3, May 12, 1980. Stewart wrote the opinion; Marshall, Brennan and Stevens dissented in part.

In this case, the court defined "interrogation" — a critical word in the controversial 1966 decision in *Miranda v. Arizona* (1966) that forbids police to continue an interrogation of a suspect in custody who indicates he wishes to remain silent or that he wishes to have his lawyer present during questioning.

The court was unanimous in declaring that "interrogation" meant more than just the direct questioning of a suspect, that it included other "techniques of persuasion," such as staged lineups, intended to evoke statements from a suspect. Interrogation, stated the court, includes "words or actions on the part of police officers that they *should have known* were reasonably likely to elicit an incriminating response."

By a vote of 6-3, however, the court refused to find that such interrogation had taken place in the case of Thomas Innis, whose incriminating statements were evoked during a ride in a police car with policemen who were conversing among themselves. Thus Innis' conviction was allowed to stand.

United States v. Henry (447 U.S. 264), decided by a vote of 6-3, June 16, 1980. Burger wrote the opinion; Blackmun, White and Rehnquist dissented.

The government denies a suspect his right to counsel when it obtains and uses incriminating statements made by him to an informer imprisoned with him prior to his trial. Such a situation clearly is intended to induce the suspect to make incriminating statements in the absence of an attorney.

Upjohn Company v. United States (449 U.S. 383), decided by a 9-0 vote, Jan. 13, 1981. Rehnquist wrote the opinion.

The attorney-client privilege protects from disclosure virtually all communications involving legal matters between a corporation's counsel and its officers and employees. The court rebuffed the government's argument for a narrower privilege protecting communications between only the attorney and a "control group" of officers and managers, the persons who in fact determine company policy.

Estelle v. Smith (451 U.S. 454), decided by a 9-0 vote, May 18, 1981. Burger wrote the opinion.

It is unconstitutional for a state to impose a sentence of death on a defendant if the decision to impose that sentence is based in part on psychiatric testimony derived from an interview of the defendant by a state-appointed psychiatrist, and if the defendant was not warned, prior to that interview, that he had the right to have his attorney present and to remain silent during the interview.

Edwards v. Arizona (451 U.S. 477), decided by a 9-0 vote, May 18, 1981. White wrote the opinion.

Once a defendant has invoked his right to have his attorney present during police questioning, all interrogation by police must cease and may not be resumed until the attorney is present or the defendant initiates a new conversation.

Eighth Amendment

Cruel and Unusual Punishment

Furman v. Georgia, Jackson v. Georgia, Branch v. Texas (408 U.S. 238), decided by a 5-4 vote, June 29, 1972. *Per curiam* (unsigned) opinion, with separate opinions filed by Douglas, Brennan, Stewart, White and Marshall in the majority; and by Burger, Blackmun, Powell and Rehnquist in dissent.

"The court holds that the imposition and carrying out of the death penalty in these cases constitutes cruel and unusual punishment in violation of the Eighth and Fourteenth Amendments." And so the death penalty, as it was at that time imposed in each of the 50 states, was declared unconstitutional.

Brennan and Marshall held executions *per se* "cruel and unusual punishment." "The calculated killing of a human being by the state," wrote Brennan, "involves, by its very nature, a denial of the executed person's humanity."

Brennan added: "The punishment of death is inconsistent with . . . four principles: Death is an unusually severe and degrading punishment; there is a strong probability that it is inflicted arbitrarily; its rejection by contemporary society is virtually total, and there is no reason to believe it serves any penal purpose more effectively than the less severe punishment of imprisonment. The function of these principles is to enable a court to determine whether a punishment comports with human dignity: Death, quite simply, does not."

Douglas found that the laws allowing imposition of the death penalty at the discretion of judge or jury provided the opportunity, which was often taken, he said, for discrimination, for imposing that sentence on the "poor and despised . . . lacking political clout . . . a member of a suspect or unpopular minority."

Stewart and White found that the present system of imposing the death penalty under which "this unique penalty . . . [is] so wantonly and freakishly imposed" clearly was unconstitutional.

Stewart wrote that these death sentences were "cruel and unusual in the same way that being struck by lightning is cruel and unusual. For all of the people convicted of rapes and murders in 1967 and 1968 . . . the petitioners are among a capriciously selected random handful upon whom the sentence of death has been imposed."

In dissent, Chief Justice Burger was quick to point out that the opinions of White and Stewart implied that states might enact a constitutional capital punishment law: "Since the two pivotal concurring opinions turn on the assumption that the punishment of death is now meted out in a random and unpredictable manner, legislative bodies may seek to bring their laws into compliance with the court's ruling by providing standards for juries and judges to follow in determining the sentences in capital cases or by more narrowly defining the crimes for which the penalty is to be imposed."

Gregg v. Georgia (428 U.S. 153), ***Proffitt v. Florida*** (428 U.S. 242), ***Jurek v. Texas*** (428 U.S. 262), decided by votes of 7-2, July 2, 1976. Stewart announced the court's decision in *Gregg*, joined in the opinion by Stevens and Powell; Stevens announced the decision in *Jurek*, joined in the opinion by Stewart and Powell; Powell announced the decision in *Proffitt*, with an opinion joined by Stewart and Stevens. White, Burger, Rehnquist and Blackmun concurred in separate statements; Brennan and Marshall dissented.

Death, as a punishment for first-degree murder, is not in and of itself cruel and unusual punishment in violation of the Eighth Amendment.

That amendment's ban on cruel and unusual punishment traditionally has been read in light of public perceptions and values. The fact that Congress and 35 state legislatures enacted new death penalty laws after the Supreme Court's 1972 ruling in *Furman v. Georgia*, which struck down all existing death penalty laws, indicated, Stewart wrote in the *Gregg* case, "that a large proportion of American society continues to regard it as an appropriate

and necessary criminal sanction."

The Eighth Amendment also requires that punishment not be "so totally without penological justification that it results in gratuitous infliction of suffering" and that it not be disproportionate to the crime for which it is imposed. When dealing with death as a punishment for deliberate murder, the social purpose of retribution and deterrence justify its use. "It is an extreme sanction, suitable to the most extreme of crimes," Stewart continued.

"We hold that the death penalty is not a form of punishment that may never be imposed regardless of the circumstances of the offense, regardless of the character of the offender and regardless of the procedure followed in reaching the decision to impose it," he concluded.

Brennan and Marshall dissented on this fundamental point, finding, according to Brennan, that capital punishment is "no longer morally tolerable in our civilized society."

Moving on to deal with the question of procedures, Stewart explained that contemporary values, reflected in the court's 1972 *Furman v. Georgia* decision, require that the death penalty be imposed fairly, not arbitrarily or capriciously. The fundamental respect for humanity that underlies the Eighth Amendment ban requires that the sentencing authority — judge or jury — consider the character and record of the individual offender and the circumstances of the particular offense before deciding whether to impose the ultimate sanction.

The court upheld, as complying with these criteria, state laws that provide for a two-part proceeding in capital cases: a trial at which the question of guilt or innocence is resolved and, if the defendant is found guilty, a subsequent proceeding at which the decision is made on an appropriate sentence. These laws also set out explicit standards to guide the judge or jury in deciding whether to impose the death sentence.

Woodson v. North Carolina (428 U.S. 280), ***Roberts v. Louisiana*** (428 U.S. 325), decided by votes of 5-4, July 2, 1976. Stewart wrote the opinion in *Woodson*; Stevens wrote the opinion in *Roberts*. Burger, White, Rehnquist and Blackmun dissented in both cases.

Laws making death the mandatory penalty for first-degree murder are unconstitutional, as they fail to meet the Eighth Amendment requirement for fair consideration of the individual defendant and the individual crime.

Roberts v. Louisiana (431 U.S. 633), decided by a 5-4 vote, June 6, 1977. *Per curiam* (unsigned) opinion; Burger, Rehnquist, White and Blackmun dissented.

State law making death the mandatory sentence for persons convicted of first-degree murder of a police officer violates the constitutional ban on cruel and unusual punishment by failing to allow for any consideration of possible mitigating circumstances or characteristics.

Coker v. Georgia (433 U.S. 583), decided by votes of 7-2 and 6-3, June 29, 1977. White wrote the opinion announcing the court's decision and setting out the views of four justices; Brennan and Marshall concurred in the result; Powell dissented in part; Burger and Rehnquist dissented.

The court overturned a death sentence imposed on a convicted rapist. Six justices declared that death is an excessive and disproportionate penalty for rape and is therefore forbidden by the Eighth Amendment as a cruel

Cruel and Unusual Punishments

Excessive bail shall not be required, nor excessive fines imposed, nor cruel and unusual punishments inflicted.

—Eighth Amendment to the U.S. Constitution

and unusual punishment for that crime.

Lockett v. Ohio, Bell v. Ohio (438 U.S. 586, 637) decided by a 7-1 vote, July 3, 1978. Burger wrote the opinion; Brennan did not participate; Rehnquist dissented.

Ohio's death penalty law, which precluded, in murder cases, consideration of a defendant's age, lack of intent to cause death and other mitigating factors by the sentencing authority, was unconstitutional. "In all but the rarest kind of capital case," the Constitution's ban on cruel and unusual punishment and its guarantees of equal protection and due process require that the sentencing judge or jury be allowed to consider, as a mitigating factor, "any aspect of a defendant's character or record and any of the circumstances of the offense...."

Rummel v. Estelle (445 U.S. 263), decided by a 5-4 vote, March 18, 1980. Rehnquist wrote the opinion; Powell, Brennan, Marshall and Stevens dissented.

The Eighth Amendment ban on cruel and unusual punishment is not violated when a state imposes a mandatory life sentence upon a "three-time loser," even when the three crimes of which the defendant has been convicted are all relatively petty, non-violent offenses.

Carlson v. Green (446 U.S. 14), decided by a vote of 7-2, April 22, 1980. Brennan wrote the opinion; Burger and Rehnquist dissented.

Persons who feel that federal officials have violated their right to be protected from cruel and unusual punishment have an implied right under that Eighth Amendment guarantee to sue those officials for damages. The court upheld the right of a mother to bring a damage suit, based on the Eighth Amendment guarantee, against the federal prison officials whom she felt had caused the death of her imprisoned son by failing to provide him with proper medical treatment.

Beck v. Alabama (447 U.S. 625), decided by a vote of 7-2, June 20, 1980. Stevens wrote the opinion; Rehnquist and White dissented.

Alabama unconstitutionally limited a jury's discretion in a capital case by requiring it to choose between convicting the defendant of a crime for which the death sentence was mandatory or acquitting him. A jury in a capital case must be given the third option of finding the defendant guilty of a similar but lesser offense. By forbidding a judge to give a jury this option, such a law enhanced the risk of an unwarranted conviction and violated the constitutional guarantee of due process.

Rhodes v. Chapman (452 U.S. 337), decided by an 8-1 vote, June 15, 1981. Powell wrote the opinion; Marshall dissented.

The constitutional ban on cruel and unusual punishment is not invariably violated by the practice in a state maximum security prison of placing two inmates in a cell designed for one person.

Enmund v. Florida (*), decided by a 5-4 vote, July 2, 1982. White wrote the opinion; O'Connor, Burger, Powell and Rehnquist dissented.

It is cruel and unusual punishment, disproportionate to the actions of the defendant, for the driver of a getaway car to be sentenced to death after he is convicted of first-degree murder and robbery though he did not himself witness the killings or kill the victims.

"Robbery is a serious crime deserving serious punishment. It is not, however ... 'so grievous an affront to humanity that the only adequate response may be the penalty of death,'" wrote the majority.

Due Process

Suspects, Defendants

In re Winship (397 U.S. 358), decided by a 5-3 vote, March 31, 1970. Brennan wrote the opinion; Burger, Black and Stewart dissented.

Due process requires that the guilt of juveniles like that of adults be found "beyond a reasonable doubt," not just "by a preponderance of the evidence."

Ward v. Village of Monroeville (409 U.S. 57), decided by a 7-2 vote, Nov. 14, 1972. Brennan wrote the opinion; White and Rehnquist dissented.

The 14th Amendment guarantee against loss of life, liberty or property without due process of law guarantees a person charged with an offense a trial before a disinterested and impartial judicial officer. This guarantee requires that traffic violators be tried before a judge other than the mayor whose government draws a substantial portion of its revenues from fines levied upon traffic offenders.

Chambers v. Mississippi (410 U.S. 284), decided by an 8-1 vote, Feb. 22, 1973. Powell wrote the opinion; Rehnquist dissented.

A defendant was denied a fair trial, and thereby deprived of his liberty without due process of law, by a judge's strict application of the hearsay rule to forbid the introduction of testimony of three men to whom another man had confessed to the crime with which the defendant was charged, and by the judge's refusal to allow the defendant to cross-examine the witness who had confessed to the crime but later repudiated that confession.

"The right of an accused in a criminal trial to due process is, in essence, the right to a fair opportunity to defend against the state's accusations," and that was denied the defendant in this case, wrote Powell. "Few rights are more fundamental than that of an accused to present witnesses in his own defense."

U.S. v. Russell (411 U.S. 423), decided by a 5-4 vote, April 24, 1973. Rehnquist wrote the opinion; Douglas, Brennan, Stewart and Marshall dissented.

A person charged with a crime can use as a defense the claim that he was "entrapped" into the incriminating activity by a government agent only if the agent could be said to have implanted the criminal design in the mind of the defendant. If the defendant already was predisposed to commit the crime, he cannot assert entrapment as a defense.

Mullaney v. Wilbur (421 U.S. 684), decided by a 9-0 vote, June 9, 1975. Powell wrote the opinion.

The guarantee of due process is violated by a state law requiring a defendant in a murder case to prove that he acted in the heat of passion or on sudden provocation in order to reduce the charge against him to manslaughter. It is the prosecution's responsibility to prove beyond a reasonable doubt every fact necessary to constitute the crime with which the defendant is charged.

Hampton v. U.S. (425 U.S. 484), decided by a 5-3 vote, April 27, 1976. Rehnquist wrote the opinion; Brennan, Stewart and Marshall dissented.

The court in *U.S. v. Russell (above)* "ruled out the possibility that the defense of entrapment could ever be based upon governmental misconduct in a case, such as this one, where the predisposition of the defendant to commit the crime was established," wrote Rehnquist, joined on this point by Burger and White.

A defendant's right to due process was not violated by the fact that a government informer had supplied him with the drug he was charged with selling illegally to two government agents, the court held. The informant, the defendant and the police acted in concert in this transaction, making the defense of entrapment unavailable.

Doyle v. Ohio, Wood v. Ohio (427 U.S. 610), decided by votes of 6-3, June 17, 1976. Powell wrote the opinion; Stevens, Blackmun and Rehnquist dissented.

Use of a defendant's silence as evidence at trial of his guilt penalizes the exercise of the constitutional right to silence and thereby violates the due process guarantee. The court held that it was unfair and unconstitutional for a prosecutor to use a defendant's silence at the time of his arrest to call into question the defendant's subsequent explanation of potentially incriminating circumstances. Once a suspect has been arrested and advised of his rights, as required in *Miranda v. Arizona* (1966), "silence . . . may be nothing more than the arrestee's exercise of these *Miranda* rights," wrote Powell.

United States v. Lovasco (431 U.S. 783), decided by an 8-1 vote, June 9, 1977. Marshall wrote the opinion; Stevens dissented.

Prosecutors do not violate the constitutional guarantee of due process by waiting as long as 18 months after the commission of a crime before lodging charges against the suspect, even if the delay deprives the defendant of the aid of defense witnesses. "Rather than deviating from elementary standards of 'fair play and decency' a prosecutor abides by them if he refuses to seek indictments until he is completely satisfied that he should prosecute and will be able promptly to establish guilt beyond a reasonable doubt," wrote Marshall.

Bordenkircher v. Hayes (434 U.S. 357), decided by a 5-4 vote, Jan. 18, 1978. Stewart wrote the opinion; Blackmun, Brennan, Marshall and Powell dissented.

Due process is not violated by a prosecutor's use, in the plea bargaining process, of a threat to bring an additional indictment against a defendant if the defendant does not accept the prosecutor's offer of a bargain. "[I]n the 'give-and-take' of plea bargaining, there is no . . . element of punishment or retaliation so long as the accused is free to accept or reject the prosecution's offer. . . . [T]he course of conduct engaged in by the prosecutor in this case, which no more than openly presented the defendant with the unpleasant alternatives of forgoing trial or facing charges on which he was plainly subject to prosecution, did not violate the due process clause of the 14th Amendment."

Bell v. Wolfish (441 U.S. 520), decided by votes of 6-3 and 5-4, May 14, 1979. Rehnquist wrote the opinion; Marshall, Stevens and Brennan dissented; Powell dissented in part.

Persons detained before trial in a federal detention center are not denied due process of law, nor any other constitutional rights, by the conditions of confinement there, which include housing two inmates in a room originally intended for single occupancy, restrictions on the books that inmates may receive, prohibitions on the receipt of packages by inmates and body-cavity searches of inmates after visits from non-inmates.

"Ensuring security and order at the institution is a permissible nonpunitive objective, whether the facility houses pretrial detainees, convicted inmates, or both. . . . [W]e think that these particular restrictions and practices were reasonable responses . . . to legitimate security concerns."

Prisoners, Probationers

Gagnon v. Scarpelli (411 U.S. 778), decided by an 8-1 vote, May 14, 1973. Powell wrote the opinion; Douglas dissented.

The guarantee that no one will be deprived of liberty without due process of law requires that two hearings — preliminary and final — be held before probation can be revoked, but it does not require that legal counsel be appointed for the probationer in all revocation proceedings. That need should be determined on a case-by-case basis, turning primarily on whether the probationer appears capable of speaking effectively for himself.

Wolff v. McDonnell (418 U.S. 539), decided by a 6-3 vote, June 26, 1974. White wrote the opinion; Marshall, Brennan and Douglas dissented.

The due process guarantee of the 14th Amendment requires prison officials to accord inmates, during prison disciplinary proceedings, certain rights. Because these proceedings could result in the loss of credits for good behavior, thereby increasing the duration of their imprisonment, prisoners should be provided advance written notice of the alleged violation and given a written statement of the fact findings and the reasons for any disciplinary action taken. At the discretion of prison officials, these inmates also might be allowed to call witnesses to testify during the proceedings and to present evidence in their behalf.

The 14th Amendment, however, does not require that inmates facing disciplinary proceedings be accorded all rights available to a defendant in a criminal trial; prisoners

Due Process, Equal Protection of the Laws

... Nor shall any State deprive any person of life, liberty, or property, without due process of law; nor deny to any person within its jurisdiction the equal protection of the laws.

—14th Amendment to the U.S. Constitution

do not have the right to confront their accusers or to cross-examine adverse witnesses, nor do they have the right to have legal counsel for these hearings.

Montanye v. Haymes, Meachum v. Fano (427 U.S. 236), decided by a vote of 6-3, June 25, 1976. White wrote the opinion; Stevens, Brennan and Marshall dissented.

The guarantee of due process does not require that a state prisoner be given a hearing before he is transferred from one institution to another for disciplinary purposes; nor is the prisoner entitled to a hearing if the transfer results in less favorable living conditions at the institution to which he is transferred.

Greenholtz v. Inmates of the Nebraska Penal and Correctional Complex (442 U.S. 1), decided by votes of 5-4 and 6-3, May 29, 1979. Burger wrote the opinion; Powell dissented in part; Marshall, Brennan and Stevens dissented in part.

The constitutional guarantee of due process applies to some state parole procedures, but it does not require that every eligible inmate be given a formal hearing, be allowed to participate in parole board hearings or be fully informed of the evidence upon which the board makes a decision not to grant him discretionary parole.

Jackson v. Virginia (443 U.S. 307), decided by a vote of 8-0, June 28, 1979. Stewart wrote the opinion; Powell did not participate.

The 14th Amendment's guarantee of due process permits a person to be convicted of a crime only if the state presents evidence of guilt beyond a reasonable doubt. Federal courts are empowered to protect this right for state, as well as federal, prisoners.

Thus, when a state prisoner seeks review by a federal judge of his conviction, arguing that he was found guilty upon insufficient evidence, the federal judge should consider whether the evidence was sufficient to justify a rational judge's or jury's finding that the defendant was guilty beyond a reasonable doubt.

The Supreme Court discarded the existing rule that a federal judge should uphold a state conviction, and deny *habeas corpus* relief to the prisoner, if he found that there was any evidence to sustain the conviction. In this particular case, the court found the evidence sufficient to justify conviction.

Connecticut Board of Pardons v. Dumschat (452 U.S. 458), decided by a 7-2 vote, June 17, 1981. Burger wrote the opinion; Stevens and Marshall dissented.

Even though the Connecticut Board of Pardons grants about three of every four applications it receives for commutation of a life sentence, the due process guarantee does not require the board to provide a written statement of the reasons for its action to every inmate denied commutation.

Contempt

Codispoti v. Pennsylvania (418 U.S. 506), decided by a 5-4 vote, June 26, 1974. White wrote the opinion; Blackmun, Burger, Stewart and Rehnquist dissented.

Due process requires that persons who are sentenced at the end of their criminal trial to aggregate sentences on contempt charges amounting to more than six months in jail should have a jury trial on those charges, even though no sentence on any single contempt charge is more than six months.

An exception is made to this holding, however, when a trial judge, to maintain order during a trial, convicts and sentences someone for contempt, imposing no more than a six-month sentence on any one charge.

Equal Protection

Williams v. Illinois (399 U.S. 235), decided by an 8-0 vote, June 29, 1970. Burger wrote the opinion; Blackmun did not take part.

Equal protection of the laws requires that the maximum imprisonment for any offense be the same for all defendants, rich and poor. Therefore, states cannot hold poor people in prison beyond the maximum sentences merely to make them work off a fine they cannot pay. (Forty-seven of the 50 states had allowed such further imprisonment.)

Tate v. Short (401 U.S. 395), decided by a 9-0 vote, March 2, 1971. Brennan wrote the opinion.

The "$30 or 30 days" sentence was ruled an unconstitutional denial of equal protection; that guarantee bars any state or municipality from limiting punishment for an offense to a fine for those who can pay, but expanding the punishment for the same offense to imprisonment for those who cannot pay.

Younger v. Gilmore (404 U.S. 15), decided by a 7-0 vote, Nov. 8, 1971. Unsigned opinion.

States must provide poor prisoners with sufficient legal research materials to ensure that they have equal access to advice and to the courts as do wealthier prisoners.

Richardson v. Ramirez (418 U.S. 24), decided by a 6-3 vote, June 24, 1974. Rehnquist wrote the opinion; Douglas, Brennan and Marshall dissented.

States do not violate the equal protection guarantee of the 14th Amendment by disenfranchising felons. The 14th Amendment implicitly recognizes the right of a state to abridge the right of a citizen to vote as a penalty "for participation in rebellion or other crime."

U.S. v. MacCollum (426 U.S. 317), decided by a 5-4 vote, June 10, 1976. Rehnquist wrote the opinion; Stevens

Brennan, White and Marshall dissented.

Indigent inmates challenging their conviction as unconstitutional do not have a constitutional right to a free transcript of their trial. Congress did not act in violation of the equal protection guarantee when it made provision of such a transcript at public expense conditional upon a finding that the challenge to the conviction was not frivolous and that the transcript was necessary to resolve the issues presented.

These conditions, the majority of the court conceded, "place an indigent in somewhat less advantageous position than a person of means. But neither the equal protection clause of the Fourteenth Amendment nor ... the Fifth Amendment ... guarantees 'absolute equality or precisely equal advantages'.... In the context of a criminal proceeding, they require only an adequate opportunity to present (one's) claim fairly...."

DECISIONS ON CIVIL RIGHTS

As the nation during the 1969-82 period continued to work toward the goal of equality for all citizens under the law, regardless of race or sex, the Supreme Court became more and more involved with civil rights issues. School desegregation, housing discrimination and job rights were the primary areas in which complaints of discrimination came to the court. Toward the end of this period, questions of sex discrimination, and of reverse discrimination, increasingly required the court's attention.

Public Schools

U.S. v. Montgomery County Board of Education (395 U.S. 225), decided by an 8-0 vote, June 2, 1969. Black wrote the opinion.

The court ruled that a federal district judge may order an Alabama school board to desegregate the faculty and staff of state schools according to specific mathematical ratios.

Swann v. Charlotte-Mecklenburg County Board of Education (402 U.S. 1), decided by a 9-0 vote, April 20, 1971. Burger wrote the opinion.

Busing, racial balance ratios and gerrymandered school districts are all permissible interim methods of eliminating the vestiges of state-imposed segregation from Southern schools.

The court said that remedies authorized under this decision as well as previous decisions may be "administratively awkward, inconvenient and even bizarre in some situations and may impose burdens on some; but all awkwardness and inconvenience cannot be avoided in the interim period when the remedial adjustments are being made to eliminate the dual school systems."

There are limits to the remedies that may be used to eliminate the vestiges of segregation, the court said, but no fixed guidelines setting such limits can be established.

The court pointed out that federal courts entered the desegregation process only when local school authorities did not fulfill their obligation to eliminate the dual school system. If school authorities failed to carry out their responsibilities — as the lower federal court had so found in the case before the court involving the school board of Charlotte, North Carolina — then the federal judge has wide discretion in selecting the means of desegregating the school system.

The court did not deal with *de facto* segregation resulting from factors other than state law. It specifically said it did not consider the question of what action would be taken concerning schools that were segregated as a result of "other types of state action, without any discriminatory action by the school authorities."

Limited use of mathematical racial ratios, as a starting point for the remedial process, is within the discretion of the federal court. But "if we were to read the holding of the district court to require, as a matter of substantive constitutional right, any particular degree of racial balance or mixing, that approach would be disapproved and we would be obliged to reverse. The constitutional command to desegregate schools does not mean that every school in every community must always reflect the racial composition of the school system as a whole."

The court said that, within an entire school system, the existence of a few schools attended almost completely by children of one race is not in itself a mark of a still-segregated system, but school authorities have to prove to the courts that such schools are not the result of present or past discriminatory action on their part.

As "an interim corrective measure" courts may order drastically gerrymandered school districts and attendance zones, and pairing, grouping or clustering of schools. Without a constitutional violation there would be no basis for court orders directing the assignment of pupils on a racial basis.

Bus transportation of students has been an "integral part of the public education system for years" and is a permissible remedial technique when ordered by a court to implement desegregation. "Desegregation plans cannot be limited to the walk-in school."

There may be some valid objections to busing when so much time or distance is involved as to risk the children's health or to impinge significantly on the education process. "Limits on time of travel will vary with many factors but probably with none more than the age of the students."

The court concluded its opinion with a statement, in an apparent reference to the resegregation that may follow the achievement of a unitary school system: "Neither school authorities nor district courts are constitutionally required to make year-by-year adjustments of the racial composition of student bodies once the affirmative duty to desegregate has been accomplished and racial discrimination through official action is eliminated from the system.

"This does not mean that federal courts are without power to deal with future problems; but in the absence of a showing that either the school authorities or some other agency of the state has deliberately attempted to fix or alter demographic patterns to affect the racial composition of the schools, further intervention by a district court should not be necessary."

U.S. v. Scotland Neck Board of Education (407 U.S. 484), decided by a 9-0 vote, **Wright v. Emporia City Council** (407 U.S. 451), decided by a 5-4 vote, June 22, 1972. Stewart wrote the opinions; Burger, Blackmun, Powell and Rehnquist dissented in the second case.

Federal courts can halt state or local action creating new school districts that have the effect of impeding school desegregation.

San Antonio Independent School District v. Rodriguez (411 U.S. 1), decided by a 5-4 vote, March 21, 1973. Powell wrote the opinion; Marshall, Douglas, Brennan and White dissented.

The right to an education is not a fundamental right guaranteed to individuals by the Constitution. Wealth is not a suspect way of classifying persons. Therefore, the equal protection guarantee does not require the courts to give the strictest scrutiny to state decisions to finance public schools from local property taxes, a decision resulting in wide disparities among districts in the amount of money spent per pupil.

States do not deny anyone the opportunity of an education by adopting this means of financing public education. This financing plan rationally furthers a legitimate state purpose and so is upheld.

"The consideration and initiation of fundamental reforms with respect to state taxation and education are matters reserved for the legislative process of the different states," wrote Powell, adding that the court's decision was not to be read as approving the status quo. "The need is apparent for reform in tax systems which may well have relied too long and too heavily on the local property tax.... But the ultimate solutions must come from the lawmakers and the democratic pressures of those who elect them."

Richmond School Board v. Virginia State Board of Education, Bradley v. Virginia State Board of Education (412 U.S. 92). The court was evenly divided, 4-4, May 21, 1973; Powell did not participate. There was no opinion.

The effect of this 4-4 vote was to overturn a federal court order of January 1972 that directed school officials to consolidate the predominantly black Richmond, Va., school district with two neighboring county systems, which were predominantly white, in order to desegregate the city schools. The U.S. Court of Appeals, Fourth Circuit, had overturned this order as too drastic; the result of the Supreme Court's tie vote was automatically to uphold the court of appeals. Such votes do not carry any weight as precedents.

Keyes v. Denver School District No. 1 (413 U.S. 189), decided by a 7-1 vote, June 21, 1973. Brennan wrote the opinion; White did not participate; Rehnquist dissented.

This was the first time the court had defined the responsibility of school officials in a district where racial segregation had not been the result of law (de jure) to take action to desegregate public schools. The court held that school officials were constitutionally obligated to desegregate a school system if the segregation had resulted from intentional school board policies. In the case of racially segregated schools within a system, the burden of proof was on the board to prove that such segregation was not a result of intentional board actions.

Lau v. Nichols (414 U.S. 563), decided by a 9-0 vote, Jan. 21, 1974. Douglas wrote the opinion.

Under the Civil Rights Act of 1964, school officials are obligated, through remedial English instruction, bilingual classes, or some other method, to provide non-English-speaking students within their system with the language skills to profit from their school attendance.

Milliken v. Bradley (418 U.S. 717), decided by a 5-4 vote, July 25, 1974. Burger wrote the opinion; Douglas, Brennan, Marshall and White dissented.

A multi-district remedy for school segregation, such as busing school children across district lines, can be ordered by a federal court only when there has been a finding that all the districts involved have been responsible for the segregation that is to be remedied.

The court reversed a lower court's order directing busing across city, county and district lines in order to desegregate the schools of Detroit, Mich. The lower court, said the majority, would have to devise a remedy for the city schools alone.

Said Chief Justice Warren E. Burger: "An inter-district remedy might be in order where the racially discriminatory acts of one or more school districts caused racial segregation in an adjacent district or where district lines have been deliberately drawn on the basis of race.... [But] without an inter-district violation and inter-district effect, there is no constitutional wrong calling for an inter-district remedy."

Pasadena City Board of Education v. Spangler (427 U.S. 424), decided by a 6-2 vote, June 28, 1976. Rehnquist wrote the opinion; Stevens did not participate; Brennan and Marshall dissented.

Once a school board has implemented a racially neutral plan for attendance of students at city schools, it is not required under the Constitution to continue juggling student assignments in order to maintain a certain racial balance in the student body of each school.

Milliken v. Bradley (433 U.S. 267), decided by a 9-0 vote, June 27, 1977. Burger wrote the opinion.

In this case, involving efforts to remedy the segregated nature of the Detroit city schools, the court held that a federal court did not exceed its power when it ordered the school board, as part of the remedy, to institute comprehensive remedial education, training, testing, counseling and guidance programs in the schools and when it directed the state to share with the city the cost of implementing these programs.

Dayton Board of Education v. Brinkman (433 U.S. 406), decided by an 8-0 vote, June 27, 1977. Rehnquist wrote the opinion; Marshall did not participate.

Remedies for school segregation must be carefully tailored to fit the scope of the constitutional violation that created the segregation. A court of appeals exceeded this limit and overstepped its proper role when it imposed upon a district court the duty of developing a system-wide remedy when system-wide violations had not been found.

Columbus Board of Education v. Penick (433 U.S. 449), decided by a vote of 7-2, July 2, 1979. White wrote the court's opinion; Powell and Rehnquist dissented.

The court upheld a massive busing order for the public schools of Columbus, Ohio. Although state law had not required the operation of racially segregated public schools since 1888, the court held that because the Columbus schools were in fact segregated in 1954 — when the court first declared segregated public schools unconstitutional —

school officials had an affirmative constitutional duty to act to terminate that segregation.

Columbus officials had not carried out that responsibility, the court found, but rather had acted to continue some degree of segregation. Because these actions had system-wide impact, the lower courts considering the case acted properly in imposing a system-wide remedy that required the reassignment of 42,000 students in the system and the additional busing of 37,000 students.

Dayton Board of Education v. Brinkman (443 U.S. 526), decided by a 5-4 vote, July 2, 1979. White wrote the opinion; Stewart, Powell, Rehnquist and Burger dissented.

The court upheld a system-wide plan for desegregating the public schools of Dayton, Ohio. Not since 1888 had there been a state law requiring racial segregation in the schools. But because Dayton officials were operating a segregated school system in 1954, and had not acted in the intervening years to end that segregation, the court majority found the system-wide desegregation order justified.

Board of Education of the City of New York v. Harris (444 U.S. 130), decided by a vote of 6-3, Nov. 28, 1979. Blackmun wrote the opinion; Stewart, Powell and Rehnquist dissented.

The court upheld the decision of the Department of Health, Education and Welfare (HEW) to deny millions of dollars in emergency federal school funds in New York City schools because the city's school board had followed a policy of assigning most black teachers to schools where most of the students were black or of another minority group.

The Emergency School Aid Act of 1972 allowed HEW to deny funds to school systems on the basis of the effect of official school board policy on desegregation, without any showing that the discriminatory effect was intended by the board.

Washington v. Seattle School District No. 1 (*), decided by a 5-4 vote, June 30, 1982. Blackmun wrote the opinion; Powell, Burger, Rehnquist and O'Connor dissented.

The court said a 1978 voter-initiated state law prohibiting school boards from voluntarily using busing and pupil reassignment to desegregate public schools violated the equal protection clause. The law, Initiative 350, was unconstitutional because it was racially discriminatory in intent and operation and because it restructured the process of deciding education policy, removing decisions about the voluntary use of busing from local school boards and transferring that authority to the state level.

Crawford v. Board of Education of City of Los Angeles (*), decided by an 8-1 vote, June 30, 1982. Powell wrote the opinion; Marshall dissented.

Proposition 1, a 1979 voter-initiated amendment to the state constitution denying state courts the power to order busing unless it is needed to remedy a specific violation of the U.S. Constitution, is permissible under the equal protection clause. This change in the state constitution simply adopts for state courts the standard federal courts use in deciding when to order busing for the purpose of school desegregation.

Private Schools

Norwood v. Harrison (413 U.S. 455), decided by a 9-0 vote, June 25, 1973. Burger wrote the opinion.

Mississippi impermissibly aided racially segregated private schools through its program of purchasing books and lending them to students in public and private schools. Private schools have the right to exist, but not to share in state aid with public schools, the court said. The state could continue its book loan program if it required all participating schools to certify they did not engage in racial discrimination.

Gilmore v. City of Montgomery (417 U.S. 556), decided by 9-0 and 8-1 votes, June 17, 1974. Blackmun wrote the opinion; Marshall dissented in part.

A city may not allow its municipal parks and recreational facilities to become "enclaves of segregation" through their exclusive use by segregated schools and affiliated groups. With Marshall dissenting, the court refused, however, to permit courts to bar all use of these parks and other facilities by segregated schools and segregated private groups.

Runyon v. McCrary, Fairfax-Brewster School, Inc. v. Gonzales, Southern Independent School Association v. McCrary (427 U.S. 160), decided by a 7-2 vote, June 25, 1976. Stewart wrote the opinion; White and Rehnquist dissented.

Racially segregated private schools that refuse to admit black students violate the Civil Rights Act of 1866, which guarantees "all persons within the jurisdiction of the United States the same right . . . to make and enforce contracts . . . as is enjoyed by white citizens."

Jobs

Griggs v. Duke Power Co. (401 U.S. 424), decided by an 8-0 vote, March 8, 1971. Burger wrote the opinion; Brennan did not participate.

The Civil Rights Act of 1964 bars employers from requiring a high school diploma or a general intelligence test score as a condition for employment or promotion, unless either is related to job skills and does not tend to disqualify more black applicants than white applicants.

McDonnell Douglas Corp. v. Green (411 U.S. 807), decided by a 9-0 vote, May 14, 1973. Powell wrote the opinion.

Title VII of the Civil Rights Act of 1964 does not compel an employer to absolve an employee who has engaged in deliberate unlawful protest against the employer and to rehire him, but neither does it allow an employer to use such activity as a pretext for a racially discriminatory employment policy.

Espinoza v. Farah Manufacturing Co., Inc. (414 U.S. 86), decided by an 8-1 vote, Nov. 19, 1973. Marshall wrote the opinion; Douglas dissented.

Employers do not violate the 1964 Civil Rights Act's Title VII ban on employment discrimination based on national origin by refusing to hire any but American citizens.

Albemarle Paper Co. v. Moody (422 U.S. 405), decided by a 7-1 vote, June 25, 1975. Stewart wrote the opinion; Powell did not participate; Burger dissented.

Back pay awards to victims of employment discrimination are the rule, not the exception, in cases won by employees under Title VII of the 1964 Civil Rights Act. Back pay awards are warranted to carry out the intent of Congress in the 1964 act to "make whole" persons who suffered because of unlawful discrimination. Back pay should not be restricted to cases in which the employer is found to have acted in bad faith.

Franks v. Bowman Transportation Co., Inc. (424 U.S. 747), decided by a 5-3 vote, March 24, 1976. Brennan wrote the opinion; Powell, Rehnquist and Burger dissented; Stevens did not participate.

Federal courts have the authority, under the Civil Rights Act of 1964, to award victims of illegal employment discrimination seniority dating back to the time when they were illegally refused a job. Congress intended such awards to be made under Title VII of the 1964 act, and they should be made in most cases where discrimination is proved.

Without such awards, the congressional intent to "make whole" victims of discrimination is frustrated, wrote Brennan, in that a victim of discrimination "will never obtain his rightful place in the hierarchy of seniority according to which various employment benefits are distributed. He will perpetually remain subordinate to persons who, but for the illegal discrimination, would have been in respect to entitlement to these benefits his inferiors."

Washington v. Davis (426 U.S. 229), decided by a 7-2 vote, June 7, 1976. White wrote the opinion; Brennan and Marshall dissented.

Job qualification tests are not unconstitutional simply because more black job applicants than white applicants fail them. Some racially discriminatory purpose must be found in order for the test to be in violation of the constitutional guarantees of due process and equal protection. "Our cases have not embraced the proposition that a law or other official act, without regard to whether it reflects a racially discriminatory purpose, is unconstitutional *solely* because it has a racially disproportionate impact," wrote White. "We have not held that a law, neutral on its face and serving ends otherwise within the power of government to pursue, is invalid under the Equal Protection Clause simply because it may affect a greater proportion of one race than another. Disproportionate impact is not irrelevant, but it is not the sole touchstone of an invidious racial discrimination forbidden by the Constitution."

McDonald v. Santa Fe Trail Transportation Co. (427 U.S. 273), decided by votes of 9-0 and 7-2, June 25, 1976. Marshall wrote the opinion; White and Rehnquist dissented in part.

The 1964 Civil Rights Act's ban on racial discrimination in employment forbids discrimination against whites as well as blacks. Therefore, white employees who charge that they have been the victim of racially discriminatory job practices can seek remedies under that law, the court held unanimously.

Teamsters v. United States, T.I.M.E.-DC v. United States (431 U.S. 324), decided by a vote of 7-2, May 31, 1977. Stewart wrote the opinion; Brennan and Marshall dissented.

Congress in the Civil Rights Act of 1964 specifically immunized existing *bona fide* seniority systems from being attacked as discriminatory. Thus, despite findings of employment discrimination on the part of a company and a union, and despite the fact that the pre-1964 seniority system perpetuates the effect of past discrimination, retroactive seniority to victims of job discrimination cannot be awarded further back than to the effective date of the 1964 act. "An otherwise neutral legitimate seniority system," wrote Stewart, "does not become unlawful under Title VII simply because it may perpetuate pre-Act discrimination. Congress did not intend to make it illegal for employees with vested seniority rights to continue to exercise those rights, even at the expense of pre-Act discriminatees."

Trans World Airlines v. Hardison, Machinists' Local 1650 v. Hardison (432 U.S. 63), decided by a 7-2 vote, June 16, 1977. White wrote the opinion; Brennan and Marshall dissented.

The 1964 Civil Rights Act ban on religious discrimination requires employers to make "reasonable accommodations" to the religious needs of their employees. It does not require them to breach otherwise valid collective bargaining agreements, to deny other employees their preferred working hours and job preferences or to deprive them of their contractual rights in order to accommodate the religious needs of others. An employer is not required to make special exceptions to its seniority policies in order to help an individual employee accommodate a religious belief that forbids him to work on Saturdays.

Furnco Construction Co. v. Waters (438 U.S. 567), decided by votes of 9-0 and 7-2, June 29, 1978. Rehnquist wrote the opinion; Marshall and Brennan dissented in part.

To rebut charges of job discrimination in violation of Title VII of the 1964 Civil Rights Act, an employer must show that he has legitimate reasons for his challenged hiring, firing or promotion decisions. In support of his defense, an employer may introduce statistics showing that he employs a substantial number of minority workers in certain jobs. However, statistics showing "a racially balanced work force cannot immunize an employer from liability for specific acts of discrimination."

New York City Transit Authority v. Beazer (440 U.S. 568), decided by votes of 6-3 and 5-4, March 21, 1979. Stevens wrote the opinion; Brennan, White and Marshall dissented; Powell dissented in part.

A city does not violate the 1964 Civil Rights Act ban on job discrimination, nor the 14th Amendment guarantee of equal protection, when it refuses to hire persons who participate in, or have completed, a methadone maintenance program. This policy was part of the transit authority's general policy against hiring drug users.

Texas Department of Community Affairs v. Burdine (450 U.S. 248), decided by a 9-0 vote, March 4, 1981. Powell wrote the opinion.

An employer charged with job discrimination must prove that he had legitimate nondiscriminatory reasons for his challenged actions, but then it is up to the person bringing the charge to show that the explanation is only a pretext for the discrimination. The court reversed a lower court's order requiring an employer charged with a discriminatory promotion to prove that the person promoted was better qualified than the one passed over.

American Tobacco Co. v. Patterson (*), decided by a 5-4 vote, April 5, 1982. White wrote the opinion; Brennan, Marshall, Blackmun and Stevens dissented.

Workers challenging a seniority system as discriminatory under the 1964 Civil Rights Act must prove both that it had an adverse effect on women or minorities and that it was adopted with the intent to discriminate against those workers.

When Congress exempted *bona fide* seniority systems from challenge under the 1964 act, unless they were adopted with the intent to discriminate, it included that exemption in both seniority systems then in effect and those adopted after the act's passage, the court held.

Kremer v. Chemical Construction Co. (*), decided by a 5-4 vote, May 17, 1982. White wrote the opinion; Blackmun, Brennan, Marshall and Stevens dissented.

Once a state court has upheld a state agency's finding that there is no basis for a charge of job discrimination, a federal court may not re-litigate that issue in a case brought under Title VII of the 1964 Civil Rights Act.

In 1790, Congress passed a law directing that all U.S. courts give the same weight to state court judgments as would the state's own courts. That law, still in effect, was not superseded by Title VII.

General Telephone Company of the Southwest v. Falcon (*), decided by votes of 9-0 and 8-1, June 14, 1982. Stevens wrote the opinion; Burger dissented in part.

An individual who alleges that he was denied a promotion because he is Mexican-American may not bring a class action on behalf of employees who were denied employment for that reason.

Sumitomo Shoji America v. Avagliano (*), decided by a 9-0 vote, June 15, 1982. Burger wrote the opinion.

A company constituted under the laws of the United States or a single state is a company of the United States, subject to the laws of the United States, and not eligible for the exemption contained in certain treaties made by the United States that allows foreign corporations operating in the United States to hire as they wish, free of the fair employment requirements of U.S. law.

Connecticut v. Teal (*), decided by a 5-4 vote, June 21, 1982. Brennan wrote the opinion; Powell, Burger, Rehnquist and O'Connor dissented.

An employer sued for violating the Civil Rights Act of 1964 by using a nonjob-related test to select candidates for promotion when that test excluded more blacks than whites from consideration for the promotion may not use as his entire defense the "bottom line" argument that in fact more qualified blacks than qualified whites are promoted by the company.

Ford Motor Co. v. Equal Employment Opportunity Commission (*), decided by a 6-3 vote, June 28, 1982. O'Connor wrote the opinion; Blackmun, Brennan and Marshall dissented.

An employer charged with discrimination in hiring can terminate the period for which he may be held liable to the claimant for back pay by unconditionally offering the claimant the job he previously had refused to offer — even if this offer does not include seniority retroactive to the date of the alleged discriminatory refusal.

Housing

Hunter v. Erickson (393 U.S. 385), decided by an 8-1 vote, Jan. 20, 1969. White wrote the opinion; Black dissented.

A city cannot constitutionally require that any local fair housing ordinance be subject to approval by referendum; such a requirement is a real, substantial and invidious denial of equal protection. Official action cannot any more disadvantage any particular group by making it difficult to enact legislation in its behalf than it can dilute any person's vote.

James v. Valtierra (402 U.S. 137), decided by a 5-3 vote, April 26, 1971. Black wrote the opinion; Douglas did not participate; Brennan, Blackmun and Marshall dissented.

The equal protection guarantee is not violated by language in a state constitution forbidding construction of any low-income housing projects not expressly approved by a referendum in the affected area.

Trafficante v. Metropolitan Life Insurance Co. (409 U.S. 205), decided by a 9-0 vote, Dec. 7, 1972. Douglas wrote the opinion.

White tenants of an apartment complex have the legal standing as "aggrieved persons" under the 1968 Civil Rights Act to sue their landlord for discriminating against prospective nonwhite tenants and thereby depriving the white tenants of the advantages of living in an integrated community.

Tillman v. Wheaton-Haven Recreational Association, Inc. (410 U.S. 431), decided by a 9-0 vote, Feb. 27, 1973. Blackmun wrote the opinion.

A community recreation association operating a swimming pool is not a private club exempt from federal civil rights laws, and it violates those laws by refusing membership to black applicants.

Village of Belle Terre v. Boraas (416 U.S. 1), decided by a 7-2 vote, April 1, 1974. Douglas wrote the opinion; Marshall and Brennan dissented.

Towns and villages do not violate the Constitution by using their zoning powers to restrict land use to one-family dwellings. So long as the classification for zoning purposes is fairly debatable, the town's decision to adopt that classification must be allowed to stand. The police power, on which the zoning power is grounded, can be used to preserve family values, seclusion and clean air. "A quiet place where yards are wide, people few and motor vehicles restricted are legitimate guidelines in a land use project," wrote Douglas.

Hills v. Gautreaux (425 U.S. 284), decided by an 8-0 vote, April 20, 1976. Stewart wrote the opinion; Stevens did not participate.

Federal courts have the power to order housing officials who have contributed to the racial segregation of public housing in a city to remedy that situation by developing public housing throughout the metropolitan area. The court upheld a federal court order for such an area-wide solution to the segregation of public housing in Chicago, a situation for which federal Housing and Urban Development (HUD) officials had been found partially responsible.

Village of Arlington Heights v. Metropolitan Housing Development Corp. (429 U.S. 252), decided by a 5-3 vote, Jan. 11, 1977. Powell wrote the opinion; Stevens did not participate; Brennan and Marshall dissented in part; White dissented.

Without any showing of a discriminatory motive, the refusal of a village to rezone property to permit building of a housing development for low- and moderate-income persons of both races does not violate the 14th Amendment.

Gladstone Realtors v. Village of Bellwood (441 U.S. 91), decided by a vote of 7-2, April 17, 1979. Powell wrote the opinion; Stewart and Rehnquist dissented.

Individuals and municipal corporations, even if they are not the direct victims of housing discrimination, have standing to sue discriminatory realtors under the Fair Housing Act of 1968 if they can demonstrate actual injury.

Havens Realty Corp. v. Coleman (*), decided by a 9-0 vote, Feb. 24, 1982. Brennan wrote the opinion.

Under the Fair Housing Act of 1968, "testers" — persons who inquire about available housing primarily to collect evidence of alleged discrimination — have legal standing to sue landlords or realtors when they uncover discriminatory practices. The law grants all persons a legal right to truthful information about available housing, and this right is violated when rental agents give false information to a black "tester."

Sex Discrimination

Phillips v. Martin Marietta Corp. (400 U.S. 542), decided by a 9-0 vote, Jan. 25, 1971. Unsigned opinion.

The Civil Rights Act of 1964 bars job discrimination on the basis of sex against a mother of pre-school children and, in absence of a *bona fide* occupational qualification, requires one hiring policy for both men and women. "The existence of such conflicting family obligations, if demonstrably more relevant to job performance for a woman than for a man could arguably be a basis for distinction."

Reed v. Reed (404 U.S. 71), decided by a 7-0 vote, Nov. 22, 1971. Burger wrote the opinion.

The guarantee of equal protection invalidates a state law that automatically favors a father over a mother as executor of their son's estate: "To give a mandatory preference to members of either sex over members of the other ... is to make the very kind of arbitrary legislative choice forbidden by the equal protection clause."

Stanley v. Illinois (405 U.S. 645), decided by a 5-2 vote, April 2, 1972. White wrote the opinion; Powell and Rehnquist did not participate; Burger and Blackmun dissented.

The guarantee of equal protection invalidates a state law that presumes that an unwed father is an unfit custodian of his child, in a custody dispute, but allows the unwed mother and all other natural parents in such a situation a hearing to determine their fitness as parents.

Frontiero v. Richardson (411 U.S. 677), decided by an 8-1 vote, May 14, 1973. Brennan wrote the opinion; Rehnquist dissented.

Federal law discriminates against women, in violation of the due process guarantee of the Fifth Amendment, by requiring women in the military to prove their husband's dependence on them in order for the husbands to receive dependents' benefits, while presuming, without such proof, that the wives of all men in the military are dependent and thus entitled to these benefits.

Cleveland Board of Education v. LaFleur, Cohen v. Chesterfield County School Board (414 U.S. 632), decided by 7-2 votes, Jan. 21, 1974. Stewart wrote the opinion; Rehnquist and Burger dissented.

Mandatory maternity leave policies that require all teachers in a school system to stop teaching five months before the expected birth of a child violates the teachers' right to due process. "Freedom of personal choice in matters of marriage and family life is one of the liberties protected by the due process clause.... Overly restrictive maternity leave regulations can constitute a heavy burden on the exercise of these protected freedoms.... The due process clause ... requires that such rules ... not needlessly, arbitrarily, or capriciously impinge upon this vital area of a teacher's constitutional liberty," wrote Stewart. The court's opinion indicated that school boards should adopt more flexible policies for determining maternity leaves on a case-by-case basis.

Kahn v. Shevin (416 U.S. 351), decided by a 6-3 vote, April 24, 1974. Douglas wrote the opinion; White, Brennan and Marshall dissented.

State law providing a special property tax exemption for widows, but not for widowers, does not violate the constitutional guarantee of equal protection. The court found such a law to be reasonably designed to aid widows, who were more likely to be left in a difficult economic situation than were widowers.

Corning Glass Works v. Brennan, Brennan v. Corning Glass Works (417 U.S. 188), decided by a 5-3 vote, June 3, 1974. Marshall wrote the opinion; Stewart did not participate; Burger, Blackmun and Rehnquist dissented.

The Equal Pay Act of 1963 requires that men and women be paid equal base wages for performing equal work, regardless of whether that work is performed during the day or night. To compensate for the less attractive night assignment, a night shift differential can be paid to all night workers, male and female, but the base wages must remain the same. This was the first time that the court had interpreted the 1963 law to require equal base wages for men and women doing the same job.

Geduldig v. Aiello (417 U.S. 484), decided by a 6-3 vote, June 17, 1974. Stewart wrote the opinion; Douglas, Brennan and Marshall dissented.

California did not violate the constitutional equal protection guarantee by excluding from its disability insurance program women unable to work because of pregnancy-related disabilities. The decision to exclude the risk of pregnancy from the risks insured by the state plan was a rational one in light of the state interest in maintaining a low-cost, self-supporting insurance fund.

Taylor v. Louisiana (419 U.S. 522), decided by an 8-1 vote, Jan. 21, 1975. White wrote the opinion; Rehnquist dissented.

State laws generally exempting women from jury duty

are unconstitutional because they violate the requirement that juries be drawn from a fair cross-section of the community.

The court overruled its 1961 decision (*Hoyt v. Florida*, 368 U.S. 57), which upheld this general exclusion of women from jury duty as rational in light of the state's interest in preventing interference with women's traditional function as wives, homemakers and mothers.

Schlesinger v. Ballard (419 U.S. 498), decided by a 5-4 vote, Jan. 15, 1975. Stewart wrote the opinion; Brennan, White, Douglas and Marshall dissented.

In light of the fact that women naval officers have fewer opportunities for promotion than their male counterparts, Congress did not act unconstitutionally when it provided female officers a maximum of 13 years of service before a discharge was mandatory if they did not win promotion, while providing male officers only nine years before such a discharge was required.

Weinberger v. Wiesenfeld (420 U.S. 636), decided by an 8-0 vote, March 19, 1975. Brennan wrote the opinion; Douglas did not participate.

A Social Security law that pays widows with small children, but not widowers with small children, survivors' benefits violates the guarantee of due process by providing working women with fewer benefits for their Social Security contributions than it provides to working men. "It is no less important for a child to be cared for by its sole surviving parent when that parent is male rather than female " wrote Brennan, pointing out that the intended purpose of this benefit was to allow a mother not to work but to stay home and care for her young children.

Stanton v. Stanton (421 U.S. 7), decided by an 8-1 vote, April 15, 1975. Blackmun wrote the opinion; Rehnquist dissented.

States cannot constitutionally set different ages at which men and women are considered adults under the law.

Utah had set the age of adulthood at 18 for women and 21 for men, reasoning that men needed a longer period of parental support in order to obtain their education. "No longer is the female destined solely for the house and the rearing of family and only the male for the marketplace and the world of ideas," wrote Blackmun.

General Electric Co. v. Gilbert, Gilbert v. General Electric Co. (429 U.S. 125), decided by a 6-3 vote, Dec. 7, 1976. Rehnquist wrote the opinion; Brennan, Marshall and Stevens dissented.

An employer does not violate the sex discrimination ban of Title VII of the 1964 Civil Rights Act by maintaining an employee disability income protection plan that excludes from coverage all pregnancy-related disabilities.

Mathews v. deCastro (429 U.S. 181), decided by a 9-0 vote, Dec. 13, 1976. Stewart wrote the opinion.

Congress did not act unconstitutionally when it provided a wife's insurance benefits to wives under 62 with their husband's dependent child in their care, while not providing those benefits to divorced wives caring for their former husband's children.

Craig v. Boren (429 U.S. 190), decided by a 7-2 vote, Dec. 20, 1976. Brennan wrote the opinion; Burger and Rehnquist dissented.

A state law permitting the sale of beer to women at age 18 but not to men until age 21 violates the equal protection guarantee of the 14th Amendment. "To withstand constitutional challenge," wrote Brennan, "classifications by gender must serve important governmental objectives and must be substantially related to achievement of those objectives."

Califano v. Goldfarb (430 U.S. 199), decided by a 5-4 vote, March 2, 1977. Brennan wrote the opinion; Stevens concurred; Rehnquist, Burger, Blackmun and Stewart dissented.

Congress acted unconstitutionally in requiring widowers, but not widows, to have been receiving one-half of their support from their spouse at the time of death in order to be eligible for survivor's benefits. Brennan, Powell, Marshall and White viewed this as discrimination against working women, who obtained less protection for their spouses although they contributed the same as men. Stevens viewed this as discrimination against widowers.

Dothard v. Rawlinson (433 U.S. 321), decided by votes of 8-1 and 7-2, June 27, 1977. Stewart wrote the opinion; White, Brennan and Marshall dissented in part.

State law setting minimum height and weight requirements for prison guards that disqualify more than 40 percent of the women in the state but fewer than 1 percent of the men constitutes sex discrimination in violation of the 1964 Civil Rights Act. The court majority said the requirements were not shown to be sufficiently related to the qualities necessary for the job. White dissented.

A state regulation that effectively excludes women from jobs as guards at all-male maximum security prisons is justified in light of the vulnerability of a woman guard to assault by male inmates and consequent risk of the loss of security in the prison. Brennan and Marshall dissented from the latter holding.

Nashville Gas Co. v. Satty (434 U.S. 136), decided by a vote of 9-0, Dec. 6, 1977. Rehnquist wrote the opinion.

The sex discrimination ban in Title VII of the 1964 Civil Rights Act forbids employers to divest women workers of their accumulated seniority when they take maternity leave, but allows them to refuse sick pay to those workers when their absence is due to pregnancy and childbirth.

Quilloin v. Walcott (434 U.S. 246), decided by a 9-0 vote, Jan. 10, 1978. Marshall wrote the opinion.

State law providing that the consent of the natural mother is sufficient for adoption of an illegitimate child does not deny the father of the illegitimate child equal protection or due process.

City of Los Angeles v. Manhart (435 U.S. 702), decided by votes of 6-2 and 7-1, April 25, 1978. Stevens wrote the opinion; Brennan did not participate; Burger, Rehnquist and Marshall dissented in part.

The fact that the average woman outlives the average man does not justify an employer requiring women to pay more into a pension fund than male workers earning the same pay, under the Civil Rights Act of 1964. The 1964 act requires that employers' decisions focus on the individual, not the generalization. "Individual risks, like individual performance, may not be predicted by resort to classifications proscribed by Title VII.... [W]hen insurance risks are grouped, the better risks always subsidize the poorer risks. . . ."

Orr v. Orr (440 U.S. 268), decided by a 6-3 vote, March 5, 1979. Brennan wrote the opinion; Burger, Powell and Rehnquist dissented.

The equal protection guarantee of the 14th Amendment prohibits states from allowing only women, and not men, to receive alimony in a divorce settlement.

Cannon v. University of Chicago (441 U.S. 677), decided by a 6-3 vote, May 14, 1979. Stevens wrote the opinion; White, Blackmun and Powell dissented.

Private individuals may bring lawsuits in federal court to enforce the ban in Title IX of the Education Amendments of 1972 on sex discrimination in education programs that receive federal financial aid. The 1972 amendments provide explicitly for enforcement of this ban only through termination of federal funds; the court held that it also could be enforced by individuals bringing lawsuits.

Davis v. Passman (442 U.S. 228), decided by a 5-4 vote, June 4, 1979. Brennan wrote the opinion; Burger, Powell, Rehnquist and Stewart dissented.

The Fifth Amendment, which protects individuals from being deprived, by federal action, of life, liberty or property without due process of law, provides congressional employees with a basis for bringing lawsuits challenging their dismissal when they argue that such dismissals violate their due process rights and that they should be awarded damages to compensate them for that violation.

Personnel Administrator of Massachusetts v. Feeney (442 U.S. 256), decided by a 7-2 vote, June 5, 1979. Stewart wrote the opinion; Marshall and Brennan dissented.

A state does not violate the 14th Amendment guarantee of equal protection when it gives veterans an absolute preference for its civil service appointments. This veterans' preference does not deny women the equal protection of the law, even though women constitute only 2 percent of the state's veterans and women applicants clearly are disadvantaged by the preference.

"[T]he Fourteenth Amendment guarantees equal laws, not equal results." The distinction in this law is not between men and women but between veterans and nonveterans. Without proof that the law was intended to discriminate against women, it is not unconstitutional.

Califano v. Westcott, Pratt v. Westcott (443 U.S. 76), decided by votes of 9-0 and 5-4, June 25, 1979. Blackmun wrote the opinion; Burger, Powell, Stewart and Rehnquist dissented in part.

The Social Security Act provision that provides for welfare benefits to a family when the father is unemployed, but not when the mother is unemployed, violates the Constitution's equal protection requirement.

Such a gender-based classification is not substantially related to the attainment of any important statutory goal, but is rather only "part of the 'baggage of sexual stereotypes,' . . . that presumes the father has the 'primary responsibility to provide a home and its essentials,' . . . while the mother is the 'center of the home and family life' . . . Legislation that rests on such presumptions, without more, cannot survive scrutiny under the Due Process Clause of the Fifth Amendment," which includes the promise of equal protection of the laws.

The majority upheld a lower court's order directing that welfare aid be extended to families where the mother is unemployed, as well as to those with unemployed fathers. The court minority said Congress should make the decision whether to expand the program or drop it altogether.

Wengler v. Druggists Mutual Insurance Company (446 U.S. 142), decided by a vote of 8-1, April 22, 1980. White wrote the opinion; Rehnquist dissented.

A state violates the 14th Amendment guarantee of equal protection when it makes widows automatically eligible for death benefits, following the work-related death of their husbands, but requires widowers — in order to be eligible for the same benefits — to prove that they were physically or mentally unable to earn a living or that they were dependent upon their wives' earnings.

Michael M. v. Superior Court of Sonoma County, Calif. (450 U.S. 464), decided by a 5-4 vote, March 23, 1981. Rehnquist wrote an opinion joined by three other justices; Blackmun concurred; Brennan, White, Marshall and Stevens dissented.

A state does not illegally discriminate against men by allowing a man to be prosecuted for having sexual relations with a girl under 18 to whom he is not married while exempting the girl involved from criminal liability. The court upheld California's statutory rape laws against constitutional challenge, finding that the distinction between that state's treatment of men and women was justified as an appropriate means of preventing illegitimate teen-age pregnancies.

County of Washington v. Gunther (452 U.S. 161), decided by a 5-4 vote, June 8, 1981. Brennan wrote the opinion; Rehnquist, Burger, Stewart and Powell dissented.

Women workers may sue their employers under the 1964 Civil Rights Act for discriminating against them on the basis of their sex without first having to prove that they were denied "equal pay for equal work," a violation of the Equal Pay Act. A violation of the Civil Rights Act's ban on sex discrimination in the workplace can be shown initially by merely demonstrating that a woman's sex, per se, was a factor in determining her pay.

Rostker v. Goldberg (453 U.S. 57), decided by a 6-3 vote, June 25, 1981. Rehnquist wrote the opinion; White, Marshall and Brennan dissented.

Congress did not violate the Constitution when it decided to exclude women from registration for the military draft. Because women are barred by law and policy from combat, they are not "similarly situated" with men for purposes of draft registration, and thus Congress may properly treat the sexes differently.

North Haven Board of Education v. Bell (*), decided by a 6-3 vote, May 17, 1982. Blackmun wrote the opinion; Powell, Burger and Rehnquist dissented.

Title IX of the Education Amendments of 1972 — which provides that "no person . . . shall, on the basis of sex, be excluded from participation in, be denied the benefits of, or be subjected to discrimination under any education program or activity receiving federal financial assistance" — authorizes federal monitoring of employment practices, as well as the treatment of students, of recipient school districts, colleges and universities.

The sanction for violating this prohibition — termination of federal funds — is program-specific; that is, funds are to be terminated only to programs in which discrimination has been found to exist, the court majority said.

Mississippi University for Women v. Hogan (*), decided by a 5-4 vote, July 1, 1982. O'Connor wrote the opinion; Burger, Blackmun, Powell and Rehnquist dissented.

A state-supported university that historically has admitted only women to its school of nursing violates the constitutional guarantee of equal protection when it denies admission to a man merely because of his sex. To justify a law that classifies individuals on the basis of sex, an "exceedingly persuasive justification" must be presented. The state did not meet that test in this case.

Affirmative Action

DeFunis v. Odegaard (416 U.S. 312), decided by a 5-4 vote, April 23, 1974. The opinion was unsigned; Burger, Stewart, Blackmun, Rehnquist and Powell formed the majority; Brennan, Douglas, White and Marshall dissented.

Citing the constitutional requirement that it deal only with live cases, the court sidestepped a major ruling on the question of reverse discrimination: Does the constitutional guarantee of equal protection of the laws prohibit the adoption of policies favoring minority group members over majority group members?

The court held that this case was moot. The white plaintiff, who charged that he was denied admission to law school so that the school could accept a less-qualified minority student, eventually was admitted under court order and was to graduate from law school in the spring of 1974. He would not, therefore, be affected by the court's decision in the case.

Regents of University of California v. Bakke (438 U.S. 265), decided by two 5-4 votes, June 28, 1978. Powell announced the judgment of the court; Stevens and Brennan filed separate opinions; Stevens was joined by Burger, Rehnquist and Stewart; Brennan was joined by Marshall, White and Blackmun.

A special admissions program for a state medical school under which a set number of places were set aside for minority group members — and white applicants were denied the opportunity to compete for those seats — clearly violated Title VI of the 1964 Civil Rights Act, which forbids the exclusion of anyone because of race from participation in a federally funded program. This view was adopted by Powell, Burger, Rehnquist, Stewart and Stevens.

Admissions programs that consider race as one of a complex of factors in the decision to admit or reject an applicant are not unconstitutional in and of themselves. "Government may take race into account when it acts not to demean or insult any racial group, but to remedy disadvantages cast on minorities by past racial prejudice, at least when appropriate findings have been made by judicial, legislative, or administrative bodies with competence to act in this area." This view was adopted by Powell, Brennan, Marshall, White and Blackmun.

United Steelworkers of America v. Weber, Kaiser Aluminum & Chemical Corp. v. Weber, United States v. Weber (443 U.S. 193), decided by a 5-2 vote, June 27, 1979. Brennan wrote the opinion; Rehnquist and Burger dissented; Powell and Stevens did not participate.

Title VII of the 1964 Civil Rights Act, which forbids employers to use race as a basis for discriminating against employees or job applicants, does not prohibit the voluntary adoption of race-conscious affirmative action plans by private employers to eliminate conspicuous racial imbalance in traditionally segregated job categories.

Fullilove v. Klutznick (448 U.S. 448), decided by a 6-3 vote, July 2, 1980. Burger wrote the opinion announcing the court's decision and setting out the views of three justices; Marshall, Brennan and Blackmun concurred; Stewart, Rehnquist and Stevens dissented.

The court upheld the power of Congress to make limited use of racial quotas to remedy past discrimination against black businesses. The court held that Congress did not violate the constitutional guarantee of equal protection when it set aside for minority businesses 10 percent of federal funds allocated for local public works projects. That provision was part of the 1977 Public Works Employment Act.

DECISIONS ON INDIVIDUAL RIGHTS

Aliens, women, students, welfare recipients, mental patients, parents and consumers all won favorable rulings from the Supreme Court during the 1969-82 period. Summaries of some of the decisions dealing with the rights of these persons follow.

Aliens

Rogers v. Bellei (401 U.S. 815), decided by a 5-4 vote, April 5, 1971. Blackmun wrote the opinion; Douglas, Black, Brennan and Marshall dissented.

A foreign-born child of alien and American parents is not a citizen within the 14th Amendment protection of due process, and he loses citizenship if he fails to live in the United States for five years between ages 14 and 28.

Graham v. Richardson (403 U.S. 365), decided by a 9-0 vote, June 14, 1971. Blackmun wrote the opinion.

The Constitution's equal protection guarantee is violated by state laws that deny welfare benefits to aliens who have lived in the United States less than 15 years and by state laws that deny benefits to all resident aliens.

In re Griffiths (413 U.S. 717), decided by a 7-2 vote, June 25, 1973. Powell wrote the opinion; Rehnquist and Burger dissented.

A state violates the equal protection guarantee by denying an applicant admission to the state bar solely because the applicant is an alien.

Sugarman v. Dougall (413 U.S. 634), decided by a 8-1 vote, June 25, 1973. Blackmun wrote the opinion;

Rehnquist dissented.

A state violates the equal protection guarantee by excluding all aliens from all permanent state civil service jobs.

Hampton v. Mow Sun Wong (426 U.S. 88), decided by a 5-4 vote, June 1, 1976. Stevens wrote the opinion; Burger, Rehnquist, White and Blackmun dissented.

All persons in the United States are protected by the Fifth Amendment from being deprived of liberty without due process of law. The Civil Service Commission violated this due process guarantee by excluding aliens from all federal jobs and by denying them the opportunity for employment in a major sector of the economy, an aspect of the Fifth Amendment's protected liberty.

Nyquist v. Mauclet (432 U.S. 1), decided by a 5-4 vote, June 13, 1977. Blackmun wrote the opinion; Powell, Burger, Stewart and Rehnquist dissented.

A state violates the equal protection guarantee by denying resident aliens who do not intend to become citizens of the United States the right to apply for state financial aid for higher education.

Foley v. Connelie (435 U.S. 291), decided by a 6-3 vote, March 22, 1978. Burger wrote the opinion; Marshall, Brennan and Stevens dissented.

States may constitutionally require that state policemen be citizens; policemen fall within the category of persons who participate in the formulation or implementation of public policy for whom a citizenship requirement may be appropriate. "[W]e extended to aliens the right to education and public welfare, along with the ability to earn a livelihood and engage in licensed professions; the right to govern [however] is reserved to citizens."

Ambach v. Norwick (441 U.S. 68), decided by a 5-4 vote, April 17, 1979. Powell wrote the opinion; Blackmun, Brennan, Marshall and Stevens dissented.

The 14th Amendment's guarantee of equal protection of the laws is not violated by a state decision forbidding aliens, unless they are applicants for U.S. citizenship, to work as public elementary or secondary school teachers. The role of public school teachers is critical in developing the attitudes of students toward government and society; therefore, it is rational for the state to decide to exclude from such jobs persons who have not become a part of the process of self-government by becoming citizens.

Cabell v. Chavez-Salido (*), decided by a 5-4 vote, Jan. 12, 1982. White wrote the opinion; Blackmun, Brennan, Marshall and Stevens dissented.

California may require that all peace officers be U.S. citizens, even when the category of peace officers is a broad one encompassing deputy probation officers. Such officers both exercise and symbolize the power of the political community, and it is reasonable that they be required to be citizens.

Plyler v. Doe, Texas v. Certain Named and Unnamed Undocumented Alien Children (*), decided by a 5-4 vote, June 15, 1982. Brennan wrote the opinion; Burger, Rehnquist, White and O'Connor dissented.

The 14th Amendment guarantees the equal protection of the laws to illegal aliens in the United States. They are clearly persons within the jurisdiction of the state in which they reside, even if they have entered the country and that state illegally. Texas, therefore, may not deny illegal alien children a free public education; there is no national policy nor sufficient state interest presented to justify denying such children a public education.

Abortion, Birth Control

Eisenstadt v. Baird (405 U.S. 438), decided by a 6-1 vote, March 22, 1972. Brennan wrote the opinion; Powell and Rehnquist did not participate; Burger dissented.

It is a violation of the equal protection guarantee for states to ban distribution of contraceptives to unmarried individuals.

Roe v. Wade (410 U.S. 113), *Doe v. Bolton* (410 U.S. 179), decided by a 7-2 vote, Jan. 22, 1973. Blackmun wrote the opinion; Rehnquist and White dissented.

The right to privacy, grounded in the 14th Amendment's due process guarantee of personal liberty, encompasses and protects a woman's decision whether or not to bear a child. This right is impermissibly abridged by state laws that make abortion a crime, except when performed to save the life of the mother.

During the first trimester of pregnancy, the decision to have an abortion should be left entirely to a woman and her physician. The state can forbid abortions by nonphysicians.

During the second trimester, the state may regulate the abortion procedure in ways reasonably related to maternal health. And during the third trimester, the state can, if it wishes, forbid all abortions except those necessary to save the mother's life or health.

Planned Parenthood of Central Missouri v. Danforth (428 U.S. 52), decided by votes of 6-3 and 5-4, July 1, 1976. Blackmun wrote the opinion; White, Burger and Rehnquist dissented, joined on one point by Stevens.

The state cannot require that a husband give his consent in order for a wife to have an abortion in the first trimester of pregnancy. "We cannot hold that the state has the constitutional authority to give the spouse unilaterally the ability to prohibit the wife from terminating her pregnancy, when the state itself lacks that right," wrote Blackmun.

White, Burger and Rehnquist dissented, saying that states should be allowed to decide this matter free of federal judicial supervision.

The state, likewise, cannot require that a parent give his or her consent before an unmarried daughter under 18 can have an abortion in the first trimester of pregnancy. "The state does not have the constitutional authority to give a third party an absolute, and possibly arbitrary, veto over the decision of the physician and his patient," wrote Blackmun. Stevens joined the dissenters — White, Burger and Rehnquist — on this point.

The court, over the dissenting votes of White, Burger and Rehnquist, also held that the state cannot ban the use of saline amniocentesis as a method of performing an abortion after the first trimester, nor can it require doctors to take as much care to preserve the life of a fetus in an abortion as they would if they expected the fetus to be born. The court upheld the requirement that a woman give her written consent to an abortion.

Beal v. Doe (432 U.S. 438), decided by a 6-3 vote, June 20, 1977. Powell wrote the opinion; Brennan, Marshall and Blackmun dissented.

The Social Security Act does not require states participating in the Medicaid program that provides medical services to indigents to finance non-therapeutic abortions.

Maher v. Roe (432 U.S. 464), decided by a 6-3 vote, June 20, 1977. Powell wrote the opinion; Blackmun, Brennan and Marshall dissented.

A state's refusal to fund non-therapeutic abortions under the Medicaid program does not violate the constitutional guarantee of equal protection of the law. A state, wrote Powell, "is free — through normal democratic processes — to decide that such benefits should be provided. We hold only that the Constitution does not require a judicially imposed resolution of these difficult issues."

Poelker v. Doe (432 U.S. 519), decided by a 6-3 vote, June 20, 1977. The opinion was unsigned (*per curiam*); Brennan, Marshall and Blackmun dissented.

A city does not act unconstitutionally when it chooses to provide publicly financed hospital services for childbirth but bars the use of its public hospitals for abortions.

Colautti v. Franklin (439 U.S. 379), decided by a 6-3 vote, Jan. 9, 1979. Blackmun wrote the opinion; Burger, White and Rehnquist dissented.

Pennsylvania interfered too much with a doctor's exercise of medical judgment regarding his patient when it, by state law, required physicians performing abortions to protect the life of the fetus whenever they had sufficient reason to believe that the fetus might be able to survive outside the mother's body. Physicians could be prosecuted for failing to comply with this requirement even in performing abortions before the seventh month of pregnancy, the usual point at which a fetus can survive.

Bellotti v. Baird, Hunerwald v. Baird (443 U.S. 622), decided by an 8-1 vote, July 2, 1979. Powell announced the decision in an opinion joined by Burger, Stewart and Rehnquist; Stevens, Brennan, Marshall and Blackmun concurred; White dissented.

A Massachusetts law requiring parental consent for an unmarried minor to have an abortion, and requiring judicial approval in the absence of parental consent, impermissibly burdens the individual's right to an abortion by requiring parental notification of any judicial proceeding concerning the minor's abortion decision and by allowing the judge, if he felt it was not in her best interest, to deny a mature and competent minor the right to have an abortion.

Harris v. McRae (448 U.S. 297), decided by a vote of 5-4, June 30, 1980. Stewart wrote the opinion; Brennan, Marshall, Blackmun and Stevens dissented.

Congress did not exceed its powers nor infringe upon the constitutional guarantees of due process, equal protection or free exercise of religion when it adopted the so-called Hyde amendment restricting federal funding of medically necessary abortions. The Hyde amendment, named for its sponsor, Rep. Henry J. Hyde, R-Ill., denies federal reimbursement for abortions under the Medicaid program except when the abortion is necessary to save the pregnant woman's life or to terminate a pregnancy caused by promptly reported rape or incest.

In addition, the court held that the Social Security Act authorizing the Medicaid program does not require states to pay for those medically necessary abortions for which federal reimbursement is unavailable because of the Hyde amendment.

Williams v. Zbaraz, Miller v. Zbaraz, United States v. Zbaraz (448 U.S. 358), decided by a vote of 5-4, June 30, 1980. Stewart wrote the opinion; Brennan, Marshall, Blackmun and Stevens dissented.

A state that adopts funding restrictions on abortions similar to those imposed by the federal Hyde amendment does not violate the 14th Amendment's equal protection guarantee by funding all other medically necessary procedures for Medicaid recipients while denying funds for medically necessary abortions.

H. L. v. Matheson (450 U.S. 398), decided by a 6-3 vote, March 23, 1981. Burger wrote the opinion; Marshall, Brennan and Blackmun dissented.

Utah law, which requires a doctor to notify the parents of a minor upon whom he is to perform an abortion, does not violate the minor's right of privacy in deciding whether to have the abortion, at least when it is applied, as in this case, to an immature minor who still is dependent upon her parents. The law does not allow the parents to veto the abortion decision; it simply requires that the parents be notified beforehand.

Consumers, Drivers, Parents, Families

Memphis Light, Gas & Water Division v. Craft (436 U.S. 1), decided by a vote of 6-3, May 1, 1978. Powell wrote the opinion; Stevens, Burger and Rehnquist dissented.

"[U]tility service is a necessity of modern life" and a state may not deprive someone of that service without due process of law. A municipally owned utility is required by the 14th Amendment to give customers full opportunity to resolve billing disputes before service is terminated.

Dixon v. Love (431 U.S. 105), decided by an 8-0 vote, May 16, 1977. Blackmun wrote the opinion; Rehnquist did not participate.

A state does not violate the constitutional guarantee of due process by authorizing the automatic suspension, based on "points" accumulated through traffic violations, of a driver's license.

Mackey v. Montrym (443 U.S. 1), decided by a 5-4 vote, June 25, 1979. Burger wrote the opinion; Stevens, Stewart, Brennan and Marshall dissented.

Massachusetts does not deny motorists due process of law when it automatically suspends for 90 days the driver's license of any driver who refuses to take a chemical or breath analysis test when arrested for drunken driving. A post-suspension hearing, at which the driver may dispute his alleged refusal, is sufficient to meet the requirements of due process; there need not be a hearing before his license is suspended.

Moore v. City of East Cleveland, Ohio (431 U.S. 494), decided by a 5-4 vote, May 31, 1977. Powell wrote the opinion; Burger, Stewart, Rehnquist and White dissented.

A city acts improperly when it enacts a housing ordinance that "slice[s] deeply into the family itself" by selecting certain categories of relatives who may live together and others who may not.

Santosky v. Kramer (*), decided by a 5-4 vote,

March 24, 1982. Blackmun wrote the opinion; Rehnquist, Burger, White and O'Connor dissented.

Natural parents have a right to due process at state proceedings on terminating their parental rights over their children. Parents have a fundamental liberty interest in the care, custody and management of their children, which they do not lose simply because they are not model parents. The interests involved in such a proceeding require that a state's contention that parents be unfit be proved by more than just a fair preponderance of the evidence.

Handicapped Persons

Board of Education of Hendrick Hudson Central School District v. Rowley (*), decided by a 6-3 vote, June 28, 1982. Rehnquist wrote the opinion; White, Brennan and Marshall dissented.

The Education for All Handicapped Children Act of 1975 obliges school districts receiving funds under the act to provide each handicapped student a free, appropriate public education. But it does not obligate the state to provide all the aid necessary to ensure that a handicapped student realizes his or her maximum potential. Instead, the law requires only that there be personal instruction accompanied by sufficient support services to permit the child to benefit educationally from that instruction.

Mentally Ill/Mentally Retarded Persons

O'Connor v. Donaldson (422 U.S. 563), decided by a 9-0 vote, June 26, 1975. Stewart wrote the opinion.

A state impermissibly deprives an individual of his liberty without due process of law when it confines him indefinitely without treatment simply because he is thought to be mentally ill — and despite the fact that he poses no danger to himself or others and is able to live safely outside an institution. "A finding of 'mental illness' alone cannot justify a state's locking a person up against his will and keeping him indefinitely in simple custodial confinement.... Mere public intolerance or animosity cannot constitutionally justify the deprivation of a person's physical liberty," wrote Stewart.

Addington v. Texas (441 U.S. 418), decided by a vote of 8-0, April 30, 1979. Burger wrote the opinion; Powell did not participate.

The court for the first time formally acknowledged that commitment to a mental institution is a deprivation of personal liberty that falls within the constitutional protection of due process.

The fact of mental illness and the need for commitment need not be proved beyond a reasonable doubt to justify an individual's involuntary civil commitment to a state mental hospital. But these elements must be proved by more than simply a preponderance of the evidence. The court suggested that an intermediate standard of proof was appropriate, such as proof by clear and convincing evidence.

Parham v. J. L. (442 U.S. 584), decided by votes of 9-0 and 6-3, June 20, 1979. Burger wrote the opinion; Brennan, Marshall and Stevens dissented in part.

A Georgia law authorizing a parent or guardian to commit a child to a state mental institution for treatment does not deny the child due process. Due process is satisfied in such cases if some kind of inquiry is made by a neutral factfinder, who may be a physician, to determine whether or not the requirements for commitment are fulfilled and if there is a periodic review of the children's continuing need for commitment. The inquiry concerning commitment need not be a formal hearing.

Pennhurst State School and Hospital v. Terri Lee Halderman, Mayor of City of Philadelphia v. Halderman, Pennsylvania Association for Retarded Citizens v. Pennhurst State School and Hospital, Commissioners and Mental Health/Mental Retardation Administrators for Bucks County v. Halderman, Pennhurst Parents-Staff Association v. Halderman (451 U.S. 1), decided by votes of 9-0 and 6-3, April 20, 1981. Rehnquist wrote the opinion; White, Brennan and Marshall dissented in part.

The Developmentally Disabled Assistance and Bill of Rights Act of 1975 (PL 94-103) did not grant to mentally retarded persons an enforceable right to be treated in the least restrictive situation. The statement in the law that persons have a right to receive treatment and housing in a setting "that is least restrictive of ... personal liberty" was a general "finding" by Congress — not an obligation imposed upon states receiving federal funds for treatment of the mentally retarded.

Youngberg v. Romeo (*), decided by a 9-0 vote, June 18, 1982. Powell wrote the opinion.

Mentally retarded persons in state institutions have a constitutional right to safe conditions, freedom of movement and sufficient training to enable them to move safely and freely within those institutions. The guarantee against deprivation of personal liberty without due process of law means that such persons can be restrained or allowed to remain in less than completely safe conditions only upon the decision of a qualified professional.

Students

Goss v. Lopez (419 U.S. 565), decided by a 5-4 vote, Jan. 22, 1975. White wrote the opinion; Powell, Burger, Blackmun and Rehnquist dissented.

Due process requires that school officials notify a public school student of charges against him, which might result in his suspension, and give him an opportunity to explain or rebut the charges before he is suspended or, if that is not feasible, as soon thereafter as practicable.

Once a state chooses to extend the right of a public education to students, it may not withdraw that right without following certain procedures to determine if suspension is justified.

Wood v. Strickland (420 U.S. 308), decided by a 5-4 vote, Feb. 25, 1975. White wrote the opinion; Powell, Burger, Blackmun and Rehnquist dissented.

School officials are not immune from civil rights damage suits brought by students for actions that the officials reasonably should have realized would violate the student's constitutional rights. The dissenting justices said the officials' liability should be limited to situations in which the challenged actions were unreasonable and taken in bad faith.

Ingraham v. Wright (430 U.S. 651), decided by a 5-4 vote, April 19, 1977. Powell wrote the opinion; White, Brennan, Marshall and Stevens dissented.

The Eighth Amendment ban on cruel and unusual punishment does not apply to corporal punishment in the public schools, but is limited to criminal law. The constitutional guarantee of due process does protect the liberty interest of a student, which is implicated in corporal punishment, but traditional common law remedies are sufficient to safeguard that interest. Prior notice and the opportunity for a hearing are not constitutionally required before a student is paddled.

Board of Curators of University of Missouri v. Horowitz (435 U.S. 78), decided by votes of 9-0 and 6-3, March 1, 1978. Rehnquist wrote the opinion; Blackmun, Marshall and Brennan dissented in part.

The constitutional guarantee of due process does not restrict the right of school officials to dismiss a student from school for poor academic performance. Due process does not require, in these circumstances, that the student be given a hearing at which he or she may contest the reasons for his or her dismissal.

Carey v. Piphus (435 U.S. 247), decided by a vote of 8-0, March 21, 1978. Powell wrote the opinion; Blackmun did not participate.

Students suspended for disciplinary reasons, without notice and a hearing as required in that circumstance by due process, may be awarded no more than nominal damages against school officials unless they are able to demonstrate that they suffered actual injury from the suspension.

Welfare Recipients

Shapiro v. Thompson*, *Washington v. Legrant*, *Reynolds v. Smith (394 U.S. 618), decided by a 6-3 vote, April 21, 1969. Brennan wrote the opinion; Warren, Black and Harlan dissented.

A state or federal requirement that persons must reside in a certain jurisdiction for one year before becoming eligible for welfare assistance violates individual rights to due process and equal protection of the laws; no compelling government interest was presented to justify this infringement of the right to travel, which includes the right to move from state to state.

Wheeler v. Montgomery*, *Goldberg v. Kelly (397 U.S. 254, 280) decided by 5-3 votes, March 23, 1970. Brennan wrote the opinion; Burger, Black and Stewart dissented.

Due process requires states to give welfare recipients whose eligibility is questioned an opportunity for a full hearing before terminating their welfare payments. The crucial factor in the situation, noted the court, was that "termination of aid pending resolution of a controversy over eligibility may deprive an eligible recipient of the very means by which to live."

Dandridge v. Williams (397 U.S. 471), decided by a 5-3 vote, April 6, 1970. Stewart wrote the opinion; Douglas, Brennan and Marshall dissented.

States do not violate federal law or the Constitution's equal protection guarantee by limiting the amount of welfare aid that one family may receive.

Lewis v. Martin (397 U.S. 552), decided by a 6-2 vote, April 20, 1970. Douglas wrote the opinion; Burger and Black dissented.

A state cannot reduce welfare aid to children because there is a man living in the same house unless he actually contributes to the support of the children. (This followed a 1968 ruling in the case of *King v. Smith* in which the court had invalidated a state regulation that terminated all welfare aid to children if a man was living in the same house.)

Wyman v. James (400 U.S. 309), decided by an 8-1 vote, Jan. 12, 1971. Blackmun wrote the opinion; Douglas dissented.

The constitutional protection against unreasonable searches does not invalidate state laws conditioning the granting of aid to dependent children on periodic, warrantless visits to the children's homes by caseworkers.

Memorial Hospital v. Maricopa County (415 U.S. 250), decided by an 8-1 vote, Feb. 26, 1974. Marshall wrote the opinion; Rehnquist dissented.

A state violates the equal protection guarantee by requiring that an indigent person live in a county for a year before he is eligible for free non-emergency medical care. A one-year requirement is not justified by any compelling state interest and impermissibly burdens the right of poor persons to move from state to state.

DECISIONS ON THE FIRST AMENDMENT

The broad sweep of the First Amendment guarantee of freedom of the press, freedom of religion, freedom of expression, and freedom of association was applied to a wide variety of situations by the court's decisions in the 1969-82 period. Among the issues brought before the court for First Amendment interpretation were court gag orders and libel suits; the "fairness" doctrine, dealing with the airing of controversial issues; flag desecration laws; the right to contribute to political election campaigns; the ever-present problems posed by the distribution of obscene material; and the efforts of many states to aid nonpublic church-related schools.

Freedom of the Press

Greenbelt Cooperative Publishing Assn. v. Bresler (398 U.S. 6), decided by an 8-0 vote, May 18, 1970. Stewart wrote the opinion.

The First Amendment guarantee of a free press protects newspapers against libel suits for accurate reporting of charges made against public figures. The fundamental meaning of a free press would be subverted if newspapers could be punished for publishing accurate, truthful reports of matters of public importance.

Monitor Patriot Co. v. Roy*, *Ocala Star-Banner Co. v. Damron (401 U.S. 265, 295), decided by 7-2 votes, Feb. 24, 1971. Stewart wrote the opinions; Black and Douglas dissented in part.

Any allegation of criminal activity, no matter how

remote, is relevant to the fitness of a candidate for office; therefore, unless such an allegation is printed with the knowledge that it is false or with actual malice, no libel judgment can be entered against a publication printing the charge.

Time Inc. v. Pape (401 U.S. 279), decided by a 8-1 vote, Feb. 24, 1971. Stewart wrote the opinion; Harlan dissented.

Mere omission of the word "alleged" from an article reporting a charge of police brutality does not show malice nor provide grounds for a libel judgment against the publisher of the article.

New York Times Co. v. U.S., *U.S. v. The Washington Post* (403 U.S. 713) decided by a 6-3 vote, June 30, 1971. The opinion was unsigned; each justice wrote a separate opinion expressing his views. Burger, Blackmun and Harlan dissented.

The government failed to show sufficient justification for its request for court orders barring publication — by *The New York Times* and *The Washington Post* — of articles based on classified documents, a multi-volume history of U.S. involvement in Indochina, popularly known as the Pentagon Papers.

Black, joined by Douglas, wrote: "I believe that every moment's continuance of the injunctions against these newspapers amounts to a flagrant, indefensible, and continuing violation of the First Amendment.... In my view, it is unfortunate that some of my brethren are apparently willing to hold that the publication of news may sometimes be enjoined. Such a holding would make a shambles of the First Amendment."

"The press was to serve the governed, not the governors. The government's power to censor the press was abolished so that the press would remain forever free to censure the government."

Marshall wrote: "The issue is whether this court or the Congress has the power to make law.... It would ... be utterly inconsistent with the concept of separation of power for this court to use its power of contempt to prevent behavior that Congress has specifically declined to prohibit.... The Constitution provides that Congress shall make laws, the President execute laws and courts interpret law.... It did not provide for government by injunction in which the courts and the executive can 'make law' without regard to the action of Congress."

White, joined by Stewart, wrote: "I concur ... but only because of the concededly extraordinary protection against prior restraints enjoyed by the press under our constitutional system. I do not say that in no circumstances would the First Amendment permit an injunction against publishing information about government plans or operations.... But ... the United States has not satisfied the very heavy burden which it must meet to warrant an injunction against publication in these cases."

And Stewart, joined by White, said: "The only effective restraint upon executive policy and power in the areas of national defense and international affairs may lie in an enlightened citizenry.... Without an informed and free press there cannot be an enlightened people."

Brennan wrote: "The error which has pervaded these cases from the outset was the granting of any injunctive relief whatsoever, interim or otherwise.... The First Amendment tolerates absolutely no prior judicial restraints of the press predicated upon surmise or conjecture that untoward consequences may result."

Douglas, joined by Black, wrote: "The dominant purpose of the First Amendment was to prohibit the widespread practice of government suppression of embarrassing information.... The First Amendment was adopted against the widespread use of the common law of seditious libel to punish the dissemination of material that is embarrassing to the powers-that-be.... The present cases will, I think, go down in history as the most dramatic example of that principle.... Secrecy in government is fundamentally antidemocratic, perpetuating bureaucratic errors."

In dissent, Harlan, joined by Burger and Blackmun, declared: "The Court has been almost irresponsibly feverish in dealing with these cases.... The scope of the judicial function in passing upon the activities of the executive branch of the government in the field of foreign affairs is very narrowly restricted."

Blackmun said: "The First Amendment, after all, is only one part of an entire Constitution. Article II ... vests in the executive branch primary power over the conduct of foreign affairs....

"Each provision ... is important and I cannot subscribe to a doctrine of unlimited absolutism for the First Amendment at the cost of downgrading other provisions."

Burger said: "To me it is hardly believable that a newspaper long regarded as a great institution in American life would fail to perform one of the basic and simple duties of every citizen with respect to the discovery or possession of stolen property or secret government documents. That duty, I had thought — perhaps naively — was to report forthwith, to responsible public officers. This duty rests on taxi drivers, justices and *The New York Times*."

Branzburg v. Hayes, *In re Pappas*, *U.S. v. Caldwell* (408 U.S. 665), decided by a 5-4 vote, June 29, 1972. White wrote the opinion; Douglas, Brennan, Stewart and Marshall dissented.

The Constitution's freedom of the press guarantee does not give newsmen a privilege to refuse — without risking contempt charges — to provide information to grand juries concerning a crime or the sources of evidence concerning a crime. White wrote that the court majority saw no basis "for holding that the public interest in law enforcement and in ensuring effective grand jury proceed-

Freedom of Religion, Speech and Press

Congress shall make no law respecting an establishment of religion, or prohibiting the free exercise thereof; or abridging the freedom of speech, or of the press; or the right of the people peaceably to assemble, and to petition the Government for a redress of grievances.

—First Amendment to the U.S. Constitution

ings is insufficient to override the consequential but uncertain burden on newsgathering which is said to result from insisting that reporters, like other citizens, respond to relevant questions put to them in the course of a valid grand jury investigation or criminal trial."

Miami Herald Publishing Co. v. Tornillo (418 U.S. 241), decided by a 9-0 vote, June 25, 1974. Burger wrote the opinion.

The First Amendment guarantee of freedom of the press is violated by a state right-of-reply law requiring that newspapers print, free of charge, the replies of candidates to articles or editorials in the newspaper critical of the candidates. The First Amendment forbids a state to dictate to a newspaper what it must print, just as it forbids a state to tell a newspaper what it may not print.

Gertz v. Welch Inc. (418 U.S. 323), decided by a 5-4 vote, June 25, 1974. Powell wrote the opinion; Burger, White, Douglas and Brennan dissented.

Private citizens involved in matters of general public interest who sue a publication for libel do not have to prove that there was actual malice on the part of the publication, as *New York Times v. Sullivan* (1964) requires of public officials. States retain substantial latitude in providing private citizens with remedies for defamation; they may allow damage awards in such cases, but such awards may exceed actual damages only when some evidence of negligence or fault on the part of the publisher is demonstrated.

Cox Broadcasting Corp. v. Cohn (420 U.S. 469), decided by an 8-1 vote, March 3, 1975. White wrote the opinion; Rehnquist dissented.

A state cannot penalize a reporter, newspaper, radio or television broadcaster for accurately reporting the name of a rape victim taken from public records. The court struck down a Georgia law forbidding publication of the name of a rape victim. "The First and Fourteenth Amendment command nothing less than that the states may not impose sanctions for the publication of truthful information contained in official court records open to public inspection."

Time, Inc. v. Firestone (424 U.S. 448), decided by a 5-3 vote, March 2, 1976. Rehnquist wrote the opinion; Stevens did not participate; White, Brennan and Marshall dissented.

Involvement in a sensational court case does not alone transform a private citizen into a public figure for the purpose of libel law. Therefore, a citizen, in bringing a libel suit charging a magazine with an inaccurate and libelous report of the suit, need not prove actual malice by the publication in order to be awarded damages, but the citizen must prove that the publication was negligent or otherwise at fault in printing the inaccurate report.

Nebraska Press Association v. Stuart (427 U.S. 539), decided by a 9-0 vote, June 30, 1976. Burger wrote the opinion.

A gag order limiting severely what the press could report about pre-trial proceedings in a mass murder case in Nebraska violated the First Amendment's free press guarantee. If ever permissible, this sort of prior restraint of publication can be justified only by the most extreme circumstances. In more usual situations, judges concerned about preserving a defendant's right to a fair trial by an unbiased jury have many, less drastic, means of ensuring

that the potential jurors are not prejudiced by publicity. "Pretrial publicity — even pervasive, adverse publicity — does not inevitably lead to an unfair trial," wrote Burger.

Burger, Blackmun, Powell and Rehnquist confined their votes in this case to the facts at hand, leaving open the possibility that gag orders might be constitutional in certain circumstances. Brennan, Stewart and Marshall said they would rule more broadly that such orders were never justified. Stevens and White indicated their inclination to accept the broader view.

Zacchini v. Scripps-Howard Broadcasting Co. (433 U.S. 562), decided by a 5-4 vote, June 28, 1977. White wrote the opinion; Brennan, Powell, Marshall and Stevens dissented.

The First Amendment does not immunize the news media from damage suits brought by performers whose entire acts have been broadcast, as part of a news show, over the performer's objection. "The Constitution," wrote White, "no more prevents a state from requiring respondent to compensate petitioner for broadcasting his act on television than it would privilege respondent to film and broadcast a copyrighted dramatic work without liability to the copyright owner...."

Landmark Communications Inc. v. Virginia (435 U.S. 829), decided by a vote of 7-0, May 1, 1978. Burger wrote the opinion; Brennan and Powell did not participate.

The First Amendment prohibits a state from penalizing a newspaper for printing a truthful and accurate report of state commission proceedings, which by state law are required to remain confidential, concerning the possible disciplining of a sitting state judge. "Whatever differences may exist about interpretations of the First Amendment, there is practically universal agreement that a major purpose of that amendment was to protect the free discussion of government affairs."

Federal Communications Commission (FCC) v. National Citizens Committee for Broadcasting (NCCB), Channel Two Television Co. v. NCCB, National Association of Broadcasters v. FCC, American Newspaper Publishers Assn. v. NCCB, Illinois Broadcasting Co. v. NCCB, The Post Co. v. NCCB (436 U.S. 775), decided by a vote of 8-0, June 12, 1978. Marshall wrote the opinion; Brennan did not participate.

The Federal Communications Commission (FCC) did not exceed its authority, nor did it infringe upon First Amendment rights, by ordering a halt to future formations of jointly owned newspaper/broadcasting station combinations in the same community, and by requiring divestiture of such combinations when they involved joint ownership of the only newspaper and only broadcast outlet in a community — unless continued existence of that monopoly was shown to be in the public interest.

Houchins v. KQED Inc. (438 U.S. 1), decided by a vote of 4-3, June 26, 1978. Burger wrote the opinion; Marshall and Blackmun did not take part in the case; Stevens, Brennan and Powell dissented.

A federal district court erred in ordering a sheriff to grant the news media greater access to a county jail facility than was granted to the public at large. "Neither the First Amendment nor 14th Amendment mandates a right of access to government information or sources of information within the government's control."

Herbert v. Lando (441 U.S. 153), decided by a 6-3 vote, April 18, 1979. White wrote the opinion; Marshall, Stewart and Brennan dissented.

The First Amendment does not protect the editorial process — the pre-publication thoughts, conclusions and conversations of editors and reporters — from scrutiny by those who charge that they were libeled by the broadcast or article that resulted.

The court rejected the media's argument that such questioning curtailed the protected freedom of the press. To the contrary, wrote Justice White, the landmark libel holding in *New York Times v. Sullivan* (1964), which gave the press constitutional protection from libel suits by public figures, requires such inquiry to ascertain whether or not a libelous publication was the result of "actual malice."

Smith v. Daily Mail Publishing Co. (443 U.S. 97), decided by a vote of 8-0, June 26, 1979. Burger wrote the court's opinion; Powell did not participate.

A state may not make it a crime for a newspaper to violate a requirement that it obtain prior judicial approval before publishing the name of a child involved in juvenile court proceedings. The First Amendment guarantee of freedom of the press forbids the imposition of a criminal penalty for the publication of truthful information in the public domain.

Wolston v. Reader's Digest Assn. Inc. (443 U.S. 157), decided by a vote of 8-1, June 26, 1979. Rehnquist wrote the opinion; Brennan dissented.

An individual whose only publicity involved a contempt conviction resulting from his failure to appear before a grand jury investigating espionage is not a public figure within the meaning of *New York Times v. Sullivan* (1964), and thus, when suing for libel, is not required to prove actual malice in order to recover damages.

Freedom of Expression

Tinker v. Des Moines Independent Community School District (393 U.S. 503), decided by a 7-2 vote, Feb. 24, 1969. Fortas wrote the opinion; Harlan and Black dissented.

Students have the right to engage in peaceful nondisruptive protest. The wearing of black armbands to protest the Vietnam War was "closely akin" to the "pure speech" protected by the First Amendment, and therefore a public school ban on this form of protest — which did not disrupt the school's work or offend the rights of others — violated these students' rights. "In the absence of a specific showing of constitutionally valid reasons to regulate their speech, students are entitled to freedom of expression of their views."

Street v. New York (394 U.S. 576), decided by a 5-4 vote, April 21, 1969. Harlan wrote the opinion; Warren, Fortas, White and Black dissented.

A state law making it a crime to "cast contempt" upon the American flag by words or acts is unconstitutional in allowing persons to be punished merely for speaking derogatory words about the flag.

Brandenburg v. Ohio (395 U.S. 444), decided by an 8-0 vote, June 9, 1969. Unsigned opinion.

A state law making it a crime to advocate violence or terrorism as a mode of reform or to meet with any group formed to advocate such ideas is an unconstitutional violation of the freedoms of speech and association.

Any law, the court held, that does not make the distinction between "mere abstract teaching" of the need for the use of force and violence and the actual preparation by a group for such violent action, impermissibly intrudes upon individual freedom and condemns constitutionally protected speech.

Red Lion Broadcasting Co. v. Federal Communications Commission and *U.S. v. Radio Television News Directors Assn.* (395 U.S. 367), decided by a 7-0 vote, June 9, 1969. White wrote the opinion; Douglas did not take part.

The court held that the general public's right to fair treatment of all aspects of important issues by news media required broadcasters to comply with the fairness doctrine set forth by the Federal Communications Commission (FCC). Therefore, the court ruled that broadcasters must continue to provide free time for persons to reply to broadcasts of political editorials or endorsements.

The right of broadcasters to free speech must be balanced with the right of the people as a whole to free speech and their "collective right to have the medium function consistently with the ends and purposes of the First Amendment." This right — of viewers and listeners — was paramount, the court held.

Schacht v. U.S. (398 U.S. 58), decided by an 8-0 vote, May 25, 1970. Black wrote the opinion.

Actors as well as other citizens have the right openly to criticize the government, the court ruled, thus invalidating a law that made it a crime for an actor to wear an official military uniform in a production that reflected unfavorably on the U.S. armed forces.

Columbia Broadcasting System, Inc. v. Democratic National Committee, American Broadcasting Companies, Inc. v. Democratic National Committee, Federal Communications Commission v. Business Executives' Move for Vietnam Peace, Post-Newsweek Stations, Inc. v. Business Executives' Move for Vietnam Peace (412 U.S. 94), decided by a 7-2 vote, May 29, 1973. Burger wrote the opinion; Brennan and Marshall dissented.

Neither the First Amendment nor the FCC's "fairness doctrine" requires broadcasters to accept paid editorial advertisements from individuals and groups who wish to expound their views on public issues across the airwaves. The majority, without Douglas, found that such a requirement might work contrary to the public interest in a fair presentation of the news; Douglas held that the First Amendment required that the government, in this case the FCC, keep its hands off the press and not require it to print or broadcast anything in particular. Brennan and Marshall dissented, seeing this refusal by broadcasters as a restriction on the right of free speech, a restriction that the government was approving in violation of the First Amendment.

Procunier v. Martinez (416 U.S. 396), decided by a 9-0 vote, April 29, 1974. Powell wrote the opinion.

State prison officials violate the First Amendment freedom of expression of inmates and persons with whom they wish to communicate by restrictive rules allowing broad censorship of letters to and from inmates and forbidding interviews between prisoners and law students or legal paraprofessionals working with lawyers representing inmates.

Federal courts traditionally have avoided the issues raised by prison regulations, recognizing that the problems of prisons are complex and not easily resolved by a court decree, explained Powell. But when a regulation offends a fundamental constitutional guarantee, it is the duty of the federal courts to intervene, as in this case, to protect constitutional rights.

Pell v. Procunier*, *Procunier v. Hillery (417 U.S. 817), ***Saxbe v. The Washington Post Co.*** (417 U.S. 843), decided by votes of 6-3 and 5-4, June 24, 1974. Stewart wrote the opinion; Brennan, Marshall and Douglas dissented; Powell dissented in part.

Prison regulations barring face-to-face interviews by newsmen with inmates whom they request by name to see do not violate the inmate's First Amendment right to free speech, which may legitimately be constrained by certain considerations of the penal system, such as security and discipline, the court held, on a 6-3 vote.

These regulations also do not violate the First Amendment rights of newsmen to freedom of the press, the court held, 5-4, with Powell joining the dissenters on this point. "Newsmen have no constitutional right of access to prisons or their inmates beyond that afforded the general public." The First Amendment does not require the government to give the press special access to information not generally available.

Spence v. Washington (418 U.S. 405), decided by a 6-3 vote, June 25, 1974. The opinion was unsigned; Burger, Rehnquist and White dissented.

A state law penalizing improper use of the American flag was applied, in violation of the First Amendment, to convict a Washington college student for displaying his flag with a large peace symbol, made of removable tape, imposed upon it. Because the purpose of this display was to express his thoughts in a peaceful way and because he had not damaged, desecrated, or disrespectfully used the flag, the Supreme Court reversed the student's conviction. The state asserted no interest in penalizing such action that was compelling enough to override the student's First Amendment freedom of expression, the court held.

Bigelow v. Virginia (421 U.S. 809), decided by a 7-2 vote, June 16, 1975. Blackmun wrote the opinion; Rehnquist and White dissented.

Commercial advertising enjoys some First Amendment protections. *Valentine v. Chrestensen* (1942) held that the manner in which such ads are distributed was subject to regulation, not that advertising itself was unprotected.

The court, in its 1975 ruling, reversed the conviction of a newspaper editor in Virginia for violating a state law against "encouraging" abortions by running an advertisement that included information on legal abortions available in New York. The law was an improper effort by the state to control what its citizens could hear or read, the court held.

Buckley v. Valeo (424 U.S. 1), decided by votes of 8-0, 7-1, and 6-2, Jan. 31, 1976. The opinion was unsigned; Stevens did not participate; Burger, Blackmun, Rehnquist, White and Marshall all dissented in part.

The First Amendment guarantee of freedom of expression requires invalidation of the limits placed by the 1974 Federal Election Campaign Act Amendments on the amounts that a candidate for federal office can spend. The vote was 7-1; White dissented. The majority, however, did find these limits permissible for candidates who accepted public financing of their campaigns for the presidency. But otherwise, the court held that "a restriction on the amount of money a person or group can spend on political communications during a campaign necessarily reduces the quantity of expression by restricting the number of issues discussed, the depth of their exploration, and the size of the audience reached."

The court, with Marshall dissenting, also struck down the law's limits on the amount of one's own money that a candidate can spend.

The court upheld, 6-2, the limits that the law placed on the amount individuals and political committees can contribute to candidates. This was only a marginal restriction on a contributor's First Amendment freedom, the majority held. Burger and Blackmun dissented.

The court upheld, 6-2, the system of public financing set up by the law for presidential campaigns and elections. Burger and Rehnquist dissented.

The court upheld the law's requirements for public disclosure of campaign contributions of more than $100 and campaign expenditures of more than $10. The vote was 7-1. Burger dissented.

The court unanimously agreed that the Federal Election Commission, as set up by the 1974 law, was unconstitutional because it violated the separation of powers. Four of the members of the commission were appointed by the leadership of Congress and two by the president, yet the commission had executive powers. The court held that the commission could properly exercise only the investigative and informational activities of a congressional committee so long as it was, in part, appointed by Congress. Only if it were presidentially appointed in its entirety could it carry out the executive, administrative and enforcement functions it was originally given under the law, the court ruled. *(Excerpts of opinion, p. 148)*

Hudgens v. National Labor Relations Board (424 U.S. 507), decided by a 6-2 vote, March 2, 1976. Stewart wrote the opinion; Stevens did not participate; Marshall and Brennan dissented.

The First Amendment bars government actions that abridge free speech; only in very unusual circumstances does it apply to private actions curtailing free expression. The First Amendment therefore provides no basis for a challenge to a ban on labor picketing within a privately owned shopping mall. Persons bringing such a challenge must base it, instead, on federal labor law. The court overruled *Food Employees Local 590 v. Logan Valley Plaza Inc.* (391 U.S. 308, 1968), which extended some First Amendment protections to labor pickets at a privately owned shopping center.

Greer v. Spock (424 U.S. 828), decided by a 6-2 vote, March 24, 1976. Stewart wrote the opinion; Stevens did not participate; Brennan and Marshall dissented.

The First Amendment does not prohibit a military base commander from barring from the base all political speeches and demonstrations and from limiting literature distributed on the base to that which he approves. Such a ban, evenhandedly applied, insulates the military from the reality and the appearance of "acting as a handmaiden for partisan political causes or candidates ... a policy wholly consistent with the American constitutional tradition of a politically neutral military establishment...."

Virginia State Board of Pharmacy v. Virginia Citizens Consumer Council, Inc. (425 U.S. 748), decided by a 7-1 vote, May 24, 1976. Blackmun wrote the opinion; Stevens did not participate; Rehnquist dissented.

The First Amendment extends some protection to commercial speech. The court struck down a state law that forbade the advertising of prices of prescription drugs and upheld a lower court ruling setting forth a consumer's First Amendment right to receive such information. "So long as we preserve a predominantly free enterprise economy, the allocation of our resources in large measure will be made through numerous private economic decisions. It is a matter of public interest that those decisions ... be intelligent and well-informed. To this end, the free flow of commercial information is indispensible," wrote Blackmun.

Wooley v. Maynard (430 U.S. 705), decided by a 6-3 vote, April 20, 1977. Burger wrote the opinion; Rehnquist, Blackmun and White dissented.

A state may not require an individual to take part in spreading an ideological message by displaying it on his car as part of his license plate; a state may not therefore penalize a person for obscuring or removing an ideological state motto from his license plate. "The right of freedom of thought protected by the First Amendment against state action includes both the right to speak freely and the right to refrain from speaking at all," wrote Burger.

Linmark Associates Inc. v. Township of Willingboro (431 U.S. 85), decided by an 8-0 vote, May 2, 1977. Marshall wrote the opinion; Rehnquist did not participate.

A town ban on the use of "for sale" signs on residential property impairs the "flow of truthful and legitimate commercial information" and thus violates the First Amendment guarantee of free speech.

Carey v. Population Services International (431 U.S. 678), decided by a 7-2 vote, June 9, 1977. Brennan wrote the opinion; Burger and Rehnquist dissented.

The right of privacy, including the freedom to make decisions about childbearing, is impermissibly burdened by a New York law forbidding anyone but licensed pharmacists to sell non-medical contraceptives and barring the distribution of contraceptives to any person under age 16. That law's ban on advertising of contraceptives is an unconstitutional infringement of First Amendment rights.

Bates v. Arizona State Bar (433 U.S. 350), decided by a vote of 5-4, June 27, 1977. Blackmun wrote the opinion; Burger, Powell, Rehnquist and Stewart dissented.

The First Amendment freedom of expression is impermissibly infringed by state bans on newspaper advertising by attorneys describing routine legal services they perform and the fees they charge for those services.

First National Bank of Boston v. Bellotti (435 U.S. 765), decided by a vote of 5-4, April 26, 1978. Powell wrote the opinion; White, Brennan, Marshall and Rehnquist dissented.

A state law banning corporate expenditures relative to referendum issues that do not materially affect the corporation's business impermissibly abridges political speech protected by the First Amendment. "If the speakers here were not corporations, no one would suggest that the state could silence their proposed speech. It is the type of speech [that is] indispensable to decision making in a democracy, and this is no less true because the speech comes from a corporation rather than an individual."

Federal Communications Commission v. Pacifica Foundation (438 U.S. 726), decided by a vote of 5-4, July 3, 1978. Stevens wrote the opinion; Brennan, Marshall, Stewart and White dissented.

The Federal Communications Commission (FCC) violates neither the First Amendment guarantee of free speech nor the Federal Communications Act by regulating the time of broadcasts of material that is offensive and indecent, yet not obscene.

Givhan v. Western Line Consolidated School District (439 U.S. 410), decided by a 9-0 vote, Jan. 9, 1979. Rehnquist wrote the opinion.

The First Amendment guarantee of free speech protects schoolteachers and other public employees from being fired for criticizing public policy in private conversations. The First Amendment protects private remarks as well as public speeches.

Village of Schaumberg v. Citizens for a Better Environment (444 U.S. 620), decided by a 8-1 vote, Feb. 20, 1980. White wrote the opinion; Rehnquist dissented.

Door-to-door fund-raising efforts by public interest groups fall within the protection of the First Amendment's guarantee of free speech.

The court struck down an ordinance adopted by a Chicago suburb that denied the right to solicit funds within the village to groups that spent more than 25 percent of the money they collected on internal costs rather than on charitable purposes. The court recognized that the village had a legitimate interest in protecting its citizens from fraud, crime and undue annoyance, but found that the 25 percent rule was only indirectly related to those interests and was an undue infringement upon freedom of speech.

Consolidated Edison of New York v. Public Service Commission of New York (447 U.S. 530), decided by a vote of 7-2, June 20, 1980. Powell wrote the opinion; Blackmun and Rehnquist dissented.

A state commission abridges the First Amendment guarantee of free speech when it forbids a utility company to send out statements of its views on controversial matters of public policy as inserts in customers' bills.

Central Hudson Gas & Electric Co. v. Public Service Commission of New York (447 U.S. 557), decided by a vote of 8-1, June 20, 1980. Powell wrote the opinion; Rehnquist dissented.

A state commission violates the First Amendment guarantee of free speech when it bans all promotional advertising by electric utilities. Such a ban is too broad, barring more than is necessary to carry out the state's legitimate interest in conserving energy.

Haig v. Agee (453 U.S. 280), decided by a 7-2 vote, June 29, 1981. Burger wrote the opinion; Brennan and

Marshall dissented.

Congress, in passing the Passport Act of 1926 authorizing the secretary of state to grant and issue passports, authorized the secretary also to revoke a citizen's passport. If the secretary may deny an application for a passport, he may revoke a passport for the same reasons.

Revocation of the passport in this case did not violate the freedom to travel outside the United States, the First Amendment freedom of expression of the person losing his passport or the guarantee of due process.

Metromedia Inc. v. City of San Diego (453 U.S. 490), decided by a 6-3 vote, July 2, 1981. White wrote an opinion joined by three other justices; Brennan and Blackmun concurred; Stevens dissented in part; Burger and Rehnquist dissented in part.

San Diego violated the First Amendment guarantee of freedom of expression when it enacted an ordinance banning most billboards within the city.

Citizens Against Rent Control/Coalition for Fair Housing v. City of Berkeley (*), decided by an 8-1 vote, Dec. 14, 1981. Burger wrote the opinion; White dissented.

Citizens have a First Amendment right to contribute as much as they wish to groups opposing or supporting ballot issues; that right is violated when a city limits such contributions to $250 each. Such a limit infringes upon the First Amendment guarantees of freedom of expression and the right of association. "Contributions by individuals to support concerted action by a committee advocating a position on a ballot measure is beyond question a very significant form of political expression," stated the court.

In re R.M.J. (*), decided by a 9-0 vote, Jan. 25, 1982. Powell wrote the opinion.

State rules governing advertising by attorneys may regulate such speech only to the extent necessary to prevent deceptive or misleading ads.

Missouri infringed too far upon the First Amendment guarantee of freedom of expression when it restricted the categories of information that could be provided in lawyers' ads and specified the phrases to be used to describe areas of legal practice.

Board of Education, Island Trees Union Free School District #26 v. Pico (*), decided by a 5-4 vote, June 25, 1982. Brennan announced the court's decision in an opinion joined by three other justices; White concurred in the decision; Burger, Powell, Rehnquist and O'Connor dissented.

The decision of a local school board to remove certain books from high school and junior high school libraries is subject to certain restrictions imposed by the First Amendment guarantee of freedom of ideas and expression. The court sent back for trial a case in which several students challenged such school board action. The justices directed the trial court to ascertain whether the board had acted to remove unpopular ideas from the library, which would be impermissible under the First Amendment, or to remove vulgar and irrelevant material from the library, which would be permissible.

National Association for the Advancement of Colored People v. Claiborne Hardware Co. (*), decided by an 8-0 vote, July 2, 1982. Stevens wrote the opinion; Marshall did not participate in the decision.

A non-violent civil rights boycott in 1966 of shops of white merchants in Port Gibson, Miss., was speech and conduct protected by the First Amendment. Violence, however, is not protected by the First Amendment, and a state court may assess damages against those responsible for such violence. But such liability must be based on a record that reflects the individuals' participation in violent activity; it may not be lodged against individuals or a group simply on the basis of association.

Freedom of Religion

Epperson v. Arkansas (393 U.S. 97), decided by a 9-0 vote, Nov. 12, 1968. Fortas wrote the opinion.

A state "monkey law" forbidding public school teaching of the Darwinian theory of evolution violates the First Amendment ban on establishment of religion and its guarantee of freedom of religion. "The First Amendment mandates governmental neutrality between religion and religion and between religion and nonreligion."

Walz v. Tax Commission of the City of New York (397 U.S. 664), decided by a 7-1 vote, May 4, 1970. Burger wrote the opinion; Douglas dissented.

Property tax exemption for church-owned land used solely for religious purposes does not violate the First Amendment guarantee against establishment of religion as applied to the states by the 14th Amendment. Such exemptions are evidence only of the state's "benevolent neutrality" toward religion, held the court.

Tilton v. Richardson (403 U.S. 672), decided by a 5-4 vote, June 28, 1971. Burger wrote the opinion; Douglas, Black, Marshall and Brennan dissented.

The Higher Education Facilities Act of 1963 — under which federal grants are provided for construction of buildings by colleges and universities, regardless of their religious affiliation, so long as the buildings are used exclusively for secular educational purposes — does not violate the First Amendment. The First Amendment does invalidate a provision of that law limiting to 20 years the restriction on use of the facility to secular education purposes.

Lemon v. Kurtzman (403 U.S. 602), decided by an 8-0 vote, June 28, 1971. Burger wrote the opinion; Marshall did not participate.

The First Amendment invalidates state laws authorizing state reimbursement to nonpublic schools of the costs of teachers' salaries, textbooks and instructional materials in secular subjects; the First Amendment invalidates state laws authorizing supplementary salary grants to nonpublic school teachers of secular subjects; such laws foster excessive entanglement between government and religion.

Wisconsin v. Yoder (406 U.S. 205), decided by a 6-1 vote, May 15, 1972. Burger wrote the opinion; Powell and Rehnquist did not participate; Douglas dissented.

The First Amendment guarantee of freedom of religion prohibits the application of a state's compulsory education law for children under 16 of the Amish sect, "whose long-established, self-sufficient agrarian lifestyle is essential to their religious faith" and is threatened by the exposure of their children to modern educational influences.

Committee for Public Education and Religious

Liberty v. Nyquist (413 U.S. 756), decided by votes of 8-1 and 6-3, June 25, 1973. Powell wrote the opinion; White dissented; Burger and Rehnquist dissented in part.

The First Amendment ban on government action "establishing" religion requires invalidation of a New York law providing state grants to nonpublic schools for maintenance and repair, state reimbursement of tuition for low-income parents with children in nonpublic schools and state tax credits for other parents with children in nonpublic schools. The vote was 8-1 on the maintenance grants, with White dissenting. The vote on the tuition reimbursement and tax credit provisions was 6-3; White in dissent was joined by Burger and Rehnquist.

Powell explained the test against which such state aid programs must be measured: "To pass muster under the Establishment Clause, the law in question, first, must reflect a clearly secular legislative purpose ... second, must have a primary effect that neither advances nor inhibits religion ... and, third, must avoid excessive government entanglement with religion." The repair grants failed the second part of this test; they could possibly be used for work on religious facilities and thus advance the religious purposes of sectarian schools. The tax and tuition reimbursement provisions failed the third part of the test; they encouraged an entangling relationship between church and state.

Sloan v. Lemon (413 U.S. 825), decided by a 6-3 vote, June 25, 1973. Powell wrote the opinion; White, Burger and Rehnquist dissented.

The First Amendment ban on government action "establishing" religion requires invalidation of a Pennsylvania law providing for state reimbursement of tuition to all parents who paid to send their children to private schools.

Levitt v. Committee for Public Education and Religious Liberty (413 U.S. 472), decided by an 8-1 vote, June 25, 1973. Burger wrote the opinion; White dissented.

The First Amendment ban on government action "establishing" religion requires invalidation of a New York law providing for state reimbursement to nonpublic schools for the costs of record-keeping and testing services that the state required them to perform.

Hunt v. McNair (413 U.S. 734), decided by a 6-3 vote, June 25, 1973. Powell wrote the opinion; Brennan, Douglas and Marshall dissented.

The First Amendment ban on government "establishment" of religion is not infringed by a state law allowing the state to issue revenue bonds that would be used to finance construction of secular facilities at colleges and universities within the state, including some church-related colleges.

Wheeler v. Barrera (417 U.S. 402), decided by an 8-1 vote, June 10, 1974. Blackmun wrote the opinion; Douglas dissented.

Title I of the 1965 Elementary and Secondary Education Act requires that comparable, but not necessarily identical, federally funded services be provided to educationally disadvantaged students in both public and parochial schools.

Meek v. Pittinger (421 U.S. 349), decided by varying 6-3 votes, May 19, 1975. Stewart wrote the opinion; Brennan, Douglas and Marshall dissented in part; Burger,

Rehnquist and White dissented in part.

The First Amendment ban on establishment of religion is violated by a Pennsylvania law allowing direct loans of instructional equipment to nonpublic schools and by allowing auxiliary staff and services to be used in nonpublic schools. Under the test set out in the 1973 *Nyquist* decision *(left column),* these forms of aid are improper because they have the primary effect of advancing religion — 75 percent of the schools aided were religiously affiliated — and because the need to monitor them would result in excessive entanglement of the state government with the schools. Burger, Rehnquist and White dissented.

The First Amendment is not violated by a state program of loaning textbooks to students from public and nonpublic schools. This aid benefited children, not schools, the court majority said. Brennan, Marshall and Douglas dissented.

Roemer v. Maryland Board of Public Works (426 U.S. 736), decided by a 5-4 vote, June 21, 1976. Blackmun announced the decision in an opinion joined by Burger and Powell; White and Rehnquist concurred in the ruling; Brennan, Marshall, Stewart and Stevens dissented.

Maryland's program of general grants to private colleges, including church-related colleges, does not offend the First Amendment ban on establishment of religion because the aid is given on the condition that it not be used for sectarian purposes.

The First Amendment does not require a "hermetic separation" of church and state, but only neutrality by the state toward church-related and non-church-related institutions. "Religious institutions need not be quarantined from public benefits that are neutrally available to all," wrote Blackmun. This form of state aid is neutral, just as federal grants to private colleges for building academic facilities were found to be neutral by the court in 1971 *(Tilton v. Richardson,* 403 U.S. 672; see p. 123)

Wolman v. Walter (433 U.S. 229), decided by votes of 8-1, 7-2, 6-3, 5-4, June 24, 1977. Blackmun wrote the opinion; Brennan, Marshall, Burger, White, Rehnquist, Powell and Stevens dissented in part.

Under the First Amendment ban on establishment of religion, the court struck down the portion of an Ohio law that provided for state loans of instructional material and equipment to pupils at nonpublic sectarian schools and to their parents, as well as the portion of the law that provided state-funded transportation for field trips for classes at nonpublic sectarian schools. Burger, White and Rehnquist dissented on both these holdings; Powell joined the dissenters on the issue of field trip transportation.

The court upheld, as not in conflict with the First Amendment ban, other provisions of the Ohio law allowing 1) the loan of textbooks to pupils at nonpublic schools, 2) the state's practice of providing testing and scoring services to nonpublic schools for standardized tests used in public schools, 3) the state's practice of providing diagnostic speech, hearing and psychological services in nonpublic schools, and 4) its practice of providing therapeutic, guidance and remedial services on a neutral site to pupils at nonpublic schools. Brennan dissented on all these points; Marshall dissented on all except the diagnostic services section; and Stevens dissented from the majority decision upholding the loan of books and the provision of testing services.

Committee for Public Education and Religious Liberty v. Regan (444 U.S. 646), decided by a 5-4 vote, Feb. 20, 1980. White wrote the opinion; Blackmun, Brennan, Marshall and Stevens dissented.

A state does not violate the First Amendment ban on establishment of religion when it reimburses church-related schools for the cost of administering, grading and reporting the results of certain standardized tests, or for the cost of reporting pupil attendance and other basic educational data required by the state.

The court pointed out that the tests for which the schools were reimbursed were prepared by the state, not by the teachers at the parochial schools.

Thomas v. Review Board of the Indiana Employment Security Division (450 U.S. 707), decided by an 8-1 vote, April 6, 1981. Burger wrote the opinion; Rehnquist dissented.

Indiana impermissibly burdened the right to free exercise of one's religion when it denied unemployment compensation benefits to a man who quit his job because his religious beliefs forbade his participation in the production of weapons.

St. Martin Evangelical Lutheran Church and Northwestern Lutheran Academy v. State of South Dakota (451 U.S. 772), decided by a 9-0 vote, May 26, 1981. Blackmun wrote the opinion.

Elementary and secondary schools that are controlled by a church, and are not separate legal entities, are exempt from the requirements that employers pay federal and state unemployment taxes.

Heffron v. International Society for Krishna Consciousness (452 U.S. 640), decided by votes of 5-4 and 9-0, June 22, 1981. White wrote the opinion; Brennan, Marshall, Stevens and Blackmun dissented in part.

Minnesota did not abridge the freedom of members of the Hare Krishna sect to exercise their religion when it made and enforced a rule that persons seeking to sell literature or solicit funds at the state fair must do so from a fixed booth. The state also was acting within constitutional limits when it restricted the free distribution of literature to a particular place on the fair grounds. Those rules were reasonable in light of the state's interest in maintaining order and avoiding congestion in a crowded public place.

Widmar v. Vincent (*), decided by an 8-1 vote, Dec. 8, 1981. Powell wrote the opinion; White dissented.

A state university violates the First Amendment guarantee of freedom of expression when it denies use of its buildings and grounds to a recognized student group — while allowing other such groups use of those facilities — just because the excluded group wishes to hold religious meetings there. Once a university creates a forum generally open for use by student groups, it may not deny access to that forum to certain groups because of the subject of their meetings.

Valley Forge Christian College v. Americans United for Separation of Church and State (*), decided by a 5-4 vote, Jan. 12, 1982. Rehnquist wrote the opinion; Brennan, Marshall, Blackmun and Stevens dissented.

A citizens' group that could not demonstrate a clear "injury" as a result of the transfer of surplus federal prop-

How to Read a Citation

The official account of Supreme Court decisions and opinions is contained in a series of volumes entitled *United States Reports*, published by the U.S. Government Printing Office.

While there are several unofficial compilations of court opinions, including *United States Law Week* published by the Bureau of National Affairs, *Supreme Court Reporter*, published by West Publishing Co., and *United States Supreme Court Reports, Lawyers' Edition*, published by Lawyers Co-operative Publishing Co., it is the official record that is generally cited. (An unofficial version or the official slip opinion might be cited if a decision has not been officially reported.)

A citation to a case includes, in order, the name of the parties to the case, the volume of *United States Reports* in which the decision appears, the page in the volume that the opinion begins on, the page from which any quoted material is taken and the year the decision is made.

erty to a church-related school lacks standing to bring a federal suit challenging that transfer as a violation of the First Amendment ban on the establishment of religion.

United States v. Lee (*), decided by a 9-0 vote, Feb. 23, 1982. Burger wrote the decision.

Congress exempted from Social Security taxes only self-employed individuals whose religious beliefs forbid them to participate in the Social Security system. This does not allow an Amish farmer and carpenter who employs other members of his sect to refuse to pay Social Security taxes on their wages. Although paying his workers' Social Security taxes may interfere with the right of the farmer to the free exercise of his religious beliefs, some burdens of this type may be justified if necessary to realize an overriding governmental interest. The federal government's interest in the fiscal vitality of Social Security is such an overriding interest, the court held.

Larson v. Valente (*), decided by a vote of 5-4, April 21, 1982. Brennan wrote the opinion; White, Rehnquist, Burger and O'Connor dissented.

Minnesota violated the Constitution's "establishment" clause and engaged in an official preference for certain denominations when it exempted from the registration and reporting requirement of state law those religious organizations that receive more than half their financial support from their members. The Supreme Court held the state law invalid in a case brought by the Unification Church.

Right of Access

Richmond Newspapers Inc. v. Commonwealth of Virginia (448 U.S. 555), decided by a vote of 7-1, July 2,

1980. Burger wrote an opinion announcing the court decision and setting out the views of three justices; Brennan, Marshall, Stewart and Blackmun concurred in the decision; Rehnquist dissented; Powell did not participate.

The First Amendment implicitly guarantees citizens and members of the press the right to attend criminal trials. The court overturned the decision of a state trial judge closing a murder trial to the press and public.

In some situations it might be necessary, in the interest of a fair trial, to limit access of the press and public to that trial, wrote Chief Justice Burger. But if a judge found such limitations necessary, he should set them out clearly and find that closing the trial, or some portion of it, was essential to preserve some overriding interest.

Globe Newspaper Co. v. Superior Court (*), decided by a 6-3 vote, June 23, 1982. Brennan wrote the opinion; Burger, Rehnquist and Stevens dissented.

The First Amendment right of access to criminal trials is violated by a Massachusetts law mandating the closing of sex-crime trials to the press and public during the testimony of a victim who is a minor.

Obscenity

Stanley v. Georgia (394 U.S. 557), decided by a 9-0 vote, April 7, 1969. Marshall wrote the opinion.

The First Amendment guarantee of freedom of expression bars states from making it a crime to privately possess obscene material. The court unanimously held: "The Constitution protects the right to receive information and ideas.... Also fundamental is the right to be free, except in very limited circumstances, from unwanted governmental intrusions into one's privacy.... Whatever may be the justifications for other statutes regulating obscenity, we do not think they reach into the privacy of one's own home.... If the First Amendment means anything, it means that the state has no business telling a man, sitting alone in his house, what books he may read or what films he may watch."

Rowan v. U.S. Post Office Dept. (397 U.S. 728), decided by an 8-0 vote, May 4, 1970. Burger wrote the opinion.

Neither freedom of the press nor freedom of speech is violated by a 1967 law authorizing individuals to request the U.S. Postmaster General to order a company to cease sending that individual obscene material. The right of privacy was paramount in this case, held the court: "To hold less would tend to license a form of trespass and would make hardly more sense than to say that a radio or television viewer may not twist the dial to cut off an offensive or boring communication."

Blount v. Rizzi, U.S. v. The Book Bin (400 U.S. 410), decided by a 9-0 vote, Jan. 14, 1971. Brennan wrote the opinion.

The court invalidated two laws — one enacted in 1950 and the other in 1960 — that allowed the Post Office to stop delivering mail to businesses under investigation for, or found to be, selling pornographic material. The laws did not contain sufficient safeguards against unconstitutional curtailment of free speech, according to the court.

U.S. v. Reidel (402 U.S. 351), decided by a 7-2 vote, May 3, 1971. White wrote the opinion; Black and Douglas dissented.

The court upheld a law that forbids use of the mails to deliver obscene material, even if the material is being distributed to willing adult recipients.

U.S. v. 37 Photographs (402 U.S. 363), decided by a 6-3 vote, May 3, 1971. White wrote the opinion; Black, Douglas and Marshall dissented.

Federal laws authorizing customs officials to seize imported obscene material do not violate the First Amendment, nor does the seizure of obscene matter privately possessed at a port of entry by a person who intends to use it for commercial distribution.

Miller v. California (413 U.S. 15), decided by a 5-4 vote, June 21, 1973. Burger wrote the opinion; Brennan, Stewart, Marshall and Douglas dissented.

States have the power, without violating the First Amendment, to regulate material that is obscene in its depiction or description of sexual conduct. Material is obscene if the average person, applying contemporary local community standards, finds that it appeals to the prurient interest, and if it depicts in a patently offensive way sexual conduct specifically defined by the applicable state law, and if the work, taken as a whole, lacks serious literary, artistic, political or scientific value.

The court with this ruling revised the definition of obscenity it had set out in 1966 in the case of *Memoirs v. Massachusetts* (383 U.S. 413), involving the book *Fanny Hill*. By its 1973 ruling the court made clear that local community standards would be used to judge offensiveness, and it substituted for the 1966 requirement that the material must be utterly without redeeming social value a less stringent one: that the material must be found lacking any serious literary, artistic, political or scientific value.

U.S. v. Orito (413 U.S. 139), ***U.S. v. 12 200-foot Reels*** (413 U.S. 123), decided by 5-4 votes, June 21, 1973. Burger wrote the opinion; Brennan, Stewart, Marshall and Douglas dissented.

Congress constitutionally can forbid the importation or interstate transportation of obscene material, even if it is intended solely for the personal use of its owner. The zone of privacy protected by *Stanley v. Georgia* (394 U.S. 557, 1969) — which forbade states to make it a crime to possess obscene materials at home for personal use — does not extend beyond the home.

Jenkins v. Georgia (418 U.S. 153), decided by a 9-0 vote, June 24, 1974. Rehnquist wrote the opinion.

Miller v. California (see above) does not give juries unbridled discretion to determine what is offensive and obscene. Juries are not the last word on whether a particular film is obscene; such decisions are subject to review by a court. A Georgia jury erred in finding the award-winning movie "Carnal Knowledge" obscene; that film did not depict sexual conduct in the patently offensive manner required by *Miller v. California* for a finding of obscenity, the court held.

Erznoznik v. City of Jacksonville (422 U.S. 205), decided by a 6-3 vote, June 23, 1975. Powell wrote the opinion; White, Burger and Rehnquist dissented.

A city ordinance infringes on the First Amendment protection of freedom of expression by making it punishable for a drive-in movie theater to show films containing nudity if the movie screen is visible from a public place. The ordinance impermissibly discriminates against movies solely on the basis of their content and is unnecessarily broad in proscribing on-screen nudity.

New York v. Ferber (*), decided by a 9-0 vote, July 2, 1982. White wrote the opinion.

Pornographic depictions of children are outside the protection of the First Amendment. State laws prohibiting the promotion of sexual performances by children under age 16 do not violate the First Amendment.

DECISIONS ON POWERS OF CONGRESS

The immunity given members of Congress by the Constitution and the reach of the constitutional powers of Congress were carefully delineated by the court in a number of major rulings in the 1969-82 period.

Immunity

U.S. v. Brewster (408 U.S. 501), decided by a 6-3 vote, June 29, 1972. Burger wrote the opinion; Brennan, Douglas and White dissented.

The constitutional immunity conferred on members of Congress does not protect them from prosecution for accepting a bribe in order to vote a certain way on a legislative matter.

Former Sen. Daniel B. Brewster, D-Md. (1963-69), was indicted in 1969 on charges of accepting $24,000 in bribes between 1966 and 1968 from the mail order firm of Spiegel Inc. During that time, Brewster was a member of the Senate Post Office and Civil Service Committee, which was considering proposed changes in postal rates. The indictment alleged he was influenced in his legislative actions on those proposals by the bribes.

In November 1970 a federal district judge in the District of Columbia, George L. Hart, dismissed the charges against Brewster, stating that the immunity granted members of Congress by the Constitution shielded him from prosecution for bribery related to performance of a legislative act. The Justice Department immediately asked the Supreme Court to review the decision.

The Supreme Court reversed the lower court ruling and held that Brewster could indeed be prosecuted on the bribery charges. The constitutional protection granting members of Congress freedom from being questioned "in any other place" for "any speech or debate in either House" did not protect members' illegal actions in accepting a bribe, even if the bribe was directed at a legislative act, such as a committee vote. Taking a bribe is illegal, is not part of the legislative process, and therefore is subject to prosecution and punishment in the nation's courts, held the court in an opinion written by Chief Justice Warren E. Burger.

The dissenting justices argued that the majority was weakening the independence of Congress and should leave the disciplining of Brewster to Congress itself: "The speech or debate clause (Article I, Section 6) does not immunize corrupt congressmen. It reserves the power to discipline [them] in the houses of Congress."

Gravel v. U.S., U.S. v. Gravel (408 U.S. 606), decided by a 5-4 vote, June 29, 1972. White wrote the opinion; Douglas, Stewart, Brennan and Marshall dissented.

The constitutional immunity of members of Congress extends also to their aides, if the conduct in question would be a protected legislative act if performed by the member himself. Immunity does not shield an aide or member from testifying to a grand jury about acts unconnected with the legislative process.

At the peak of the controversy over publication of the Pentagon Papers in 1971, Sen. Mike Gravel, D-Alaska (1969-81), called a nocturnal meeting of the Senate Public Works subcommittee of which he was chairman. At the meeting, attended by members of the press and the general public, Gravel read, hour after hour, from the classified documents. Later he arranged for the Beacon Press to publish the record of these hearings, the Gravel version of the Pentagon Papers.

In August 1971 a grand jury investigating the leak of the documents called Leonard S. Rodberg, an aide to Gravel, to appear before it. Rodberg moved to quash his subpoena on the basis that he was protected by congressional immunity from such questioning. Gravel backed that motion; the Justice Department opposed it.

A federal district court held that no witness, including Rodberg, could be questioned about Gravel's conduct at the subcommittee meeting or about preparations for the meeting. The Court of Appeals, First Circuit, held that Gravel and Rodberg could be questioned about the subsequent publication of the subcommittee record.

White, for the court, made clear that neither Gravel nor Rodberg could be questioned about the events at the subcommittee meeting. However, the court majority agreed that this protection did not extend to arrangements that were made for publication of the papers nor information about the source of the classified documents. Gravel, as well as Rodberg, could be required to testify about these nonlegislative matters, held the majority.

Stewart dissented from the ruling insofar as it held that a member of Congress could be forced to tell a grand jury about the sources of information used to prepare for legislative activity. Douglas, Brennan and Marshall held that the constitutional immunity also would protect Gravel and Rodberg as well as Beacon Press from questions concerning the publication of the papers.

Doe v. McMillan (412 U.S. 306), decided by a 5-4 vote, May 29, 1973. White wrote the opinion; Blackmun, Rehnquist, Burger and Stewart dissented.

There are limits to the protection extended to members of Congress and employees of Congress by the Constitution's prescription that "for any speech or debate in either house, they shall not be questioned in any other place." That clause protects only actions taken in the "legislative sphere."

The court held that members of Congress and their employees — in this particular case Rep. John L. McMillan, D-S.C. (1939-73), chairman of the House District of Columbia Committee, the committee's members and employees — were immune from charges that they violated the rights of certain children to privacy by naming them as disciplinary problems in a committee report on the District of Columbia school system. But the court held that this immunity might not extend to the public printer and the superintendent of documents, also named in the suit. This protection did not cover persons, held the court, "who publish and distribute otherwise actionable materials beyond the reasonable requirements of the legislative function." It was left to the trial court to determine if these defendants had gone beyond those requirements.

"Everything a member of Congress may regularly do is not a legislative act within the protection" of the speech or debate clause, wrote White. "The business of Congress is to legislate; Congressmen and aides are absolutely immune when they are legislating. But when they act outside the 'sphere of legitimate legislative activity' ... they enjoy no special immunity from local laws protecting the good name or the reputation of the ordinary citizen."

Eastland v. U.S. Servicemen's Fund (421 U.S. 491), decided by an 8-1 vote, May 27, 1975. Burger wrote the opinion; Douglas dissented.

The Constitution's speech or debate clause precludes a federal court from interfering with a valid subpoena from a congressional committee even if it is claimed that the subpoena is intended to impede the exercise of First Amendment rights. The subpoena falls within the protected sphere of legislative activity.

"Once it is determined that members are acting within the 'legitimate legislative sphere,' the speech or debate clause is an absolute bar to interference."

The case arose from a subpoena issued by Sen. James O. Eastland, D-Miss. (1941, 1943-78), chairman of the Senate Judiciary Subcommittee on Internal Security, for the bank records of the United States Servicemen's Fund as part of the subcommittee's inquiry into the enforcement of the Internal Security Act of 1950. The servicemen's fund set up coffee houses and aided underground military base newspapers, both of which were vehicles for protest against U.S. military involvement in Indochina.

The constitutional protection in this case extended to the subcommittee's chief counsel as well as to Eastland himself, held the court. The courts could not investigate the propriety of the inquiry into the fund's activities beyond determining that such an inquiry was within the jurisdiction of the subcommittee.

United States v. Helstoski (442 U.S. 477), decided by a vote of 5-3, June 18, 1979. Burger wrote the opinion; Powell did not participate; Stevens, Stewart and Brennan dissented.

The speech or debate clause of the Constitution prohibits government prosecutors from using in the bribery trial of a former member of Congress any evidence referring to his performance of a legislative act.

Chief Justice Burger wrote that the speech or debate clause "was designed to preclude prosecution of Members for legislative acts.... [R]eferences to past legislative acts of a Member cannot be admitted without undermining the values protected by the Clause."

The majority did hold, however, that the constitutional protection did not extent to "a promise to deliver a speech, to vote, or to solicit other votes at some future date ... a *promise* to introduce a bill is not a legislative act." Evidence of such a promise could be used by the prosecution without violating the Constitution.

'Speech or Debate' Clause

[The Senators and Representatives] ... shall in all Cases, except Treason, Felony, and Breach of the Peace, be Privileged from Arrest during their attendance at the Session of their respective Houses and in going to and returning from the same; and for any Speech or Debate in either House, they shall not be questioned in any other place.

—Article I, Section 6, of the U.S. Constitution

Hutchinson v. Proxmire (443 U.S. 111), decided by votes of 8-1 and 7-2, June 26, 1979. Burger wrote the opinion; Brennan dissented; Stewart dissented in part.

The immunity extended by the speech or debate clause to the legislative actions of members of Congress protects libelous remarks included in a speech on the floor of the House or Senate, but it does not protect those remarks when they are republished in a senator's press releases or newsletters. This immunity also does not extend to efforts by the senator or his staff to influence the conduct of executive agencies or to libelous comments made by the senator or his staff in conversations with agency officials.

A scientist thrust into the public eye as a result of such libelous remarks, and his response to them, is not a "public figure" within the meaning of *New York Times Co. v. Sullivan* (1964), and therefore he is not required to prove that the remarks were motivated by "actual malice" in order to prevail in his suit for damages.

Powers

Powell v. McCormack (395 U.S. 486), decided by a 7-1 vote, June 16, 1969. Warren wrote the opinion; Stewart dissented.

The House of Representatives does not have the authority to exclude from membership a duly elected representative who meets the three constitutional qualifications of age, residence and citizenship.

Adam Clayton Powell Jr., D-N.Y. (1945-67, 1969-71) in 1966 was elected to his 12th term as representative from New York's 18th Congressional District (Harlem).

On the first day of the 90th Congress, Jan. 10, 1967, the House decided (H Res 1) that Powell's eligibility to be sworn in and seated as a member should be determined by a select committee.

The committee, on Feb. 23, 1967, concluded that Powell had claimed an unwarranted immunity from the New York courts, submitted false expense reports to the Committee on House Administration and misused House funds. The House March 1, 1967, voted 307-116 to exclude Powell from the 90th Congress.

Powell and a number of his constituents March 8 filed suit in federal district court for the District of Columbia against House Speaker John W. McCormack, D-Mass. (1928-71), and other House leaders and officials.

The suit requested a declaratory judgment that the exclusion of Powell by the House was unconstitutional, and it sought a permanent order forbidding McCormack to refuse to administer the oath to Powell. The suit also asked the court to order the clerk of the House to perform duties due a representative, the sergeant-at-arms to pay Powell his salary, and the doorkeeper to admit him to the House chamber.

The federal district court dismissed the suit because, it said, it did not have jurisdiction over its subject matter.

The Court of Appeals, District of Columbia Circuit, on Feb. 28, 1968, affirmed the action of the lower court in dismissing the suit. The Court of Appeals held that the lower court did have jurisdiction over the subject matter but that the case involved a political question, which if decided, would constitute a violation of the separation of powers principle and produce an embarrassing confrontation between Congress and the courts. Judge Warren E. Burger wrote the court of appeals opinion.

While *Powell v. McCormack* was pending on the court's docket, the 90th Congress ended. Powell was elected again to represent New York's 18th District in the House. He was seated in January 1969 by the 91st Congress and fined $25,000.

Chief Justice Earl Warren, speaking for the court, ruled that the House had improperly excluded Powell, a duly elected representative who met all the constitutional requirements.

Warren then proceeded to the question whether the speech or debate clause of the Constitution protected those named by Powell in his suit from judicial review of their actions.

Freedom of legislative activity, the objective of the constitutional clause, was protected, the court held, so long as legislators were not forced to defend themselves for their legislative actions. Therefore, the action against McCormack and the other members was dismissed. The court, however, allowed Powell to maintain the suit against the House employees.

The Constitution, the court ruled, in giving to the House the power to "be the Judge of the . . . Qualifications of its own Members" (Article I, Section 5, clause 1), left the House without the authority to exclude any duly elected representative who met the requirements for membership expressly stated in the Constitution.

The court did not deny the unquestionable interest of Congress in maintaining its own integrity. In most cases, however, the court felt that that interest could be properly safeguarded by the use of each House's power to punish or expel its members. "The Constitution does not vest in the Congress a discretionary power to deny membership by a majority vote."

The court dismissed the argument that the case presented a "political question" which, if decided by the court, could produce an explosive confrontation between the legislative and judicial branches. Determination of Powell's right to his seat in the 90th Congress, the court held, required only the interpretation of the Constitution, the traditional function of the court.

The Supreme Court sent the case back to the court of appeals with instructions to enter a declaratory judgment stating that the House action was unconstitutional and to conduct further proceedings on the unresolved issues of seniority, back pay and the $25,000 fine.

Stewart dissented, holding that the end of the 90th Congress and the seating of Powell in the 91st Congress rendered the case moot.

Oregon v. Mitchell, Texas v. Mitchell, U.S. v. Idaho, U.S. v. Arizona (400 U.S. 112), decided by a 5-4 vote on the issue of a lower voting age, by an 8-1 vote on residency requirements, and by a 9-0 vote on a literacy test ban, Dec. 21, 1970. Black wrote the opinion; Stewart, Burger, Harlan and Blackmun dissented on the question of age; Harlan alone dissented on the residency issue.

Congress has the power to lower the voting age to 18 for federal elections, but not for state and local elections; Congress has the power to restrict state residency requirements to 30 days for persons wishing to vote in presidential elections; Congress has the power to ban the use of literacy tests as voter qualification devices in any national, state or local election.

Black wrote the court's opinion and cast the pivotal vote. His position — that Congress had the power to lower the voting age in federal, but not in state or local, elections — prevailed, although he was the only justice holding that view in its entirety.

Four justices, Brennan, Douglas, Marshall and White, considered the 18-year-old vote provision fully constitutional for federal and state elections. None agreed completely with Black's position.

"I believe that Congress has the final authority over federal elections," Black said, but "I would hold that Congress has exceeded its powers in attempting to lower the voting age in state and local elections."

Stewart in dissent emphasized that the Supreme Court was not attempting to determine the value of lowering the voting age. "Our single duty as judges is to determine whether the legislation before us was within the constitutional power of Congress to enact. . . . A casual reader could easily get the impression that what we are being asked in these cases is whether or not we think allowing people 18 years old to vote is a good idea. Nothing could be wider of the mark."

Stewart, joined by Burger and Blackmun, argued that state laws that deny the vote to persons under 21 "do not invidiously discriminate against any discrete and insular minority." They concluded that the laws do not violate the 14th Amendment's antidiscrimination ban and thus Congress was in error when it passed the law to combat "discrimination" against youths.

California Bankers Association v. Shultz, Shultz v. California Bankers Association, Stark v. Shultz (416 U.S. 21), decided by a 6-3 vote, April 1, 1974. Rehnquist wrote the opinion; Douglas, Brennan and Marshall dissented.

The Bank Secrecy Act of 1970 (PL 91-508), which requires banks to maintain certain records on depositors that can be made available to the government and to report to the government certain large foreign and domestic transactions by customers, is a reasonable exercise of Congress' power to deal with crime affecting foreign and interstate commerce. These recordkeeping and reporting requirements do not violate — for either the banks or depositors — the constitutional guarantee of due process, nor the Fourth Amendment guarantee against unreasonable search and seizure, nor the Fifth Amendment protection against compulsory self-incrimination.

Fry v. U.S. (421 U.S. 542), decided by a 7-2 vote, May 27, 1975. Marshall wrote the opinion; Rehnquist and Douglas dissented.

Congress did not exceed its power to regulate interstate commerce when it set wage ceilings for state employees as part of an emergency economic stabilization program. The court struck down Ohio's effort to give its employees a larger pay increase than allowed by federal wage-price regulations.

The sovereign status of the states does not protect them from all federal regulations under the commerce clause, wrote Marshall, citing *Maryland v. Wirtz* (392 U.S. 183, 1968) in which the court upheld the extension of the Fair Labor Standards Act to employees of state-run schools and hospitals. "The interference with state affairs incident to the uniform implementation of federal economic controls was of no consequence since Congress had a rational basis upon which to conclude that the state activity substantially affected commerce." The pay boost that Ohio wanted to give its employees would have injected millions of dollars of purchasing power into the economy, Marshall noted. "The effectiveness of federal action would have been drastically impaired if wage increases to this sizeable group of employees were left outside the reach of these emergency federal wage controls."

National League of Cities v. Usery, California v. Usery

National League of Cities v. Usery, California v. Usery (426 U.S. 833), decided by a 5-4 vote, June 24, 1976. Rehnquist wrote the opinion; Brennan, White, Marshall and Stevens dissented.

Congress exceeded its power to regulate commerce when it extended federal minimum wage and overtime provisions — through the 1974 amendments to the Fair Labor Standards Act — to state and local government employees.

"Congress may not exercise that power so as to force directly upon the states its choices as to how essential decisions regarding the conduct of integral governmental functions are to be made," held the court. "We have repeatedly recognized that there are attributes of sovereignty attaching to every state government which may not be impaired by Congress. . . . One undoubted attribute of state sovereignty is the states' power to determine the wages which shall be paid to those whom they employ in order to carry out their governmental functions, what hours those persons will work, and what compensation will be provided where these employees may be called upon to work overtime. . . . If Congress may withdraw from the states the authority to make those fundamental employment decisions upon which their systems for performance of these functions rest, we think there would be little left of the states' 'separate and independent existence.' "

Maryland v. Wirtz (1968) is overruled; *Fry v. U.S.* (421 U.S. 542, 1975) is not in conflict with this ruling because it involves a temporary and limited federal intervention in state wage matters, required by a national crisis. *(Excerpts from ruling, p. 152)*

Usery v. Turner Elkhorn Mining Co.

Usery v. Turner Elkhorn Mining Co. (428 U.S. 1), decided by votes of 8-0 and 6-2, July 1, 1976. Marshall wrote the opinion; Stevens did not participate; Stewart and Rehnquist dissented in part.

Congress did not deprive coal mine operators of their property without due process of law when it set up the black lung benefits program for coal miners. Congress acted rationally in basing eligibility for black lung benefits on certain assumptions concerning the extent of disability and the cause of respiratory or pulmonary impairment in miners and in providing for payment of benefits to employees or their survivors who had left the coal mining industry before passage of the law.

Nixon v. General Services Administration

Nixon v. General Services Administration (433 U.S. 425), decided by a 7-2 vote, June 28, 1977. Brennan wrote the opinion; Burger and Rehnquist dissented.

Congress, in enacting the Presidential Recordings and Materials Preservation Act of 1974, which placed the tapes and papers of the Nixon administration in federal custody, did not violate the principle of separation of powers, the presidential privilege of confidentiality, the right of privacy, the First Amendment rights of free speech and freedom of political association, or the constitutional guarantees of equal protection of the law and due process. The act did not constitute an unlawful bill of attainder; it did not constitute legislative punishment of President Richard M. Nixon. Congress had a valid reason for considering Nixon a legitimate "class of one" because only he, among the presidents, had entered into a depository agreement concerning these materials that provided for the eventual destruction of some of them.

Duke Power Co. v. Carolina Environmental Study Group, Nuclear Regulatory Commission v. Carolina Environmental Study Group

Duke Power Co. v. Carolina Environmental Study Group, Nuclear Regulatory Commission v. Carolina Environmental Study Group (438 U.S. 59), decided by a vote of 9-0, June 26, 1978. Burger wrote the opinion.

Congress did not act unconstitutionally when it enacted a $560 million ceiling on the liability of the nuclear power industry for damages resulting from an accident at a nuclear power plant. That limitation does not deprive citizens of life, liberty or property without due process of law or take private property without just compensation. The decision to impose such a limit and the limit adopted were neither arbitrary nor irrational, and thus were well within the power of Congress.

United States v. Will

United States v. Will (449 U.S. 200), decided by an 8-0 vote, Dec. 15, 1980. Burger wrote the opinion; Blackmun did not participate.

Congress may not rescind cost-of-living adjustments in the salaries of federal judges after those increases actually take effect; such an after-the-fact rescission violates the Constitution's guarantee that judicial salaries "shall not be diminished during their Continuance in Office." Congress may rescind such adjustments if it acts before the beginning of the fiscal year in which they take effect.

The court held that Congress had properly rescinded cost-of-living increases for fiscal 1978 and 1979, acting before the first day of the new fiscal year, but had improperly tried to cancel those increases for fiscal 1977 and 1980, when the rescissions were not enacted until after Oct. 1. The effect of this ruling was to increase the salaries of all federal judges, including members of the Supreme Court, by about 12 percent.

Hodel v. Virginia Surface Mining and Reclamation Assn., Virginia Surface Mining and Reclamation Assn. v. Hodel

Hodel v. Virginia Surface Mining and Reclamation Assn., Virginia Surface Mining and Reclamation Assn. v. Hodel (452 U.S. 264), decided by a 9-0 vote, June 15, 1981. Marshall wrote the opinion.

Congress did not exceed its authority to regulate interstate commerce when it enacted the Surface Mining Control and Reclamation Act of 1977 (PL 95-87). On its face, the strip mining law, which imposes severe land use restrictions and strict reclamation requirements, does not violate the Constitution.

Railway Labor Executives Association v. Gibbons (*), decided by a vote of 9-0, March 2, 1982. Rehnquist wrote the opinion.

Congress may not pass bankruptcy laws that apply to the affairs of only one bankrupt organization. The Constitution gives Congress the power to "establish . . . uniform Laws on the subject of bankruptcies throughout the United States."

The Rock Island Transition and Employee Assistance Act of 1980 (PL 96-254) applied only to the Rock Island Railroad, providing special protection to its employees not available to the employees of other bankrupt railroads. Thus that law violated the uniformity standard of the Constitution's bankruptcy clause.

Federal Energy Regulatory Commission v. Mississippi (*), decided by votes of 9-0 and 5-4, June 1, 1982. Blackmun wrote the opinion; Powell, O'Connor, Burger and Rehnquist dissented in part.

Congress acted within its power to regulate interstate commerce when it passed the Public Utility Regulatory Policies Act of 1978 (PL 95-617) directing state utility regulatory commissions to consider adopting certain rate-design and regulatory standards and to follow certain procedures when acting on those standards. The majority held that PL 95-617 did not infringe upon powers reserved to the states under the 10th Amendment.

Northern Pipeline Construction Co. v. Marathon Pipe Line Co., United States v. Marathon Pipe Line Co. (*), decided by a 6-3 vote, June 28, 1982. Brennan announced the decision in an opinion joined by three other justices; Rehnquist and O'Connor concurred in the judgment; White, Burger and Powell dissented.

Congress acted in violation of Article III of the Constitution, which provides that federal judicial power should be exercised only by federal judges whose independence is assured by life tenure and fixed compensation, when it enacted provisions of the 1978 Bankruptcy Reform Act creating a new corps of bankruptcy judges who lack these guarantees of independence but nevertheless have jurisdiction over all civil cases related to a bankrupt person or organization.

DECISIONS ON EXECUTIVE POWERS

The single most significant ruling by the Supreme Court in the 1969-82 period resulted in the first presidential resignation in history. Rebuffing a claim of absolute executive immunity from judicial demands for information, the court unanimously held that President Richard M. Nixon had to comply with a subpoena requiring him to surrender certain tapes to the Watergate special prosecutor for use in a *criminal* case. Two weeks later, aware of the incriminating nature of those tapes, Nixon resigned.

Eight years later, the court ruled that presidents were immune from *civil* damage suits for all their official actions.

The court dealt with several other issues of executive power during this period: the power of the president to pardon, to impound funds appropriated by Congress, to use import fees as a means of controlling the nation's imports of oil, and to reach settlements with foreign governments.

U.S. v. Nixon (418 U.S. 683), decided by an 8-0 vote, July 24, 1974. Burger wrote the opinion; Rehnquist did not participate.

Neither the doctrine of separation of powers nor the need to preserve the confidentiality of presidential communications can, alone, justify an absolute executive privilege of immunity from judicial demands under all circumstances.

The court held that President Richard M. Nixon was obligated to comply with a subpoena from the Watergate special prosecutor for certain tapes of White House conversations. The tapes were to be turned over to a federal judge for private examination and excision of irrelevant portions before they were given to the special prosecutor. These tapes were sought for use as evidence in the criminal proceedings against former White House aides concerning the effort to cover up White House involvement in the break-in at the Democratic Party headquarters in the Watergate building, in Washington, D.C., in 1972.

"The President's need for complete candor and objectivity from advisers calls for great deference from the courts," wrote the chief justice. "However, when the privilege depends solely on the broad undifferentiated claim of public interest in the confidentiality of such conversations, a confrontation with other values arises. Absent a claim of need to protect military, diplomatic or sensitive national security secrets, we find it difficult to accept the argument that even the very important interest in confidentiality . . . is significantly diminished by production of such material for *in camera* inspection. . . .

"To read the Article II powers of the President as providing an absolute privilege as against a subpoena essential to enforcement of criminal statutes on no more than a generalized claim of the public interest in confidentiality of nonmilitary and nondiplomatic discussions would upset the constitutional balance of 'a workable government' and gravely impair the role of the courts under Article III" of the Constitution.

"When the ground for asserting privilege as to subpoenaed materials sought for use in a criminal trial is based only on the generalized interest in confidentiality, it cannot prevail over the fundamental demands of due process of law in the fair administration of criminal justice. The generalized assertion of privilege must yield to the demonstrated specific need for evidence in a pending criminal trial." *(Excerpts from ruling, p. 144)*

Schick v. Reed (419 U.S. 256), decided by a 6-3 vote, Dec. 23, 1974. Burger wrote the opinion; Marshall, Douglas and Brennan dissented.

The power to pardon is granted to the president of the United States by the Constitution, and the only limits on its use are those set out in the Constitution. President Eisenhower did not exceed those limits when he commuted a murderer's death sentence to one of life imprisonment with no possibility of parole — even though at the time there was no such no-parole life imprisonment penalty provided by law for murder.

Train v. City of New York (420 U.S. 35), ***Train v. Campaign Clean Water*** (420 U.S. 136), decided by a 9-0 vote, Feb. 19, 1975. White wrote the opinion.

Congress, in enacting the Water Pollution Control Act of 1972 (PL 92-500) over President Nixon's veto, left the president no leeway to withhold or impound the funds it authorized to be spent. Nixon therefore exceeded his authority when he refused to allocate to the states $9 billion provided by that law. The court carefully limited its holding to the question of the impoundment of funds provided under PL 92-500, avoiding a ruling on the broader issue of the president's power to withhold funds authorized and appropriated by Congress.

Federal Energy Administration v. Algonquin SNG Inc. (426 U.S. 548), decided by a 9-0 vote, June 17, 1976. Marshall wrote the opinon.

Congress, in the Trade Expansion Act of 1962, granted the president the authority to adjust imports of any item being imported into the United States in such quantities or under such circumstances that it threatens the national security. This grant of authority is broad enough to allow the president to use import fees, as well as import quotas, to control the import of oil. The court upheld the decisions of Presidents Nixon and Gerald R. Ford to use import fees rather than quotas, a more direct means, to attempt to reduce U.S. dependence on imported oil.

Dames & Moore v. Regan (453 U.S. 654), decided by a 9-0 vote, July 2, 1981. Rehnquist wrote the opinion.

President Jimmy Carter acted within his statutory power to conduct foreign affairs when he concluded the financial agreement with the Iranian government that resulted in the release of 52 Americans held hostage in Iran for more than 14 months.

Carter was within his power when he agreed 1) to nullify all federal court orders attaching the assets of Iranian businesses and of the Iranian government in the United States and 2) to transfer those assets back to Iran. It was also within the president's power to agree that all pending claims against Iran would be transferred to an international tribunal and would be heard and resolved there, rather than in the U.S. courts.

Congress, in the International Emergency Economic Powers Act of 1977 (PL 95-223), and in a number of other earlier laws, gave the president powers broad enough to take these actions, the court held.

Immunity

Nixon v. Fitzgerald (*), decided by a 5-4 vote, June 24, 1982. Powell wrote the opinion; White, Brennan, Marshall and Blackmun dissented.

Presidents are absolutely immune from civil damage suits for all official actions taken while in office. The court ruled in a case involving the claim of former Defense Department cost analyst A. Ernest Fitzgerald that he lost his job through a White House conspiracy involving former President Nixon, who wished to punish him for his disclosure to a congressional committee of massive cost overruns on a military transport plane, the C-5A. The majority said the electoral process and the impeachment mechanism provide sufficient remedy for presidential wrongdoing. The four dissenters said the ruling "places the president above the law" and was "a reversion to the old notion that the king can do no wrong."

Harlow v. Fitzgerald (*), decided by an 8-1 vote, June 24, 1982. Powell wrote the opinion; Burger dissented.

Presidential aides do not have absolute immunity from civil rights damage suits by individuals who claim they have been denied their rights by those aides acting in their official capacity. A presidential aide can establish such immunity if he shows that the "responsibilities of his office embrace a function so sensitive as to require a total shield from liability."

Presidential aides, like other executive officials, enjoy qualified immunity from such damage suits. The court set out a new standard for courts to use in weighing a qualified immunity defense. The court held that "government officials performing discretionary functions generally are shielded from liability for civil damages insofar as their conduct does not violate clearly established statutory or constitutional rights of which a reasonable person would have known." The court abandoned an earlier test that had required inquiry into the motivation of the official committing the challenged act.

Appendix

Constitution of the United States

We the People of the United States, in Order to form a more perfect Union, establish Justice, insure domestic Tranquility, provide for the common defence, promote the general Welfare, and secure the Blessings of Liberty to ourselves and our Posterity, do ordain and establish this Constitution for the United States of America.

Article I

Section 1. All legislative Powers herein granted shall be vested in a Congress of the United States, which shall consist of a Senate and House of Representatives.

Section 2. The House of Representatives shall be composed of Members chosen every second Year by the People of the several States, and the Electors in each State shall have the Qualifications requisite for Electors of the most numerous Branch of the State Legislature.

No Person shall be a Representative who shall not have attained to the age of twenty five Years, and been seven Years a Citizen of the United States, and who shall not, when elected, be an Inhabitant of that State in which he shall be chosen.

[Representatives and direct Taxes shall be apportioned among the several States which may be included within this Union, according to their respective Numbers, which shall be determined by adding to the whole Number of free Persons, including those bound to Service for a Term of Years, and excluding Indians not taxed, three fifths of all other Persons.][1] The actual Enumeration shall be made within three Years after the first Meeting of the Congress of the United States, and within every subsequent Term of ten Years, in such Manner as they shall by Law direct. The Number of Representatives shall not exceed one for every thirty Thousand, but each State shall have at Least one Representative; and until such enumeration shall be made, the State of New Hampshire shall be entitled to chuse three, Massachusetts eight, Rhode-Island and Providence Plantations one, Connecticut five, New-York six, New Jersey four, Pennsylvania eight, Delaware one, Maryland six, Virginia ten, North Carolina five, South Carolina five, and Georgia three.

When vacancies happen in the Representation from any State, the Executive Authority thereof shall issue Writs of Election to fill such Vacancies.

The House of Representatives shall chuse their Speaker and other Officers; and shall have the sole Power of Impeachment.

Section 3. The Senate of the United States shall be composed of two Senators from each State, [chosen by the Legislature thereof,][2] for six Years; and each Senator shall have one Vote.

Immediately after they shall be assembled in Consequence of the first Election, they shall be divided as equally as may be into three Classes. The Seats of the Senators of the first Class shall be vacated at the Expiration of the second Year, of the second Class at the Expiration of the fourth Year, and of the third Class at the Expiration of the sixth Year, so that one third may be chosen every second Year; [and if Vacancies happen by Resignation, or otherwise, during the Recess of the Legislature of any State, the Executive thereof may make temporary Appointments until the next Meeting of the Legislature, which shall then fill such Vacancies.][3]

No Person shall be a Senator who shall not have attained to the Age of thirty Years, and been nine Years a Citizen of the United States, and who shall not, when elected, be an Inhabitant of that State for which he shall be chosen.

The Vice President of the United States shall be President of the Senate, but shall have no Vote, unless they be equally divided.

The Senate shall chuse their other Officers, and also a President pro tempore, in the Absence of the Vice President, or when he shall exercise the Office of President of the United States.

The Senate shall have the sole Power to try all Impeachments. When sitting for that Purpose, they shall be on Oath or Affirmation. When the President of the United States is tried the Chief Justice shall preside: And no Person shall be convicted without the Concurrence of two thirds of the Members present.

Judgment in Cases of Impeachment shall not extend further than to removal from Office, and disqualification to hold and enjoy any Office of honor, Trust or Profit under the United States: but the Party convicted shall nevertheless be liable and subject to Indictment, Trial, Judgment and Punishment, according to Law.

Section 4. The Times, Places and Manner of holding Elections for Senators and Representatives, shall be prescribed in each State by the Legislature thereof; but the Congress may at any time by Law make or alter such Regulations, except as to the Places of chusing Senators.

The Congress shall assemble at least once in every Year, and such Meeting shall [be on the first Monday in December],[4] unless they shall by Law appoint a different Day.

Section 5. Each House shall be the Judge of the Elections, Returns and Qualifications of its own Members, and a Majority of each shall constitute a Quorum to do Business; but a smaller Number may adjourn from day to day, and may be authorized to compel the Attendance of absent Members, in such Manner, and under such Penalties as each House may provide.

Each House may determine the Rules of its Proceedings, punish its Members for disorderly Behaviour, and, with the Concurrence of two thirds, expel a Member.

Each House shall keep a Journal of its Proceedings, and from time to time publish the same, excepting such Parts as may in their Judgment require Secrecy; and the Yeas and Nays of the Members of either House on any question shall, at the Desire of one fifth of those Present, be entered on the Journal.

Neither House, during the Session of Congress, shall, without the Consent of the other, adjourn for more than three days, nor to any other Place than that in which the two Houses shall be sitting.

Section 6. The Senators and Representatives shall receive a Compensation for their Services, to be ascertained by Law, and paid out of the Treasury of the United States. They shall in all Cases, except Treason, Felony and Breach of the Peace, be privileged from Arrest during their Attendance at the Session of their respective Houses, and in going to and returning from the same; and for any Speech or Debate in either House, they shall not be questioned in any other Place.

No Senator or Representative shall, during the Time for which he was elected, be appointed to any civil Office under the Authority of the United States, which shall have been created, or the Emoluments whereof shall have been encreased during such time; and no Person holding any Office under the United States, shall be a Member of either House during his Continuance in Office.

Section 7. All Bills for raising Revenue shall originate in the House of Representatives; but the Senate may propose or concur with amendments as on other Bills.

Every Bill which shall have passed the House of Representatives and the Senate, shall, before it become a Law, be presented to the President of the United States; If he approve he shall sign it, but if not he shall return it, with his Objections to that House in which it shall have originated, who shall enter the Objections at large on their Journal, and proceed to reconsider it. If after such Reconsideration two thirds of that House shall agree to pass the Bill, it shall be sent, together with the Objections, to the other House, by which it shall likewise be reconsidered, and if approved by two thirds of that House, it shall become a Law. But in all such Cases the Votes of both Houses shall be determined by yeas and Nays, and the Names of the Persons voting for and against the Bill shall be entered on the Journal of each House respectively. If any Bill shall not be returned by the President within ten Days (Sunday excepted) after it shall have been presented to him, the Same shall be a Law, in like Manner as if he had signed it, unless the Congress by their Adjournment prevent its Return, in which Case it shall not be a Law.

Every Order, Resolution, or Vote to which the Concurrence of the Senate and House of Representatives may be necessary (except on a question of Adjournment) shall be presented to the President of the United States; and before the Same shall take Effect, shall be approved by him, or being disapproved by him, shall be repassed by two thirds of the Senate and House of Representatives, according to the Rules and Limitations prescribed in the Case of a Bill.

Section 8. The Congress shall have Power To lay and collect Taxes, Duties, Imposts and Excises, to pay the Debts and provide for the common Defence and general Welfare of the United States; but all Duties, Imposts and Excises shall be uniform throughout the United States;

To borrow Money on the credit of the United States;

To regulate Commerce with foreign Nations, and among the several States, and with the Indian Tribes;

To establish an uniform Rule of Naturalization, and uniform Laws on the subject of Bankruptcies throughout the United States;

To coin Money, regulate the Value thereof, and of foreign Coin, and fix the Standard of Weights and Measures;

To provide for the Punishment of counterfeiting the Securities and current Coin of the United States;

To establish Post Offices and post Roads;

To promote the Progress of Science and useful Arts, by securing for limited Times to Authors and Inventors the exclusive Right to their respective Writings and Discoveries;

To constitute Tribunals inferior to the supreme Court;

To define and punish Piracies and Felonies commited on the high Seas, and Offences against the Law of Nations;

To declare War, grant Letters of Marque and Reprisal, and make Rules concerning Captures on Land and Water;

To raise and support Armies, but no Appropriation of Money to that Use shall be for a longer Term than two Years;

To provide and maintain a Navy;

To make Rules for the Government and Regulation of the land and naval Forces;

To provide for calling forth the Militia to execute the Laws of the Union, suppress Insurrections and repel Invasions;

To provide for organizing, arming, and displining the Militia, and for governing such Part of them as may be employed in the Service of the United States, reserving to the States respectively, the Appointment of the Officers, and the Authority of training the Militia according to the discipline prescribed by Congress;

To exercise exclusive Legislation in all Cases whatsoever, over such District (not exceeding ten Miles square) as may, by Cession of Particular States, and the Acceptance of Congress, become the Seat of the Government of the United States, and to exercise like Authority over all Places purchased by the Consent of the Legislature of the State in which the Same shall be, for the Erection of Forts, Magazines, Arsenals, dock-Yards, and other needful Buildings; — And

To make all Laws which shall be necessary and proper for carrying into Execution the foregoing Powers, and all other Powers vested by this Constitution in the Government of the United States, or in any Department or Officer thereof.

Section 9. The Migration or Importation of such Persons as any of the States now existing shall think proper to admit, shall not be prohibited by the Congress prior to the Year one thousand eight hundred and eight, but a Tax or duty may be imposed on such Importation, not exceeding ten dollars for each Person.

The Privilege of the Writ of Habeas Corpus shall not be suspended, unless when in Cases of Rebellion or Invasion the public Safety may require it.

No Bill of Attainder or ex post facto Law shall be passed.

No capitation, or other direct, Tax shall be laid, unless in Proportion to the Census of Enumeration herein before directed to be taken.[5]

No Tax or Duty shall be laid on Articles exported from any State.

No Preference shall be given by any Regulation of Commerce or Revenue to the Ports of one State over those of another; nor shall Vessels bound to, or from, one State, be obliged to enter, clear or pay Duties in another.

No Money shall be drawn from the Treasury, but in Consequence of Appropriations made by Law; and a regular Statement and Account of the Receipts and Expenditures of all public Money shall be published from time to time.

No Title of Nobility shall be granted by the United States: And no Person holding any Office of Profit or Trust under them, shall, without the Consent of the Congress, accept of any present, Emolument, Office, or Title, of any kind whatever, from any King, Prince or foreign State.

Section 10. No State shall enter into any Treaty, Alliance, or Confederation; grant Letters of Marque and Reprisal; coin Money; emit Bills of Credit; make any Thing but gold and silver Coin a Tender in Payment of Debts; pass any Bill of Attainder, ex post facto Law, or Law impairing the Obligation of Contracts, or grant any Title of Nobility.

No State shall, without the Consent of the Congress, lay any Imposts or Duties on Imports or Exports, except what may be absolutely necessary for executing it's inspection Laws: and the net Produce of all Duties and Imposts, laid by any State on Imports or Exports, shall be for the Use of the Treasury of the United States; and all such Laws shall be subject to the Revision and Controul of the Congress.

No State shall, without the Consent of Congress, lay any Duty of Tonnage, keep Troops, or Ships of War in time of Peace, enter into any Agreement or Compact with another State, or with a foreign Power, or engage in War, unless actually invaded, or in such imminent Danger as will not admit of delay.

Article II

Section 1. The executive Power shall be vested in a President of the United States of America. He shall hold his Office during the Term of four Years, and, together with the Vice President, chosen for the same Term, be elected, as follows.

Each State shall appoint, in such Manner as the Legislature thereof may direct, a Number of Electors, equal to the whole Number of Senators and Representatives to which the State may be entitled in the Congress: but no Senator or Representative, or Person holding an Office of Trust or Profit under the United States, shall be appointed an Elector.

[The Electors shall meet in their respective States, and vote by Ballot for two Persons, of whom one at least shall not be an Inhabitant of the same State with themselves. And they shall make a List of all the Persons voted for, and of the Number of Votes for each; which List they shall sign and certify, and transmit sealed to the Seat of the Government of the United States, directed to the President of the Senate. The President of the Senate shall, in the Presence of the Senate and House of Representatives, open all the Certificates, and the Votes shall then be counted. The Person having the greatest Number of Votes shall be the President, if such Number be a Majority of the whole Number of Electors appointed; and if there be more than one who have such Majority, and have an equal Number of Votes, then the House of Representatives shall immediately chuse by Ballot one of them for President; and if no Person have a Majority, then from the five highest on the list the said House shall in like Manner chuse the President. But in chusing the President, the Votes shall be

taken by States, the Representation from each State having one Vote; a quorum for this Purpose shall consist of a Member or Members from two thirds of the States, and a Majority of all the States shall be necessary to a Choice. In every Case, after the Choice of the President, the Person having the greatest Number of Votes of the Electors shall be the Vice President. But if there should remain two or more who have equal Votes, the Senate shall chuse from them by Ballot the Vice President.][6]

The Congress may determine the Time of chusing the Electors, and the Day on which they shall give their Votes; which Day shall be the same throughout the United States.

No Person except a natural born Citizen, or a Citizen of the United States, at the time of the Adoption of this Constitution, shall be eligible to the Office of President; neither shall any Person be eligible to that Office who shall not have attained to the Age of thirty five Years, and been fourteen Years a Resident within the United States.

In Case of the Removal of the President from Office, or of his Death, Resignation, or Inability to discharge the Powers and Duties of the said Office,[7] the Same shall devolve on the Vice President, and the Congress may by Law provide for the Case of Removal, Death, Resignation or Inability, both of the President and Vice President, declaring what Officer shall then act as President, and such Officer shall act accordingly, until the Disability be removed, or a President shall be elected.

The President shall, at stated Times, receive for his Services, a Compensation, which shall neither be increased nor diminished during the Period for which he shall have been elected, and he shall not receive within that Period any other Emolument from the United States, or any of them.

Before he enter on the Execution of his Office, he shall take the following Oath or Affirmation: — "I do solemnly swear (or affirm) that I will faithfully execute the Office of President of the United States, and will to the best of my Ability, preserve, protect and defend the Constitution of the United States."

Section 2. The President shall be Commander in Chief of the Army and Navy of the United States, and of the Militia of the several States, when called into the actual Service of the United States; he may require the Opinion, in writing, of the principal Officer in each of the executive Departments, upon any Subject relating to the Duties of their respective Offices, and he shall have Power to grant Reprieves and Pardons for Offenses against the United States, except in Cases of Impeachment.

He shall have Power, by and with the Advice and Consent of the Senate, to make Treaties, provided two thirds of the Senators present concur; and he shall nominate, and by and with the Advice and Consent of the Senate, shall appoint Ambassadors, other public Ministers and Consuls, Judges of the supreme Court, and all other Officers of the United States, whose Appointments are not herein otherwise provided for, and which shall be established by Law: but the Congress may by Law vest the Appointment of such inferior Officers, as they think proper, in the President alone, in the Courts of Law, or in the Heads of Departments.

The President shall have Power to fill up all Vacancies that may happen during the Recess of the Senate, by granting Commissions which shall expire at the End of their next Session.

Section 3. He shall from time to time give to the

Congress Information of the State of the Union, and recommend to their Consideration such Measures as he shall judge necessary and expedient; he may, on extraordinary Occasions, convene both Houses, or either of them, and in Case of Disagreement between them, with Respect to the Time of Adjournment, he may adjourn them to such Time as he shall think proper; he shall receive Ambassadors and other public Ministers; he shall take Care that the Laws be faithfully executed, and shall Commission all the Officers of the United States.

Section 4. The President, Vice President and all Civil Officers of the United States, shall be removed from office on Impeachment for, and Conviction of, Treason, Bribery, or other high Crimes and Misdemeanors.

Article III

Section 1. The judicial Power of the United States, shall be vested in one supreme Court, and in such inferior Courts as the Congress may from time to time ordain and establish. The Judges, both of the supreme and inferior Courts, shall hold their Offices during good Behaviour, and shall, at stated Times, receive for their Services, a Compensation, which shall not be diminished during their Continuance in Office.

Section 2. The judicial Power shall extend to all Cases, in Law and Equity, arising under this Constitution, the Laws of the United States, and Treaties made, or which shall be made, under their Authority; — to all Cases affecting Ambassadors, other public Ministers and Consuls; — to all Cases of admiralty and maritime Jurisdiction; — to Controversies to which the United States shall be a Party; — to Controversies between two or more States; — between a State and Citizens of another State;[8] — between Citizens of different States; — between Citizens of the same State claiming Lands under Grants of different States, and between a State, or the Citizens thereof, and foreign States, Citizens or Subjects.[8]

In all Cases affecting Ambassadors, other public Ministers and Consuls, and those in which a State shall be Party, the supreme Court shall have original Jurisdiction. In all the other Cases before mentioned, the supreme Court shall have appellate Jurisdiction, both as to Law and Fact, with such Exceptions, and under such Regulations as the Congress shall make.

The Trial of all Crimes, except in cases of Impeachment, shall be by Jury; and such Trial shall be held in the State where the said Crimes shall have been committed; but when not committed within any State, the Trial shall be at such Place or Places as the Congress may by Law have directed.

Section 3. Treason against the United States, shall consist only in levying War against them, or in adhering to their Enemies, giving them Aid and Comfort. No Person shall be convicted of Treason unless on the Testimony of two Witnesses to the same overt Act, or on Confession in open Court.

The Congress shall have Power to declare the Punishment of Treason, but no Attainder of Treason shall work Corruption of Blood, or Forfeiture except during the Life of the Person attainted.

Article IV

Section 1. Full Faith and Credit shall be given in each State to the public Acts, Records, and judicial Proceedings of every other State. And the Congress may by general Laws prescribe the Manner in which such Acts, Records and Proceedings shall be proved, and the Effect thereof.

Section 2. The Citizens of each State shall be entitled to all Privileges and Immunities of Citizens in the several States.

A Person charged in any State with Treason, Felony, or other Crime, who shall flee from Justice, and be found in another State, shall on Demand of the executive Authority of the State from which he fled, be delivered up, to be removed to the State having Jurisdiction of the Crime.

[No Person held to Service or Labour in one State, under the Laws thereof, escaping into another, shall, in Consequence of any Law or Regulation therein, be discharged from such Service or Labour, but shall be delivered up on Claim of the Party to whom such Service or Labour may be due.][9]

Section 3. New States may be admitted by the Congress into this Union; but no new State shall be formed or erected within the Jurisdiction of any other State; nor any State be formed by the Junction of two or more States, or Parts of States, without the Consent of the Legislatures of the States concerned as well as of the Congress.

The Congress shall have Power to dispose of and make all needful Rules and Regulations respecting the Territory or other Property belonging to the United States; and nothing in this Constitution shall be so construed as to Prejudice any Claims of the United States, or of any particular State.

Section 4. The United States shall guarantee to every State in this Union a Republican Form of Government, and shall protect each of them against Invasion; and on Application of the Legislature, or of the Executive (when the Legislature cannot be convened) against domestic Violence.

Article V

The Congress, whenever two thirds of both Houses shall deem it necessary, shall propose Amendments to this Constitution, or, on the Application of the Legislatures of two thirds of the several States, shall call a Convention for proposing Amendments, which, in either Case, shall be valid to all Intents and Purposes, as Part of this Constitution, when ratified by the Legislatures of three fourths of the several States, or by Conventions in three fourths thereof, as the one or the other Mode of Ratification may be proposed by the Congress; Provided [that no Amendment which may be made prior to the Year One thousand eight hundred and eight shall in any Manner affect the first and fourth Clauses in the Ninth Section of the first Article; and][10] that no State, without its Consent, shall be deprived of its equal Suffrage in the Senate.

Article VI

All Debts contracted and Engagements entered into, before the Adoption of this Constitution, shall be as valid against the United States under this Constitution, as under the Confederation.

This Constitution, and the Laws of the United States which shall be made in Pursuance thereof; and all Treaties made, or which shall be made, under the Authority of the United States, shall be the supreme Law of the Land; and the Judges in every State shall be bound thereby, any Thing in the Constitution or Laws of any State to the Contrary notwithstanding.

The Senators and Representatives before mentioned, and the Members of the several State Legislatures, and all executive and judicial Officers, both of the United States and of the several States, shall be bound by Oath or Affirmation, to support this Constitution; but no religious Test shall ever be required as a Qualification to any Office or public Trust under the United States.

Article VII

The Ratification of the Conventions of nine States, shall be sufficient for the Establishment of this Constitution between the States so ratifying the Same. Done in Convention by the Unanimous Consent of the States present the Seventeenth Day of September in the Year of our Lord one thousand seven hundred and Eighty seven and of the Independence of the United States of America the Twelfth In witness whereof We have hereunto subscribed our Names, George Washington, President and deputy from Virginia.

New Hampshire: John Langdon,
Nicholas Gilman.

Massachusetts: Nathaniel Gorham,
Rufus King.

Connecticut: William Samuel Johnson,
Roger Sherman.

New York: Alexander Hamilton

New Jersey: William Livingston,
David Brearley,
William Paterson,
Jonathan Dayton.

Pennsylvania: Benjamin Franklin,
Thomas Mifflin,
Robert Morris,
George Clymer,
Thomas FitzSimons,
Jared Ingersoll,
James Wilson,
Gouverneur Morris.

Delaware: George Read,
Gunning Bedford Jr.,
John Dickinson,
Richard Bassett,
Jacob Broom.

Maryland: James McHenry,
Daniel of St. Thomas Jenifer,
Daniel Carroll.

Virginia: John Blair,
James Madison Jr.

North Carolina: William Blount,
Richard Dobbs Spaight,
Hugh Williamson.

South Carolina: John Rutledge,
Charles Cotesworth Pinckney,
Charles Pinckney,
Pierce Butler.

Georgia: William Few,
Abraham Baldwin.

[The language of the original Constitution, not including the Amendments, was adopted by a convention of the states on Sept. 17, 1787, and was subsequently ratified by the states on the following dates: Delaware, Dec. 7, 1787; Pennsylvania, Dec. 12, 1787; New Jersey, Dec. 18, 1787; Georgia, Jan. 2, 1788; Connecticut, Jan. 9, 1788; Massachusetts, Feb. 6, 1788; Maryland, April 28, 1788; South Carolina, May 23, 1788; New Hampshire, June 21, 1788.

Ratification was completed on June 21, 1788.

The Constitution subsequently was ratified by Virginia, June 25, 1788; New York, July 26, 1788; North Carolina, Nov. 21, 1789; Rhode Island, May 29, 1790; and Vermont, Jan. 10, 1791.]

Amendments

Amendment I
(First ten amendments ratified Dec. 15, 1791.)

Congress shall make no law respecting an establishment of religion, or prohibiting the free exercise thereof; or abridging the freedom of speech, or of the press; or the right of the people peaceably to assemble, and to petition the Government for a redress of grievances.

Amendment II

A well regulated Militia, being necessary to the security of a free State, the right of the people to keep and bear Arms, shall not be infringed.

Amendment III

No Soldier shall, in time of peace be quartered in any house, without the consent of the Owner, nor in time of war, but in a manner to be prescribed by law.

Amendment IV

The right of the people to be secure in their persons, houses, papers, and effects, against unreasonable searches and seizures, shall not be violated, and no Warrants shall issue, but upon probable cause, supported by Oath or affirmation, and particularly describing the place to be searched, and the persons or things to be seized.

Amendment V

No person shall be held to answer for a capital, or otherwise infamous crime, unless on a presentment or indictment of a Grand Jury, except in cases arising in the land or naval forces, or in the Militia, when in actual service in time of War or public danger; nor shall any person be subject for the same offence to be twice put in jeopardy of life or limb; nor shall be compelled in any criminal case to be a witness against himself, nor be deprived of life, liberty, or property, without due process of law; nor shall private property be taken for public use, without just compensation.

Amendment VI

In all criminal prosecutions, the accused shall enjoy

the right to a speedy and public trial, by an impartial jury of the State and district wherein the crime shall have been committed, which district shall have been previously ascertained by law, and to be informed of the nature and cause of the accusation; to be confronted with the witnesses against him; to have compulsory process for obtaining witnesses in his favor, and to have the Assistance of Counsel for his defence.

Amendment VII

In Suits at common law, where the value in controversy shall exceed twenty dollars, the right of trial by jury shall be preserved, and no fact tried by a jury, shall be otherwise re-examined in any Court of the United States, than according to the rules of the common law.

Amendment VIII

Excessive bail shall not be required, nor excessive fines imposed, nor cruel and unusual punishments inflicted.

Amendment IX

The enumeration in the Constitution, of certain rights, shall not be construed to deny or disparage others retained by the people.

Amendment X

The powers not delegated to the United States by the Constitution, nor prohibited by it to the States, are reserved to the States respectively, or to the people.

Amendment XI *(Ratified Feb. 7, 1795)*

The Judicial power of the United States shall not be construed to extend to any suit in law or equity, commenced or prosecuted against one of the United States by Citizens of another State, or by Citizens or Subjects of any Foreign State.

Amendment XII *(Ratified June 15, 1804)*

The Electors shall meet in their respective states and vote by ballot for President and Vice-President, one of whom, at least, shall not be an inhabitant of the same state with themselves; they shall name in their ballots the person voted for as President, and in distinct ballots the person voted for as Vice-President, and they shall make distinct lists of all persons voted for as President, and of all persons voted for as Vice-President, and of the number of votes for each, which lists they shall sign and certify, and transmit sealed to the seat of the government of the United States, directed to the President of the Senate; — The President of the Senate shall, in the presence of the Senate and House of Representatives, open all the certificates and the votes shall then be counted; — The person having the greatest number of votes for President, shall be the President, if such number be a majority of the whole number of Electors appointed; and if no person have such majority, then from the persons having the highest numbers not exceeding three on the list of those voted for as President, the House of Representatives shall choose immediately, by ballot, the President. But in choosing the President, the votes shall be taken by states, the representation from each state having one vote; a quorum for this purpose shall

consist of a member or members from two-thirds of the states, and a majority of all the states shall be necessary to a choice. [And if the House of Representatives shall not choose a President whenever the right of choice shall devolve upon them, before the fourth day of March next following, then the Vice-President shall act as President, as in the case of the death or other constitutional disability of the President —][11] The person having the greatest number of votes as Vice-President, shall be the Vice-President, if such number be a majority of the whole number of Electors appointed, and if no person have a majority, then from the two highest numbers on the list, the Senate shall choose the Vice-President; a quorum for the purpose shall consist of two-thirds of the whole number of Senators, and a majority of the whole number shall be necessary to a choice. But no person constitutionally ineligible to the office of President shall be eligible to that of Vice-President of the United States.

Amendment XIII *(Ratified Dec. 6, 1865)*

Section 1. Neither slavery nor involuntary servitude, except as a punishment for crime whereof the party shall have been duly convicted, shall exist within the United States, or any place subject to their jurisdiction.

Section 2. Congress shall have power to enforce this article by appropriate legislation.

Amendment XIV *(Ratified July 9, 1868)*

Section 1. All persons born or naturalized in the United States and subject to the jurisdiction thereof, are citizens of the United States and of the State wherein they reside. No State shall make or enforce any law which shall abridge the privileges or immunities of citizens of the United States; nor shall any State deprive any person of life, liberty, or property, without due process of law; nor deny to any person within its jurisdiction the equal protection of the laws.

Section 2. Representatives shall be apportioned among the several States according to their respective numbers, counting the whole number of persons in each State, excluding Indians not taxed. But when the right to vote at any election for the choice of electors for President and Vice President of the United States, Representatives in Congress, the Executive and Judicial officers of a State, or the members of the Legislature thereof, is denied to any of the male inhabitants of such State, being twenty-one years of age,[12] and citizens of the United States, or in any way abridged, except for participation in rebellion, or other crime, the basis of representation therein shall be reduced in the proportion which the number of such male citizens shall bear to the whole number of male citizens twenty-one years of age in such State.

Section 3. No person shall be a Senator or Representative in Congress, or elector of President and Vice President, or hold any office, civil or military, under the United States, or under any State, who, having previously taken an oath, as a member of Congress, or as an officer of the United States, or as a member of any State legislature, or as an executive or judicial officer of any State, to support the Constitution of the United States, shall have engaged in insurrection or rebellion against the same, or given aid or comfort to the enemies thereof. But Congress may by a vote of two-thirds of each House, remove such disability.

Section 4. The validity of the public debt of the United States, authorized by law, including debts incurred for payment of pensions and bounties for services in suppressing insurrection or rebellion, shall not be questioned. But neither the United States nor any State shall assume or pay any debt or obligation incurred in aid of insurrection or rebellion against the United States, or any claim for the loss or emancipation of any slave; but all such debts, obligations and claims shall be held illegal and void.

Section 5. The Congress shall have power to enforce, by appropriate legislation, the provisions of this article.

Amendment XV *(Ratified Feb. 3, 1870)*

Section 1. The right of citizens of the United States to vote shall not be denied or abridged by the United States or by any State on account of race, color, or previous condition of servitude.

Section 2. The Congress shall have power to enforce this article by appropriate legislation.

Amendment XVI *(Ratified Feb. 3, 1913)*

The Congress shall have power to lay and collect taxes on incomes, from whatever source derived, without apportionment among the several States, and without regard to any census or enumeration.

Amendment XVII *(Ratified April 8, 1913)*

The Senate of the United States shall be composed of two Senators from each State, elected by the people thereof, for six years; and each Senator shall have one vote. The electors in each State shall have the qualifications requisite for electors of the most numerous branch of the State legislatures.

When vacancies happen in the representation of any State in the Senate, the executive authority of such State shall issue writs of election to fill such vacancies: *Provided,* That the legislature of any State may empower the executive thereof to make temporary appointments until the people fill the vacancies by election as the legislature may direct.

This amendment shall not be so construed as to affect the election or term of any Senator chosen before it becomes valid as part of the Constitution.

Amendment XVIII *(Ratified Jan. 16, 1919)*

Section. 1. After one year from the ratification of this article the manufacture, sale, or transportation of intoxicating liquors within, the importation thereof into, or the exportation thereof from the United States and all territory subject to the jurisdiction thereof for beverage purposes is hereby prohibited.

Section 2. The Congress and the several States shall have concurrent power to enforce this article by appropriate legislation.

Section 3. This article shall be inoperative unless it shall have been ratified as an amendment to the Constitution by the legislatures of the several States, as provided in the Constitution, within seven years from the date of the submission hereof to the States by the Congress.][13]

Amendment XIX *(Ratified Aug. 18, 1920)*

The right of citizens of the United States to vote shall not be denied or abridged by the United States or by any State on account of sex.

Congress shall have power to enforce this article by appropriate legislation.

Amendment XX *(Ratified Jan. 23, 1933)*

Section 1. The terms of the President and Vice President shall end at noon on the 20th day of January, and the terms of Senators and Representatives at noon on the 3d day of January, of the years in which such terms would have ended if this article had not been ratified; and the terms of their successors shall then begin.

Section 2. The Congress shall assemble at least once in every year, and such meeting shall begin at noon on the 3d day of January, unless they shall by law appoint a different day.

Section 3.[14] If, at the time fixed for the beginning of the term of the President, the President elect shall have died, the Vice President elect shall become President. If a President shall not have been chosen before the time fixed for the beginning of his term, or if the President elect shall have failed to qualify, then the Vice President elect shall act as President until a President shall have qualified; and the Congress may by law provide for the case wherein neither a President elect nor a Vice President elect shall have qualified, declaring who shall then act as President, or the manner in which one who is to act shall be selected, and such person shall act accordingly until a President or Vice President shall have qualified.

Section 4. The Congress may by law provide for the case of the death of any of the persons from whom the House of Representatives may choose a President whenever the right of choice shall have devolved upon them, and for the case of the death of any of the persons from whom the Senate may choose a Vice President whenever the right of choice shall have devolved upon them.

Section 5. Sections 1 and 2 shall take effect on the 15th day of October following the ratification of this article.

Section 6. This article shall be inoperative unless it shall have been ratified as an amendment to the Constitution by the legislatures of three-fourths of the several States within seven years from the date of its submission.

Amendment XXI *(Ratified Dec. 5, 1933)*

Section 1. The eighteenth article of amendment to the Constitution of the United States is hereby repealed.

Section 2. The transportation or importation into any State, Territory or possession of the United States for delivery or use therein of intoxicating liquors, in violation of the laws thereof, is hereby prohibited.

Section 3. This article shall be inoperative unless it shall have been ratified as an amendment to the Constitution by conventions in the several States, as provided in the Constitution, within seven years from the date of the submission hereof to the States by the Congress.

Amendment XXII *(Ratified Feb. 27, 1951)*

Section 1. No person shall be elected to the office of the President more than twice, and no person who has held the office of President, or acted as President, for more than two years of a term to which some other person was elected President shall be elected to the office of the President more than once. But this Article shall not apply to any person holding the office of President when this Article was proposed by the Congress, and shall not prevent any person who may be holding the office of President, or acting as President, during the term within which this Article become operative from holding the office of President or acting as President during the remainder of such term.

Section 2. This Article shall be inoperative unless it shall have been ratified as an amendment to the Constitution by the legislatures of three-fourths of the several States within seven years from the date of its submission to the States by the Congress.

Amendment XXIII *(Ratified March 29, 1961)*

Section 1. The District constituting the seat of Government of the United States shall appoint in such manner as the Congress may direct:

A number of electors of President and Vice President equal to the whole number of Senators and Representatives in Congress to which the District would be entitled if it were a State, but in no event more than the least populous State; they shall be in addition to those appointed by the States, but they shall be considered, for the purposes of the election of President and Vice President, to be electors appointed by a State; and they shall meet in the District and perform such duties as provided by the twelfth article of amendment.

Section 2. The Congress shall have power to enforce this article by appropriate legislation.

Amendment XXIV *(Ratified Jan. 23, 1964)*

Section 1. The right of citizens of the United States to vote in any primary or other election for President or Vice President, for electors for President or Vice President, or for Senator or Representative in Congress, shall not be denied or abridged by the United States or any State by reason of failure to pay any poll tax or other tax.

Section 2. The Congress shall have power to enforce this article by appropriate legislation.

Amendment XXV *(Ratified Feb. 10, 1967)*

Section 1. In case of the removal of the President from office or of his death or resignation, the Vice President shall become President.

Section 2. Whenever there is a vacancy in the office of the Vice President, the President shall nominate a Vice President who shall take office upon confirmation by a majority vote of both Houses of Congress.

Section 3. Whenever the President transmits to the President pro tempore of the Senate and the Speaker of the House of Representatives his written declaration that he is unable to discharge the powers and duties of his office, and until he transmits to them a written declaration to the contrary, such powers and duties shall be discharged by the Vice President as Acting President.

Section 4. Whenever the Vice President and a major-

ity of either the principal officers of the executive departments or of such other body as Congress may by law provide, transmit to the President pro tempore of the Senate and the Speaker of the House of Representatives their written declaration that the President is unable to discharge the powers and duties of his office, the Vice President shall immediately assume the powers and duties of the office as Acting President.

Thereafter, when the President transmits to the President pro tempore of the Senate and the Speaker of the House of Representatives his written declaration that no inability exists, he shall resume the powers and duties of his office unless the Vice President and a majority of either the principal officers of the executive department or of such other body as Congress may by law provide, transmit within four days to the President pro tempore of the Senate and the Speaker of the House of Representatives their written declaration that the President is unable to discharge the powers and duties of his office. Thereupon Congress shall decide the issue, assembling within forty-eight hours for that purpose if not in session. If the Congress, within twenty-one days after receipt of the latter written declaration, or, if Congress is not in session, within twenty-one days after Congress is required to assemble, determines by two-thirds vote of both houses that the President is unable to discharge the powers and duties of his office, the Vice President shall continue to discharge the same as Acting President; otherwise, the President shall resume the powers and duties of his office.

Amendment XXVI *(Ratified July 1, 1971)*

Section 1. The right of citizens of the United States, who are eighteen years of age or older, to vote shall not be denied or abridged by the United States or by any State on account of age.

Section 2. The Congress shall have power to enforce this article by appropriate legislation.

Footnotes

1. The part in brackets was changed by section 2 of the 14th Amendment.
2. The part in brackets was changed by section 1 of the 17th Amendment.
3. The part in brackets was changed by the second paragraph of the 17th Amendment.
4. The part in brackets was changed by section 2 of the 20th Amendment.
5. The 16th Amendment gave Congress the power to tax incomes.
6. The material in brackets has been superseded by the 12th Amendment.
7. This provision has been affected by the 25th Amendment.
8. These clauses were affected by the 11th Amendment.
9. This paragraph has been superseded by the 13th Amendment.
10. Obsolete.
11. The part in brackets has been superseded by section 3 of the 20th Amendment.
12. See the 26th Amendment.
13. This Amendment was repealed by section 1 of the 21st Amendment.
14. See the 25th Amendment.

Source: U.S. Congress, House, Committee on the Judiciary, *The Constitution of the United States of America, As Amended Through July 1971*, H. Doc. 93-215, 93rd Cong., 2nd sess., 1974.

Historic Supreme Court Rulings

Excerpts of Chief Justice Marshall's Opinion in *Marbury v. Madison*

Following is the section of Chief Justice Marshall's opinion in Marbury v. Madison *(1803), dealing with the question of the power of the courts to invalidate an act of Congress.*

...The authority, therefore, given to the Supreme Court, by the act establishing the judicial courts of the United States, to issue writs of mandamus to public officers, appears not to be warranted by the constitution; and it becomes necessary to inquire whether a jurisdiction so conferred can be exercised.

The question, whether an act, repugnant to the constitution, can become the law of the land, is a question deeply interesting to the United States; but, happily, not of an intricacy proportioned to its interest. It seems only necessary to recognize certain principles, supposed to have been long and well established, to decide it.

That the people have an original right to establish, for their future government, such principles, as, in their opinion, shall most conduce to their own happiness is the basis on which the whole American fabric has been erected. The exercise of this original right is a very great exertion; nor can it, nor ought it, to be frequently repeated. The principles, therefore, so established, are deemed fundamental. And as the authority from which they proceed is supreme, and can seldom act, they are designed to be permanent.

This original and supreme will organizes the government, and assigns to different departments their respective powers. It may either stop here, or establish certain limits not to be transcended by those departments.

The government of the United States is of the latter description. The powers of the legislature are defined and limited; and that those limits may not be mistaken, or forgotten, the constitution is written. To what purpose are powers limited, and to what purpose is that limitation committed to writing, if these limits may, at any time, be passed by those intended to be restrained? The distinction between a government with limited and unlimited powers is abolished, if those limits do not confine the persons on whom they are imposed, and if acts prohibited and acts allowed, are of equal obligation. It is a proposition too plain to be contested, that the constitution controls any legislative act repugnant to it; or, that the legislature may alter the constitution by an ordinary act.

Between these alternatives there is no middle ground. The constitution is either a superior paramount law, unchangeable by ordinary means, or it is on a level with ordinary legislative acts, and, like other acts, is alterable when the legislature shall please to alter it.

If the former part of the alternative be true, then a legislative act contrary to the constitution is not law: if the latter part be true, then written constitutions are absurd attempts, on the part of the people, to limit a power in its own nature illimitable.

Certainly all those who have framed written constitutions contemplate them as forming the fundamental and paramount law of the nation, and consequently, the theory of every such government must be that an act of the legislature, repugnant to the constitution, is void.

This theory is essentially attached to a written constitution, and is, consequently, to be considered, by this court, as one of the fundamental principles of our society. It is not therefore to be lost sight of in the further consideration of this subject.

If an act of the legislature, repugnant to the constitution, is void, does it, notwithstanding its invalidity, bind the courts, and oblige them to give it effect? Or, in other words, though it be not law, does it constitute a rule as operative as if it was a law? This would be to overthrow in fact what was established in theory; and would seem, at first view, an absurdity too gross to be insisted on. It shall, however, receive a more attentive consideration.

It is emphatically the province and duty of the judicial department to say what the law is. Those who apply the rule to particular cases, must of necessity expound and interpret that rule. If two laws conflict with each other, the courts must decide on the operation of each.

So if a law be in opposition to the constitution; if both the law and the constitution apply to a particular case, so that the court must either decide that case conformably to the law, disregarding the constitution; or conformably to the constitution, disregarding the law; the court must determine which of these conflicting rules governs the case. This is of the very essence of judicial duty.

If, then, the courts are to regard the constitution, and the constitution is superior to any ordinary act of the legislature, the constitution, and not such ordinary act, must govern the case to which they both apply.

Those, then, who controvert the principle that the constitution is to be considered, in court, as a paramount law, are reduced to the necessity of maintaining that courts must close their eyes on the constitution, and see only the law.

This doctrine would subvert the very foundation of all written constitutions. It would declare that an act which, according to the principles and theory of our government, is entirely void, is yet, in practice, completely obligatory. It would declare that if the legislature shall do what is expressly forbidden, such act, notwithstanding the express prohibition, is in reality effectual. It would be giving to the legislature a practical and real omnipotence, with the same breath which professes to restrict their powers within narrow limits. It is prescribing limits, and declaring that those limits may be passed at pleasure.

That it thus reduces to nothing what we have deemed the greatest improvement on political institutions — a written constitution — would of itself be sufficient, in America, where written constitutions have been viewed with so much reverence, for rejecting the construction. But the peculiar expressions of the constitution of the United States furnish additional arguments in favour of its rejection.

The judicial power of the United States is extended to all cases arising under the constitution.

Could it be the intention of those who gave this power, to say that in using it the constitution should not be looked into? That a case arising under the constitution should be decided without examining the instrument under which it arises?

This is too extravagant to be maintained.

In some cases, then, the constitution must be looked into by the judges. And if they can open it at all, what part of it are they forbidden to read or to obey?

There are many other parts of the constitution which serve to illustrate this subject. It is declared, that "no tax or duty shall be laid on articles exported from any state." Suppose, a duty on the export of cotton, of tobacco or of flour; and a suit instituted to recover it. Ought judgment to be rendered in such a case? Ought the judges to close their eyes on the constitution, and only see the law?

The constitution declares "that no bill of attainder or ex post facto law shall be passed."

If, however, such a bill should be passed, and a person should be prosecuted under it; must the court condemn to death those victims whom the constitution endeavors to preserve?

"No person," says the constitution, "shall be convicted of treason unless on the testimony of two witnesses to the same overt act, or on confession in open court."

Here the language of the constitution is addressed especially to the courts. It prescribes, directly for them, a rule of evidence not to be departed from. If the legislature should change that rule, and declare *one* witness, or a confession *out* of court, sufficient for conviction, must the constitutional principle yield to the legislative act?

From these, and many other selections which might be made, it is apparent, that the framers of the constitution contemplated that instrument as a rule for the government of *courts*, as well as of the legislature.

Why otherwise does it direct the judges to take an oath to support it? This oath certainly applies in an especial manner, to their conduct in their official character. How immoral to impose it on them, if they were to be used as the instruments, and the knowing instruments, for violating what they swear to support!

The oath of office, too, imposed by the legislature, is completely demonstrative of the legislative opinion on this subject. It is in these words: "I do solemnly swear that I will administer justice without respect to persons, and do equal right to the poor and to the rich; and that I will faithfully and impartially discharge all the duties incumbent on me as —, according to the best of my abilities and understanding agreeably to the *constitution* and laws of the United States."

Why does a judge swear to discharge his duties agreeably to the constitution of the United States, if that constitution forms no rule for his government? If it is closed upon him, and cannot be inspected by him?

If such be the real state of things, this is worse than solemn mockery. To prescribe, or to take this oath, becomes equally a crime.

It is also not entirely unworthy of observation, that in declaring what shall be the *supreme* law of the land, the *constitution* itself is first mentioned; and not the laws of the United States generally, but those only which shall be made in *pursuance* of the constitution, have that rank.

Thus, the particular phraseology of the constitution of the United States confirms and strengthens the principle, supposed to be essential to all written constitutions, that a law repugnant to the constitution is void; and that *courts*, as well as other departments, are bound by that instrument.

The rule must be discharged.

Excerpts From Decision On Subpoena for Nixon Tapes

Following are excerpts from the opinion issued by the Supreme Court July 24, 1974, in U.S. v. Nixon, *upholding a lower court decision ordering President Nixon to comply with the Watergate special prosecutor's subpoena for presidential tape recordings and documents.*

MR. CHIEF JUSTICE BURGER delivered the opinion of the Court.

These cases present for review the denial of a motion, filed on behalf of the President of the United States, in the case of *United States v. Mitchell et al.* (D.C. Crim. No. 74-110), to quash a third-party subpoena duces tecum issued by the United States District Court for the District of Columbia, pursuant to Fed. Rule Crim. Proc. 17 (c). The subpoena directed the President to produce certain tape recordings and documents relating to his conversations with aides and advisors. The court rejected the President's claims of absolute executive privilege, of lack of jurisdiction, and of failure to satisfy the requirements of Rule 17 (c). The President appealed to the Court of Appeals. We granted the United States' petition for certiorari before judgment, and also the President's responsive cross-petition for certiorari before judgment, because of the public importance of the issues presented and the need for their prompt resolution. —U.S.—, —(1974).

On March 1, 1974, a grand jury of the United States District Court for the District of Columbia returned an indictment charging seven named individuals with various offenses, including conspiracy to defraud the United States and to obstruct justice. Although he was not designated as such in the indictment, the grand jury named the President, among others, as an unindicted co-conspirator. On April 18, 1974, upon motion of the Special Prosecutor, see n. 8, infra, a subpoena duces tecum was issued pursuant to Rule 17 (c) to the President by the United States District Court and made returnable on May 2, 1974. This subpoena required the production, in advance of the September 9 trial date, of certain tapes, memoranda, papers, transcripts, or other writings relating to certain precisely identified meetings between the President and others. The Special Prosecutor was able to fix the time, place and persons present at these discussions because the White House daily logs and appointment records had been delivered to him. On April 30, the President publicly released edited transcripts of 43 conversations; portions of 20 conversations subject to subpoena in the present case were included. On May 1, 1974, the President's counsel, filed a "special appearance" and a motion to quash the subpoena, under Rule 17 (c). This motion was accompanied by a formal claim of privilege. At a subsequent hearing, further motions to expunge the grand jury's action naming the President as an unindicted co-conspirator and for protective orders against the disclosure of that information were filed or raised orally by counsel for the President.

On May 20, 1974, the District Court denied the motion to quash and the motions to expunge and for protective orders. —F. Supp.—(1974). It further ordered "the President or any subordinate officer, official or employee with custody or control of the documents or objects subpoenaed," id., at—, to deliver to the District Court, on or before May 31, 1974, the originals of all subpoenaed items, as well as an index and analysis of those items, together with tape copies of those portions of the subpoenaed recordings for which transcripts had been released to the public by the President on April 30. The District Court rejected jurisdictional challenges based on a contention that the dispute was nonjusticiable because it was between the Special Prosecutor and the Chief Executive and hence "intra-executive" in character; it also rejected the contention that the judiciary was without authority to review an assertion of executive privilege by the President. The court's rejection of the first challenge was based on the authority and powers vested in the Special Prosecutor by the regulation promulgated by the Attorney General; the court concluded that a justiciable controversy was presented. The second challenge was held to be foreclosed by the decision in *Nixon v. Sirica,*—U.S. App. D.C.—, 487 F. 2d 700 (1973).

The District Court held that the judiciary, not the President was the final arbiter of a claim of executive privilege. The court concluded that, under the circumstances of this case, the presumptive privilege was overcome by the Special Prosecutor's prima facie "demonstration of need sufficiently compelling to warrant judicial examination in chambers...."—F. Supp., at—. The court held, finally, that the Special Prosecutor had satisfied the requirements of Rule 17 (c)....

On May 24, 1974, the President filed a timely notice of appeal from the District Court order, and the certified record from the

District Court was docketed in the United States Court of Appeals for the District of Columbia Circuit. On the same day, the President also filed a petition for writ of mandamus in the Court of Appeals seeking review of the District Court order.

Later on May 24, the Special Prosecutor also filed, in this Court, a petition for a writ of certiorari before judgment. On May 31, the petition was granted with an expedited briefing schedule.—U.S.—(1974). On June 6, the President filed, under seal, a cross-petition for writ or certiorari before judgment. This cross-petition was granted June 15, 1974,—U.S.—(1974), and the case was set for argument on July 8, 1974.

I
Jurisdiction

The threshold question presented is whether the May 20, 1974, order of the District Court was an appealable order and whether this case was properly "in," 28 U.S.C. 1254, the United States Court of Appeals when the petition for certiorari was filed in this Court. Court of Appeals jurisdiction under 28 U.S.C. 1291 encompasses only "final decisions of the district courts...."

The finality requirement of 28 U.S.C. 1291 embodies a strong congressional policy against piecemeal reviews, and against obstructing or impeding an ongoing judicial proceeding by interlocutory appeals. See, e.g., *Cobbledick v. United States,* 309 U.S. 323, 324-326 (1940). This requirement ordinarily promotes judicial efficiency and hastens the ultimate termination of litigation....

The requirement of submitting to contempt, however, is not without exception and in some instances the purposes underlying the finality rule require a different result....

Here too the traditional contempt avenue to immediate appeal is peculiarly inappropriate due to the unique setting in which the question arises. To require a President of the United States to place himself in the posture of disobeying an order of a court merely to trigger the procedural mechanism for review of the ruling would be unseemly, and present an unnecessary occasion for constitutional confrontation between two branches of the Government. Similarly, a federal judge should not be placed in the posture of issuing a citation to a President simply in order to invoke review....

II
Justiciability

In the District Court the President's counsel argued that the Court lacked jurisdiction to issue the subpoena because the matter was an intra-branch dispute between a subordinate and superior officer of the Executive Branch and hence not subject to judicial resolution. That argument has been renewed in this Court with emphasis on the contention that the dispute does not present a "case" or "controversy" which can be adjudicated in the federal courts. The President's counsel argues that the federal courts should not intrude into areas committed to the other branches of Government. He views the present dispute as essentially a "jurisdictional" dispute within the Executive Branch which he analogizes to a dispute between two congressional committees. Since the Executive Branch has exclusive authority and absolute discretion to decide whether to prosecute a case, *Confiscation Cases,* 7 Wall. 454 (1869), *United States v. Cox,* 342 F. 2d 167, 171 (CA 5), cert. denied, 381 U.S. 935 (1965), it is contended that a President's decision is final in determining what evidence is to be used in a given criminal case. Although his counsel concedes the President has delegated certain specific powers to the Special Prosecutor, he has not "waived nor delegated to the Special Prosecutor the President's duty to claim privileges as to all materials ... which fall within the President's inherent authority to refuse to disclose to any executive officer." Brief for the President 47. The Special Prosecutor's demand for the items therefore presents, in the view of the President's counsel, a political question under *Baker v. Carr,* 369 U.S. 186 (1962), since it involves a "textually demonstrable" grant of power under Art. II.

The mere assertion of a claim of an "intra-branch dispute," without more, has never operated to defeat federal jurisdiction; justiciability does not depend on such a surface inquiry. In *United States v. ICC,* 337 U.S. 426 (1949), the Court observed, "courts must look behind names that symbolize the parties to determine whether a justiciable case or controversy is presented." Id., at 430....

Our starting point is the nature of the proceeding for which the evidence is sought — here a pending criminal prosecution. It is a judicial proceeding in a federal court alleging violation of federal laws and is brought in the name of the United States as sovereign. *Berger v. United States,* 295 U.S. 78, 88 (1935). Under the authority of Art. II, 2, Congress has vested in the Attorney General the power to conduct the criminal litigation of the United States Government. 28 U.S.C. 516. It has also vested in him the power to appoint subordinate officers to assist him in the discharge of his duties. 28 U.S.C. 509, 510, 515, 533. Acting pursuant to those statutes, the Attorney General has delegated the authority to represent the United States in these particular matters to a Special Prosecutor with unique authority and tenure. The regulation gives the Special Prosecutor explicit power to contest the invocation of executive privilege in the process of seeking evidence deemed relevant to the performance of these specially delegated duties 38 Fed. Reg. 30739....

So long as this regulation remains in force the Executive Branch is bound by it, and indeed the United States as the sovereign composed of the three branches is bound to respect and enforce it. Moreover, the delegation of authority to the Special Prosecutor in this case is not an ordinary delegation by the Attorney General to a subordinate officer; with the authorization of the President, the Acting Attorney General provided in the regulation that the Special Prosecutor was not to be removed without the "consensus" of eight designated leaders of Congress....

The demands of and the resistance to the subpoena present an obvious controversy in the ordinary sense, but that alone is not sufficient to meet constitutional standards. In the constitutional sense, controversy means more than disagreement and conflict; rather it means the kind of controversy courts traditionally resolve. Here at issue is the production or nonproduction of specified evidence deemed by the Special Prosecutor to be relevant and admissible in a pending criminal case. It is sought by one official of the Government within the scope of his express authority; it is resisted by the Chief Executive on the ground of his duty to preserve the confidentiality of the communications of the President. Whatever the correct answer on the merits, these issues are "of a type which are traditionally justiciable...."

In light of the uniqueness of the setting in which the conflict arises, the fact that both parties are officers of the Executive Branch cannot be viewed as a barrier to justiciability. It would be inconsistent with the applicable law and regulation, and the unique facts of this case to conclude other than that the Special Prosecutor has standing to bring this action and that a justiciable controversy is presented for decision.

III
Rule 17 (c)

The subpoena duces tecum is challenged on the ground that the Special Prosecutor failed to satisfy the requirements of Fed. Rule Crim. Proc. 17 (c), which governs the issuance of subpoenas duces tecum in federal criminal proceedings. If we sustained this challenge, there would be no occasion to reach the claim of privilege asserted with respect to the subpoenaed material....

Against this background, the Special Prosecutor, in order to carry his burden, must clear three hurdles: (1) relevancy; (2) admissibility; (3) specificity....

With respect to many of the tapes, the Special Prosecutor offered the sworn testimony or statements of one or more of the participants in the conversations as to what was said at the time. As for the remainder of the tapes, the identity of the participants and the time and place of the conversations, taken in their total context, permit a rational inference that at least part of the conversations relate to the offenses charged in the indictment....

We also conclude there was a sufficient preliminary showing that each of the subpoenaed tapes contains evidence admissible with respect to the offenses charged in the indictment. The most cogent objection to the admissibility of the taped conversations here at issue is that they are a collection of out-of-court statements by declarants who will not be subject to the cross-examination and that the statements are therefore inadmissible hearsay. Here, however, most of the tapes apparently contain conversations to which one or more of the defendants named in the indictment were party. . . .

Here, however, there are valid potential evidentiary uses for the same material and the analysis and possible transcription of the tapes may take a significant period of time. Accordingly, we cannot say that the District Court erred in authorizing the issuance of the subpoena duces tecum. . . .

In a case such as this, however, where a subpoena is directed to a President of the United States, appellate review in deference to a coordinate branch of government, should be particularly meticulous to ensure that the standards of Rule 17 (c) have been correctly applied *United States v. Burr,* 25 Fed. Cas. 30, 34 (No. 14,692) (1807). From our examination of the materials submitted by the Special Prosecutor to the District Court in support of his motion for the subpoena, we are persuaded that the District Court's denial of the President's motion to quash the subpoena was consistent with Rule 17 (c). We also conclude that the Special Prosecutor has made a sufficient showing to justify a subpoena for production before trial. . . .

IV
The Claim of Privilege

Having determined that the requirements of Rule 17 (c) were satisfied, we turn to the claim that the subpoena should be quashed because it demands "confidential conversations between a President and his close advisors that it would be inconsistent with the public interest to produce" App. 48a. The first contention is a broad claim that the separation of powers doctrine precludes judicial review of a President's claim of privilege. The second contention is that if he does not prevail on the claim of absolute privilege, the court should hold as a matter of constitutional law that the privilege prevails over the subpoena duces tecum.

In the performance of assigned constitutional duties each branch of the Government must initially interpret the Constitution and the interpretation of its powers by any branch is due great respect from the others. The President's counsel, as we have noted, reads the Constitution as providing an absolute privilege of confidentiality for all presidential communications. Many decisions of this Court, however, have unequivocally reaffirmed the holding of *Marbury v. Madison,* 1 Cranch 137 (1803), that "it is emphatically the province and duty of the judicial department to say what the law is." Id., at 177.

No holding of the Court has defined the scope of judicial power specifically relating to the enforcement of a subpoena for confidential presidential communications for use in criminal prosecution, but other exercises of powers by the Executive Branch and the Legislative Branch have been found invalid as in conflict with the Constitution *Powell v. McCormack* supra; *Youngstown,* supra. In a series of cases, the Court interpreted the explicit immunity conferred by express provisions of the Constitution on Members of the House and Senate by the Speech or Debate Clause, U.S. Const. Art. I, 6. *Doe v. McMillan,* 412 U.S. 306 (1973), *Gravel v. United States,* 408 U.S. 606 (1973); *United States v. Brewster,* 408 U.S. 501 (1972), *United States v. Johnson,* 383 U.S. 169 (1966). Since this Court has consistently exercised the power to construe and delineate claims arising under express powers, it must follow that the Court has authority to interpret claims with respect to powers alleged to derive from enumerated powers. . . . Notwithstanding the deference each branch must accord the others, the "judicial power of the United States" vested in the federal courts by Art. III, 1 of the Constitution can no more be shared with the Executive Branch than the Chief Executive, for example, can share with the Judiciary the veto power, or the Congress share with the Judiciary the power to override a presidential veto. Any other conclusion would be contrary to the basic concept of separa-

tion of powers and the checks and balances that flow from the scheme of a tripartite government. The Federalist, No. 47, p. 313 (C. F. Mittel ed. 1938). We therefore reaffirm that it is "emphatically the province and the duty" of this Court "to say what the law is" with respect to the claim of privilege presented in this case. *Marbury v. Madison,* supra, at 177.

B

In support of his claim of absolute privilege, the President's counsel urges two grounds one of which is common to all governments and one of which is peculiar to our system of separation of powers. The first ground is the valid need for protection of communications between high government officials and those who advise and assist them in the performance of their manifold duties; the importance of this confidentiality is too plain to require further discussion. Human experience teaches that those who expect public dissemination of their remarks may well temper candor with a concern for appearances and for their own interests to the detriment of the decision-making process. Whatever the nature of the privilege of confidentiality of presidential communications in the exercise of Art. II powers the privilege can be said to derive from the supremacy of each branch within its own assigned area of constitutional duties. Certain powers and privileges flow from the nature of enumerated powers; the protection of the confidentiality of presidential communications has similar constitutional underpinnings.

The second ground asserted by the President's counsel in support of the claim of absolute privilege rests on the doctrine of separation of powers. Here it is argued that the independence of the Executive Branch within its own sphere *Humphrey's Executor v. United States,* 295 U.S. 602, 629-630; *Kilbourn v. Thompson,* 103 U.S. 168, 190-191 (1880), insulates a president from a judicial subpoena in an ongoing criminal prosecution, and thereby protects confidential presidential communications.

However, neither the doctrine of separation of powers, nor the need for confidentiality of high level communications without more can sustain an absolute, unqualified presidential privilege of immunity from judicial process under all circumstances. The President's need for complete candor and objectivity from advisers calls for great deference from the courts. However, when the privilege depends solely on the broad, undifferentiated claim of public interest in the confidentiality of such conversations, a confrontation with other values arises. Absent a claim of need to protect military, diplomatic or sensitive national security secrets, we find it difficult to accept the argument that even the very important interest in confidentiality of presidential communications is significantly diminished by production of such material for in camera inspection with all the protection that a district court will be obliged to provide.

The impediment that an absolute unqualified privilege would place in the way of the primary constitutional duty of the Judicial Branch to do justice in criminal prosecutions would plainly conflict with the function of the courts under Art. III. In designing the structure of our Government and dividing and allocating the sovereign power among three coequal branches, the Framers of the Constitution sought to provide a comprehensive system, but the separate powers were not intended to operate with absolute independence. . . . To read the Art. II powers of the President as providing an absolute privilege as against a subpoena essential to enforcement of criminal statutes on no more than a generalized claim of the public interest in confidentiality and nondiplomatic discussions would upset the constitutional balance of "a workable government" and gravely impair the role of the courts under Art. III.

C

Since we conclude that the legitimate needs of the judicial process may outweigh presidential privilege, it is necessary to resolve those competing interests in a manner that preserves the essential functions of each branch. The right and indeed the duty to resolve that question does not free the judiciary from according high respect to the representations made on behalf of the President. *United States v. Burr,* 25 Fed. Cas. 187, 190, 191-192 (No. 14, 694) (1807).

The expectation of a President to the confidentiality of his conversations and correspondence, like the claim of confidentiality of judicial deliberations, for example, has all the values to which we accord deference for the privacy of all citizens and added to those values the necessity for protection of the public interest in candid, objective, and even blunt or harsh opinions in presidential decision-making. A President and those who assist him must be free to explore alternatives in the process of shaping policies and making decisions and to do so in a way many would be unwilling to express except privately. These are the considerations justifying a presumptive privilege for presidential communications. The privilege is fundamental to the operation of government and inextricably rooted in the separation of powers under the Constitution. In *Nixon v. Sirica,*—U.S. App. D.C.—, 487 F. 2d 700 (1973), the Court of Appeals held that such presidential communications are "presumptively privileged," id., at 717, and this position is accepted by both parties in the present litigation. We agree with Mr. Chief Justice Marshall's observation, therefore, that "in no case of this kind would a court be required to proceed against the President as against an ordinary individual." *United States v. Burr,* 25 Fed. Cas. 187, 191 (No. 14,694) (CCD Va. 1807).

But this presumptive privilege must be considered in light of our historic commitment to the rule of law. This is nowhere more profoundly manifest than in our view that "the twofold aim [of criminal justice] is that guilt shall not escape or innocence suffer." *Berger v. United States,* 295 U.S. 78, 88 (1935). We have elected to employ an adversary system of criminal justice in which the parties contest all issues before a court of law. The need to develop all relevant facts in the adversary system is both fundamental and comprehensive. The ends of criminal justice would be defeated if judgments were to be founded on a partial or speculative presentation of the facts. The very integrity of the judicial system and public confidence in the system depend on full disclosure of all the facts, within the framework of the rules of evidence. To ensure that justice is done, it is imperative to the function of courts that compulsory process be available for the production of evidence needed either by the prosecution or by the defense.

Only recently, the Court restated the ancient proposition of law, albeit in the context of a grand jury inquiry rather than a trial, " 'that the public ... has a right to every man's evidence' except for those persons protected by a constitutional, common law, or statutory privilege, *United States v. Bryan,* 339 U.S., at 331 (1949); *Blackmer v. United States,* 284 U.S. 421, 328, *Branzburg v. United States,* 408 U.S. 665, 688 (1973)." The privileges referred to by the Court are designed to protect weighty and legitimate competing interests. Thus the Fifth Amendment to the Constitution provides that no man "shall be compelled in any criminal case to be a witness against himself." And, generally, an attorney or a priest may not be required to disclose what has been revealed in professional confidence. These and other interests are recognized in law by privileges against forced disclosure, established in the Constitution, by statute, or at common law. Whatever their origins, these exceptions to the demand for every man's evidence are not lightly created nor expansively construed, for they are in derogation of the search for truth.

In this case, the President challenges a subpoena served on him as a third party requiring the production of materials for use in a criminal prosecution on the claim that he has a privilege against disclosure of confidential communications. He does not place his claim of privilege on the grounds they are military or diplomatic secrets. As to these areas of Art. II duties, the courts have traditionally shown the utmost deference to presidential responsibilities. In *C & S. Air Lines v. Waterman Steamship Corp.,* 333 U.S. 103, 111 (1948), dealing with presidential authority involving foreign policy considerations, the Court said:

"The President, both as a Commander-in-Chief and as the Nation's organ for foreign affairs, has available intelligence services whose reports are not and ought not to be published to the world. It would be intolerable that courts, without the relevant information, should review and perhaps nullify actions of the Executive taken on information properly held secret." Id., at 111.

In *United States v. Reynolds,* 345 U.S. 1 (1952), dealing with a claimant's demand for evidence in a damage case against the Government the Court said:

"It may be possible to satisfy the court, from all the circumstances of the case, that there is a reasonable danger that compulsion of the evidence will expose military matters which, in the interest of national security, should not be divulged. When this is the case, the occasion for the privilege is appropriate, and the court should not jeopardize the security which the privilege is meant to protect by insisting upon an examination of the evidence, even by the judge alone, in chambers."

No case of the Court, however, has extended this high degree of deference to a President's generalized interest in confidentiality. Nowhere in the Constitution as we have noted earlier, is there any explicit reference to a privilege of confidentiality, yet to the extent this interest relates to the effective discharge of a President's powers, it is constitutionally based.

The right to the production of all evidence at a criminal trial similarly has constitutional dimensions. The Sixth Amendment explicitly confers upon every defendant in a criminal trial the right "to be confronted with the witnesses against him" and "to have compulsory process for obtaining witnesses in his favor." Moreover, the Fifth Amendment also guarantees that no person shall be deprived of liberty without due process of law. It is the manifest duty of the courts to vindicate those guarantees and to accomplish that it is essential that all relevant and admissible evidence be produced.

In this case, we must weigh the importance of the general privilege of confidentiality of presidential communications in performance of his responsibilities against the inroads of such a privilege on the fair administration of criminal justice. The interest in preserving confidentiality is weighty indeed and entitled to great respect. However, we cannot conclude that advisers will be moved to temper the candor of their remarks by the infrequent occasions of disclosure because of the possibility that such conversations will be called for in the context of a criminal prosecution.

On the other hand, the allowance of the privilege to withhold evidence that is demonstrably relevant in a criminal trial would cut deeply into the guarantee of due process of law and gravely impair the basic function of the courts. A President's acknowledged need for confidentiality in the communications of his office is general in nature, whereas the constitutional need for production of relevant evidence in a criminal proceeding is specific and central to the fair adjudication of a particular criminal case in the administration of justice. Without access to specific facts a criminal prosecution may be totally frustrated. The President's broad interest in confidentiality of communications will not be vitiated by disclosure of a limited number of conversations preliminarily shown to have some bearing on the pending criminal cases.

We conclude that when the ground for asserting privilege as to subpoenaed materials sought for use in a criminal trial is based only on the generalized interest in confidentiality, it cannot prevail over the fundamental demands of due process of law in the fair administration of criminal justice. The generalized assertion of privilege must yield to the demonstrated, specific need for evidence in a pending criminal trial.

D

We have earlier determined that the District Court did not err in authorizing the issuance of the subpoena. If a president concludes that compliance with a subpoena would be injurious to the public interest he may properly, as was done here, invoke a claim of privilege on the return of the subpoena. Upon receiving a claim of privilege from the Chief Executive, it became the further duty of the District Court to treat the subpoenaed material as presumptively privileged and to require the Special Prosecutor to demonstrate that the presidential material was "essential to the justice of the [pending criminal] case," *United States v. Burr,* supra, at 192. Here the District Court treated the material as presumptively privileged, proceeded to find that the Special Prosecutor had made a sufficient showing to rebut the presumption and ordered an in camera examination of the subpoenaed material. On the basis of our examination of the record, we are unable to conclude that the District Court erred in ordering the inspection. Accordingly, we affirm the order of the District Court that subpoenaed materials be transmitted to that court. We now turn to the important question of the District Court's responsibilities in conducting the in camera examination of presidential materials or communications delivered under the compulsion of the subpoena duces tecum.

E

Enforcement of the subpoena duces tecum was stayed pending this Court's resolution of the issues raised by the petitions for certiorari. Those issues now having been disposed of, the matter of implementation will rest with the District Court. "[T]he guard, furnished to [President] to protect him from being harassed by vexations and unnecessary subpoenas, is to be looked for in the conduct of the [district] court after the subpoenas have issued; not in any circumstances which is to precede their being issued." *United States v. Burr,* supra, at 34. Statements that meet the test of admissibility and relevance must be isolated; all other material must be excised. At this stage the District Court is not limited to representations of the Special Prosecutor as to the evidence sought by the subpoena; the material will be available to the District Court. It is elementary that in camera inspection of evidence is always a procedure calling for scrupulous protection against any release or publication of material not found by the court, at that stage, probably admissible in evidence and relevant to the issues of the trial for which it is sought. That being true of an ordinary situation, it is obvious that the District Court has a very heavy responsibility to see to it that presidential conversations, which are either not relevant or not admissible, are accorded that high degree of respect due the President of the United States. Mr. Chief Justice Marshall sitting as a trial judge in the Burr case, supra, was extraordinarily careful to point out that:

> "[I]n no case of this kind would a Court be required to proceed against the President as against an ordinary individual." *United States v. Burr,* 25 Fed. Cases 187, 191 (No. 14,694).

Marshall's statement cannot be read to mean in any sense that a President is above the law, but relates to the singularly unique role under Art. II of a President's communications and activities related to the performance of duties under that Article. Moreover a President's communications and activities encompass a vastly wider range of sensitive material than would be true of any "ordinary individual." It is therefore necessary in the public interest to afford presidential confidentiality the greatest protection consistent with the fair administration of justice. The need for confidentiality even as to idle conversations with associates in which casual reference might be made concerning political leaders within the country or foreign statesmen is too obvious to call for further treatment. We have no doubt that the District Judge will at all times accord to presidential records that high degree of deference suggested in *United States v. Burr,* supra, and will discharge his responsibility to see to it that until released to the Special Prosecutor no in camera material is revealed to anyone. This burden applies with even greater force to excised material: once the decision is made to excise, the material is restored to its privileged status and should be returned under seal to its lawful custodian.

Since this matter came before the Court during the pendency of a criminal prosecution, and on representations that time is of the essence, the mandate shall issue forthwith.

Affirmed

Excerpts From Decision On Campaign Spending

Following are excerpts from the Supreme Court's opinion in the case of Buckley v. Valeo, *decided Jan. 30, 1976, striking down portions of the Federal Election Campaign Act Amendments of 1974, which set limits on the amounts of money a candidate for federal office could spend, but upholding the law's limitations on the amounts that an individual could contribute to a campaign. The opinion was unsigned* (per curiam). *The justices divided differently on various aspects of the law.*

PER CURIAM. [MR. JUSTICE STEVENS took no part in the consideration or decision of these cases.]

These appeals present constitutional challenges to the key provisions of the Federal Election Campaign Act of 1971, as amended in 1974.

The Court of Appeals, in sustaining the Act in large part against various constitutional challenges, viewed it as "by far the most comprehensive reform legislation [ever] passed by Congress concerning the election of the President, Vice-President, and members of Congress." ... The Act, summarized in broad terms, contains the following provisions: (a) individual political contributions are limited to $1,000 to any single candidate per election, with an overall annual limitation of $25,000 by any contributor; independent expenditures by individuals and groups "relative to a clearly identified candidate" are limited to $1,000 a year; campaign spending by candidates for various federal offices and spending for national conventions by political parties are subject to prescribed limits; (b) contributions and expenditures above certain threshold levels must be reported and publicly disclosed; (c) a system for public funding of Presidential campaign activities is established by Subtitle H of the Internal Revenue Code; and (d) a Federal Election Commission is established to administer and enforce the Act....

I. Contribution and Expenditure Limitations

The intricate statutory scheme adopted by Congress to regulate federal election campaigns includes restrictions on political contributions and expenditures that apply broadly to all phases of and all participants in the election process. The major contribution and expenditure limitations in the Act prohibit individuals from contributing more than $25,000 in a single year or more than $1,000 to any single candidate for an election campaign and from spending more than $1,000 a year "relative to a clearly identified candidate." Other provisions restrict a candidate's use of personal and family resources in his campaign and limit the overall amount that can be spent by a candidate in campaigning for federal office.

The constitutional power of Congress to regulate federal elections is well established and is not questioned by any of the parties in this case. Thus, the critical constitutional questions presented here go not to the basic power of Congress to legislate in this area, but to whether the specific legislation that Congress has enacted interferes with First Amendment freedoms or invidiously discriminates against nonincumbent candidates and minor parties in contravention of the Fifth Amendment.

The Act's contribution and expenditure limitations operate in an area of the most fundamental First Amendment activities. Discussion of public issues and debate on the qualifications of candidates are integral to the operation of the system of government established by our Constitution. The First Amendment affords the broadest protection to such political expression in order "to assure the unfettered interchange of ideas for the bringing about of political and social changes desired by the people." *Roth* v. *United States* . . . (1957). . . .

The First Amendment protects political association as well as political expression. . . .

. . . A restriction on the amount of money a person or group can spend on political communication during a campaign necessarily reduces the quantity of expression by restricting the number of issues discussed, the depth of their exploration, and the size of the audience reached. This is because virtually every means of communicating ideas in today's mass society requires the expenditure of money. The distribution of the humblest handbill or leaflet entails printing, paper, and circulation costs. Speeches and rallies generally necessitate hiring a hall and publicizing the event. The electorate's increasing dependence on television, radio, and other mass media for news and information has made these expensive modes of communication indispensable instruments of effective political speech. . . .

By contrast with a limitation upon expenditures for political expression, a limitation upon the amount that any one person or group may contribute to a candidate or political committee entails only a marginal restriction upon the contributor's ability to engage in free communication. A contribution serves as a general expression of support for the candidate and his views, but does not communicate the underlying basis for the support. The quantity of communication by the contributor does not increase perceptibly with the size of his contribution, since the expression rests solely on the undifferentiated, symbolic art of contributing. At most, the size of the contribution provides a very rough index of the intensity of the contributor's support for the candidate. A limitation on the amount of money a person may give to a candidate or campaign organization thus involves little direct restraint on his political communication, for it permits the symbolic expression of support evidenced by a contribution but does not in any way infringe the contributor's freedom to discuss candidates and issues. . . .

Given the important role of contributions in financing political campaigns, contribution restrictions could have a severe impact on political dialogue if the limitations prevented candidates and political committees from amassing the resources necessary for effective advocacy. There is no indication, however, that the contribution limitations imposed by the Act would have any dramatic adverse effect on the funding of campaigns and political associations. The overall effect of the Act's contribution ceilings is merely to require candidates and political committees to raise funds from a greater number of persons and to compel people who would otherwise contribute amounts greater than the statutory limits to expend such funds on direct political expression, rather than to reduce the total amount of money potentially available to promote political expression.

The Act's contribution and expenditure limitations also impinge on protected associational freedoms. Making a contribution, like joining a political party, serves to affiliate a person with a candidate. In addition, it enables like-minded persons to pool their resources in furtherance of common political goals. The Act's contribution ceilings thus limit one important means of associating with a candidate or committee, but leave the contributor free to become a member of any political association and to assist personally in the association's efforts on behalf of candidates. . . .

In sum, although the Act's contribution and expenditure limitations both implicate fundamental First Amendment interests, its expenditure ceilings impose significantly more severe restrictions on protected freedoms of political expression and association than do its limitations on financial contributions. . . .

It is unnecessary to look beyond the Act's primary purpose . . . in order to find a constitutionally sufficient justification for the $1,000 contribution limitation. Under a system of private financing of elections, a candidate lacking immense personal or family wealth must depend on financial contributions from others to provide the resources necessary to conduct a successful campaign. The increasing importance of the communications media and sophisticated mass mailing and polling operations to effective cam-

paigning make the raising of large sums of money an ever more essential ingredient of an effective candidacy. To the extent that large contributions are given to secure political *quid pro quos* from current and potential office holders, the integrity of our system of representative democracy is undermined. Although the scope of such pernicious practices can never be reliably ascertained, the deeply disturbing examples surfacing after the 1972 election demonstrate that the problem is not an illusory one. . . .

The Act's $1,000 contribution limitation focuses precisely on the problem of large campaign contributions — the narrow aspect of political association where the actuality and potential for corruption have been identified — while leaving persons free to engage in independent political expression, to associate actively through volunteering their services, and to assist to a limited but nonetheless substantial extent in supporting candidates and committees with financial resources. Significantly, the Act's contribution limitations in themselves do not undermine to any material degree the potential for robust and effective discussion of candidates and campaign issues by individual citizens, associations, the institutional press, candidates, and political parties.

We find that, under the rigorous standard of review established by our prior decisions, the weighty interests served by restricting the size of financial contributions to political candidates are sufficient to justify the limited effect upon First Amendment freedoms caused by the $1,000 contribution ceiling. . . .

The Act's expenditure ceilings impose direct and substantial restraints on the quantity of political speech. The most drastic of the limitations restricts individuals and groups, including political parties that fail to place a candidate on the ballot, to an expenditure of $1,000 "relative to a clearly identified candidate during a calendar year." § 608 (e)(1) Other expenditure ceilings limit spending by candidates . . . their campaigns . . . and political parties in connection with election campaigns. . . . It is clear that a primary effect of these expenditure limitations is to restrict the quantity of campaign speech by individuals, groups, and candidates. The restrictions, while neutral as to the ideas expressed, limit political expression "at the core of our electoral process and of First Amendment freedoms. . . ." *Williams* v. *Rhodes* . . . (1968). . . .

We find that the governmental interest in preventing corruption and the appearance of corruption is inadequate to justify [the] ceiling on independent expenditures. . . .

. . . [T]he independent advocacy restricted by the provision does not presently appear to pose dangers of real or apparent corruption comparable to those identified with large campaign contributions. . . . The absence of prearrangement and coordination of an expenditure with the candidate or his agent not only undermines the value of the expenditure to the candidate, but also alleviates the danger that expenditures will be given as a *quid pro quo* for improper commitments from the candidate. . . .

While the independent expenditure ceiling thus fails to serve any substantial governmental interest in stemming the reality or appearance of corruption in the electoral process, it heavily burdens core First Amendment expression. . . . Advocacy of the election or defeat of candidates for federal office is no less entitled to protection under the First Amendment than the discussion of political policy generally or advocacy of the passage or defeat of legislation.

It is argued, however, that the ancillary governmental interest in equalizing the relative ability of individuals and groups to influence the outcome of elections serves to justify the limitation on express advocacy of the election or defeat of candidates imposed by [the] expenditure ceiling. But the concept that government may restrict the speech of some elements of our society in order to enhance the relative voice of others is wholly foreign to the First Amendment. . . . The First Amendment's protection against governmental abridgement of free expression cannot properly be made to depend on a person's financial ability to engage in public discussion. . . .

. . . For the reasons stated, we conclude that [the] independent expenditure limitation is unconstitutional under the First Amendment. . . .

The Act also sets limits on expenditures by a candidate "from his personal funds, or the personal funds of his immediate family, in connection with his campaigns during any calendar year." . . . These ceilings vary from $50,000 for Presidential or Vice Presidential candidates to $35,000 for Senate candidates, and $25,000 for most candidates for the House of Representatives.

The ceiling on personal expenditure by candidates on their own behalf, like the limitations on independent expenditures . . . imposes a substantial restraint on the ability of persons to engage in protected First Amendment expression. The candidate, no less than any other person, has a First Amendment right to engage in the discussion of public issues and vigorously and tirelessly to advocate his own election and the election of other candidates. Indeed, it is of particular importance that candidates have the unfettered opportunity to make their views known so that the electorate may intelligently evaluate the candidates' personal qualities and their positions on vital public issues before choosing among them on election day. . . . [The] ceiling on personal expenditures by a candidate in furtherance of his own candidacy thus clearly and directly interferes with constitutionally protected freedoms.

The primary governmental interest served by the Act — the prevention of actual and apparent corruption of the political process — does not support the limitation on the candidate's expenditure of his own personal funds. . . . Indeed, the use of personal funds reduces the candidate's dependence on outside contributions and thereby counteracts the coercive pressures and attendant risks of abuse to which the Act's contribution limitations are directed.

The ancillary interest in equalizing the relative financial resources of candidates competing for elective office . . . is clearly not sufficient to justify the provision's infringement of fundamental First Amendment rights. First, the limitation may fail to promote financial equality among candidates. A candidate who spends less of his personal resources on his campaign may nonetheless outspend his rival as a result of more successful fundraising efforts. . . . Second, and more fundamentally, the First Amendment simply cannot tolerate . . . [a] restriction upon the freedom of a candidate to speak without legislative limit on behalf of his own candidacy. We therefore hold that . . . [the] restrictions on a candidate's personal expenditures is [sic] unconstitutional. . . .

Section 608 (c) of the Act places limitations on overall campaign expenditures by candidates seeking nomination for election and election to federal office. . . .

No governmental interest that has been suggested is sufficient to justify the restriction on the quantity of political expression imposed by § 608 (c)'s campaign expenditure limitations. The major evil associated with rapidly increasing campaign expenditures is the danger of candidate dependence on large contributions. The interest in alleviating the corrupting influence of large contributions is served by the Act's contribution limitations and disclosure provisions. . . .

The interest in equalizing the financial resources of candidates competing for federal office is no more convincing a justification for restricting the scope of federal election campaigns. Given the limitation on the size of outside contributions, the financial resources available to a candidate's campaign, like the number of volunteers recruited, will normally vary with the size and intensity of the candidate's support. . . .

The campaign expenditure ceilings appear to be designed primarily to serve the governmental interests in reducing the allegedly skyrocketing costs of political campaigns. . . . [T]he mere growth in the cost of federal election campaigns in and of itself provides no basis for governmental restrictions on the quantity of campaign spending and the resulting limitations on the scope of federal campaigns. The First Amendment denies government the power to determine that spending to promote one's political views is wasteful, excessive, or unwise. . . .

For these reasons we hold that § 608 (c) is constitutionally invalid.

In sum, the provisions of the Act that impose a $1,000 limitation on contributions to a single candidate, § 608 (b)(1), a $5,000 limitation on contributions by a political committee to a single candidate, § 608 (b)(2), and a $25,000 limitation on total contribu-

tions by an individual during any calendar year, § 608 (b)(3), are constitutionally valid. These limitations along with the disclosure provisions, constitute the Act's primary weapons against the reality or appearance of improper influence stemming from the dependence of candidates on large campaign contributions. The contribution ceilings thus serve the basic governmental interest in safeguarding the integrity of the electoral process without directly impinging upon the rights of individual citizens and candidates to engage in political debate and discussion. By contrast, the First Amendment requires the invalidation of the Act's independent expenditure ceiling, § 608 (e)(1), its limitation on a candidate's expenditures from his own personal funds, § 608 (c). These provisions place substantial and direct restrictions on the ability of candidates, citizens, and associations to engage in protected political expression, restrictions that the First Amendment cannot tolerate.

II. Reporting and Disclosure Requirements

. . . Unlike the overall limitations on contributions and expenditures, the disclosure requirements impose no ceiling on campaign-related activities. But we have repeatedly found that compelled disclosure, in itself, can seriously infringe on privacy of association and belief guaranteed by the First Amendment. . . .

. . . [C]ompelled disclosure has the potential for substantially infringing the exercise of First Amendment rights. But we have acknowledged that there are governmental interests sufficiently important to outweigh the possibility of infringement, particularly when the "free functioning of our national institutions" is involved. . . .

The governmental interests sought to be vindicated by the disclosure requirements are of this magnitude. They fall into three categories. First, disclosure provides the electorate with information "as to where political campaign money comes from and how it is spent by the candidate" in order to aid the voters in evaluating those who seek Federal office. . . .

Second, disclosure requirements deter actual corruption and avoid the appearance of corruption by exposing large contributions and expenditures to the light of publicity. This exposure may discourage those who would use money for improper purposes either before or after the election. . . .

Third, and not least significant, record-keeping, reporting and disclosure requirements are an essential means of gathering the data necessary to detect violations of the contribution limitations described above.

In summary, we find no constitutional infirmities in the record-keeping, reporting, and disclosure provisions of the act.

III. Public Financing of Presidential Election Campaigns

A series of statutes for the public financing of Presidential election campaigns produced the scheme now found in 26 U.S.C. § 6096 and Subtitle H, §§ 9001-9042, of the Internal Revenue Code of 1954. . . .

Appellants argue that Subtitle H is invalid (1) as "contrary to the 'general welfare,' " Art. I, § 8, (2) because any scheme of public financing of election campaigns is inconsistent with the First Amendment, and (3) because Subtitle H invidiously discriminates against certain interests in violation of the Due Process Clause of the Fifth Amendment. We find no merit in these contentions.

Appellants' "general welfare" contention erroneously treats the General Welfare Clause as a limitation upon congressional power. It is rather a grant of power, the scope of which is quite expansive, particularly in view of the enlargement of power by the Necessary and Proper Clause. . . . Congress has power to regulate Presidential elections and primaries, . . . and public financing of Presidential elections as a means to reform the electoral process was clearly a choice within the granted power. It is for Congress to decide which expenditures will promote the general welfare. "[T]he power of Congress to authorize expenditure of public moneys for public purposes is not limited by the direct grants of legislative power found in the Constitution." *United States* v. *Butler* ... (1936). ... Any limitations upon the exercise of that granted power must be found elsewhere in the Constitution. In this case, Congress was legislating for the "general welfare" — to reduce the deleterious influence of large contributions on our political process, to facilitate communication by candidates with the electorate, and to free candidates from the rigors of fundraising.... Whether the chosen means appear "bad," "unwise," or "unworkable" to us is irrelevant; Congress has concluded that the means are "necessary and proper" to promote the general welfare, and we thus decline to find this legislation without the grant of power in Art. I, § 8....

... [P]ublic financing as a means of eliminating the improper influence of large private contributions furthers a significant governmental interest.... In addition, ... Congress properly regarded public financing as an appropriate means of relieving major-party Presidential candidates from the rigors of soliciting private contributions.... Congress' interest in not funding hopeless candidacies with large sums of public money ... necessarily justifies the withholding of public assistance from candidates without significant public support....

IV. The Federal Election Commission

The 1974 Amendments to the Act created an eight-member Federal Election Commission, and vest in it primary and substantial responsibility for administering and enforcing the Act. The question that we address in this portion of the opinion is whether, in view of the manner in which a majority of its members are appointed, the Commission may under the Constitution exercise the powers conferred upon it....

Beyond these recordkeeping, disclosure, and investigative functions, however, the Commission is given extensive rulemaking and adjudicative powers....

The Commission's enforcement power is both direct and wide-ranging....

... The body in which this authority is reposed consists of eight members. The Secretary of the Senate and the Clerk of the House of Representatives are *ex officio* members of the Commission without the right to vote. Two members are appointed by the President *pro tempore* of the Senate "upon the recommendations of the majority leader of the Senate and the minority leader of the Senate." Two more are to be appointed by the Speaker of the House of Representatives, likewise upon the recommendations of its respective majority and minority leaders. The remaining two members are appointed by the President. Each of the six voting members of the commission must be confirmed by the majority of both Houses of Congress....

Appellants urge that since Congress has given the Commission wideranging rule-making and enforcement powers with respect to the substantive provisions of the Act, Congress is precluded under the principle of separation of powers from vesting in itself the authority to appoint those who will exercise such authority. Their argument is based on the language of Art. II, § 2, cl. 2, of the Constitution, which provides in pertinent part as follows:

> "[The President] shall nominate, and by and with the Advice and Consent of the Senate, shall appoint ... all other Officers of the United States, whose Appointments are not herein otherwise provided for, and which shall be established by Law: but the Congress may by Law vest the Appointment of such inferior Officers, as they think proper, in the President alone, in the Courts of Law, or in the Heads of Departments."

Appellants' argument is that this provision is the exclusive method by which those charged with executing the laws of the United States may be chosen. Congress, they assert, cannot have it both ways. If the legislature wishes the Commission to exercise all

of the conferred powers, then its members are in fact "Officers of the United States" and must be appointed under the Appointments Clause. But if Congress insists upon retaining the power to appoint, then the members of the Commission may not discharge those many functions of the Commission which can be performed only by "Officers of the United States," as that term must be construed within the doctrine of separation of powers....

... [T]he Framers of the Constitution, while mindful of the need for checks and balances among the three branches of the National Government, had no intention of denying to the Legislative Branch authority to appoint its own officers. Congress, either under the Appointments Clause or under its grants of substantive legislative authority and the Necessary and Proper Clause in Art. I, is in their view empowered to provide for the appointment to the Commission in the manner which it did because the Commission is performing "appropriate legislative functions."...

Insofar as the powers confided in the Commission are essentially of an investigative and informative nature, falling in the same general category as those powers which Congress might delegate to one of its own committees, there can be no question that the Commission as presently constituted may exercise them....

But when we go beyond this type of authority to the more substantial powers exercised by the Commission, we reach a different result. The Commission's enforcement power, exemplified by its discretionary power to seek judicial relief, is authority that cannot possibly be regarded as merely in aid of the legislative function of Congress. A law suit is the ultimate remedy for a breach of the law, and it is to the President, and not to the Congress, that the Constitution entrusts the responsibility to "take Care that the Laws be faithfully executed." Art. II, § 3.

Congress may undoubtedly under the Necessary and Proper Clause create "offices" in the generic sense and provide such method of appointment to those "offices" as it chooses. But Congress' power under that Clause is inevitably bounded by the express language of Art. II, § 2, cl. 2, and unless the method it provides comports with the latter, the holders of those offices will not be "Officers of the United States." They may, therefore, properly perform duties only in aid of those functions that Congress may carry out by itself, or in an area sufficiently removed from the administration and enforcement of the public law as to permit them being performed by persons not "Officers of the United States."...

... We hold that these provisions of the Act, vesting in the Commission primary responsibility for conducting civil litigation in the courts of the United States for vindicating public rights, violate Art. II, cl 2, § 2, of the Constitution. Such functions may be discharged only by persons who are "Officers of the United States" within the language of that section.

All aspects of the Act are brought within the Commission's broad administrative powers: rule-making, advisory opinions, and determinations of eligibility for funds and even for federal elective office itself. These functions, exercised free from day-to-day supervision of either Congress or the Executive Branch, are more legislative and judicial in nature than are the Commission's enforcement powers, and are of kinds usually performed by independent regulatory agencies or by some department in the Executive Branch under the direction of an Act of Congress. Congress viewed these broad powers as essential to effective and impartial administration of the entire substantive framework of the Act. Yet each of these functions also represents the performance of a significant governmental duty exercised pursuant to a public law.... [N]one of them operates merely in aid of congressional authority to legislate or is sufficiently removed from the administration and enforcement of public law to allow it to be performed by the present Commission. These administrative functions may therefore be exercised only by persons who are "Officers of the United States."

Conclusion

In summary, we sustain the individual contribution limits, the disclosure and reporting provisions, and the public financing scheme. We conclude, however, that the limitations on campaign expenditures, on independent expenditures by individuals and groups, and on expenditures by a candidate from his personal funds are constitutionally infirm. Finally, we hold that most of the powers conferred by the Act upon the Federal Election Commission can be exercised only by "Officers of the United States," appointed in conformity with Art. II, § 2, cl. 2, of the Constitution, and therefore cannot be exercised by the Commission as presently constituted. . . .

Excerpts From Decision On Minimum Wage Law

Following are excerpts from the majority opinion issued by the Supreme Court June 24, 1976, striking down the provision of the Fair Labor Standards Act Amendments of 1974 that extended minimum wage and overtime pay requirements to the employees of state and local governments. Justice William H. Rehnquist wrote the opinion, joined by Justices Potter Stewart, Harry A. Blackmun, Lewis F. Powell Jr. and Chief Justice Warren E. Burger. Dissenting were Justices William J. Brennan Jr., Byron R. White, Thurgood Marshall and John Paul Stevens. The case was entitled The National League of Cities v. W. J. Usery Jr., Secretary of Labor.

Nearly 40 years ago, Congress enacted the Fair Labor Standards Act, and required employers covered by the Act to pay their employees a minimum hourly wage and to pay them at one and one-half times their regular rate of pay for hours worked in excess of 40 during a work week. . . . This Court unanimously upheld the Act as a valid exercise of congressional authority under the commerce power in *United States v. Darby* . . . (1941), observing:

"Whatever their motive and purpose, regulations of commerce which do not infringe some constitutional prohibition are within the plenary power conferred on Congress by the Commerce Clause." . . .

The original Fair Labor Standards Act passed in 1938 specifically excluded the States and their political subdivisions from its coverage. In 1974, however, Congress enacted the most recent of a series of broadening amendments to the Act. By these amendments, Congress has extended the minimum wage and maximum hour provisions to almost all public employees employed by the States and by their various political subdivisions. Appellants in these cases include individual cities and States, the National League of Cities, and the National Governors' Conference. . . . The gist of their complaint was not that the conditions of employment of such public employees were beyond the scope of the commerce power had those employees been employed in the private sector, but that the established constitutional doctrine of intergovernmental immunity consistently recognized in a long series of our cases affirmatively prevented the exercise of this authority in the manner which Congress chose in the 1974 Amendments.

I

In a series of amendments beginning in 1961 Congress began to extend the provisions of the Fair Labor Standards Act to some types of public employees. The 1961 amendment to the Act extended its coverage to persons who were employed in "enterprises" engaged in commerce or in the production of goods for commerce. And in 1966, with the amendment of the definition of employers under the Act, the exemption heretofore extended to the States and their political subdivisions was removed with respect to employees of state hospitals, institutions, and schools. We nevertheless sustained the validity of the combined effect of these two amendments in *Maryland v. Wirtz* . . . (1968). . . .

II

It is established beyond preadventure that the Commerce Clause of Art. I of the Constitution is a grant of plenary authority to Congress. That authority is, in the words of Chief Justice Marshall in *Gibbons v. Ogden,* . . . (1824), ". . . the power to regulate; that is to prescribe the rule by which commerce is to be governed." . . .

When considering the validity of asserted applications of this power to wholly private activity, the Court has made it clear that

"[e]ven activity that is purely intrastate in character may be regulated by Congress, where the activity, combined with like conduct by others similarly situated, affects commerce among the states or with foreign nations." *Fry v. United States* . . . (1975).

Congressional power over areas of private endeavor, even when its exercise may not be exempt state law determinations contrary to the result which has commended itself to collective wisdom of Congress, has been held to be limited only by the requirement that "the means chosen by [Congress] must be reasonably adapted to the end permitted by the Constitution." . . . *Heart of Atlanta Motel, Inc. v. United States* . . . (1964).

Appellants in no way challenge these decisions establishing the breadth of authority granted Congress under the commerce power. Their contention, on the contrary is that when Congress seeks to regulate directly the activities of States as public employers, it transgresses an affirmative limitation on the exercise of its power akin to other commerce power affirmative limitations contained in the Constitution. . . . Appellants' essential contention is that the 1974 amendments to the Act, while undoubtedly within the scope of the Commerce Clause, encounter a . . . constitutional barrier because they are to be applied directly to the States and subdivisions of States as employers.

This Court has never doubted that there are limits upon the power of Congress to override state sovereignty, even when exercising its otherwise plenary powers to tax or to regulate commerce which are conferred by Art. I of the Constitution. . . .

. . . It is one thing to recognize the authority of Congress to enact laws regulating individual businesses necessarily subject to the dual sovereignty of the government of the Nation and of the State in which they reside. It is quite another to uphold a similar exercise of congressional authority directed not to private citizens, but to the States as States. We have repeatedly recognized that there are attributes of sovereignty attaching to every state government which may not be impaired by Congress, not because Congress may lack an affirmative grant of legislative authority to reach the matter, but because the Constitution prohibits it from exercising the authority in that matter. . . .

One undoubted attribute of state sovereignty is the States' power to determine the wages which shall be paid to those whom they employ in order to carry out their governmental functions, what hours those persons will work, and what compensation will be provided where these employees may be called upon to work overtime. The question we must resolve in this case, then, is whether these determinations are "functions essential to separate and independent existence." *Coyle v. Smith* . . . [1911], quoting from *Lane County v. Oregon* [1869], so that Congress may not abrogate the States' otherwise plenary authority to make them. . . .

. . . Quite apart from the substantial costs imposed upon the States and their political subdivisions, the Act displaces state policies regarding the manner in which they will structure delivery of those governmental services which their citizens require. The Act, speaking directly to the States *qua* States, requires that they shall pay all but an extremely limited minority of their employees the minimum wage rates currently chosen by Congress. It may well be that as a matter of economic policy it would be desirable that States, just as private employers, comply with these minimum wage requirements. But it cannot be gainsaid that the federal requirements directly supplants the considered policy choices of the States' elected officials and administrators as to how they wish to structure pay scales in state employment. The State might wish to employ persons with little or no training or those who wish to work on a casual basis, or those who for some other reason do not possess minimum employment requirements, and pay them less than the federally prescribed minimum wage. It may wish to offer part time or summer employment to teenagers at a figure less than the minimum wage, and if unable to do so may decline to offer such employment at all. But the Act would forbid such choices by the States. The only "discretion" left to them under the Act is either to attempt to increase their revenue to meet the additional financial burden imposed upon them by paying congressionally prescribed wages to their existing complement of employees, or to reduce that complement to a number which can be paid the federal minimum wage without increasing revenue.

This dilemma presented by the minimum wage restrictions may seem not immediately different from that faced by private employers, who have long been covered by the Act and who must find ways to increase their gross income if they are to pay higher wages while maintaining current earnings. The difference, however, is that a State is not merely a factor in the "shifting economic arrangements" of the private sector of the economy, *Kovacs v. Cooper* ... (1940) ... but is itself a coordinate element in the system established by the framers for governing our federal union.

The degree to which the FLSA amendments would interfere with traditional aspects of state sovereignty can be seen even more clearly upon examining the overtime requirements of the Act. The general effect of these provisions is to require the States to pay their employees at premium rates whenever their work exceeds a specified number of hours in a given period.... [L]ike the minimum wage provisions, the vice of the Act as sought to be applied here is that it directly penalizes the States for choosing to hire governmental employees on terms different from those which Congress has sought to impose.

This congressionally imposed displacement of state decisions may substantially restructure traditional ways in which the local governments have arranged their affairs. Although at this point many of the actual effects under the proposed Amendments remain a matter of some dispute among the parties, enough can be satisfactorily anticipated for an outline discussion of their general import. The requirement imposing premium rates upon any employment in excess of what Congress has decided is appropriate for a governmental employee's workweek, for example, appears likely to have the effect of coercing the States to structure work periods in some employment areas, such as police and fire protection, in a manner substantially different from practices which have long been commonly accepted among local governments of this Nation....

Our examination of the effect of the 1974 amendments, as sought to be extended to the States and their political subdivisions, satisfies us that both the minimum wage and the maximum hour provisions will impermissibly interfere with the integral governmental functions of these bodies.... If Congress may withdraw from the States the authority to make those fundamental employment decisions upon which their systems for performance of these functions must rest, we think there would be little left of the States' "separate and independent existence." *Coyle, supra.* Thus, even if appellants may have overestimated the effect which the Act will have upon their current levels and patterns of governmental activity, the dispositive factor is that Congress has attempted to exercise its Commerce Clause authority to prescribe minimum wages and maximum hours to be paid by the States in their capacities as sovereign governments. In so doing, Congress has sought to wield its power in a fashion that would impair the States' "ability to function effectively within a federal system." *Fry, supra....* This exercise of congressional authority does not comport with the federal system of government embodied in the Constitution. We hold that insofar as the challenged amendments operate to directly displace the States' of freedom to structure integral operations in areas of traditional government functions, they are not within the authority granted Congress by Art. I, § 8, cl. 3.

III

... We have reaffirmed today that the States as States stand on a quite different footing than an individual or a corporation when challenging the exercise of Congress' power to regulate commerce.... Congress may not exercise that power so as to force directly upon the States its choices as to how essential decisions regarding the conduct of integral governmental functions are to be made. We agree that such assertions of power, if unchecked, would indeed, as Mr. Justice Douglas cautioned in his dissent in *Wirtz,* allow "the National Government [to] devour the essentials of state sovereignty." ..., and would therefore transgress the bounds of the authority granted Congress under the Commerce Clause. While there are obvious differences between the schools and hospitals involved in *Wirtz,* and the fire and police departments affected here, each provides an integral portion of those governmental services which the States and their political subdivisions have traditionally afforded their citizens. We are therefore persuaded that *Wirtz* must be overruled....

Excerpts From Decision On Public Funding Of Abortions

Following are excerpts from the majority opinion issued by the Supreme Court June 30, 1980, upholding the power of Congress to curtail severely federal funding of abortions under the Medicaid program. Justice Potter Stewart wrote the opinion, joined by Chief Justice Warren E. Burger, Justices Byron R. White, Lewis F. Powell Jr. and William H. Rehnquist. Dissenting were Justices William J. Brennan Jr., Thurgood Marshall, Harry A. Blackmun and John Paul Stevens. The case was entitled Harris v. McRae.

This case presents statutory and constitutional questions concerning the public funding of abortions under Title XIX of the Social Security Act, commonly known as the "Medicaid" Act, and recent annual appropriations acts containing the so-called "Hyde Amendment." The statutory question is whether Title XIX requires a State that participates in the Medicaid program to fund the cost of medically necessary abortions for which federal reimbursement is unavailable under the Hyde Amendment. The constitutional question, which arises only if Title XIX imposes no such requirement, is whether the Hyde Amendment, by denying public funding for certain medically necessary abortions, contravenes the liberty or equal protection guarantees of the Due Process Clause of the Fifth Amendment, or either of the Religion Clauses of the First Amendment.

I

The Medicaid program was created in 1965, when Congress added Title XIX to the Social Security Act ... for the purpose of providing federal financial assistance to States that choose to reimburse certain costs of medical treatment for needy persons. Although participation in the Medicaid program is entirely optional, once a State elects to participate, it must comply with the requirements of Title XIX.

One such requirement is that a participating State agree to provide financial assistance to the "categorically needy" with respect to five general areas of medical treatment: (1) inpatient hospital services, (2) outpatient hospital services, (3) other laboratory and X-ray services, (4) skilled nursing facilities services, periodic screening and diagnosis of children, and family planning services, and (5) services of physicians.... Although a participating State need not "provide funding for all medical treatment falling within the five general categories, [Title XIX] does require that [a] state Medicaid plan [] establish 'reasonable standards . . . for determining . . . the extent of medical assistance under the plan which . . . are consistent with the objectives of [Title XIX].'. . ." *Beal* v. *Doe,* 432 U.S. 438, 441.

Since September 1976, Congress has prohibited — either by an amendment to the annual appropriations bill for the Department of Health, Education, and Welfare or by a joint resolution — the use of any federal funds to reimburse the cost of abortions under the Medicaid program except under certain specified circumstances. This funding restriction is commonly known as the "Hyde Amendment," after its original congressional sponsor, Representative Hyde. The current version of the Hyde Amendment, applicable for fiscal year 1980, provides:

> "[N]one of the funds provided by this joint resolution shall be used to perform abortions except where the life of the mother would be endangered if the fetus were carried to term; or except for such medical procedures necessary for the victims of rape or incest when such rape or incest has been reported promptly to a law enforcement agency or public health service." Pub. L. No. 96-123, § 109, 93 Stat. 926. See also Pub. L. No. 96-86, § 118, 93 Stat. 662.

On September 30, 1976, the day on which Congress enacted the initial version of the Hyde Amendment, these consolidated cases were filed in the District Court for the Eastern District of New York. The plantiffs — Cora McRae, a New York Medicaid recipient then in the first trimester of a pregnancy that she wished to terminate, the New York City Health and Hospitals Corp., a public benefit corporation that operates 16 hospitals, 12 of which provide abortion services, and others — sought to enjoin the enforcement of the funding restriction on abortions. They alleged that the Hyde Amendment violated the First, Fourth, Fifth, and Ninth Amendments of the Constitution insofar as it limited the funding of abortions to those necessary to save the life of the mother, while permitting the funding of costs associated with childbirth. Although the sole named defendant was the Secretary of Health, Education, and Welfare, the District Court permitted Senators James L. Buckley and Jesse A. Helms and Representative Henry J. Hyde to intervene as defendants. . . .

After a lengthy trial, which inquired into the medical reasons for abortions and the diverse religious views on the subject, the District Court filed an opinion and entered a judgment invalidating all versions of the Hyde Amendment on constitutional grounds . . . the District Court concluded that the Hyde Amendment, though valid under the Establishment Clause, violates the equal protection component of the Fifth Amendment's Due Process clause and the Free Exercise clause of the First Amendment. With regard to the Fifth Amendment, the District Court noted that when an abortion is "medically necessary to safeguard the pregnant woman's health, . . . the disentitlement to [M]edicaid assistance impinges directly on the woman's right to decide, in consultation with her physician and in reliance on his judgment, to terminate her pregnancy in order to preserve her health." The court concluded that the Hyde Amendment violates the equal protection guarantee because, in its view, the decision of Congress to fund medically necessary services generally but only certain medically necessary abortions serves no legitimate governmental interest. As to the Free Exercise Clause of the First Amendment, the court held that insofar as a woman's decision to seek a medically necessary abortion may be a product of her religious beliefs under certain Protestant and Jewish tenets, the funding restrictions of the Hyde Amendment violate that constitutional guarantee as well. . . .

II

It is well settled that if a case may be decided on either statutory or constitutional grounds, this Court, for sound jurisprudential reasons, will inquire first into the statutory question. This practice reflects the deeply rooted doctrine "that we ought not to pass on questions of constitutionality . . . unless such adjudication is unavoidable." *Spector Motor Co.* v. *McLaughlin,* 323 U.S. 101, 105. Accordingly, we turn first to the question whether Title XIX requires a State that participates in the Medicaid program to continue to fund those medically necessary abortions for which federal reimbursement is unavailable under the Hyde Amendment. If a participating State is under such an obligation, the constitutionality of the Hyde Amendment need not be drawn into question in the present case, for the availability of medically necessary abortions under Medicaid would continue, with the participating State shouldering the total cost of funding such abortions.

Since the Congress that enacted Title XIX did not intend a participating State to assume a unilateral funding obligation for any health service in an approved Medicaid plan, it follows that Title XIX does not require a participating State to include in its plan any services for which a subsequent Congress has withheld federal funding. Title XIX was designed as a cooperative program of shared financial responsibility, not as a device for the federal Government to compel a State to provide services that Congress itself is unwilling to fund. Thus, if Congress chooses to withdraw federal funding for a particular service, a State is not obliged to continue to pay for that service as a condition of continued federal financial support of other services. . . .

Thus, by the normal operation of Title XIX, even if a State were otherwise required to include medically necessary abortions in its Medicaid plan, the withdrawal of federal funding under the Hyde Amendment would operate to relieve the State of that obligation for those abortions for which federal reimbursement is unavailable. . . . Accordingly, we conclude that Title XIX does not require a participating State to pay for those medically necessary abortions for which federal reimbursement is unavailable under the Hyde Amendment.

III

Having determined that Title XIX does not obligate a participating State to pay for those medically necessary abortions for which Congress has withheld federal funding, we must consider the constitutional validity of the Hyde Amendment. . . .

A

We address first the appellees' argument that the Hyde Amendment, by restricting the availability of certain medically necessary abortions under Medicaid, impinges on the "liberty" protected by the Due Process Clause as recognized in *Roe* v. *Wade,* 410 U.S. 113, and its progeny. . . .

. . . The Hyde Amendment . . . places no governmental obstacle in the path of a woman who chooses to terminate her pregnancy, but rather, by means of unequal subsidization of abortion and other medical services, encourages alternative activity deemed in the public interest. . . .

It is evident that a woman's interest in protecting her health was an important theme in *Wade.* In concluding that the freedom of a woman to decide whether to terminate her pregnancy falls within the personal liberty protected by the Due Process Clause, the Court in *Wade* emphasized the fact that the woman's decision carries with it significant personal health implications — both physical and psychological. . . . Because even the compelling interest of the State in protecting potential life after fetal viability was held to be insufficient to outweigh a woman's decision to protect her life or health, it could be argued that the freedom of a woman to decide whether to terminate her pregnancy for health reasons does in fact lie at the core of the constitutional liberty identified in *Wade.*

But, regardless of whether the freedom of a woman to choose to terminate her pregnancy for health reasons lies at the core or the periphery of the due process liberty recognized in *Wade,* it simply does not follow that a woman's freedom of choice carries with it a constitutional entitlement to the financial resources to avail herself of the full range of protected choices . . . although government may not place obstacles in the path of a woman's exercise of her freedom of choice, it need not remove those not of its own creation. Indigency falls in the latter category. The financial constraints that restrict an indigent woman's ability to enjoy the full range of constitutionally protected freedom of choice are the product not of governmental restrictions on access to abortions, but rather of her indigency. Although Congress has opted to subsidize medically necessary services generally, but not certain medically necessary abortions, the fact remains that the Hyde Amendment leaves an indigent woman with at least the same range of choice in deciding whether to obtain a medically necessary abortion as she would have had if Congress had chosen to subsidize no health care costs at all. We are thus not persuaded that the Hyde Amendment impinges on the constitutionally protected freedom of choice recognized in *Wade.*. . .

Although the liberty protected by the Due Process Clause affords protection against unwarranted government interference with freedom of choice in the context of certain personal decisions, it does not confer an entitlement to such funds as may be necessary to realize all the advantages of that freedom. To hold otherwise would mark a drastic change in our understanding of the Constitution. . . . To translate the limitation on governmental power implicit in the Due Process Clause into an affirmative funding obligation would require Congress to subsidize the medically necessary abortion of an indigent woman even if Congress had not enacted a Medicaid program to subsidize other medically necessary services. Nothing in the Due Process Clause supports such an extraordinary result. Whether freedom of choice that is constitutionally protected warrants federal subsidization is a question for Congress to answer, not a matter of constitutional entitlement. Accordingly, we conclude that the Hyde Amendment does not impinge on the due process liberty recognized in *Wade.*

B

The appellees also argue that the Hyde Amendment contravenes rights secured by the Religion Clauses of the First Amendment. It is the appellees' view that the Hyde Amendment violates the Establishment Clause because it incorporates into law the doctrines of the Roman Catholic Church concerning the sinfulness of abortion and the time at which life commences. Moreover, insofar as a woman's decision to seek a medically necessary abortion may be a product of her religious beliefs under certain Protestant and Jewish tenets, the appellees assert that the funding limitations of the Hyde Amendment impinge on the freedom of religion guaranteed by the Free Exercise Clause.

1

It is well settled that "a legislative enactment does not contravene the Establishment Clause if it has a secular legislative purpose, if its principal or primary effect neither advances nor inhibits religion, and if it does not foster an excessive governmental entanglement with religion.". . . we are convinced that the fact that the funding restrictions in the Hyde Amendment may coincide with the religious tenets of the Roman Catholic Church does not, without more, contravene the Establishment Clause.

2

We need not address the merits of the appellees' arguments concerning the Free Exercise Clause, because the appellees lack standing to raise a free exercise challenge to the Hyde Amendment. . . .

C

It remains to be determined whether the Hyde Amendment violates the equal protection component of the Fifth Amendment. This challenge is premised on the fact that, although federal reimbursement is available under Medicaid for medically necessary services generally, the Hyde Amendment does not permit federal reimbursement of all medically necessary abortions. The District Court held, and the appellees argue here, that this selec-

tive subsidization violates the constitutional guarantee of equal protection.

The guarantee of equal protection under the Fifth Amendment is not a source of substantive rights or liberties, but rather a right to be free from invidious discrimination in statutory classifications and other governmental activity. It is well-settled that where a statutory classification does not itself impinge on a right or liberty protected by the Constitution, the validity of classification must be sustained unless "the classification rests on grounds wholly irrelevant to the achievement of [any legitimate governmental] objective." *McGowan* v. *Maryland, supra*, 366 U.S., at 425. This presumption of constitutional validity, however, disappears if a statutory classification is predicated on criteria that are, in a constitutional sense, "suspect," the principal example of which is a classification based on race, *e.g., Brown* v. *Board of Education,* 347 U.S. 483.

1

For the reasons stated above, we have already concluded that the Hyde Amendment violates no constitutionally protected substantive rights. We now conclude as well that it is not predicated on a constitutionally suspect classification. . .

Gerem, . . . the principal impact of the Hyde Amendment falls on the indigent. But that fact does not itself render the funding restriction constitutionally invalid, for this Court has held repeatedly that poverty, standing alone, is not a suspect classification. . . .

2

The remaining question then is whether the Hyde Amendment is rationally related to a legitimate governmental objective. It is the Government's position that the Hyde Amendment bears a rational relationship to its legitimate interest in protecting the potential life of the fetus. We agree, ...

. . . The Hyde Amendment, by encouraging childbirth except in the most urgent circumstances, is rationally related to the legitimate governmental objective of protecting potential life. By subsidizing the medical expenses of indigent women who carry their pregnancies to term while not subsidizing the comparable expenses of women who undergo abortions (except those whose lives are threatened), Congress has established incentives that make childbirth a more attractive alternative than abortion for persons eligible for Medicaid. These incentives bear a direct relationship to the legitimate congressional interest in protecting potential life. Nor is it irrational that Congress has authorized federal reimbursement for medically necessary services generally, but not for certain medically necessary abortions. Abortion is inherently different from other medical procedures, because no other procedure involves the purposeful termination of a potential life.

After conducting an extensive evidentiary hearing into issues surrounding the public funding of abortions, the District Court concluded that "[t]he interests of . . . the federal government . . . in the fetus and in preserving it are not sufficient, weighed in the balance with the woman's threatened health, to justify withdrawing medical assistance unless the woman consents . . . to carry the fetus to term." In making an independent appraisal of the competing interests involved here, the District Court went beyond the judicial function. Such decisions are entrusted under the Constitution to Congress, not the courts. It is the role of the courts only to ensure that congressional decisions comport with the Constitution.

Where, as here, the Congress has neither invaded a substantive constitutional right or freedom, nor enacted legislation that purposefully operates to the detriment of a suspect class the only requirement of equal protection is that congressional action be rationally related to a legitimate governmental interest. The Hyde Amendment satisfies that standard. It is not the mission of this Court or any other to decide whether the balance of competing interests reflected in the Hyde Amendment is wise social policy. If that were our mission, not every Justice who has subscribed to the judgment of the Court today could have done so. But we cannot, in the name of the Constitution, overturn duly enacted statutes simply "because they may be unwise, improvident, or out of harmony with a particular school of thought." *Williamson* v. *Lee Optical Co.*, 348 U.S. 483, 488, quoted in *Dandridge* v. *Williams*, 397 U.S. 471, 484. Rather, "when an issue involves policy choices as sensitive as those implicated [here] . . ., the appropriate forum for their resolution in a democracy is the legislature." *Maher* v. *Roe, supra,* at *479.*

IV

For the reasons stated in this opinion, we hold that a State that participates in the Medicaid program is not obligated under Title XIX to continue to fund those medically necessary abortions for which federal reimbursement is unavailable under the Hyde Amendment. We further hold that the funding restrictions of the Hyde Amendment violate neither the Fifth Amendment nor the Establishment Clause of the First Amendment. It is also our view that the appellees lack standing to raise a challenge to the Hyde Amendment under the Free Exercise Clause of the First Amendment. Accordingly, the judgment of the District Court is reversed, and the case is remanded to that court for further proceedings consistent with this opinion.

(It is so ordered)

Excerpts From Decision Upholding Male-Only Military Draft

Following are excerpts from the opinion issued by the Supreme Court June 25, 1981, upholding the decision of Congress to exclude women from the military draft, thus requiring only men to register for the draft. Justice William H. Rehnquist wrote the majority opinion, joined by Chief Justice Burger, Justices Potter Stewart, Harry A. Blackmun, Lewis F. Powell Jr. and John Paul Stevens. Dissenting were Justices William J. Brennan Jr., Thurgood Marshall and Byron R. White. The case was entitled Rostker v. Goldberg.

The question presented is whether the Military Selective Service Act, 50 U.S.C. App. § 451 *et seq.,* violates the Fifth Amendment to the United States Constitution in authorizing the President to require the registration of males and not females.

I

Congress is given the power under the Constitution "To raise and support Armies," "To provide and maintain a Navy," and "To make Rules for the Government and Regulation of the land and naval Forces." Art. I, § 8, cls. 12-14. Pursuant to this grant of authority Congress has enacted the Military Selective Service Act, 50 U.S.C. App. § 451 *et seq.* ("the MSSA" or "the Act"). Section 3 of the Act, 50 U.S.C. App. § 453, empowers the President, by proclamation, to require the registration of "every male citizen" and male resident aliens between the ages of 18 and 26. The purpose of this registration is to facilitate any eventual conscription: pursuant to § 4 (a) of the Act, 50 U.S.C. App. § 454 (a), those persons required to register under § 3 are liable for training and service in the Armed Forces. The MSSA registration provision serves no other purpose beyond providing a pool for subsequent induction.

Registration for the draft under § 3 was discontinued in 1975.

Presidential Proclamation No. 4360, 11 Weekly Comp. of Pres. Doc. 318 (April 7, 1975). In early 1980, President Carter determined that it was necessary to reactivate the draft registration process. The immediate impetus for this decision was the Soviet armed invasion of Afghanistan. . . . The Selective Service System had been inactive, however, and funds were needed before reactivating registration. The President therefore recommended that funds be transferred from the Department of Defense to the separate Selective Service System. H. R. Doc. No. 96-267, 96th Cong., 2d Sess., 2 (1980). He also recommended that Congress take action to amend the MSSA to permit the registration and conscription of women as well as men. . . .

Congress agreed that it was necessary to reactivate the registration process, and allocated funds for that purpose. . . . Although Congress considered the question at great length . . . it declined to amend the MSSA to permit the registration of women.

On July 2, 1980, the President, by proclamation, ordered the registration of specified groups of young men pursuant to the authority conferred by § 3 of the Act. Registration was to commence on July 21, 1980. . . .

These events of last year breathed new life into a lawsuit which had been essentially dormant in the lower courts for nearly a decade. It began in 1971 when several men subject to registration for the draft and subsequent induction into the Armed Services filed a complaint in the United States District Court for the Eastern District of Pennsylvania challenging the MSSA on several grounds. . . .

On Friday, July 18, 1980, three days before registration was to commence, the District Court issued an opinion finding that the Act violated the Due Process Clause of the Fifth Amendment and permanently enjoined the Government from requiring registration under the Act. . . . The court stressed that it was not deciding whether or to what extent women should serve in combat, but only the issue of registration, and felt that this "should dispel any concern that we are injecting ourselves in an inappropriate manner in military affairs." 509 F. Supp., at 597. See also *id.,* at 599, nn. 17 and 18. The court proceeded to examine the testimony and hearing evidence presented to Congress by representatives of the military and the Executive Branch, and concluded on the basis of this testimony that "military opinion, backed by extensive study, is that the availability of women registrants would materially increase flexibility, not hamper it." *Id.,* at 603. It rejected Congress' contrary determination in part because of what it viewed as Congress' "inconsistent positions" in declining to register women yet spending funds to recruit them and expand their opportunities in the military. *Id.,* at 603.

The United States immediately filed a notice of appeal and the next day, Saturday, July 19, 1980, Justice Brennan, acting in his capacity as Circuit Justice for the Third Circuit, stayed the District Court's order enjoining commencement of registration. — U.S. —. Registration began the next Monday. . . .

II

Whenever called upon to judge the constitutionality of an Act of Congress — "the gravest and most delicate duty that this Court is called upon to perform," *Blodgett* v. *Holden,* 275 U.S. 142, 148 (1927) (Holmes, J.) — the Court accords "great weight to the decisions of Congress." *CBS, Inc.* v. *Democratic National Committee,* 412 U.S. 94, 102 (1973). The Congress is a coequal branch of government whose members take the same oath we do to uphold the Constitution of the United States. As Justice Frankfurter noted in *Joint Anti-Fascist Refugee Committee* v. *McGrath,* 341 U.S. 123, 164 (1951) (concurring opinion), we must have "due regard to the fact that this Court is not exercising a primary judgment but is sitting in judgment upon those who also have taken the oath to observe the Constitution and who have the responsibility for carrying on government." The customary deference accorded the judgments of Congress is certainly appropriate when, as here, Congress specifically considered the question of the Act's constitutionality. . . .

This is not, however, merely a case involving the customary deference accorded congressional decisions. The case arises in the context of Congress' authority over national defense and military affairs, and perhaps in no other area has the Court accorded Congress greater deference. In rejecting the registration of women, Congress explicitly relied upon its constitutional powers under Art. I, § 8, cls. 12-14.

Not only is the scope of Congress' constitutional power in this area broad, but the lack of competence on the part of the courts is marked. In *Gilligan* v. *Morgan*, 413 U.S. 1, 10 (1973), the Court noted:

> "It is difficult to conceive of an area of governmental activity in which the courts have less competence. The complex, subtle, and professional decisions as to the composition, training, equipping, and control of a military force are essentially professional military judgments, subject always to civilian control of the Legislative and Executive branches."

The operation of a healthy deference to legislative and executive judgments in the area of military affairs is evident in several recent decisions of this Court. In *Parker* v. *Levy*, 417 U.S. 733, 756 (1974), the court rejected both vagueness and overbreadth challenges to army regulations, noting that "Congress is permitted to legislate both with greater breadth and with greater flexibility" when the statute governs military society, and that "[w]hile the members of the military are not excluded from the protection granted by the First Amendment, the different character of the military community and of the military mission requires a different application of those protections." In *Middendorf* v. *Henry*, 425 U.S. 25 (1976), the Court noted that in considering due process claims in the context of summary court martial it "must give particular deference to the determination of Congress, made under its military authority to regulate the land and naval forces, U.S. Const., Art. I, § 8," concerning what rights were available. *Id.*, at 43. See also *id.*, at 49-50 (Powell, J. concurring). Deference to the judgment of other branches in the area of military affairs also played a major role in *Greer* v. *Spock*, 424 U.S. 828, 837-838 (1976), where the Court upheld a ban on political speeches by civilians on a military base, and *Brown* v. *Glines*, 444 U.S. 348 (1980), where the Court upheld regulations imposing a prior restraint on the right to petition of military personnel. See also *Burns* v. *Wilson*, 346 U.S. 137 (1953); *United States* v. *MacIntosh*, 283 U.S. 605, 622 (1931).

In *Schlesinger* v. *Ballard*, 419 U.S. 498 (1975), the Court considered a due process challenge, brought by males, to the navy policy of according females a longer period than males in which to attain promotions necessary to continued service. The Court distinguished previous gender-based discrimination held unlawful in *Reed* v. *Reed*, 404 U.S. 71 (1971) and *Frontiero* v. *Richardson*, 411 U.S. 677 (1973). In those cases, the classifications were based on "overbroad generalizations." See 419 U.S., at 506-507. In the case before it, however, the Court noted:

> "the different treatment of men and women naval officers ... reflects, not archaic and overbroad generalizations, but, instead, the demonstrable fact that male and female line officers in the Navy are not similarly situated with respect to opportunities for professional service. Appellee has not challenged the current restrictions on women officers' participation in combat and in most sea duty." *Id.*, at 508.

In light of the combat restrictions, women did not have the same opportunities for promotion as men, and therefore it was not unconstitutional for Congress to distinguish between them.

None of this is to say that Congress is free to disregard the Constitution when it acts in the area of military affairs. In that area as any other Congress remains subject to the limitations of the Due Process Clause, *see Ex parte Milligan*, 4 Wall. 2 (1866); *Hamilton* v. *Kentucky Distilleries & Warehouse Co.*, 251 U.S. 146, 156 (1919), but the tests and limitations to be applied may differ because of the military context. We of course do not abdicate our ultimate responsibility to decide the constitutional question, but simply recognize that the Constitution itself requires such deference to congressional choice. See *CBS, Inc.* v. *Democratic National Committee*, 412 U.S., at 103. In deciding the question before us we must be particularly careful not to substitute our judgment of what is desirable for that of Congress, or our own evaluation of evidence for a reasonable evaluation by the Legislative Branch.

The District Court purported to recognize the appropriateness of deference to Congress when that body was exercising its constitutionally delegated authority over military affairs, 509 F. Supp., at 596, but it stressed that "[w]e are not here concerned with military operations or day-to-day conduct of the military into which we have no desire to intrude." *Ibid.* Appellees also stress that this case involves civilians, not the military, and that "the impact of registration on the military is only indirect and attenuated." Brief for Appellees 19. We find these efforts to divorce registration from the military and national defense context, with all the deference called for in that context, singularly unpersuasive. *United States* v. *O'Brien, supra*, recognized the broad deference due Congress in the selective service area before us in this case. Registration is not an end in itself in the civilian world but rather the first step in the induction process into the military one, and Congress specifically linked its consideration of registration to induction, see, *e. g.*, S. Rep. No. 96-826, *supra*, at 156, 160. Congressional judgments concerning registration and the draft are based on judgments concerning military operations and needs, see, *e. g.*, *id.*, at 157 ("the starting point for any discussion of the appropriateness of registering women for the draft is the question of the proper role of women in combat"), and the deference unquestionably due the latter judgments is necessarily required in assessing the former as well. Although the District Court stressed that it was not intruding on military questions, its opinion was based on assessments of military need and flexibility in a time of mobilization. See, *e.g.*, 509 F. Supp., at 600-605. It would be blinking reality to say that our precedents requiring deference to Congress in military affairs are not implicated by the present case.

No one could deny that ... the Government's interest in raising and supporting armies is an "important governmental interest." Congress and its committees carefully considered and debated two alternative means of furthering that interest: the first was to register only males for potential conscription, and the other was to register both sexes. Congress chose the former alternative. When that decision is challenged on equal protection grounds, the question a court must decide is not which alternative it would have chosen, had it been the primary decision-maker, but whether that chosen by Congress denies equal protection of the laws.

Nor can it be denied that the imposing number of cases from this Court previously cited suggest that judicial deference to such congressional exercise of authority is at its apogee when legislative action under the congressional authority to raise and support armies and make rules and regulations for their governance is challenged. As previously noted, *ante*, at 9, deference does not mean abdication. The reconciliation between the deference due Congress and our own constitutional responsibility is perhaps best instanced in *Schlesinger* v. *Ballard*, 419 U.S., at 510, where we stated:

> "This Court has recognized that 'it is the primary business of armies and navies to fight or be ready to fight wars should the occasion arise.' *U.S. ex rel. Toth* v. *Quarles*, 350 U.S. 11, 17. See also *Orloff* v. *Willoughby*, 345 U.S. 83, 94 (1953). The responsibility for determining how best our Armed Forces shall attend to that business rests with Congress, see U.S. Const., Art. I, § 8, cls. 12-14, and with the President. See U.S. Const., Art. II, § 2, cl. 1. We cannot say that, in exercising its broad constitutional power here, Congress has violated the Due Process Clause of the Fifth Amendment."

Or, as put a generation ago in a case not involving any claim of gender-based discrimination:

> "[J]udges are not given the task of running the Army. The responsibility for setting up channels through which ... grievances can be considered and fairly settled rests upon the Congress and upon the President of the United States and his subordinates. The military constitutes a specialized community governed by a separate discipline from that of the civil-

ian. Orderly government requires that the judiciary be as scrupulous not to interefere with legitimate Army matters as the Army must be scrupulous not to intervene in judicial matters." *Orloff* v. *Willoughby,* 345 U.S., at 93-94.

Schlesinger v. Ballard did not purport to apply a different equal protection test because of the military context, but did stress the deference due congressional choices among alternatives in exercising the congressional authority to raise and support armies and make rules for their governance. In light of the floor debate and the report of the Senate Armed Services Committee hereinafter discussed, it is apparent that Congress was fully aware not merely of the many facts and figures presented to it by witnesses who testified before its committees, but of the current thinking as to the place of women in the Armed Services. In such a case, we cannot ignore Congress' broad authority conferred by the Constitution to raise and support armies when we are urged to declare unconstitutional its studied choice of one alternative in preference to another for furthering that goal.

III

This case is quite different from several of the gender-based discrimination cases we have considered in that, despite appellees' assertions, Congress did not act "unthinkingly" or "reflexively and not for any considered reason." ... The question of registering women for the draft not only received considerable national attention and was the subject of wide-ranging public debate, but also was extensively considered by Congress in hearings, floor debate, and in committee....

... the decision to exempt women from registration was not the "accidental by-product of a traditional way of thinking about women." The issue was considered at great length, and Congress clearly expressed its purpose and intent....

The MSSA established a plan for maintaining "adequate armed strength ... to ensure the security of [the] nation...." Registration is the first step "in a united and continuous process designed to raise an army speedily and efficiently,"... and Congress provided for the reactivation of registration in order to "provide the means for the early delivery of inductees in an emergency."... Although the three-judge District Court often tried to sever its consideration of registration from the particulars of induction, see, *e. g.,* 509 F. Supp., at 604-605, Congress rather clearly linked the need for renewed registration with its views on the character of a subsequent draft.... Any assessment of the congressional purpose and its chosen means must therefore consider the registration scheme as a prelude to a draft in a time of national emergency. Any other approach would not be testing the Act in light of the purposes Congress sought to achieve.

Congress determined that any future draft, which would be facilitated by the registration scheme, would be characterized by a need for combat troops....

Women as a group, however, unlike men as a group, are not eligible for combat.... The Army and Marine Corps preclude the use of women in combat as a matter of established policy.... Congress specifically recognized and endorsed the exclusion of women from combat in exempting women from registration. In the words of the Senate Report:

"The principle that women should not intentionally and routinely engage in combat is fundamental, and enjoys wide support among our people. It is universally supported by military leaders who have testified before the Committee.... Current law and policy exclude women from being assigned to combat in our military forces, and the Committee reaffirms this policy."

... The existence of the combat restrictions clearly indicates

the basis for Congress' decision to exempt women from registration. The purpose of registration was to prepare for a draft of combat troops. Since women are excluded from combat, Congress concluded that they would not be needed in the event of a draft, and therefore decided not to register them. Again turning to the Senate Report:

"In the Committee's view, the starting point for any discussion of the appropriateness of registering women for the draft is the question of the proper role of women in combat.... The policy precluding the use of women in combat is, in the Committee's view, the most important reason for not including women in a registration system."

The district court stressed that the military need for women was irrelevant to the issue of their registration. As that court put it: "Congress could not constitutionally require registration under MSSA of only black citizens or only white citizens, or single out any political or religious group simply because those groups contained sufficient persons to fill the needs of the Selective Service System." 509 F. Supp., at 596. This reasoning is beside the point. The reason women are exempt from registration is not because military needs can be met by drafting men. This is not a case of Congress arbitrarily choosing to burden one of two similarly situated groups, such as would be the case with an all-black or all-white, or an all-Catholic or all-Lutheran, or an all-Republican or all-Democratic registration. Men and women, because of the combat restrictions on women, are simply not similarly situated for purposes of a draft or registration for a draft.

Congress' decision to authorize the registration of only men, therefore, does not violate the Due Process Clause. The exemption of women from registration is not only sufficiently but closely related to Congress' purpose in authorizing registration.... The fact that Congress and the Executive have decided that women should not serve in combat fully justifies Congress in not authorizing their registration, since the purpose of registration is to develop a pool of potential combat troops. As was the case in *Schlesinger* v. *Ballard, supra,* "the gender classification is not invidious, but rather realistically reflects the fact that the sexes are not similarly situated" in this case.... The Constitution requires that Congress treat similarly situated persons similarly, not that it engage in gestures of superficial equality.

In holding the MSSA constitutionally invalid the District Court relied heavily on the President's decision to seek authority to register women and the testimony of members of the Executive Branch and the military in support of that decision.... As stated by the Administration's witnesses before Congress, however, the President's "decision to ask for authority to register women is based on equity." The Senate Report, evaluating the testimony before the Committee, recognized that "the argument for registration and induction of women ... is not based on military necessity, but on considerations of equity."... Congress was certainly entitled, in the exercise of its constitutional powers to raise and regulate armies and navies, to focus on the question of military need rather than "equity."...

In sum, Congress carefully evaluated the testimony that 80,000 women conscripts could be usefully employed in the event of a draft and rejected it in the permissible exercise of its constitutional responsibility.... The District Court was quite wrong in undertaking an independent evaluation of this evidence, rather than adopting an appropriately deferential examination of *Congress'* evaluation of that evidence.

In light of the foregoing, we conclude that Congress acted well within its constitutional authority when it authorized the registration of men, and not women, under the Military Selective Service Act. The decision of the District Court holding otherwise is accordingly

Reversed.

Acts Declared Unconstitutional

Following is a list of acts of Congress that have been held unconstitutional in whole or in part by the Supreme Court. The material is compiled from the Library of Congress, The Constitution of the United States of America; Analysis and Interpretation, *S. Doc., 92-82, 92d Cong., 2d sess., 1973; 1976 Supplement, S. Doc. 94-200, 94th Cong. 2d sess., 1976; and Library of Congress, Congressional Research Service.*

1. Act of September 24, 1789 (1 Stat. 81, § 13, in part).

    Provision that "... [the Supreme Court] shall have power to issue ... writs of mandamus, in cases warranted by the principles and usages of law, to any ... persons holding office, under authority of the United States" as applied to the issue of mandamus to the Secretary of State requiring him to deliver to plaintiff a commission (duly signed by the President) as justice of the peace in the District of Columbia, *held* an attempt to enlarge the original jurisdiction of the Supreme Court, fixed by Article III, § 2.

    Marbury v. *Madison,* 1 Cr. (5 U.S.) 137 (1803).

2. Act of February 20, 1812 (2 Stat. 677).

    Provisions establishing board of revision to annul titles conferred many years previously by governors of the Northwest Territory were *held* violative of the due process clause of the Fifth Amendment.

    Reichart v. *Felps,* 6 Wall. (73 U.S.) 160 (1868).

3. Act of March 6, 1820 (3 Stat. 548, § 8, proviso).

    The Missouri Compromise, prohibiting slavery within the Louisiana Territory north of 36° 30', except Missouri, *held* not warranted as a regulation of Territory belonging to the United States under Article IV, § 3, clause 2 (and *see* Fifth Amendment).

    Scott v. *Sandford,* 19 How. (60 U.S.) 393 (1857).

4. Act of February 25, 1862 (12 Stat. 345, § 1); July 11, 1862 (12 Stat. 532, § 1); March 3, 1863 (12 Stat. 711, § 3), each in part only.

    "Legal tender clauses," making noninterest-bearing United States notes legal tender in payment of "all debts, public and private," so far as applied to debts contracted before passage of the act, *held* not within express or implied powers of Congress under Article I, § 8, and inconsistent with Article I, § 10, and Fifth Amendment.

    Hepburn v. *Griswold,* 8 Wall. (75 U.S.) 603 (1870); overruled in *Knox* v. *Lee (Legal Tender Cases),* 12 Wall. (79 U.S.) 457 (1871).

5. Act of March 3, 1863 (12 Stat. 756, § 5).

    "So much of the fifth section ... as provides for the removal of a judgment in a State court, and in which the cause was tried by a jury to the circuit court of the United States for a retrial on the facts and law, is not in pursuance of the Constitution, and is void" under the Seventh Amendment.

    The Justices v. *Murray,* 9 Wall. (76 U.S.) 274 (1870).

6. Act of March 3, 1863 (12 Stat. 766, § 5).

    Provision for an appeal from the Court of Claims to the Supreme Court — there being, at the time, a further provision (§ 14) requiring an estimate by the Secretary of the Treasury before payment of final judgments, *held* to contravene the judicial finality intended by the Constitution, Article III.

    Gordon v. *United States,* 2 Wall. (69 U.S.) 561 (1865). (Case was dismissed without opinion; the grounds upon which this decision was made were stated in a posthumous opinion by Chief Justice Taney printed in the appendix to volume 117 U.S. 697.)

7. Act of June 30, 1864 (13 Stat. 311, § 13).

    Provision that "any prize cause now pending in any circuit court shall, on the application of all parties in interest ... be transferred by that court to the Supreme Court...," as applied in a case where no action had been taken in the Circuit Court on the appeal from the district court, *held* to propose an appeal procedure not within Article III, § 2.

    The Alicia, 7 Wall. (74 U.S.) 571 (1869).

8. Act of January 24, 1865 (13 Stat. 424).

    Requirement of a test oath (disavowing actions in hostility to the United States) before admission to appear as attorney in a federal court by virtue of any previous admission, *held* invalid as applied to an attorney who had been pardoned by the President for all offenses during the Rebellion — as *ex post facto* (Article I, § 9, clause 3) and an interference with the pardoning power (Article II, § 2, clause 1).

    Ex parte Garland, 4 Wall. (71 U.S.) 333 (1867).

9. Act of March 2, 1867 (14 Stat. 484, § 29).

    General prohibition on sale of naphtha, etc., for illuminating purposes, if inflammable at less temperature than 110° F., *held* invalid "except so far as the section named operates within the United States, but without the limits of any State," as being a mere police regulation.

    United States v. *Dewitt,* 9 Wall. (76 U.S.) 41 (1870).

10. Act of May 31, 1870 (16 Stat. 140, §§ 3, 4).

    Provisions penalizing (1) refusal of local election officials to permit voting by persons offering to qualify under State laws, applicable to any citizens; and (2) hindering of any person from qualifying or voting, *held* invalid under Fifteenth Amendment.

    United States v. *Reese,* 92 U.S. 214 (1876).

11. Act of July 12, 1870 (16 Stat. 235).

    Provision making Presidential pardons inadmissible in evidence in Court of Claims, prohibiting their use by that court in deciding claims or appeals, and requiring dismissal of appeals by the Supreme Court in cases where proof of loyalty had been made otherwise than as prescribed by law, *held* an interference with judicial power under Article III, § 1, and with the pardoning power under Article II, § 2, clause 1.

    United States v. *Klein,* 13 Wall. (80 U.S.) 128 (1872).

12. Act of June 22, 1874 (18 Stat. 1878, § 4).

    Provision authorizing federal courts, in suits for forfeitures under revenue and custom laws, to require production of documents, with allegations expected to be proved therein to be taken as proved on failure to produce such documents, was *held* violative of the search and seizure provision of the Fourth Amendment and the self-incrimination clause of the Fifth Amendment.

    Boyd v. *United States,* 116 U.S. 616 (1886).

13. Revised Statutes 1977 (Act of May 31, 1870, 16 Stat. 144).

    Provision that "all persons within the jurisdiction of the United States shall have the same right in every State and Territory to make and enforce contracts ... as is enjoyed by white citizens...," *held* invalid under the Thirteenth Amendment.

    Hodges v. *United States,* 203 U.S. 1 (1906).

14. Revised Statutes 4937-4947 (Act of July 8, 1870, 16 Stat. 210), and Act of August 14, 1876 (19 Stat. 141).

    Original trademark law, applying to marks "for exclusive use within the United States," and a penal act designed solely for the protection of rights defined in the earlier measure, *held* not supportable by Article I, § 8, clause 8 (copyright clause), nor Article I, § 8, clause 3, by reason of its application to intrastate as well as interstate commerce.

    Trade-Mark Cases, 100 U.S. 82 (1879).

15. Revised Statutes 5132, subdivision 9 (Act of March 2, 1867, 14 Stat. 539).

    Provision penalizing "any person respecting whom bankruptcy proceedings are commenced ... who, within 3 months before the commencement of proceedings in bankruptcy, under the false color and pretense of carrying on business and dealing in the ordinary course of trade, obtains on credit from any person any goods or chattels with intent to defraud...," *held* a police regulation not within the bankruptcy power (Article I, § 4, clause 4).

    United States v. *Fox,* 95 U.S. 670 (1878).

16. Revised Statutes 5507 (Act of May 31, 1870, 16 Stat. 141, § 4).

    Provision penalizing "every person who prevents, hinders, controls, or intimidates another from exercising ... the right of suffrage, to whom that right is guaranteed by the Fifteenth Amendment to the Constitution of the United States, by means of bribery...," *held* not authorized by the Fifteenth Amendment.

    James v. *Bowman,* 190 U.S. 127 (1903).

17. Revised Statutes 5519 (Act of April 20, 1871, 17 Stat. 13, § 2).

    Section providing punishment in case "two or more persons in any State ... conspire ... for the purpose of depriving ... any person ... of the equal protection of the laws ... or for the purpose of preventing or hindering the constituted authorities of any State ... from giving or securing to all persons within such State ... the equal protection of the laws....," *held* invalid as not being directed at state action proscribed by the Fourteenth Amendment.

United States v. *Harris,* 106 U.S. 629 (1883).

In *Baldwin* v. *Franks,* 120 U.S. 678 (1887), an attempt was made to distinguish the *Harris* case and to apply the statute to a conspiracy directed at aliens within a State, but the provision was *held* not enforceable in such limited manner.

18. Revised Statutes of the District of Columbia, § 1064 (Act of June 17, 1870, 16 Stat. 154 § 3).

Provision that "prosecutions in the police court [of the District of Columbia] shall be by information under oath, without indictment by grand jury or trial by petit jury," as applied to punishment for conspiracy held to contravene Article III, § 2, requiring jury trial of all crimes.

Callan v. *Wilson,* 127 U.S. 540 (1888).

19. Act of March 1, 1875 (18 Stat. 336, §§ 1, 2).

Provision "That all persons within the jurisdiction of the United States shall be entitled to the full and equal enjoyment of the accommodations ... of inns, public conveyances on land or water, theaters, and other places of public amusement; subject only to the conditions and limitations established by law, and applicable alike to citizens of every race and color, regardless of any previous condition of servitude" — subject to penalty, *held* not to be supported by the Thirteenth or Fourteenth Amendments.

Civil Rights Cases, 109 U.S. 3 (1883), as to operation within States.

20. Act of March 3, 1875 (18 Stat. 479, § 2).

Provision that "if the party [i.e., a person stealing property from the United States] has been convicted, then the judgment against him shall be conclusive evidence in the prosecution against [the] receiver that the property of the United States therein described has been embezzled, stolen, or purloined," *held* to contravene the Sixth Amendment.

Kirby v. *United States,* 174 U.S. 47 (1899).

21. Act of July 12, 1876 (19 Stat. 80, sec. 6, in part).

Provision that "postmasters of the first, second, and third classes ... may be removed by the President by and with the advice and consent of the Senate," *held* to infringe the executive power under Article II, § 1, clause 1.

Myers v. *United States,* 272 U.S. 52 (1926).

22. Act of August, 14, 1876 (19 Stat. 141, Trademark Act). *See* Revised Statutes 4937, above, No. 14.

23. Act of August 11, 1888 (25 Stat. 411).

Clause, in a provision for the purchase or condemnation of a certain lock and dam in the Monongahela River, that "...in estimating the sums to be paid by the United States, the franchise of said corporation to collect tolls shall not be considered or estimated...," *held* to contravene the Fifth Amendment.

Monongahela Navigation Co. v. *United States,* 148 U.S. 312 (1893).

24. Act of May 5, 1892 (27 Stat. 25, § 4).

Provision of a Chinese exclusion act, that Chinese persons "convicted and adjudged to be not lawfully entitled to be or remain in the United States shall be imprisoned at hard labor for a period not exceeding 1 year and thereafter removed from the United States ... (such conviction and judgment being had before a justice, judge, or commissioner upon a summary hearing), *held* to contravene the Fifth and Sixth Amendments.

Wong Wing v. *United States,* 163 U.S. 228 (1896).

25. Joint Resolution of August 4, 1894 (28 Stat. 1018, No. 41).

Provision authorizing the Secretary of the Interior to approve a second lease of certain land by an Indian chief in Minnesota (granted to lessor's ancestor by art. 9 of a treaty with the Chippewa Indians), *held* an interference with judicial interpretation of treaties under Article III, § 2, clause 1 (and repugnant to the Fifth Amendment).

Jones v. *Meehan,* 175 U.S. 1 (1899).

26. Act of August 27, 1894 (28 Stat. 553-560, §§ 27-37).

Income tax provisions of the tariff act of 1894. "The tax imposed by §§ 27 and 37, inclusive ... so far as it falls on the income of real estate and of personal property, being a direct tax within the meaning of the Constitution, and, therefore, unconstitutional and void because not apportioned according to representation [Article I, § 2, clause 3], all those sections, constituting one entire scheme of taxation, are necessarily invalid" (158 U.S. 601, 637).

Pollock v. *Farmers' Loan & Trust Co.,* 157 U.S. 429 (1895), and rehearing, 158 U.S. 601 (1895).

27. Act of January 30, 1897 (29 Stat. 506).

Prohibition on sale of liquor "... to any Indian to whom allotment of land has been made while the title to the same shall be held in trust by the Government...," *held* a police regulation infringing state powers, and not warranted by the commerce clause, Article I, § 8, clause 3.

Matter of Heff, 197 U.S. 488 (1905), overruled in *United States* v. *Nice,* 241 U.S. 591 (1916).

28. Act of June 1, 1898 (30 Stat. 428).

Section 10, penalizing "any employer subject to the provisions of this act" who should "threaten any employee with loss of employment ... because of his membership in ... a labor corporation, association, or organization" (the act being applicable "to any common carrier ... engaged in the transportation of passengers or property ... from one State ... to another State...," etc.), *held* an infringement of the Fifth Amendment and not supported by the commerce clause.

Adair v. *United States,* 208 U.S. 161 (1908).

29. Act of June 13, 1898 (30 Stat. 451, 459).

Stamp tax on foreign bills of lading, *held* a tax on exports in violation of Article I, § 9.

Fairbank v. *United States,* 181 U.S. 283 (1901).

30. Same (30 Stat. 451, 460).

Tax on charter parties, as applied to shipments exclusively from ports in United States to foreign ports, *held* a tax on exports in violation of Article I, § 9.

United States v. *Hvoslef,* 237 U.S. 1 (1915).

31. Act of June 6, 1900 (31 Stat. 359, § 171).

Section of the Alaska Code providing for a six-person jury in trials for misdemeanors, *held* repugnant to the Sixth Amendment, requiring "jury" trial of crimes.

Rassmussen v. *United States,* 197 U.S. 516 (1905).

32. Act of March 3, 1901 (31 Stat. 1341, § 935).

Section of the District of Columbia Code granting the same right of appeal, in criminal cases, to the United States or the District of Columbia as to the defendant, but providing that a verdict was not to be set aside for error found in rulings during trial, *held* an attempt to take an advisory opinion, contrary to Article III, § 2.

United States v. *Evans,* 213 U.S. 297 (1909).

33. Act of June 11, 1906 (34 Stat. 232).

Act providing that "every common carrier engaged in trade or commerce in the District of Columbia ... or between the several States ... shall be liable to any of its employees ... for all damages which may result from the negligence of any of its officers ... or by reason of any defect ... due to its negligence in its cars, engines ... roadbed," etc., *held* not supportable under Article I, § 8, clause 3 because it extended to intrastate as well as interstate commercial activities.

The Employers' Liability Cases, 207 U.S. 463 (1908). (The act was upheld as to the District of Columbia in *Hyde* v. *Southern R. Co.,* 31 App. D.C. 466 (1908); and as to the Territories, in *El Paso & N.E. Ry.* v. *Gutierrez,* 215 U.S. 87 (1909).)

34. Act of June 16, 1906 (34 Stat. 269, § 2).

Provision of Oklahoma Enabling Act restricting relocation of the State capital prior to 1913, *held* not supportable by Article IV, § 3, authorizing admission of new States.

Coyle v. *Smith,* 221 U.S. 559 (1911).

35. Act of February 20, 1907 (34 Stat. 889, § 3).

Provision in the Immigration Act of 1907 penalizing "whoever ... shall keep, maintain, control, support, or harbor in any house or other place, for the purpose of prostitution ... any alien woman or girl, within 3 years after she shall have entered the United States," *held* an exercise of police power not within the control of Congress over immigration (whether drawn from the commerce clause or based on inherent sovereignty).

Keller v. *United States,* 213 U.S. 138 (1909).

36. Act of March 1, 1907 (34 Stat. 1028).

Provisions authorizing certain Indians "to institute their suits in the Court of Claims to determine the validity of any acts of Congress passed since ... 1902, insofar as said acts ... attempt to increase or extend the restrictions upon alienation ... of allotments of lands of Cherokee citizens....," and giving a right of appeal to the Supreme Court, *held* an attempt to enlarge the judicial power restricted by Article III, § 2, to cases and controversies.

Muskrat v. *United States,* 219 U.S. 346 (1911).

37. Act of May 27, 1908 (35 Stat. 313, § 4).

Provision making locally taxable "all land [of Indians of the Five Civilized Tribes] from which restrictions have been or shall be removed," *held* a violation of the Fifth Amendment, in view of the Atoka Agreement, embodied in the Curtis Act of June 28, 1898, providing tax-exemption for allotted lands while title in original allottee, not exceeding 21 years.

Choate v. *Trapp,* 224 U.S. 665 (1912).

38. Act of February 9, 1909, § 2, 35 Stat. 614, as amended.

Provision of Narcotic Drugs Import and Export Act creating a presumption that possessor of cocaine knew of its illegal importation into the United States, *held,* in light of the fact that more cocaine is produced domestically than is brought into the country and in absence of any showing that defendant could have known his cocaine was imported, if it was, inapplicable to support conviction from mere possession of cocaine.

Turner v. *United States,* 396 U.S. 398 (1970).

39. Act of August 19, 1911 (37 Stat. 28).

A proviso in § 8 of the Federal Corrupt Practices Act fixing a maximum authorized expenditure by a candidate for Senator "in any campaign for his nomination and election," as applied to a primary election, *held* not supported by Article I, § 4, giving Congress power to regulate the manner of holding elections for Senators and Representatives.

Newberry v. *United States,* 256 U.S. 232 (1921), overruled in *United States* v. *Classic,* 313 U.S. 299 (1941).

40. Act of June 18, 1912 (37 Stat. 136, § 8).

Part of § 8 giving the Juvenile Court of the District of Columbia (proceeding upon information) concurrent jurisdiction of desertion cases (which were, by law, punishable by fine or imprisonment in the workhouse at hard labor for 1 year), *held* invalid under the Fifth Amendment, which gives right to presentment by a grand jury in case of infamous crimes.

United States v. *Moreland,* 258 U.S. 433 (1922).

41. Act of March 4, 1913 (37 Stat. 988, part of par. 64).

Provision of the District of Columbia Public Utility Commission Act authorizing appeal to the United States Supreme Court from decrees of the District of Columbia Court of Appeals modifying valuation decisions of the Utilities Commission, *held* an attempt to extend the appellate jurisdiction of the Supreme Court to cases not strictly judicial within the meaning of Article III, § 2.

Keller v. *Potomac Elec. Co.,* 261 U.S. 428 (1923).

42. Act of September 1, 1916 (39 Stat. 675).

The original Child Labor Law, providing "that no producer ... shall ship ... in interstate commerce ... any article or commodity the product of any mill ... in which within 30 days prior to the removal of such product therefrom children under the age of 14 years have been employed or permitted to work more than 8 hours in any day or more than 6 days in any week...," *held* not within the commerce power of Congress.

Hammer v. *Dagenhart,* 247 U.S. 251 (1918).

43. Act of September 8, 1916 (39 Stat. 757, § 2(a), in part).

Provision of the income tax law of 1916, that a "stock dividend shall be considered income, to the amount of its cash value," *held* invalid (in spite of the Sixteenth Amendment) as an attempt to tax something not actually income, without regard to apportionment under Article I, § 2, clause 3.

Eisner v. *Macomber,* 252 U.S. 189 (1920).

44. Act of October 6, 1917 (40 Stat. 395).

The amendment of §§ 24 and 256 of the Judicial Code (which prescribe the jurisdiction of district courts) "saving ... to claimants the rights and remedies under the workmen's compensation law of any State," *held* an attempt to transfer federal legislative powers to the States — the Constitution, by Article III, § 2, and Article I, § 8, having adopted rules of general maritime law.

Knickerbocker Ice Co. v. *Stewart,* 253 U.S. 149 (1920).

45. Act of September 19, 1918 (40 Stat. 960).

Specifically, that part of the Minimum Wage Law of the District of Columbia which authorized the Wage Board "to ascertain and declare ... (a) Standards of minimum wages for women in any occupation within the District of Columbia, and what wages are inadequate to supply the necessary cost of living to any such women workers to maintain them in good health and to protect their morals...," *held* to interfere with freedom of contract under the Fifth Amendment.

Adkins v. *Children's Hospital,* 261 U.S. 525 (1923), overruled in *West Coast Hotel Co.* v. *Parrish,* 300 U.S. 379 (1937).

46. Act of February 24, 1919 (40 Stat. 1065, § 213, in part).

That part of § 213 of the Revenue Act of 1918 which provided that "... for the purposes of this title ... the term 'gross income' ... includes gains, profits, and income derived from salaries, wages, or compensation for personal service (including in the case of ... judges of the Supreme and inferior courts of the United States ... the compensation received as such)..." as applied to a judge in office when the act was passed, *held* a violation of the guaranty of judges' salaries, in Article III, § 1.

Evans v. *Gore,* 253 U.S. 245 (1920).

Miles v. *Graham,* 268 U.S. 51 (1925), held it invalid as applied to a judge taking office subsequent to the date of the act.

47. Act of February 24, 1919 (40 Stat. 1097, § 402(c)).

That part of the estate tax law providing that "gross estate" of a decedent should include value of all property "to the extent of any interest therein of which the decedent has at any time made a transfer or with respect to which he had at any time created a trust, in contemplation of or intended to take effect in possession or enjoyment at or after his death (whether such transfer or trust is made or created before or after the passage of this act), except in

case of a *bona fide* sale..." as applied to a transfer of property made prior to the act and intended to take effect "in possession or enjoyment" at death of grantor, but not in fact testamentary or designed to evade taxation, *held* confiscatory, contrary to Fifth Amendment.

Nicholds v. *Coolidge,* 274 U.S. 531 (1927).

48. Act of February 24, 1919, title XII (40 Stat. 1138, entire title).

The Child Labor Tax Act, providing that "every person ... operating ... any ... factory ... in which children under the age of 14 years have been employed or permitted to work ... shall pay ... in addition to all other taxes imposed by law, an excise tax equivalent to 10 percent of the entire net profits received ... for such year from the sale ... of the product of such ... factory...," *held* beyond the taxing power under Article I, §, 8, clause 1, and an infringement of state authority.

Bailey v. *Drexel Furniture Co. (Child Labor Tax Case),* 259 U.S. 20 (1922).

49. Act of October 22, 1919 (41 Stat. 298, § 2), amending Act of August 10, 1917 (40 Stat. 277, § 4).

(a) § 4 of the Lever Act, providing in part "that it is hereby made unlawful for any persons willfully ... to make any unjust or unreasonable rate or charge in handling or dealing in or with any necessaries..." and fixing a penalty, *held* invalid to support an indictment for charging an unreasonable price on sale — as not setting up an ascertainable standard of guilt within the requirement of the Sixth Amendment.

United States v. *Cohen Grocery Co.,* 255 U.S. 81 (1921).

(b) That provision of § 4 making it unlawful "to conspire, combine, agree, or arrange with any other person to ... exact excessive prices for any necessaries" and fixing a penalty, *held* invalid to support an indictment, on the reasoning of the *Cohen Grocery* case.

Weeds, Inc. v. *United States,* 255 U.S. 109 (1921).

50. Act of August 24, 1921 (42 Stat. 187, Future Trading Act).

(a) § 4 (and interwoven regulations) providing a "tax of 20 cents a bushel on every bushel involved therein, upon each contract of sale of grain for future delivery, except ... where such contracts are made by or through a member of a board of trade which has been designated by the Secretary of Agriculture as a 'contract market'...," *held* not within the taxing power under Article I, § 8.

Hill v. *Wallace,* 259 U.S. 44 (1922).

(b) § 3, providing "That in addition to the taxes now imposed by law there is hereby levied a tax amounting to 20 cents per bushel on each bushel involved therein, whether the actual commodity is intended to be delivered or only nominally referred to, upon each ... option for a contract either of purchase or sale of grain...," *held* invalid on the same reasoning.

Trusler v. *Crooks,* 269 U.S. 475 (1926).

51. Act of November 23, 1921 (42 Stat. 261, § 245, in part).

Provision of Revenue Act of 1921 abating the deduction (4 percent of mean reserves) allowed from taxable income of life insurance companies in general by the amount of interest on their tax-exempts, and so according no relative advantage to the owners of the tax-exempt securities, *held* to destroy a guaranteed exemption.

National Life Ins. v. *United States,* 277 U.S. 508 (1928).

52. Act of June 10, 1922 (42 Stat. 634).

A second attempt to amend §§ 24 and 256 of the Judicial Code, relating to jurisdiction of district courts, by saving "to claimants for compensation for injuries to or death of persons other than the master or members of the crew of a vessel, their rights and remedies under the workmen's compensation law of any State..." *held* invalid on authority of *Knickerbocker Ice Co.* v. *Stewart.*

Washington v. *Dawson & Co.,* 264 U.S. 219 (1924).

53. Act of June 2, 1924 (43 Stat. 313).

The gift tax provisions of the Revenue Act of 1924, applicable to gifts made during the calendar year, were *held* invalid under the Fifth Amendment insofar as they applied to gifts made before passage of the act.

Untermeyer v. *Anderson,* 276 U.S. 440 (1928).

54. Act of February 26, 1926 (44 Stat. 70, § 302, in part).

Stipulation creating a conclusive presumption that gifts made within two years prior to the death of the donor were made in contemplation of death of donor and requiring the value thereof to be included in computing the death transfer tax on decedent's estate was *held* to effect an invalid deprivation of property without due process.

Heiner v. *Donnan,* 285 U.S. 312 (1932).

55. Act of February 26, 1926 (44 Stat. 95, § 701).

Provision imposing a special excise tax of $1,000 on liquor dealers operating in States where such business is illegal, was *held* a penalty, without constitutional support following repeal of the Eighteenth Amendment.

United States v. *Constantine,* 296 U.S. 287 (1935).

56. Act of March 20, 1933 (48 Stat. 11, § 17, in part).

Clause in the Economy Act of 1933 providing "... all laws

granting or pertaining to yearly renewable term war risk insurance are hereby repealed," *held* invalid to abrogate an outstanding contract of insurance, which is a vested right protected by the Fifth Amendment.

Lynch v. *United States,* 292 U.S. 571 (1934).

57. Act of May 12, 1933 (48 Stat. 31).

Agricultural Adjustment Act providing for processing taxes on agricultural commodities and benefit payments therefrom to farmers, *held* not within the taxing power under Article I, § 8, clause 1.

United States v. *Butler,* 297 U.S. 1 (1936).

58. Joint Resolution of June 5, 1933 (48 Stat. 113, § 1).

Abrogation of gold clause in Government obligations, *held* a repudiation of the pledge implicit in the power to borrow money (Article 1, § 8, clause 2), and within the prohibition of the Fourteenth Amendment, against questioning the validity of the public debt. (The majority of the Court, however, held plaintiff not entitled to recover under the circumstances.)

Perry v. *United States,* 294 U.S. 330 (1935).

59. Act of June 16, 1933 (48 Stat. 195, the National Industrial Recovery Act).

(a) Title I, except § 9.

Provisions relating to codes of fair competition, authorized to be approved by the President in his discretion "to effectuate the policy" of the act, *held* invalid as a delegation of legislative power (Article I, § 1) and not within the commerce power (Article I, § 8, clause 3).

Schechter Corp. v. *United States,* 295 U.S. 495 (1935).

(b) § 9(c).

Clause of the oil regulation section authorizing the President "to prohibit the transportation in interstate . . . commerce of petroleum . . . produced or withdrawn from storage in excess of the amount permitted . . . by any State law. . ." and prescribing a penalty for violation of orders issued thereunder, *held* invalid as a delegation of legislative power.

Panama Refining Co. v. *Ryan,* 293 U.S. 388 (1935).

60. Act of June 16, 1933 (48 Stat. 307, § 13).

Temporary reduction of 15 percent in retired pay of judges, retired from service but subject to performance of judicial duties under the Act March 1, 1929 (45 Stat. 1422), was *held* a violation of the guaranty of judges' salaries in Article III, § 1.

Booth v. *United States,* 291 U.S. 339 (1934).

61. Act of April 27, 1934 (48 Stat. 646, § 6) amending § 5(i) of Home Owners' Loan Act of 1933.

Provision for conversion of state building and loan associations into federal associations, upon vote of 51 percent of the votes cast at a meeting of stockholders called to consider such action, *held* an encroachment on reserved powers of State.

Hopkins Savings Assn. v. *Cleary,* 296 U.S. 315 (1935).

62. Act of May 24, 1934 (48 Stat. 798).

Provision for readjustment of municipal indebtedness, though "adequately related" to the bankruptcy power, was *held* invalid as an interference with state sovereignty.

Ashton v. *Cameron County Dist.,* 298 U.S. 513 (1936).

63. Act of June 27, 1934 (48 Stat. 1283).

The Railroad Retirement Act, establishing a detailed compulsory retirement system for employees of carriers subject to the Interstate Commerce Act, *held* not a regulation of commerce within the meaning of Article I, § 8, clause 3, and violative of the due process clause (Fifth Amendment).

Railroad Retirement Board v. *Alton R. Co.,* 295 U.S. 330 (1935).

64. Act of June 28, 1934 (48 Stat. 1289, ch. 869).

The Frazier-Lemke Act, adding subsection (5) to § 75 of the Bankruptcy Act, designed to preserve to mortgagors the ownership and enjoyment of their farm property and providing specifically, in paragraph 7, that a bankrupt left in possession has the option at any time within 5 years of buying at the appraised value — subject meanwhile to no monetary obligation other than payment of reasonable rental, *held* a violation of property rights, under the Fifth Amendment.

Louisville Bank v. *Radford,* 295 U.S. 555 (1935).

65. Act of August 24, 1935 (49 Stat. 750).

Amendments of Agricultural Adjustment Act *held* not within the taxing power.

Rickert Rice Mills v. *Fontenot,* 297 U.S. 110 (1936).

66. Act of August 30, 1935 (49 Stat. 991).

Bituminous Coal Conservation Act of 1935, *held* to impose, not a tax within Article I, § 8, but a penalty not sustained by the commerce clause (Article I, § 8, clause 3).

Carter v. *Carter Coal Co.,* 298 U.S. 238 (1936).

67. Act of June 25, 1938 (52 Stat. 1040).

Federal Food, Drug, and Cosmetic Act of 1938, § 301(f), prohib-

iting the refusal to permit entry or inspection of premises by federal officers *held* void for vagueness and as violative of the due process clause of the Fifth Amendment.

United States v. *Cardiff,* 344 U.S. 174 (1952).

68. Act of June 30, 1938 (52 Stat. 1251).

Federal Firearms Act, § 2(f), establishing a presumption of guilt based on a prior conviction and present possession of a firearm, *held* to violate the test of due process under the Fifth Amendment.

Tot v. *United States,* 319 U.S. 463 (1943).

69. Act of August 10, 1939 (53 Stat. 1362 as amended).

Provision of Social Security Act that grants survivors' benefits based on the earnings of a deceased husband and father covered by the Act to his widow and to the couple's children in her care but that grants benefits based on the earnings of a covered deceased wife and mother only to the minor children and not to the widower violates the right to equal protection secured by the Fifth Amendment's due process clause, since it unjustifiably discriminates against female wage earners required to pay social security taxes by affording them less protection for their survivors than is provided for male wage earners.

Weinberger v. *Wiesenfeld,* 420 U.S. 636 (1975).

70. Act of October 14, 1940 (54 Stat. 1169, § 401(g)); as amended by Act of January 20, 1944 (58 Stat. 4, § 1).

Provision of Aliens and Nationality Code (8 U.S.C. § 1481(a) (8)), derived from the Nationality Act of 1940, as amended, that citizenship shall be lost upon conviction by court martial and dishonorable discharge for deserting the armed services in time of war, *held* invalid as imposing a cruel and unusual punishment barred by the Eighth Amendment and not authorized by the war powers conferred by Article I, § 8, clauses 11 to 14.

Trop v. *Dulles,* 356 U.S. 86 (1958).

71. Act of November 15, 1943 (57 Stat. 450).

Urgent Deficiency Appropriation Act of 1943, § 304, providing that no salary should be paid to certain named federal employees out of moneys appropriated, *held* to violate Article I, § 9, clause 3, forbidding enactment of bill of attainder or *ex post facto* law.

United States v. *Lovett,* 328 U.S. 303 (1946).

72. Act of September 27, 1944 (58 Stat. 746, § 401 (J)); and Act of June 27, 1952 (66 Stat. 163, 267-268, § 349(a) (10)).

§ 401 (J) of Immigration and Nationality Act of 1940, added in 1944, and § 49(a) (10) of the Immigration and Nationality Act of 1952 depriving one of citizenship, without the procedural safeguards guaranteed by the Fifth and Sixth Amendments, for the offense of leaving or remaining outside the country, in time of war or national emergency, to evade military service *held* invalid.

Kennedy v. *Mendoza-Martinez,* 372 U.S. 144 (1963).

73. Act of July 31, 1946 (ch. 707, § 7, 60 Stat. 719).

District court decision holding invalid under First and Fifth Amendments statute prohibiting parades or assemblages on United States Capitol grounds is summarily affirmed.

Chief of Capitol Police v. *Jeanette Rankin Brigade,* 409 U.S. 972 (1972).

74. Act of June 25, 1948 (62 Stat. 760).

Provision of Lindbergh Kidnapping Act which provided for the imposition of the death penalty only if recommended by the jury *held* unconstitutional inasmuch as it penalized the assertion of a defendant's assertion of his Sixth Amendment right to a jury trial.

United States v. *Jackson,* 390 U.S. 570 (1968).

75. Act of May 5, 1950 (64 Stat. 107).

Article 3(a) of the Uniform Code of Military Justice subjecting civilian ex-servicemen to court martial for crime committed while in military service *held* to violate Article III, § 2, and the Fifth and Sixth Amendments.

Toth v. *Quarles,* 350 U.S. 11 (1955).

76. Act of May 5, 1950 (64 Stat. 107).

Insofar as Article 2(11) of the Uniform Code of Military Justice subjects civilian dependents accompanying members of the armed forces overseas in time of peace, in capital cases, by court martial, it is violative of Article III, § 2, and the Fifth and Sixth Amendments.

Reid v. *Covert,* 354 U.S. 1 (1957).

Insofar as the aforementioned provision is invoked in time of peace for the trial of noncapital offenses committed on land bases overseas by employees of the armed forces who have not been inducted or who have not voluntarily enlisted therein, it is violative of the Sixth Amendment.

McElroy v. *United States,* 361 U.S. 281 (1960).

Insofar as the aforementioned provision is invoked in time of peace for the trial of noncapital offense committed by civilian dependents accompanying members of the armed forces overseas, it is violative of Article III, § 2, and the Fifth and Sixth Amendments.

Kinsella v. *United States,* 361 U.S. 234 (1960).

Insofar as the aforementioned provision is invoked in time of peace for the trial of a capital offense committed by a civilian employee of the armed forces overseas, it is violative of Article III, § 2, and the Fifth and Sixth Amendments.

Grisham v. *Hogan*, 361 U.S. 278 (1960).

77. Act of August 16, 1950 (64 Stat. 451, as amended).

Statutory scheme authorizing the Postmaster General to close the mails to distributors of obscene materials *held* unconstitutional in the absence of procedural provisions which would assure prompt judicial determination that protected materials were not being restrained.

Blount v. *Rizzi*, 400 U.S. 410 (1971).

78. Act of August 28, 1950 (§ 202(f)(1)(E), 64 Stat. 485, 42 U.S.C. § 402(f)(1)(D)).

Social Security Act provision awarding survivors' benefits based on the earnings of a deceased wife to widower only if he was receiving at least half of his support from her at the time of her death, whereas widow receives benefits regardless of dependency violates equal protection element of Fifth Amendment's due process clause because of its impermissible gender classification.

Califano v. *Goldfarb*, 430 U.S. 199 (1977).

79. Act of September 23, 1950 (Title 1, § 5, 64 Stat. 992).

Provision of Subversive Activities Control Act making it unlawful for member of Communist front organization to work in a defense plant *held* to be an overbroad infringement of the right of association protected by the First Amendment.

United States v. *Robel*, 389 U.S. 258 (1967).

80. Act of September 23, 1950 (64 Stat. 993, § 6).

Subversive Activities Control Act of 1950, § 6, providing that any member of a Communist organization, which has registered or has been ordered to register, commits a crime if he attempts to obtain or use a passport, *held* violative of due process under the Fifth Amendment.

Aptheker v. *Secretary of State*, 378 U.S. 500 (1964).

81. Act of September 23, 1950 (Title I, §§ 7, 8, 64 Stat. 993).

Provisions of Subversive Activities Control Act of 1950 requiring registration by party members in lieu of registration by the Communist Party may not be applied to compel registration of, or to prosecute for refusal to register, alleged members who have asserted their privilege against self-incrimination inasmuch as registration would expose such persons to criminal prosecution under other laws.

Albertson v. *Subversive Activities Control Board*, 382 U.S. 70 (1965).

82. Act of October 30, 1951 (§ 5(f) ii), 65 Stat. 683, 45 U.S.C. § 231a(c)(3) (ii)).

Provision of Railroad Retirement Act similar to section voided in *Goldfarb*. See Act of August 28, 1950, above No. 78.

Railroad Retirement Board v. *Kalina*, 431 U.S. 909 (1977).

83. Act of June 27, 1952 (Title III, § 349, 66 Stat. 267).

Provision of Immigration and Nationality Act of 1952 providing for revocation of United States citizenship of one who votes in a foreign election *held* unconstitutional under § 1 of the Fourteenth Amendment.

Afroyim v. *Rusk*, 387 U.S. 253 (1967).

84. Act of June 27, 1952 (66 Stat. 163, 269, § 352(a) (1)).

§ 352(a) (1) of the Immigration and Nationality Act of 1952 depriving a naturalized person of citizenship for "having a continuous residence for three years" in state of his birth or prior nationality *held* violative of the due process clause of the Fifth Amendment.

Schneider v. *Rusk*, 377 U.S. 163 (1964).

85. Act of August 16, 1954 (68A Stat. 525, Int. Rev. Code of 1954, §§ 4401-4423).

Provisions of tax laws requiring gamblers to pay occupational and excise taxes may not be used over an assertion of one's privilege against self-incrimination either to compel extensive reporting of activities, leaving the registrant subject to prosecution under the laws of all the States with the possible exception of Nevada, or to prosecute for failure to register and report, because the scheme abridged the Fifth Amendment privilege.

Marchetti v. *United States*, 390 U.S. 39 (1968), and *Grosso* v. *United States*, 390 U.S. 62 (1968).

86. Act of August 16, 1954 (68A Stat. 560, Marijuana Tax Act, §§ 4741, 4744, 4751, 4753).

Provisions of tax laws requiring possessors of marijuana to register and to pay a transfer tax may not be used over an assertion of the privilege against self-incrimination to compel registration or to prosecute for failure to register.

Leary v. *United States*, 395 U.S. 6 (1969).

87. Act of August 16, 1954 (68A Stat. 728, Int. Rev. Code of 1954, §§ 5841, 5851).

Provisions of tax laws requiring the possessor of certain firearms, which it is made illegal to receive or to possess, to register with

the Treasury Department may not be used over an assertion of the privilege against self-incrimination to prosecute one for failure to register or for possession of an unregistered firearm since the statutory scheme abridges the Fifth Amendment privilege.

Haynes v. *United States*, 390 U.S. 85 (1968).

88. Act of August 16, 1954 (68A Stat. 867, Int. Rev. Code of 1954, § 7302).

Provisions of tax laws providing for forfeiture of property used in violating internal revenue laws may not be constitutionally used in face of invocation of privilege against self-incrimination to condemn money in possession of gambler who had failed to comply with the registration and reporting scheme held void in *Marchetti* v. *United States*, 390 U.S. 39 (1968).

United States v. *United States Coin & Currency*, 401 U.S. 715 (1971).

89. Act of July 18, 1956 (§ 106, Stat. 570).

Provision of Narcotic Drugs Import and Export Act creating a presumption that possessor of marijuana knew of its illegal importation into the United States *held*, in absence of showing that all marijuana in United States was of foreign origin and that domestic users could know that their marijuana was more likely than not of foreign origin, unconstitutional under the due process clause of the Fifth Amendment.

Leary v. *United States*, 395 U.S. 6 (1969).

90. Act of August 10, 1956 (70A Stat. 65, Uniform Code of Military Justice, Articles 80, 130, 134).

Servicemen may not be charged under the Act and tried in military courts because of the commission of non-service connected crimes committed off-post and off-duty which are subject to civilian court jurisdiction where the guarantees of the Bill of Rights are applicable.

O'Callahan v. *Parker*, 395 U.S. 258 (1969).

91. Act of August 10, 1956 (70A Stat. 35, § 772(f)).

Provision of statute permitting the wearing of United States military apparel in theatrical productions only if the portrayal does not tend to discredit the armed force imposes an unconstitutional restraint upon First Amendment freedoms and precludes a prosecution under 18 U.S.C. § 702 for unauthorized wearing of uniform in a street skit disrespectful of the military.

Schacht v. *United States*, 398 U.S. 58 (1970).

92. Act of September 2, 1958 (§ 5601(b) (1), 72 Stat. 1399).

Provision of Internal Revenue Code creating a presumption that one's presence at the site of an unregistered still shall be sufficient for conviction under a statute punishing possession, custody, or control of an unregistered still unless defendant otherwise explained his presence at the site to the jury is unconstitutional because the presumption is not a legitimate, rational, or reasonable inference that defendant was engaged in one of the specialized functions proscribed by the statute.

United States v. *Romano*, 382 U.S. 136 (1965).

93. Act of September 2, 1958 (§ 1(25) (b), 72 Stat. 1446), and Act of September 7, 1962 (§ 401, 76 Stat. 469).

Federal statutes providing that spouses of female members of the Armed Forces must be dependent in fact in order to qualify for certain dependent's benefits, whereas spouses of male members are statutorily deemed dependent and automatically qualified for allowances, whatever their actual status, is an invalid gender classification under the equal protection principles of the Fifth Amendment's due process Clause.

Frontiero v. *Richardson*, 411 U.S. 677 (1973).

94. Act of September 14, 1959 (§ 504, 73 Stat. 536).

Provision of Labor-Management Reporting and Disclosure Act of 1959 making it a crime for a member of the Communist Party to serve as an officer or, with the exception of clerical or custodial positions, as an employee of a labor union *held* to be a bill of attainder and unconstitutional.

United States v. *Brown*, 381 U.S. 437 (1965).

95. Act of October 11, 1962 (§ 305, 76 Stat. 840).

Provision of Postal Services and Federal Employees Salary Act of 1962 authorizing Post Office Department to detain material determined to be "communist political propaganda" and to forward it to the addressee only if he requested it after notification by the Department, the material to be destroyed otherwise, *held* to impose on the addressee an affirmative obligation which amounted to an abridgment of First Amendment rights.

Lamont v. *Postmaster General*, 381 U.S. 301 (1965).

96. Act of October 15, 1962 (76 Stat. 914).

Provision of District of Columbia laws requiring that a person to be eligible to receive welfare assistance must have resided in the District for at least one year impermissibly classified persons on the basis of an assertion of the right to travel interstate and therefore *held* to violate the due process clause of the Fifth Amendment.

Shapiro v. *Thompson*, 394 U.S. 618 (1969).

97. Act of December 16, 1963 (77 Stat. 378, 20 U.S.C. § 754).

Provision of Higher Education Facilities Act of 1963 which in effect removed restriction against religious use of facilities constructed with federal funds after 20 years *held* to violate the establishment clause of the First Amendment inasmuch as the property will still be of considerable value at the end of the period and removal of the restriction would constitute a substantial governmental contribution to religion.

Tilton v. *Richardson,* 403 U.S. 672 (1971).

98. Act of July 30, 1965 (§ 339, 79 Stat. 409).

Section of Social Security Act qualifying certain illegitimate children for disability insurance benefits by presuming dependence but disqualifying other illegitimate children, regardless of dependency, if the disabled wage earner parent did not contribute to the child's support before the onset of the disability or if the child did not live with the parent before the onset of disability denies latter class of children equal protection as guaranteed by the due process clause of the Fifth Amendment.

Jimenez v. *Weinberger,* 417 U.S. 628 (1974).

99. Act of September 3, 1966 (§ 102(b), 80 Stat. 831), and Act of April 8, 1974 (§§ 6(a)(1) (amending § 3(d) of Act), 6(a)(2) (amending 3(e) (2)(C), 6(a) (5) (amending 3(5)(5), and 6(a) (6) (amending § 3(x)).

Those sections of the Fair Labor Standards Act extending wage and hour coverage to the employees of state and local governments are invalid because Congress lacks the authority under the commerce clause to regulate employee activities in areas of traditional governmental functions of the States.

National League of Cities v. *Usery,* 426 U.S. 833 (1976).

100. Act of January 2, 1968 (§ 163(a) (2), 81 Stat. 872).

District court decisions holding unconstitutional under Fifth Amendment's due process clause section of Social Security Act that reduced, perhaps to zero, benefits coming to illegitimate children upon death of parent in order to satisfy the maximum payment due the wife and legitimate children are summarily affirmed.

Richardson v. *Davis,* 409 U.S. 1069 (1972).

Richardson v. *Griffin,* 409 U.S. 1069 (1972).

101. Act of January 2, 1968 (§ 203, 81 Stat. 882).

Provision of Social Security Act extending benefits to families when dependent children have been deprived of parental support because of the unemployment of the father but not giving benefits when the mother becomes unemployed violates the equal protection principle of the Fifth Amendment's due process clause because of the impermissible gender classification.

Califano v. *Westcott,* 443 U.S. 76 (1979).

102. Act of June 22, 1970 (ch. III, 84 Stat. 318).

Provision of Voting Rights Act Amendments of 1970 which set a minimum voting age qualification of 18 in state and local elections *held* to be unconstitutional because beyond the powers of Congress to legislate.

Oregon v. *Mitchell,* 400 U.S. 112 (1970).

103. Act of December 29, 1970 (§ 8(a), 84 Stat. 1598, 29 U.S.C. § 637 (a)).

Provision of Occupational Safety and Health Act authorizing inspections of covered work places in industry without warrants violates Fourth Amendment.

Marshall v. *Barlow's, Inc.,* 436 U.S. 307 (1978).

104. Act of January 11, 1971 (§ 2, 84 Stat. 2048).

Provision of Food Stamp Act disqualifying from participation in program any household containing an individual unrelated by birth, marriage, or adoption to any other member of the household violates the due process clause of the Fifth Amendment.

Department of Agriculture v. *Moreno,* 413 U.S. 528 (1973).

105. Act of January 11, 1971 (§ 4, 84 Stat. 2049).

Provision of Food Stamp Act disqualifying from participation in program any household containing a person 18 years or older who had been claimed as a dependent child for income tax purposes in the present or preceding tax year by a taxpayer not a member of the household violates the due process clause of the Fifth Amendment.

Dept. of Agriculture v. *Murry,* 413 U.S. 508 (1973).

106. Act of December 10, 1971 (85 Stat. 570)

Supreme Court affirms, by an equal division of the justices, judgment of district court holding unconstitutional provision limiting to $1,000 the amount that independent committees could expend on behalf of presidential candidate as an impermissible limitation of freedom of speech and association protected by the First Amendment.

Common Cause v. *Schmitt,* 455 U.S. 129 (1982).

107. Federal Election Campaign Act of February 7, 1972 (86 Stat. 3), as amended by the Federal Election Campaign Act Amendments of 1974 (88 Stat. 1263), adding or amending 18 U.S.C. §§ 608(a), 608(e), and 2 U.S.C. § 437c.

Provisions of election law that forbid a candidate or the members of his immediate family from expending personal funds in excess of specified amounts, that limit to $1,000 the independent expenditures of any person relative to an identified candidate, and that forbid expenditures by candidates for federal office in excess of specified amounts violate the First Amendment speech guarantees; provisions of the law creating a commission to oversee enforcement of the Act are an invalid infringement of constitutional separation of powers in that they devolve responsibilities upon a commission four of whose six members are appointed by Congress and all six of whom are confirmed by the House of Representatives as well as by the Senate, not in compliance with the appointments clause.

Buckley v. *Valeo,* 424 U.S. 1 (1976).

108. Act of October 1, 1976 (Title II, part, 90 Stat. 1446), Act of October 12, 1979 (§ 101(c), 93 Stat. 657).

Provisions of Legislative Appropriations Act rolling back automatic pay increases for federal officer and employees is unconstitutional as to Article III judges because, the increases having gone into effect, they violate security of compensation Clause of Article III.

United States v. *Will,* 449 U.S. 200 (1980).

109. Act of November 6, 1978 (92 Stat. 2549, § 251 (a)).

Vesting of certain traditional judicial powers in a court the judges of which are not endowed with security of tenure and compensation violates Article III of the Constitution.

Northern Pipeline Construction Co. v. *Marathon Pipe Line Co.,* 458 U.S. 000 (1982).

110. Act of May 30, 1980 (94 Stat. 399) as amended by the Act of October 14, 1980 (94 Stat. 1959)

Acts of Congress applying to bankruptcy reorganization of one railroad and guaranteeing employee benefits is repugnant to the requirement of Article I, Sec. 8, clause 4, that bankruptcy legislation be "uniform."

Railroad Labor Executives' Assn. v. *Gibbons,* 455 U.S. 000 (1982).

Supreme Court Justices: 1969-83

The following sketches provide biographical information about each person who has served on the Supreme Court since 1969.

The biographies of the nine sitting justices (as of March 1983) precede those of the six men who served for part of this period and then resigned from the court.

Warren Earl Burger
(1969-   )

Born: Sept. 17, 1907, St. Paul, Minn.

Education: Attended the University of Minnesota, 1925-27; St. Paul College of Law (now Mitchell College of Law), LL.B., magna cum laude, 1931.

Religion: Presbyterian.

Official Positions: U.S. assistant attorney general, civil division, Justice Department, 1953-56; judge, U.S. Court of Appeals for the District of Columbia, 1956-69.

Supreme Court Appointment: Nominated at age 61 to be chief justice of the United States by President Richard M. Nixon May 21, 1969, to replace Chief Justice Earl Warren, who resigned; confirmed by the Senate June 9, 1969, by a 74-3 vote.

Family: Married Elvera Stromberg, Nov. 8, 1933; one son, one daughter.

Personal Background

Burger is the fourth of seven children of Swiss and German parents. Financially unable to attend college full time, Burger spent the years following his 1925 graduation from high school attending evening classes at college and law school: two years at the University of Minnesota and four years at St. Paul College of Law. To support himself, Burger sold life insurance during the day.

After graduating with honors from law school in 1931, Burger joined a respected law firm in Minnesota, where he practiced until 1953. He also taught part time at his alma mater, St. Paul College of Law, from 1931 to 1948.

Burger developed a deep interest in art and is an accomplished sculptor; as chief justice, he serves as chairman of the board of the National Gallery of Art. He is also an antiques buff and a connoisseur of wines. He serves as chancellor of the Smithsonian Institution.

Public Career

Soon after beginning his law career in Minnesota, Burger became involved in state Republican politics. In 1938 he assisted Harold E. Stassen in his successful campaign for governor of Minnesota.

It was during Stassen's unsuccessful bid for the Republican presidential nomination 10 years later that Burger met a man who was to figure largely in his career — Herbert Brownell, campaign manager for GOP presidential nominee Thomas E. Dewey, then governor of New York. It was Brownell, later the attorney general in the Eisenhower administration, who brought Burger to Washington in 1953 to serve as assistant attorney general in charge of the claims division (now the civil division).

Burger's stint as assistant attorney general from 1953 to 1956 was not without controversy. His decision to defend the government's action in dismissing John F. Peters, a part-time federal employee, on grounds of disloyalty — after Solicitor General Simon E. Sobeloff had refused to do so on grounds of conscience — won Burger the enmity of many liberals.

But Burger's overall record as assistant attorney general apparently won President Eisenhower's approval. In 1956 Burger was appointed to the U.S. Court of Appeals for the District of Columbia Circuit. As an appeals court judge, Burger developed a reputation as a conservative, especially in criminal justice cases. He did not hesitate to criticize the "liberal" rulings of the Warren court, particularly in the area of criminal law.

President Nixon's appointment of Burger as chief justice on May 21, 1969, caught most observers by surprise. Despite the white-haired nominee's years of service in the Justice Department and on the court of appeals, he was little known outside the legal community. But Nixon apparently was impressed by Burger's consistent argument as an appeals judge that the Constitution should be read narrowly — a belief Nixon had stressed during his 1968 presidential campaign.

Off the bench, Burger became an outspoken advocate of major administrative reform of the judicial system. Due in large part to Burger's efforts, the American Bar Association and other legal groups established the Institute of Court Management to train court executive officers, bring new management techniques to the courts, and relieve judges of paper work.

During Burger's years as chief justice, Congress also approved a number of measures to streamline and modernize the operations of the federal judiciary. Among these measures were the creation of the post of administrative assistant to the chief justice, creation of a similar post — circut court executive — for each appellate court, elimination of certain special short routes through which certain cases moved more quickly than others to the Supreme Court, and expansion of the functions and powers of U.S. magistrates.

William Hubbs Rehnquist
(1971-   )

Justice Department's office of legal counsel as an assistant attorney general.

Rehnquist quickly became one of the Nixon administration's chief spokesmen on Capitol Hill, commenting on issues ranging from wiretapping to the rights of the accused. It was Rehnquist's job to review the legality of all presidential executive orders and other constitutional law questions involving the executive branch. He frequently testified before congressional committees in support of the administration's policies, most of which matched his own conservative philosophy. So tightly reasoned and articulate was his testimony — backing such controversial matters as government surveillance of American citizens and tighter curbs on obscene materials — that his ability impressed many members of Congress, both liberal and conservative.

In 1971 the once-obscure Phoenix lawyer was nominated by Nixon to the Supreme Court. By the mid-1970s it was clear that Rehnquist was the court's most consistently conservative member.

Born: Oct. 1, 1924, Milwaukee, Wis.

Education: Stanford University, B.A., Phi Beta Kappa, "with great distinction" 1948, M.A., 1948; Harvard University, M.A. in political science, 1950; Stanford University Law School, LL.B., 1952.

Religion: Lutheran.

Official Positions: Law clerk to Supreme Court Justice Robert H. Jackson, 1952-53; U.S. assistant attorney general, office of legal counsel, 1969-71.

Supreme Court Appointment: Nominated at age 47 to be an associate justice by President Nixon Oct. 21, 1971, to replace John Marshall Harlan, who resigned; confirmed by the Senate Dec. 10, 1971, by a 68-26 vote.

Family: Married Natalie Cornell, Aug. 29, 1953; one son, two daughters.

John Paul Stevens
(1975-   )

Personal Background

Rehnquist was born in Milwaukee and grew up there. After World War II service in the Air Force, he entered Stanford University, where he received both a B.A. and an M.A. in 1948. He earned another M.A. in political science at Harvard University (conferred in 1950) before returning to Stanford to attend law school. He was graduated first in his class in 1952.

Public Career

After finishing law school, Rehnquist became a law clerk to Supreme Court Justice Robert H. Jackson. In 1952 he wrote a memorandum for Jackson that would later haunt him during his Senate confirmation hearing. The memorandum favored separate but equal schools for blacks and whites. Asked about those views by the Senate Judiciary Committee in 1971, Rehnquist repudiated them, declaring that they were Justice Jackson's, not his own.

After his clerkship, Rehnquist began law practice in the economically burgeoning Southwest. In 1953 he moved to Phoenix, Ariz., and immediately became immersed in state Republican politics. From his earliest days in the state, he was associated with the party's most conservative wing. A 1957 speech denouncing the liberalism of the Warren court typified his views at the time.

During the 1964 presidential election campaign, Rehnquist worked ardently for GOP candidate Sen. Barry Goldwater. It was during that campaign that Rehnquist met Richard G. Kleindienst, who, as President Nixon's deputy attorney general, later appointed Rehnquist to head the

Born: April 20, 1920, Chicago, Ill.

Education: University of Chicago, B.A., Phi Beta Kappa, 1941; Northwestern University School of Law, J.D. magna cum laude, 1947.

Religion: Protestant.

Official Positions: Law clerk to Supreme Court Justice Wiley B. Rutledge, 1947-48; minority (Republican) counsel, Subcommittee on the Study of Monopoly Power, House Judiciary Committee, 1951; member, U.S. Attorney General's National Committee to Study the Antitrust Laws, 1953-55; judge, U.S. Court of Appeals for the Seventh Circuit, 1970-75.

Supreme Court Appointment: Nominated at age 55 to be an associate justice by President Gerald R. Ford Nov. 28, 1975, to replace William O. Douglas, who resigned; confirmed by the Senate Dec. 17, 1975, by a 98-0 vote.

Family: Married Elizabeth Jane Sheeren, 1942; one son, three daughters; divorced 1979; married Maryan Mulholland Simon, 1980.

Personal Background

A member of a prominent Chicago family, Stevens graduated from the University of Chicago in 1941. After wartime service in the Navy during which he earned the Bronze Star, Stevens returned to Chicago and entered Northwestern University Law School, graduating first in his class in 1947. He was co-editor of the school's Law Review. Stevens then served as a law clerk to Supreme

Court Justice Wiley B. Rutledge. He left Washington to join a prominent Chicago law firm that specialized in antitrust law. He became the firm's leading antitrust expert.

Developing a reputation as a pre-eminent antitrust lawyer, Stevens left to form his own law firm. He also taught antitrust law part time at the Northwestern and University of Chicago law schools until his appointment by President Nixon in 1970 to the U.S. Court of Appeals for the Seventh Circuit.

An enthusiastic pilot, Stevens flies his own small plane. He is low-keyed and soft-spoken. He underwent open heart surgery in the early 1970s, but recovered fully.

Public Career

Stevens developed a reputation as a political moderate during his undergraduate days at the University of Chicago, then a predominately liberal campus. A registered Republican, he was never active in partisan politics. Nevertheless, Stevens in 1951 served as Republican counsel to the House Judiciary Committee's Subcommittee on the Study of Monopoly Power. He also served from 1953 to 1955, during the Eisenhower administration, as a member of the attorney general's National Committee to Study the Antitrust Laws.

When President Ford nominated Stevens to the Supreme Court seat vacated by William O. Douglas, court watchers tried without success to pin an ideological label on the new nominee. He soon became known as a centrist, whose well-crafted, scholarly opinions gave him the reputation as a "judge's judge." He was unanimously confirmed. The most original thinker on the present court, Stevens is an iconoclastic loner who often files separate opinions that challenge old assumptions, even when his conclusions coincide with those of his colleagues.

Sandra Day O'Connor
(1981-   )

Born: March 26, 1930, El Paso, Texas.

Education: Stanford University, B.A. magna cum laude, 1950; Stanford University Law School, LL.B., with high honors, 1952.

Religion: Episcopal.

Official Positions: Deputy county attorney, San Mateo, Calif., 1952-53; assistant attorney general, Arizona, 1965-69; Arizona state senator, 1969-75, Senate majority leader, 1972-75; judge, Maricopa County Superior Court, Arizona, 1974-79; judge, Arizona Court of Appeals, 1979-81.

Supreme Court Appointment: Nominated at age 51 to be an associate justice by President Ronald Reagan Aug. 19, 1981, to replace Potter Stewart, who retired; con-

firmed by the Senate Sept. 21, 1981, by a 99-0 vote.

Family: Married John J. O'Connor III, Dec. 20, 1952; three sons.

Personal Background

Sandra Day spent her early years on the Lazy B Ranch, a 162,000-acre spread that her grandfather had established in southeastern Arizona, straddling the New Mexico-Arizona border. It had been in the family since 1881. She spent the school year in El Paso, living with her grandmother. After graduating from high school in 1946 at age 16, she entered Stanford University.

Within six years, by 1952, she had earned degrees from the university (in economics) and from Stanford Law School. At law school she met John J. O'Connor III, her future husband. During her law school years, she was an editor of the Stanford Law Review. She ranked in the top 10 in her class scholastically. So did William H. Rehnquist, who graduated six months before O'Connor.

Despite her outstanding law school record, she found it difficult to locate a job as an attorney in 1952, when relatively few women were practicing law. She applied to the firm in which William French Smith — the attorney general in the Reagan administration — was a partner, only to be offered a job as a legal secretary.

After a short stint as deputy county attorney for San Mateo County, Calif., while her husband completed law school at Stanford, the O'Connors moved to Frankfurt, Germany, where her husband served a tour of duty with the U.S. Army. During their stay, Sandra Day O'Connor worked as a civilian attorney for the Army.

After her husband left the Army in 1957 they moved to Phoenix, where their three sons were born and raised. O'Connor practiced law in partnership with another attorney for a few years, but after the birth of her second son decided to curtail her legal career for a time to stay at home with her children.

Public Career

In 1965 O'Connor resumed her legal career, taking a job as an assistant attorney general for Arizona. After four years in the post, she was appointed to fill a vacancy in the state Senate, where she served on the judiciary committee. In 1970 she was elected to the state Senate, and two years later was elected its majority leader, the first woman in the nation to hold such a post and the only sitting Supreme Court justice in 1982 to have been elected to legislative office.

O'Connor was active in Republican Party politics and was co-chairman of the Arizona Committee to Re-Elect the President in 1972. In the 1960s, she served as president of the Junior League of Phoenix and served on the boards of the Arizona chapters of the Salvation Army, the YMCA and the National Conference of Christians and Jews.

In 1974 she was elected to the Superior Court for Maricopa County, where she served for five years. Then in 1979 Gov. Bruce Babbitt, acting, according to some observers, to remove a potential rival for the governorship, appointed O'Connor to the Arizona Court of Appeals. It was from that seat that President Reagan chose her as his first nominee to the Supreme Court. On nominating her, he described O'Connor as "a person for all seasons" with "unique qualities of temperament, fairness and intellectual capacity."

William Joseph Brennan Jr.
(1956-   )

Born: April 25, 1906, Newark, N.J.

Education: University of Pennsylvania, B.S., 1928; Harvard Law School, LL.B., 1931.

Religion: Roman Catholic.

Official Positions: New Jersey superior court judge, 1949-50; appellate division, 1950-52; associate justice, New Jersey Supreme Court, 1952-56.

Supreme Court Appointment: Received a recess appointment at age 50 as an associate justice by President Dwight D. Eisenhower Oct. 16, 1956, and began service on that date, replacing Sherman Minton, who resigned; nominated as an associate justice by President Eisenhower Jan. 14, 1957; confirmed March 19, 1957, by voice vote.

Family: Married Marjorie Leonard May 5, 1928; died December 1982; two sons, one daughter. Married Mary Fowler March 9, 1983.

Personal Background

Brennan is the second of eight children of Irish parents who immigrated to the United States in 1890. Brennan displayed impressive academic abilities early in life. He was an outstanding student in high school and an honors student at the University of Pennsylvania's Wharton School of Finance and was graduated in the top 10 percent of his Harvard Law School class in 1931.

After law school Brennan returned to Newark, where he joined a prominent law firm. After passage of the Wagner Labor Act in 1935, he began to specialize in labor law.

With the outbreak of World War II, Brennan entered the Army, serving as a manpower trouble-shooter on the staff of the under secretary of war, Robert B. Patterson. At the conclusion of the war, Brennan returned to his old law firm. But as his practice swelled, Brennan, a dedicated family man, began to resent the demands that it placed on his time.

Public Career

A desire to temper the pace of his work was one of the reasons Brennan accepted an appointment to the newly created New Jersey superior court in 1949. Brennan had been a leader of the movement to establish the court as part of a large program of judicial reform in the state. Thus it was not surprising that Republican Gov. Alfred E. Driscoll named Brennan, a registered but inactive Democrat, to the court.

During his tenure on the superior court, Brennan's use of pretrial procedures to speed up the disposition of cases brought him to the attention of New Jersey Supreme Court Justice Arthur T. Vanderbilt. It was reportedly at Vanderbilt's suggestion that Brennan, in 1950, moved to the appellate division of the superior court and then, in 1952, to the state Supreme Court. Late in 1956, when President Eisenhower was looking for a justice to replace Sherman Minton, Vanderbilt and others strongly recommended Brennan for the post, and Eisenhower gave him a recess appointment that October. There was some criticism that Eisenhower was seeking to curry favor with Catholic voters by nominating a Roman Catholic Democrat to the bench so close to the November general election. But Brennan's established integrity and non-political background minimized the impact of the charges, and his nomination was confirmed early in 1957.

Brennan spoke for the Warren court on some of the major issues of the 1960s. He wrote the court's opinion in the landmark reapportionment case of *Baker v. Carr* (1962). On the more conservative court of the 1970s and 1980s, Brennan has been a staunchly liberal, dissenting voice.

Byron Raymond White
(1962-   )

Born: June 8, 1917, Fort Collins, Colo.

Education: University of Colorado, B.A., Phi Beta Kappa, 1938; Rhodes Scholar, Oxford University, 1939; Yale Law School, LL.B., magna cum laude, 1946.

Official Positions: Law clerk to Chief Justice Fred M. Vinson, 1946-47; U.S. deputy attorney general, 1961-62.

Supreme Court Appointment: Nominated at the age of 44 to be an associate justice by President John F. Kennedy March 30, 1962, to replace Charles E. Whittaker, who resigned; confirmed by the Senate April 11, 1962, by a voice vote.

Family: Married Marion Stearns, 1946; one son, one daughter.

Personal Background

White grew up in Wellington, Colo., a small town in the state's sugar beet area. His father was in the lumber business and was the Republican mayor of Wellington.

Ranking first in his high school class, White in 1934 won a scholarship to the University of Colorado, where he earned a reputation as an outstanding scholar-athlete. He was first in his class, a member of Phi Beta Kappa and the winner of three varsity letters in football, four in basketball and three in baseball. By the end of his college career in 1938 he had been dubbed "Whizzer" White for his prowess as a football player, a performance that earned him both a national reputation and a one-year contract with the old Pittsburgh Pirates professional football team.

After a year as a pro football player, White sailed for England to attend Oxford University, where he had received a coveted Rhodes Scholarship. When World War II broke out in September 1939, White returned to the United States and enrolled in Yale Law School, alternating law study with playing professional football for the Detroit Lions.

When the United States entered the war, White served in the Navy in the South Pacific. He returned to Yale after the war, earning his law degree magna cum laude.

Public Career

After graduation from law school, White served as law clerk to Chief Justice Fred M. Vinson. In 1947 he returned to his native Colorado, where for the next 14 years he practiced law with a prominent Denver law firm.

Several times during his adult life, White crossed paths with John F. Kennedy. The two first met when White was studying at Oxford and Kennedy's father, Joseph, was ambassador to the Court of St. James. They met again during White's wartime service in the South Pacific. And when White clerked for Vinson in Washington, in 1946-47, he renewed his acquaintance with Kennedy, then a freshman U.S. representative.

In 1960, when Kennedy ran for president, White joined the campaign and headed the pre-convention Kennedy effort in Colorado. After Kennedy's nomination, White became chairman of the National Citizens for Kennedy organization, designed to attract independents and Republicans.

After his election, Kennedy named White to the post of deputy attorney general. From that post Kennedy named him to the Supreme Court in 1962.

Thurgood Marshall
(1967-   )

Born: July 2, 1908, Baltimore, Md.

Education: Lincoln University, A.B., cum laude, 1930; Howard University Law School, LL.B., 1933.

Religion: Episcopal.

Official Positions: Judge, Court of Appeals for the Second Circuit, 1961-65; Solicitor General, 1965-67.

Supreme Court Appointment: Nominated at age 59 to be an associate justice by President Lyndon B. Johnson June 13, 1967, to replace Tom C. Clark, who resigned; confirmed by the Senate Aug. 30, 1967, by a 69-11 vote.

Family: Married Vivian Burey, Sept. 4, 1929, who died February 1955; two sons; married Cecelia Suryat, Dec. 17, 1955.

Personal Background

Marshall, a black, is the son of a primary school teacher and a club steward. In 1926 he left Baltimore to attend all-black Lincoln University in Chester, Pa., where he developed a reputation as an outstanding debater. After graduating cum laude in 1930, he studied law at Howard University in Washington, D.C.

During his law-school years, Marshall developed an interest in civil rights. After graduating first in his law school class in 1933, Marshall began a long and historic involvement with the National Association for the Advancement of Colored People (NAACP). In 1940 he became the head of the newly formed NAACP Legal Defense and Education Fund, a position he held for more than 20 years.

Over those two decades, Marshall coordinated the fund's attack on segregation in voting, housing, public accommodations and education. The culmination of his career as a civil rights attorney came in 1954 as chief counsel in the *Brown v. Board of Education* case. In that historic case, which Marshall argued before the Supreme Court, the court declared that separate public schools for black and white students were inherently unequal and that state-sanctioned segregation in the schools violated the equal protection guarantee of the 14th Amendment.

Public Career

In 1961 President Kennedy appointed Marshall to the U.S. Court of Appeals for the Second Circuit, but because of heated opposition from Southern Democrats in the Senate, he was not confirmed until a year later.

In 1966 President Lyndon B. Johnson chose Marshall to be the nation's first black solicitor general. During his years as the government's chief advocate before the Supreme Court, Marshall scored impressive victories in the areas of civil and constitutional rights: he was successful in persuading the Supreme Court to uphold the constitutionality of the 1965 Voting Rights Act, voluntarily informed the court that the government had used electronic eavesdropping devices in two cases, and joined in a suit that successfully overturned a California constitutional amendment that prohibited open housing legislation.

On June 13, 1967, President Johnson chose Marshall to be an associate justice of the Supreme Court. During his years on the court, he has compiled a consistently liberal record.

Harry Andrew Blackmun
(1970-   )

Born: Nov. 12, 1908, Nashville, Ill.

Education: Harvard University, B.A., Phi Beta

Kappa, summa cum laude in mathematics, 1929; Harvard Law School, LL.B., 1932.

Religion: Methodist.

Official Positions: Law clerk, U.S. Court of Appeals, Eighth Circuit, 1932-33; judge, U.S. Court of Appeals for the Eighth Circuit, 1959-70.

Supreme Court Appointment: Nominated at age 61 to be an associate justice by President Richard M. Nixon April 14, 1970, to replace Abe Fortas, who resigned; confirmed by the Senate May 12, 1970, by a 94-0 vote.

Family: Married Dorothy E. Clark, June 21, 1941; three daughters.

Personal Background

Blackmun spent most of his early years in the Minneapolis-St. Paul area, where his father was an official of the Twin Cities Savings and Loan Company. It was in grade school that Blackmun began a lifelong friendship with Warren E. Burger.

After showing an early aptitude for mathematics, Blackmun attended Harvard University on a scholarship. At Harvard Blackmun majored in mathematics and thought briefly of becoming a physician.

But Blackmun chose the law instead. After graduating Phi Beta Kappa from Harvard in 1929, Blackmun entered Harvard Law School, from which he was graduated in 1932. During his law school years, Blackmun supported himself with a variety of odd jobs, including tutoring in math and driving the launch for the college crew team.

After law school, Blackmun returned to St. Paul, where he served for a year and a half as a law clerk to United States Circuit Court Judge John B. Sanborn, whom Blackmun succeeded on the court 26 years later. He left the clerkship in 1933 to teach at Mitchell College of Law in St. Paul, Chief Justice Burger's alma mater.

After a year of teaching, Blackmun opted for private practice. In 1934 he joined a Minneapolis law firm, where he remained for 16 years. In 1950 he accepted a post as resident legal counsel for the world famous Mayo Clinic in Rochester, Minn. There, Blackmun quickly developed a reputation among his colleagues as a serious man totally engrossed in his profession. He served in that post for nine years.

Public Career

That reputation followed him to the bench of the U.S. Court of Appeals for the Eighth Circuit. President Eisenhower appointed him to that post in 1959. As an appeals court judge, Blackmun became known for his scholarly and thorough opinions.

Blackmun's nomination to the Supreme Court was President Nixon's third try at filling the seat vacated by Justice Abe Fortas' resignation in May 1969. The Senate had refused to confirm Nixon's first two nominees — Clement F. Haynsworth Jr. of South Carolina and G. Harrold Carswell of Florida. Nixon then turned to Blackmun, who was confirmed without opposition. Although during Blackmun's first years on the court, he and Burger were often described as the "Minnesota Twins," he has since demonstrated that his views are considerably more liberal than those of the chief justice. Blackmun was the court's spokesman in 1973 when, in the case of *Roe v. Wade*, it declared that states could not ban abortion as a crime.

Lewis Franklin Powell Jr.
(1971-   )

Born: Sept. 19, 1907, Suffolk, Va.

Education: Washington and Lee University, B.S., Phi Beta Kappa, 1929; Washington and Lee University Law School, LL.B., 1931; Harvard Law School, LL.M., 1932.

Religion: Presbyterian.

Official Positions: President of the Richmond, Va., School Board, 1952-61; member, 1961-69, and president, 1968-69, Virginia State Board of Education; president of the American Bar Association, 1964-65; president, American College of Trial Lawyers, 1968-69.

Supreme Court Appointment: Nominated at age 64 to be an associate justice by President Nixon Oct. 21, 1971, to replace Hugo L. Black, who resigned; confirmed by the Senate Dec. 6, 1971, by an 89-1 vote.

Family: Married Josephine M. Rucker, May 2, 1936; three daughters, one son.

Personal Background

Powell has spent much of his life in Virginia. After attending college and law school in the state he went to Harvard. Upon completion of his law studies there, he returned to Virginia, where he joined one of the state's oldest and most prestigious Richmond law firms. Powell eventually became a senior partner, continuing his association with the firm until his nomination to the Supreme Court.

Over the years, Powell's practice made him a familiar figure in blue-chip boardrooms. Among the companies represented during Powell's years with the law firm were the Baltimore and Ohio Railroad Co., the Prudential Insurance Company of America and the Virginia Electric and Power Co.

Public Career

By the time Nixon picked him for the Supreme Court, Powell generally was recognized as a first-rate attorney and a political moderate. His views had been shaped by his long practice of law in Richmond, years of active participation in the American Bar Association, and deep involvement in the sensitive question of desegregating the public schools of Virginia. In the face of intense pressure for "massive" resistance to desegregation, Powell consistently advocated keeping the schools open.

A one-year stint in 1964-65 as president of the American Bar Association (ABA) provided Powell with a national platform from which to express his views on a variety of subjects and to enhance his reputation as a moderate. On the liberal side, Powell spoke out against inadequate legal services for the poor and worked to create the legal services program of the Office of Economic Opportunity. A more conservative tone characterized his views of social ills caused by parental permissiveness and his stern denunciations of civil disobedience and other forms of civil demonstrations. And as a member in 1966 of President Lyndon B. Johnson's Crime Commission, Powell helped write a minority statement criticizing Supreme Court rulings upholding the right of criminal suspects to remain silent.

Powell was the only Democrat among President Nixon's four Supreme Court appointees. On the court, he continued to reflect a generally moderate outlook on most issues.

Potter Stewart
(1958-1981)

Born: Jan. 23, 1915, Jackson, Mich.
Education: Yale University, B.A., cum laude, 1937; Yale Law School, LL.B., cum laude, 1941; fellow, Cambridge University, Cambridge, England, 1937-38.
Religion: Episcopal.
Official Positions: Member, Cincinnati, Ohio, City Council 1950-53; vice mayor of Cincinnati, 1952-53; judge, U.S. Court of Appeals for the Sixth Circuit, 1954-58.
Supreme Court Career: Received recess appointment at age 43 as an associate justice from President Dwight D. Eisenhower Oct. 14, 1958, replacing Harold H. Burton, who resigned; nominated to be an associate justice by President Eisenhower Jan. 17, 1959; confirmed by the Senate May 5, 1959, by a 70-17 vote; retired on July 3, 1981. Replaced on the court by Sandra Day O'Connor.
Family: Married Mary Ann Bertles, April 24, 1943; two sons, one daughter.

Personal Background

Stewart was the son of an established middle-class Cincinnati family with a strong tradition of public service and a respect for the benefits of a good education. Stewart's father, James Garfield Stewart, was mayor of Cincinnati from 1938 to 1947 and was the Republican nominee for governor of Ohio in 1944. He lost. His father served on the Ohio Supreme Court from 1947 until his death in 1959.

After early schooling in Cincinnati, Potter Stewart attended two of the most prestigious Eastern schools — Hotchkiss preparatory and Yale University, where he received numerous academic honors and was graduated Phi Beta Kappa in 1937. After completing his undergraduate work at Yale, he spent a year abroad doing postgraduate

work at Cambridge University in England. Returning to the United States in 1938, he began law school at Yale. After graduating in 1941, Stewart moved to New York, where he joined a Wall Street law firm. Soon after he began work there, however, the United States entered World War II, and Stewart joined the Navy and was a deck officer aboard oil tankers plying the Atlantic and Mediterranean.

After the war, Stewart returned to his New York law practice but soon moved to his hometown of Cincinnati, where he joined one of its leading law firms.

Public Career

Once Stewart settled in Cincinnati, he took up the family tradition of public service. He was twice elected to the City Council and served one term as vice mayor. He also was actively involved in the 1948 and 1952 Republican presidential campaigns, supporting Sen. Robert A. Taft, R-Ohio (1939-53). When Eisenhower won the party's endorsement in 1952, Stewart actively supported him in the fall campaign.

Stewart's appointment in 1954 to the U.S. Court of Appeals for the Sixth Circuit ended his participation in politics. He was Eisenhower's fifth and last appointment to the Supreme Court. He received a recess appointment in 1958, and Eisenhower sent his nomination to the new Congress in 1959.

Because of his tendency to vote sometimes with the court's liberals and sometimes with the conservatives, Stewart often was referred to as a "swing vote." He earned a reputation as a legal craftsman, writing well-reasoned, concisely worded opinions.

Stewart retired July 3, 1981, saying he wished to leave the court while he was still relatively young and healthy enough to enjoy additional time with his family.

Abe Fortas
(1965-1969)

Born: June 19, 1910, Memphis, Tenn.
Education: Southwestern College, A.B., 1930; Yale Law School, LL.B., 1933.
Religion: Jewish.
Official Positions: Assistant director, corporate reorganization study, Securities and Exchange Commission (SEC), 1934-37; assistant director, public utilities division, SEC, 1938-39; general counsel, Public Works Administration, 1939-40, and counsel to the bituminous coal division, 1939-41; director, division of power, Department of the Interior, 1941-42; under secretary of the interior, 1942-46.
Supreme Court Career: Nominated at age 55 to be an associate justice by President Johnson July 28, 1965, to

replace Arthur J. Goldberg, who resigned; confirmed by the Senate Aug. 11, 1965, by a voice vote; resigned May 14, 1969; replaced on the court by Harry A. Blackmun.

Family: Married Carolyn Eugenia Agger, July 9, 1935. No children.

Died: April 5, 1982, in Washington, D.C.

Personal Background

Fortas was the son of an English immigrant cabinetmaker. After working his way through Southwestern College in Memphis, from which he received a B.A. in 1930, Fortas went to Yale Law School. He served as editor of the school's law journal and was graduated in 1933.

Fortas developed an interest in music and began to play the violin in various string quartets, a practice he continued throughout his life. In 1935 he married Carolyn Eugenia Agger, who became a renowned tax lawyer.

Upon graduation, Fortas was made an associate professor of law at Yale. But the excitement and activity generated by President Franklin D. Roosevelt's New Deal in Washington soon enticed the young lawyer away from academic pursuits and into public affairs.

Public Career

Throughout the 1930s Fortas held various jobs in the Roosevelt administration, mostly involving detailed legal work in such newly created agencies as the Securities and Exchange Commission and the Public Works Administration. In 1942 Roosevelt appointed him under secretary of the Interior Department. In that post he served under the controversial and irascible Secretary Harold L. Ickles.

After the Second World War, Fortas and other former New Dealers helped found the law firm of Arnold, Fortas and Porter, which quickly became one of Washington's most prestigious legal institutions. The firm specialized in corporation law, but its members, including Fortas, found time to litigate some important civil and individual rights cases.

Named by the Supreme Court to represent an indigent named Clarence Earl Gideon, Fortas argued Gideon's case, *Gideon v. Wainwright,* brilliantly and won for him — and other poor people charged with serious crimes under state law — the right to the aid of an attorney in preparing his defense. This ruling was issued by the court in 1963.

In 1948 Fortas had successfully defended a representative from Texas, Lyndon B. Johnson, when Johnson's election victory in the Texas Democratic senatorial primary was challenged. That defense was the basis for an enduring friendship between the two men, and Fortas became one of Johnson's most trusted advisers.

Preferring his role as confidential adviser, Fortas in 1964 declined Johnson's offer to name him attorney general. But when Arthur J. Goldberg resigned from the court in 1965 to become U.S. representative to the United Nations, Johnson ignored Fortas' opposition and appointed him to the Supreme Court. He was 55.

When Chief Justice Earl Warren voiced his intention to resign in 1968, Johnson decided to elevate Fortas to the chief justiceship. But amid charges of "cronyism," events began to unfold that ultimately led to Fortas' undoing.

In the face of strong opposition from Republicans and conservative Democrats, Johnson was forced to withdraw the nomination, but not before it was revealed that Fortas had received $15,000 to teach a course at a local university.

Then, in May of 1969, *Life* magazine revealed that

after he was appointed to the court Fortas had accepted, and then returned several months later, $20,000 from a charitable foundation controlled by the family of an indicted stock manipulator.

The allegations touched off talk of impeachment proceedings against Fortas. In mid-May, despite his denial of any "wrongdoing on my part," Fortas resigned from the court. He then returned to private law practice in Washington in partnership with another attorney.

In March 1982 he argued a case before the Supreme Court for the first time since his resignation. Two weeks later, he died suddenly after suffering a massive heart attack. He was 71.

John Marshall Harlan
(1955-1971)

Born: May 20, 1899, Chicago, Ill.

Education: Princeton Universtiy, B.A., 1920; Rhodes Scholar, Balliol College, Oxford University, Oxford, England, B.A. in jurisprudence, 1923; New York Law School, LL.B., 1924.

Religion: Presbyterian.

Official Positions: Assistant U.S. attorney, Southern District of New York, 1925-27; special assistant attorney general of New York state, 1928-30; chief counsel, New York State Crime Commission, 1951-53; judge, U.S. Court of Appeals for the Second Circuit, 1954-55.

Supreme Court Career: Nominated at age 55 to be an associate justice by President Dwight D. Eisenhower Nov. 8, 1954, to replace Robert H. Jackson, who died; Senate consideration postponed; formally nominated Jan. 10, 1955; confirmed by the Senate March 16, 1955, by a 71-11 vote; retired Sept. 23, 1971, after serving 16 years on the court; replaced on the court by William H. Rehnquist.

Family: Married Ethel Andrews Nov. 10, 1928; one daughter.

Died: Dec. 29, 1971, Washington, D.C.

Personal Background

The namesake and grandson of Supreme Court Justice John Marshall Harlan (1877-1911), Harlan was born in Chicago, where his father, John Maynard Harlan, was a prominent attorney. His father also was involved in politics, losing two races for mayor of Chicago near the turn of the century.

Harlan attended Princeton University, graduating in 1920. Awarded a Rhodes scholarship, he spent the next three years studying jurisprudence at Balliol College, Oxford. Returning to the United States, he earned his law degree in 1924 from New York Law School.

Public Career

For the next 25 years Harlan was a member of a prominent Wall Street law firm, taking periodic leaves to serve in various public positions. In 1925 he became an assistant U.S. attorney for the Southern District of New York. He returned to private practice but soon left again, this time to serve as one of the special prosecutors in a state investigation of municipal graft.

During World War II, Harlan served as head of the Operational Analysis Section of the Eighth Air Force. After the war he returned to private practice, but was soon called again to public service. From 1951 to 1953 he was chief counsel to the New York State Crime Commission, which Gov. Thomas E. Dewey had created to investigate the relationship between organized crime and state government.

During the same period, Harlan became active in various professional organizations, serving as chairman of the committee on professional ethics of the Association of the Bar of the City of New York and later as chairman of its committee on the judiciary and as vice president of the association.

A lifelong Republican, Harlan was nominated at age 54 by President Eisenhower to the U.S. Court of Appeals for the Second Circuit in January 1954. Harlan had hardly begun his work there when the president named him in November 1954 to the U.S. Supreme Court. The Senate, then in special session to consider the censure of Sen. Joseph R. McCarthy, R-Wis. (1947-57), postponed consideration of the nomination until the next Congress convened in 1955. Harlan remained on the appeals court until he was confirmed by the Senate in March 1955.

During his 16 years on the court, Harlan functioned as a dignified gadfly, often reminding his activist colleagues that the court, in his view, had only a limited role to play in reshaping American society.

He resigned in failing health in September 1971, and died three months later.

**William Orville
Douglas**
(1939-1975)

Born: Oct. 16, 1898, Maine, Minn.

Education: Whitman College, BA., 1920, Phi Beta Kappa; Columbia Law School, LL.B., 1925.

Religion: Presbyterian.

Official Positions: Member, Securities and Exchange Commission, 1936-39, chairman, 1937-39.

Supreme Court Career: Nominated at age 40 to be an associate justice by President Franklin D. Roosevelt,

March 20, 1939, to replace Louis D. Brandeis, who retired; confirmed by the Senate April 4, 1939, by a 62-4 vote; retired Nov. 12, 1975, at age 77 after 36 years of service; replaced on the court by John Paul Stevens.

Family: Married Mildred Riddle Aug. 16, 1923, divorced 1954; one son, one daughter; married Mercedes Hester Dec. 14, 1954, divorced 1963; married Joan Martin, August 1963, divorced 1966; married Cathleen Heffernan, July 1966.

Died: Jan. 19, 1980, Washington, D.C.

Personal Background

Born into an impoverished farm family in Minnesota shortly before the turn of the 20th century, Douglas spent his early years in Yakima, Washington. A polio attack as a child sparked Douglas' lifelong passion for the outdoors. He hiked the mountains near his home to strengthen his weakened legs.

After graduating from Whitman College in Walla Walla, Wash., in 1920, Douglas decided to pursue a law career. Despite his lack of funds, he was determined to study law at Columbia University Law School. Once there, Douglas quickly became one of the school's top students.

After law school, a two-year stint with a prestigious Wall Street law firm convinced Douglas that representing corporate clients would not be to his liking. He returned to Yakima, but after a year moved back East to join the law faculty at Columbia University. In 1929 he moved to New Haven, Conn., to teach law at Yale.

Public Career

By the time the Depression struck in 1929, Douglas already had developed a reputation as one of the country's foremost financial law experts. Thus when President Roosevelt needed staff for the newly formed Securities and Exchange Commission (SEC), created in 1934, he called on Douglas, who joined the commission in 1936. He became SEC chairman in 1937.

Douglas, at 40, became the youngest man in the 20th century to be named to the court.

His 1939 Supreme Court nomination sailed through the Senate without difficulty. Such easy relations with Congress, however, were not to mark Douglas' forthcoming years in Washington. Twice he faced the threat of impeachment, in 1953 and in 1970. On neither occasion, however, did the move gain solid congressional support.

Four times married, three times divorced, ardent conservationist and absolute defender of the First Amendment, Douglas is likely to be remembered as the 20th century's most colorful Supreme Court justice. His controversial lifestyle and liberal political views, plus conservative resentment at the Senate's rejection of two of President Nixon's Supreme Court nominees, created much hostility toward Douglas in Congress and led to the 1970 impeachment attempt, led by House Republican leader Gerald R. Ford Jr., R-Mich. (1949-73).

Douglas' relations with the Parvin Foundation, recipient of considerable income from gambling interests, were scrutinized. Anti-establishment sentiments expressed in one of his many books further fueled the animosity. But a special House Judiciary Subcommittee created to investigate the charges found no grounds for impeachment.

Douglas suffered a paralytic stroke in January 1975. He attempted to stay on the court, but in November 1975 he resigned, citing the continuing pain and physical disability. He had served 36 years and seven months, longer than any other justice. He died five years later, in January 1980, at the age of 81.

Hugo Lafayette Black
(1937-71)

Born: Feb. 27, 1886, Harlan, Ala.
Education: Birmingham Medical College, 1903-04; University of Alabama, LL.B., 1906.
Religion: Baptist.
Official Positions: Police court judge, Birmingham, 1910-11; solicitor, Jefferson County, Ala., 1915-17; U.S. senator, D-Ala., 1927-37.
Supreme Court Career: Nominated to be an associate justice at age 51 by President Franklin D. Roosevelt Aug. 12, 1937, to replace Willis Van Devanter, who retired; confirmed by the Senate Aug. 17, 1937, by a 63-16 vote; retired Sept. 17, 1971, at age 85 after serving 34 years; replaced by Lewis F. Powell Jr.
Family: Married Josephine Foster in February 1921, died in 1951; two sons, one daughter; married Elizabeth Seay DeMeritte Sept. 11, 1957.
Died: Sept. 25, 1971, Washington, D.C.

Personal Background

The eighth child of a Baptist storekeeper and farmer, Hugo Black spent the first years of his life in the hill country near Harlan, Ala. When he was still a youngster, his family moved to Ashland, a larger community, where his father's business prospered. Black attended the local schools in Ashland and after attending Birmingham Medical College for a year decided to study law. At 18 he entered the University of Alabama Law School at Tuscaloosa.

Upon receipt of his LL.B., Black returned to Ashland and set up his first law practice. The following year, after a fire destroyed his office and library, Black moved to Birmingham. There, he quickly established a relationship with labor by defending the United Mine Workers strikers in 1908. Black also developed an expertise in arguing personal injury cases.

Public Career

He was a part-time police court judge in Birmingham in 1911 and was elected county solicitor (public prosecutor) for Jefferson County in 1914. As solicitor, he gained a measure of local fame for investigating reports of brutality by the police in questioning suspects at the notorious Bessemer jail.

When he left the solicitor's post to enter the Army in

World War I, Black had successfully emptied a docket that had once held as many as 3,000 pending cases.

His brief military career kept him in the United States. He returned to law practice in Birmingham in 1918 and married a local woman the following year. He continued to specialize in labor law and personal injury cases. In 1923 he joined the Ku Klux Klan, but resigned from the organization two years later just before announcing his intention to run for the Democratic nomination for the Senate seat held by Oscar W. Underwood, D-Ala. (1915-27). Campaigning as the poor man's candidate, Black won the party's endorsement and the subsequent election. He entered the Senate in 1927 and immediately began to study history and the classics at the Library of Congress to compensate for his lack of formal education.

During his two terms in the Senate, Black used committee hearings to investigate several issues, including abuses of marine and airline subsidies and the activities of various lobbying groups. In 1933 he introduced a bill to create a 30-hour workweek. This legislation, after several alterations, eventually was passed in 1938 as the Fair Labor Standards Act.

One of the Senate's strongest supporters of President Roosevelt, Black spoke out in favor of Roosevelt's 1937 court-packing scheme and other New Deal programs. His support for the administration and his strong liberal instincts led the president to pick Black as his choice to fill the Supreme Court seat vacated by the retirement of Willis Van Devanter.

Black's previous affiliation with the Ku Klux Klan was widely reported in the national news media after his Senate confirmation. The furor quickly quieted, however, when the new justice admitted in a dramatic radio broadcast that he had indeed once been a member of the Klan but had resigned from the organization many years earlier. During his court career Black always carried in his pocket a copy of the U.S. Constitution.

He is ranked by virtually all legal scholars as one of the court's most influential justices and one of its staunchest liberals.

Black retired from the court Sept. 17, 1971, after suffering an impairing stroke. He died eight days later.

Earl Warren
(1953-1969)

Born: March 19, 1891, Los Angeles, Calif.
Education: University of California, B.L., 1912, J.D., 1914.
Religion: Protestant.
Official Positions: Deputy city attorney of Oakland, Calif., 1919-20; deputy assistant district attorney, Alameda

County, Calif., 1920-23; chief deputy district attorney, Alameda County, 1923-25; district attorney, Alameda County, 1925-39; attorney general of California, 1939-43; governor of California, 1943-53.

Supreme Court Career: Nominated at age 62 to be chief justice by President Dwight D. Eisenhower Sept. 30, 1953, to replace Chief Justice Fred M. Vinson, who died; confirmed March 1, 1954, by a voice vote; retired June 23, 1969, after 16 years on the court; replaced as chief justice by Warren E. Burger.

Family: Married Nina P. Meyers Oct. 14, 1925; three sons, three daughters.

Died: July 9, 1974, Washington, D.C.

Personal Background

Warren was born in Los Angeles, Calif., the son of Scandinavian immigrant parents. Soon afterwards, the family moved to Bakersfield, where his father worked as a railroad car repairman. In 1938, after Warren had become active in politics, his father was bludgeoned to death in a crime that was never solved.

Warren worked his way through college and law school at the University of California. After graduation, he worked in law offices in San Francisco and Oakland, the only time in his career that he engaged in private practice.

Public Career

From 1920 until his retirement from the court in 1969, Warren held public office without interruption. His first post was deputy city attorney for Oakland. Warren then was named a deputy district attorney for Alameda County, which embraces the cities of Oakland, Alameda, and Berkeley.

In 1925 Warren was appointed district attorney when the incumbent resigned. He won election to the post in his own right in 1926, 1930, and 1934. During his 14 years as district attorney, Warren developed a reputation as a crime fighter, sending a city manager and several councilmen to jail on graft charges and smashing an illegal deal involving garbage collection.

A Republican, Warren decided in 1938 to run for state attorney general. He cross-filed and won three primaries —

his own party's, as well as the Democratic and Progressive Party contests.

In 1942 Warren ran for governor of California. Although he was at first rated the underdog, he ended up defeating the incumbent Democratic governor, Culbert Olson, by a margin of 342,000 votes, winning 57.1 percent of the vote. He was twice re-elected, winning the Democratic as well as the Republican nomination in 1946 and defeating Democrat James Roosevelt, son of the late President Franklin D. Roosevelt, by an almost two-to-one margin in 1950.

At first viewed as a conservative governor — he denounced "communistic radicals" and supported the wartime federal order to move all persons of Japanese ancestry away from the West Coast — Warren developed a progressive image after the war. In 1945 he proposed a state program of prepaid medical insurance and later championed liberal pension and welfare benefits.

Warren made two bids for national political office. In 1948 he ran for vice president on the Republican ticket with Gov. Thomas E. Dewey of New York. In 1952 he sought the Republican presidential nomination. But with little chance of winning, he threw his support at a crucial moment behind Dwight D. Eisenhower, helping him win the battle for the nomination against Sen. Robert A. Taft, R-Ohio (1939-53).

As a result of that support, Eisenhower was politically indebted to Warren. After the death of Chief Justice Vinson in 1953, Eisenhower nominated the Californian to replace Vinson. Reflecting on his choice years later in light of the Warren court's liberal record, Eisenhower called the appointment "the biggest damn-fool mistake I ever made."

During his 16-year tenure as chief justice, Warren, who had no previous experience as a judge, contributed profoundly to the reshaping of American political and social institutions. The court he led expanded greatly the role of the federal courts as the protector of individual and civil rights.

In addition to his work on the court, Warren headed the commission that investigated the assassination of President John F. Kennedy. Warren retired in 1969 after 16 years on the court and died five years later at the age of 83.

Supreme Court Nominations, 1789-1983**

Name	State	Date of Birth	Nomi- nated by	To Replace	Date of Appointment	Confirmation or Other Action*	Date Resigned	Date of Death	Years Service
John Jay	N.Y.	12/12/1745	Washington		9/24/1789	9/26/1789	6/29/1795	5/17/1829	6
John Rutledge	S.C.	1739	Washington		9/24/1789	9/26/1789	3/5/1791	6/21/1800	1
William Cushing	Mass.	3/1/1732	Washington		9/24/1789	9/26/1789		9/13/1810	21
Robert H. Harrison	Md.	1745	Washington		9/24/1789	9/26/1789 (D)		4/20/1790	
James Wilson	Pa.	9/14/1742	Washington		9/24/1789	9/26/1789		8/21/1798	9
John Blair	Va.	1732	Washington		9/24/1789	9/26/1789	1/27/1796	8/31/1800	6
James Iredell	N.C.	10/5/1751	Washington	Harrison	2/8/1790	2/10/1790		10/20/1799	9
Thomas Johnson	Md.	11/4/1732	Washington	Rutledge	11/1/1791	11/7/1791	3/4/1793	10/26/1819	1
William Paterson	N.J.	12/24/1745	Washington	Johnson	2/27/1793	2/28/1793 (W)			
William Paterson†			Washington	Johnson	3/4/1793	3/4/1793		9/9/1806	13
John Rutledge#			Washington	Jay	7/1/1795	12/15/1795 (R, 10-14)			
William Cushing#			Washington	Jay	1/26/1796	1/27/1796 (D)			
Samuel Chase	Md.	4/17/1741	Washington	Blair	1/26/1796	1/27/1796		6/19/1811	15
Oliver Ellsworth	Conn.	4/29/1745	Washington	Jay	3/3/1796	3/4/1796 (21-1)	9/30/1800	11/26/1807	4
Bushrod Washington	Va.	6/5/1762	Adams	Wilson	12/19/1798	12/20/1798		11/26/1829	31
Alfred Moore	N.C.	5/21/1755	Adams	Iredell	12/6/1799	12/10/1799	1/26/1804	10/15/1810	4
John Jay#			Adams	Ellsworth	12/18/1800	12/19/1800 (D)			
John Marshall	Va.	9/24/1755	Adams	Ellsworth	1/20/1801	1/27/1801		7/6/1835	34
William Johnson	S.C.	12/27/1771	Jefferson	Moore	3/22/1804	3/24/1804		8/4/1834	30
Brockholst Livingston	N.Y.	11/25/1757	Jefferson	Paterson	12/13/1806	12/17/1806		3/18/1823	16
Thomas Todd	Ky.	1/23/1765	Jefferson	New Seat	2/28/1807	3/3/1807		2/7/1826	19
Levi Lincoln	Mass.	5/15/1749	Madison	Cushing	1/2/1811	1/3/1811 (D)		4/14/1820	
Alexander Wolcott	Conn.	9/15/1758	Madison	Cushing	2/4/1811	2/13/1811 (R, 9-24)		6/26/1828	
John Quincy Adams	Mass.	7/11/1767	Madison	Cushing	2/21/1811	2/22/1811 (D)		2/23/1848	
Joseph Story	Mass.	9/18/1779	Madison	Cushing	11/15/1811	11/18/1811		9/10/1845	34
Gabriel Duvall	Md.	12/6/1752	Madison	Chase	11/15/1811	11/18/1811	1/10/1835	3/6/1844	23
Smith Thompson	N.Y.	1/17/1768	Monroe	Livingston	12/8/1823	12/19/1823		12/18/1843	20
Robert Trimble	Ky.	11/17/1776	J. Q. Adams	Todd	4/11/1826	5/9/1826 (27-5)		8/25/1828	2
John J. Crittenden	Ky.	9/10/1787	J. Q. Adams	Trimble	12/17/1828	2/12/1829 (P)		7/26/1863	
John McLean	Ohio	3/11/1785	Jackson	Trimble	3/6/1829	3/7/1829		4/4/1861	32
Henry Baldwin	Pa.	1/14/1780	Jackson	Washington	1/4/1830	1/6/1830 (41-2)		4/21/1844	14
James M. Wayne	Ga.	1790	Jackson	Johnson	1/7/1835	1/9/1835		7/5/1867	32
Roger B. Taney	Md.	3/17/1777	Jackson	Duvall	1/15/1835	3/3/1835 (P)			
Roger B. Taney†			Jackson	Marshall	12/28/1835	3/15/1836 (29-15)		10/12/1864	28
Philip P. Barbour	Va.	5/25/1783	Jackson	Duvall	12/28/1835	3/15/1836 (30-11)		2/25/1841	5
William Smith	Ala.	1762	Jackson	New Seat	3/3/1837	3/8/1837 (23-18) (D)		6/10/1840	
John Catron	Tenn.	1786	Jackson	New Seat	3/3/1837	3/8/1837 (28-15)		5/30/1865	28
John McKinley	Ala.	5/1/1780	Van Buren	New Seat	9/18/1837	9/25/1837		7/19/1852	15
Peter V. Daniel	Va.	4/24/1784	Van Buren	Barbour	2/26/1841	3/2/1841 (22-5)		5/31/1860	19
John C. Spencer	N.Y.	1/8/1788	Tyler	Thompson	1/9/1844	1/31/1844 (R, 21-26)		5/18/1855	
Reuben Walworth	N.Y.	10/26/1788	Tyler	Thompson	3/13/1844	6/17/1844 (W)		11/27/1867	
Edward King	Pa.	1/31/1794	Tyler	Baldwin	6/5/1844	6/15/1844 (P)			
Edward King†			Tyler	Baldwin	12/4/1844	2/7/1845 (W)		5/8/1873	
Samuel Nelson	N.Y.	11/10/1792	Tyler	Thompson	2/4/1845	2/14/1845	11/28/1872	12/13/1873	27
John M. Read	Pa.	2/21/1797	Tyler	Baldwin	2/7/1845	No action		11/29/1874	
George Woodward	Pa.	3/26/1809	Polk	Baldwin	12/23/1845	1/22/1846 (R, 20-29)		5/10/1875	
Levi Woodbury	N.H.	12/22/1789	Polk	Story	12/23/1845	1/3/1846		9/4/1851	5
Robert C. Grier	Pa.	3/5/1794	Polk	Baldwin	8/3/1846	8/4/1846	1/31/1870	9/26/1870	23
Benjamin R. Curtis	Mass.	11/4/1809	Fillmore	Woodbury	12/11/1851	12/29/1851	9/30/1857	9/15/1874	5
Edward A. Bradford	La.	9/27/1813	Fillmore	McKinley	8/16/1852	No action		11/22/1872	
George E. Badger	N.C.	4/13/1795	Fillmore	McKinley	1/10/1853	2/11/1853 (P)		5/11/1866	
William C. Micou	La.	1806	Fillmore	McKinley	2/24/1853	No action		4/16/1854	

Name	State	Date of Birth	Nomi-nated by	To Replace	Date of Appointment	Confirmation or Other Action*	Date Resigned	Date of Death	Years Service
John A. Campbell	Ala.	6/24/1811	Pierce	McKinley	3/22/1853	3/25/1853	4/26/1861	3/13/1889	8
Nathan Clifford	Maine	8/18/1803	Buchanan	Curtis	12/9/1857	1/12/1858 (26-23)		7/25/1881	23
Jeremiah S. Black	Pa.	1/10/1810	Buchanan	Daniel	2/5/1861	2/21/1861 (R, 25-26)		8/19/1883	
Noah H. Swayne	Ohio	12/7/1804	Lincoln	McLean	1/21/1862	1/24/1862 (38-1)	1/24/1881	6/8/1884	19
Samuel F. Miller	Iowa	4/5/1816	Lincoln	Daniel	7/16/1862	7/16/1862		10/13/1890	28
David Davis	Ill.	3/9/1815	Lincoln	Campbell	12/1/1862	12/8/1862	3/7/1877	6/26/1886	14
Stephen J. Field	Calif.	11/4/1816	Lincoln	New Seat	3/6/1863	3/10/1863	12/1/1897	4/9/1899	34
Salmon P. Chase	Ohio	1/13/1808	Lincoln	Taney	12/6/1864	12/6/1864		5/7/1873	8
Henry Stanbery	Ohio	2/20/1803	Johnson	Catron	4/16/1866	No action		6/26/1881	
Ebenezer R. Hoar	Mass.	2/21/1816	Grant	New Seat	12/15/1869	2/3/1870 (R, 24-33)		1/31/1895	
Edwin M. Stanton	Pa.	12/19/1814	Grant	Grier	12/20/1869	12/20/1869 (46-11)		12/24/1869	
William Strong	Pa.	5/6/1808	Grant	Grier	2/7/1870	2/18/1870	12/14/1880	8/19/1895	10
Joseph P. Bradley	N.J.	3/14/1813	Grant	New Seat	2/7/1870	3/21/1870 (46-9)		1/22/1892	21
Ward Hunt	N.Y.	6/14/1810	Grant	Nelson	12/3/1872	12/11/1872	1/7/1882	3/24/1886	9
George H. Williams	Ore.	3/23/1823	Grant	Chase	12/1/1873	1/8/1874 (W)		4/4/1910	
Caleb Cushing	Mass.	1/17/1800	Grant	Chase	1/9/1874	1/13/1874 (W)		1/2/1879	
Morrison R. Waite	Ohio	11/29/1816	Grant	Chase	1/19/1874	1/21/1874 (63-0)		3/23/1888	14
John M. Harlan	Ky.	6/1/1833	Hayes	Davis	10/17/1877	11/29/1877		10/14/1911	34
William B. Woods	Ga.	8/3/1824	Hayes	Strong	12/15/1880	12/21/1880 (39-8)		5/14/1887	6
Stanley Matthews	Ohio	7/21/1824	Hayes	Swayne	1/26/1881	No action			
Stanley Matthews†			Garfield	Swayne	3/14/1881	5/12/1881 (24-23)		3/22/1889	7
Horace Gray	Mass.	3/24/1828	Arthur	Clifford	12/19/1881	12/20/1881 (51-5)	7/9/1902	9/15/1902	20
Roscoe Conkling	N.Y.	10/30/1829	Arthur	Hunt	2/24/1882	3/2/1882 (39-12) (D)		4/18/1888	
Samuel Blatchford	N.Y.	3/9/1820	Arthur	Hunt	3/13/1882	3/27/1882		7/7/1893	11
Lucius Q. C. Lamar	Miss.	9/17/1825	Cleveland	Woods	12/6/1887	1/16/1888 (32-28)		1/23/1893	5
Melville W. Fuller	Ill.	2/11/1833	Cleveland	Waite	4/30/1888	7/20/1888 (41-20)		7/4/1910	22
David J. Brewer	Kan.	1/20/1837	Harrison	Matthews	12/4/1889	12/18/1889 (53-11)		3/28/1910	20
Henry B. Brown	Mich.	3/2/1836	Harrison	Miller	12/23/1890	12/29/1890	5/28/1906	9/4/1913	15
George Shiras Jr.	Pa.	1/26/1832	Harrison	Bradley	7/19/1892	7/26/1892	2/23/1903	8/2/1924	10
Howell E. Jackson	Tenn.	4/8/1832	Harrison	Lamar	2/2/1893	2/18/1893		8/8/1895	2
William Hornblower	N.Y.	5/13/1851	Cleveland	Blatchford	9/19/1893	1/15/1894 (R, 24-30)		6/16/1914	
Wheeler H. Peckham	N.Y.	1/1/1833	Cleveland	Blatchford	1/22/1894	2/16/1894 (R, 32-41)		9/27/1905	
Edward D. White	La.	11/3/1845	Cleveland	Blatchford	2/19/1894	2/19/1894		5/19/1921	17
Rufus W. Peckham	N.Y.	11/8/1838	Cleveland	Jackson	12/3/1895	12/9/1895		10/24/1909	13
Joseph McKenna	Calif.	8/10/1843	McKinley	Field	12/16/1897	1/21/1898	1/5/1925	11/21/1926	26
Oliver W. Holmes	Mass.	3/8/1841	Roosevelt	Gray	12/2/1902	12/4/1902	1/12/1932	3/6/1935	29
William R. Day	Ohio	4/17/1849	Roosevelt	Shiras	2/19/1903	2/23/1903	11/13/1922	7/9/1923	19
William H. Moody	Mass.	12/23/1853	Roosevelt	Brown	12/3/1906	12/12/1906	11/20/1910	7/2/1917	3
Horace H. Lurton	Tenn.	2/26/1844	Taft	Peckham	12/13/1909	12/20/1909		7/12/1914	4
Edward D. White#			Taft	Fuller	12/12/1910	12/12/1910			10#
Charles E. Hughes	N.Y.	4/11/1862	Taft	Brewer	4/25/1910	5/2/1910	6/10/1916	8/27/1948	6
Willis Van Devanter	Wyo.	4/17/1859	Taft	Moody	12/12/1910	12/15/1910	6/2/1937	2/8/1941	26
Joseph R. Lamar	Ga.	10/14/1857	Taft	White	12/12/1910	12/15/1910		1/2/1916	5
Mahlon Pitney	N.J.	2/5/1858	Taft	Harlan	2/19/1912	3/13/1912 (50-26)	12/31/1922	12/9/1924	10
James McReynolds	Tenn.	2/3/1862	Wilson	Lurton	8/19/1914	8/29/1914 (44-6)	1/31/1941	8/24/1946	26
Louis D. Brandeis	Mass.	11/13/1856	Wilson	Lamar	1/28/1916	6/1/1916 (47-22)	2/13/1939	10/5/1941	22
John H. Clarke	Ohio	9/18/1857	Wilson	Hughes	7/14/1916	7/24/1916	7/18/1922	3/22/1945	6
William H. Taft	Ohio	9/15/1857	Harding	White	6/30/1921	6/30/1921	2/3/1930	3/8/1930	8
George Sutherland	Utah	3/25/1862	Harding	Clarke	9/5/1922	9/5/1922	1/17/1938	7/18/1942	15
Pierce Butler	Minn.	3/17/1866	Harding	Day	11/23/1922	12/21/1922 (61-8)		11/16/1939	17
Edward T. Sanford	Tenn.	7/23/1865	Harding	Pitney	1/24/1923	1/29/1923		3/8/1930	7

Name	State	Date of Birth	Nomi-nated by	To Replace	Date of Appointment	Confirmation or Other Action*	Date Resigned	Date of Death	Years Service
Harlan F. Stone	N.Y.	10/11/1872	Coolidge	McKenna	1/5/1925	2/5/1925 (71-6)		4/22/1946	16
Charles E. Hughes#			Hoover	Taft	2/3/1930	2/13/1930 (52-26)	7/1/1941	8/27/1948	11#
John J. Parker	N.C.	11/20/1885	Hoover	Sanford	3/21/1930	5/7/1930 (R, 39-41)		3/17/1958	
Owen J. Roberts	Pa.	5/2/1875	Hoover	Sanford	5/9/1930	5/20/1930	7/31/1945	5/17/1955	15
Benjamin N. Cardozo	N.Y.	5/24/1870	Hoover	Holmes	2/15/1932	2/24/1932		7/9/1938	6
Hugo L. Black	Ala.	2/27/1886	Roosevelt	Van Devanter	8/12/1937	8/17/1937 (63-16)	9/17/1971	9/25/1971	34
Stanley F. Reed	Ky.	12/31/1884	Roosevelt	Sutherland	1/15/1938	1/25/1938	2/26/1957	4/2/1980	19
Felix Frankfurter	Mass.	11/15/1882	Roosevelt	Cardozo	1/5/1939	1/17/1939	8/28/1962	2/22/1965	23
William O. Douglas	Conn.	10/16/1898	Roosevelt	Brandeis	3/20/1939	4/4/1939 (62-4)	11/12/1975	1/19/1980	36
Frank Murphy	Mich.	4/13/1890	Roosevelt	Butler	1/4/1940	1/15/1940		7/19/1949	9
Harlan F. Stone#			Roosevelt	Hughes	6/12/1941	6/27/1941		4/22/1946	5#
James F. Byrnes	S.C.	5/2/1879	Roosevelt	McReynolds	6/12/1941	6/12/1941	10/3/1942	4/9/1972	1
Robert H. Jackson	N.Y.	2/13/1892	Roosevelt	Stone	6/12/1941	7/7/1941		10/9/1954	13
Wiley B. Rutledge	Iowa	7/20/1894	Roosevelt	Byrnes	1/11/1943	2/8/1943		9/10/1949	6
Harold H. Burton	Ohio	6/22/1888	Truman	Roberts	9/19/1945	9/19/1945	10/13/1958	10/28/1964	13
Fred M. Vinson	Ky.	1/22/1890	Truman	Stone	6/6/1946	6/20/1946		9/8/1953	7
Tom C. Clark	Texas	9/23/1899	Truman	Murphy	8/2/1949	8/18/1949 (73-8)	6/12/1967	6/13/1977	18
Sherman Minton	Ind.	10/20/1890	Truman	Rutledge	9/15/1949	10/4/1949 (48-16)	10/15/1956	4/9/1965	7
Earl Warren	Calif.	3/19/1891	Eisenhower	Vinson	9/30/1953	3/1/1954	6/23/1969	7/9/1974	15
John M. Harlan	N.Y.	5/20/1899	Eisenhower	Jackson	1/10/1955	3/16/1955 (71-11)	9/23/1971	12/29/1971	16
William J. Brennan	N.J.	4/25/1906	Eisenhower	Minton	1/14/1957	3/19/1957			
Charles E. Whittaker	Mo.	2/22/1901	Eisenhower	Reed	3/2/1957	3/19/1957	4/1/1962	11/26/1973	5
Potter Stewart	Ohio	1/23/1915	Eisenhower	Burton	1/17/1959	5/5/1959 (70-17)	7/3/1981		22
Byron R. White	Colo.	6/8/1917	Kennedy	Whittaker	3/30/1962	4/11/1962			
Arthur J. Goldberg	Ill.	8/8/1908	Kennedy	Frankfurter	8/29/1962	9/25/1962	7/25/1965		3
Abe Fortas	Tenn.	6/19/1910	Johnson	Goldberg	7/28/1965	8/11/1965	5/14/1969	4/5/1982	4
Thurgood Marshall	N.Y.	7/2/1908	Johnson	Clark	6/13/1967	8/30/1967 (69-11)			
Abe Fortas#			Johnson	Warren	6/26/1968	10/4/1968 (W)	5/14/1969	4/5/1982	
Homer Thornberry	Texas	1/9/1909	Johnson	Fortas	6/26/1968	No action			
Warren E. Burger	Minn.	9/17/1907	Nixon	Warren	5/21/1969	6/9/1969 (74-3)			
Clement Haynsworth	S.C.	10/30/1912	Nixon	Fortas	8/18/1969	11/21/1969 (R, 45-55)			
G. Harrold Carswell	Fla.	12/22/1919	Nixon	Fortas	1/19/1970	4/8/1970 (R, 45-51)			
Harry A. Blackmun	Minn.	11/12/1908	Nixon	Fortas	4/14/1970	5/12/1970 (94-0)			
Lewis F. Powell Jr.	Va.	9/19/1907	Nixon	Black	10/21/1971	12/6/1971 (89-1)			
William H. Rehnquist	Ariz.	10/1/1924	Nixon	Harlan	10/21/1971	12/10/1971 (68-26)			
John Paul Stevens	Ill.	4/20/1920	Ford	Douglas	11/28/75	12/17/1975 (98-0)			
Sandra Day O'Connor	Ariz.	3/26/1930	Reagan	Stewart	8/19/1981	9/21/1981 (99-0)			

Sources: Leon Friedman and Fred L. Israel, eds., *The Justices of the United States Supreme Court, 1789-1969;* Executive Journal of the U.S. Senate, 1789-1975; *Congressional Quarterly Almanacs 1971, 1975, 1981.*

Boldface - Chief Justice.
Italics - Did not serve.
Boldface italic - Chief Justice, did not serve.
Earlier court service. See above.
† Earlier nomination not confirmed. See above.

D Declined
W Withdrawn
P Postponed
R Rejected
 * Where no vote is listed, confirmation was by voice vote or otherwise unrecorded vote.
** As of March 10, 1983.

Glossary of Common Legal Terms

Accessory. In criminal law, a person not present at the commission of an offense who commands, advises, instigates or conceals the offense.

Acquittal. Discharge of a person from a charge of guilt. A person is acquitted when a jury returns a verdict of not guilty. However, a person may also be acquitted when a judge determines that there is insufficient evidence to convict or that a violation of due process precludes a fair trial. *(See Due Process)*

Adjudicate. To determine finally by the exercise of judicial authority; as to decide a case.

Affidavit. A voluntarily made written statement of facts or charges affirmed under oath.

Amicus Curiae. "A friend of the court." A person, not a party to the litigation, who volunteers or is invited by the court to give advice on a matter pending before it.

Appeal. To take a case to a higher court for review. Generally, a party losing in a trial court may appeal once to an appellate court as a matter of right. If he loses in the appellate court, appeal to a higher court is within the discretion of the higher court. Most appeals to the U.S. Supreme Court are within the court's discretion. *(See Writ of Certiorari)*
However, when the highest court in a state rules that a U.S. statute is unconstitutional or upholds a state statute against the claim that it is unconstitutional, appeal to the Supreme Court is a matter of right.

Appellant. The party that appeals a lower court decision to a higher court. *(See Appellee, Appeal)*

Appellee. One who has an interest in upholding the decision of a lower court and is compelled to respond when the case is appealed to a higher court by the appellant. *(See Appellant, Appeal)*

Arraignment. Process of calling an indicted person before the court, reading him the indictment, asking whether he pleads guilty or not guilty, and entering his plea. *(See Indictment, Pleas)*

Bail. The security, usually money, given as assurance of a prisoner's due appearance at a designated time and place (as in court) in order to procure in the interim his release from jail.

Bailiff. A minor officer of a court usually serving as an usher or a messenger.

Brief. A document prepared by counsel to serve as the basis for an argument in an appellate court.

Case Law. As distinguished from statutes and other sources of law, case law is the law as defined by previously decided cases. *(See Code, Statutes, Common Law)*

Civil Law. Body of law dealing with the private rights of individuals, as distinguished from criminal law.

Class Action. A lawsuit brought by one person or group on behalf of all persons similarly situated.

Code. A collection of laws, arranged systematically.

Common Law. Collection of principles and rules of action, particularly from unwritten English law, which derive their authority from longstanding usage and custom or from courts recognizing and enforcing these customs. Sometimes used synonymously with case law. *(See Civil Law, Criminal Law, Statute Case Law)*

Consent Decree. A court-sanctioned agreement entered into by the consent of the parties.

Contempt (Civil and Criminal). Civil contempt consists in the failure to do something which the party is ordered by the court to do for the benefit of another party. Criminal contempt occurs when a person willfully exhibits disrespect for the court or obstructs the administration of justice.

Conviction. Final judgment or sentence that the defendant is guilty as charged.

Criminal Law. That branch of law which deals with the enforcement of laws and the punishment of persons who, by breaking laws, commit crimes. *(See Civil Law)*

Declaratory Judgment. A court pronouncement declaring a legal right or interpretation but not ordering a specific action.

Defendant. In a civil action, the party denying or defending itself against charges brought by a plaintiff. In a criminal action, the person indicted for commission of an offense. *(See Plaintiff)*

Deposition. Oral testimony from a witness taken out of court in response to written or oral questions, committed to writing, and intended to be used in the preparation of a case.

Dicta. Opinions of a judge which are not part of the

Sources for Definitions

Black's Law Dictionary. West Publishing Company, St. Paul, Minn. 1968.
Random House Dictionary. Random House, New York, N.Y., 1966.
Webster's Third International Dictionary. G. & C. Merriam Company, Springfield, Mass., 1961.

resolution or determination of the court; non-binding statements included in a court decision.

Dismissal. Order disposing of a case without a trial.

Docket. See Trial Docket.

Due Process. Constitutional guarantee of the Fifth and Fourteenth Amendments providing that a person may not be "deprived of life, liberty or property" without opportunity to prepare a defense and present it.

Ex Parte. "On one side only." Application to a court on behalf of only one party.

Grand Jury. Group of 12 to 23 persons impaneled to hear in private evidence presented by the state against persons accused of crime and to issue indictments when a majority of the jurors find that probable cause exists to believe that the accused has committed a crime. Called a "grand" jury because it has more members than a "petit jury." *(See Petit Jury)*

Grand Jury Report. A public report released by a grand jury after an investigation into activities of public officials that fall short of criminal actions. Grand jury reports are often called "presentments."

Guilty. A word used by a defendant in entering a plea or by a jury in returning a verdict, indicating that the defendant is legally responsible as charged for a crime or other wrongdoing.

Habeas Corpus. A writ to inquire whether a person is lawfully imprisoned or detained. *(See Writ)*

Immunity. A grant of exemption from prosecution in return for evidence or testimony. *(See Transactional Immunity and Use Immunity)*

In Camera. "In chambers." Refers to court hearings in private without spectators.

In Re. In the affair; concerning. Frequent title of judicial proceedings where there are no adversaries, but rather where a matter itself requires judicial actions, as a bankrupt's estate.

Indictment. A formal written statement based on evidence presented by the prosecutor from a grand jury decided by a majority vote, charging one or more persons with specified offenses. *(See Grand Jury)*

Information. A written set of accusations, similar to an indictment, but filed directly by a prosecutor without intervention by a grand jury.

Injunction. A court order prohibiting the person to whom it is directed from performing a particular act.

Interlocutory Decree. A provisional decision of the court before completion of a legal action which temporarily settles an intervening matter.

Judgment. Official decision of a court based on the rights and claims of the parties to a case which was submitted for determination.

Jurisdiction. Exists when a court has the right and power to hear a case in question, when the proper parties are present, and when the point to be decided is within the issues authorized to be handled by the particular court.

Juries. See Grand Jury and Petit Jury.

Magistrate. A judicial officer having jurisdiction to try minor criminal cases and conduct preliminary examinations of persons charged with serious crimes.

Mandamus. "We command." An order issued from a superior court directing a lower court or other authority to perform a particular act.

Moot. Unsettled; undecided. A moot question is also one which is no longer material.

Motion. Written or oral application to a court or a judge to obtain a rule or an order.

Nolo Contendere. "I will not contest it." A plea entered by a defendant at the discretion of the judge with the same legal effect as a plea of guilty, but it may not be cited in other proceedings as an admission of guilt.

Parole. A conditional release from imprisonment under conditions that if the prisoner abides by the law and other restrictions that may be placed upon him, he will not have to serve the remainder of his sentence. But if he does not abide by specified rules, he will be returned to prison to finish his time.

Per Curiam. "By the court." An unsigned opinion of the court, or an opinion written by the whole court.

Petit Jury. Originally, a panel of 12 persons who tried to reach a unanimous verdict on questions of fact in criminal and civil proceedings. Since 1970 the Supreme Court has upheld the legality of state juries with fewer than 12 persons and of non-unanimous verdicts. Because it comprises fewer persons than a "grand jury," it is called a "petit" jury. *(See Grand Jury)*

Petitioner. One who files a petition with a court seeking action or relief, including a plaintiff or an appellant. But a petitioner is also a person who files for other court action where charges are not necessarily made; for example, a party may petition the court for an order requiring another person or party to produce documents. The opposite party is called the respondent.

When writ of certiorari is granted by the Supreme Court, parties to the case are called petitioner and respondent in contrast to the appellant and appellee terms used in an appeal. *(See Appeal, Respondent, Writ of Certiorari)*

Plaintiff. A party who brings a civil action or sues to obtain a remedy for injury to his rights. The party against whom action is brought is termed the defendant.

Plea Bargaining. Negotiations between prosecutors and the defendant aimed at eliciting a plea of guilty from the defendant in exchange for concessions by the prosecutors, such as reduction of charges or a request for leniency. Plea bargains often are used in federal and state courts to settle criminal cases before trial.

Pleas. See Guilty and Nolo Contendere.

Presentment. See Grand Jury Report.

Prima Facie. "At first sight." Referring to a fact or other evidence presumably sufficient to establish a defense or a claim unless otherwise contradicted.

Probation. Process under which a person convicted of an offense, usually a first offense, receives a suspended sentence and is given his freedom, usually under the guardianship of a probation officer.

Quash. To overthrow, annul or vacate; as to quash a subpoena. *(See Vacate)*

Recognizance. An obligation entered into before a court or magistrate requiring the performance of a specified act — usually to appear in court at a later date. It is an alternative to bail for pretrial release.

Remand. To send back. In the event of a case being remanded, it is sent back by a higher court to the court from which it came for further action.

Respondent. One who is compelled to answer the claims or questions posed in court by a petitioner. A defendant and an appellee may be called respondents, but the term also includes those parties who answer in court during actions where charges are not necessarily brought or where the Supreme Court has granted a writ of certiorari. *(See Petitioner, Appeal, Writ of Certiorari)*

Stare Decisis. The doctrine of law under which principles of law established by judicial decision are to be accepted as authoritative in cases similar to those from which such principles were established.

Statute. A written law enacted by a legislature. A collection of statutes for a particular governmental division is called a code. *(See Code)*

Stay. To halt or suspend further judicial proceedings.

Subpoena. An order to present one's self before a grand jury, court or legislative hearing.

Subpoena Duces Tecum. An order to produce specified documents or papers.

Transactional Immunity. Protects a witness from prosecution for any offense mentioned in or related to his testimony, regardless of independent evidence against him.

Trial Docket. A calendar prepared by the clerks of the court listing the cases to be tried.

Use Immunity. Protects a witness against the use of his own testimony against him in prosecution.

Vacate. To make void, annul or rescind.

Writ. A written court order commanding the designated recipient to perform or not perform acts specified in the order.

Writ of Certiorari. Discretionary writ issued from the Supreme Court of the United States or a state Supreme Court to an inferior court ordering the lower court to prepare the records of a case and to send them up for review.

Selected Bibliography

Books

Abraham, Henry J. *Justices and Presidents: A Political History of Appointments to the Supreme Court.* New York: Oxford University Press, 1974.

Beard, Charles A. *The Supreme Court and the Constitution.* New York: Macmillan, 1912.

Berger, Raoul. *Congress v. The Supreme Court.* Cambridge: Harvard University Press, 1969.

Berle, Adolf A. *The Three Faces of Power.* New York: Harcourt, Brace and World, 1967.

Bickel, Alexander M. *The Least Dangerous Branch.* Indianapolis: Bobbs-Merrill, 1962.

_____. *Politics and the Warren Court.* New York: Harper & Row, 1965 ed.

Binkley, Wilfred E. and Moos, Malcolm C. *A Grammar of American Politics.* New York: Alfred A. Knopf, 1958 ed.

Boudin, Louis B. *Government by the Judiciary.* New York: Russell & Russell, 1968.

Breckenridge, Adam C. *Congress Against the Court.* Lincoln: University of Nebraska Press, 1970.

Congressional Quarterly's Guide to the Supreme Court. Washington, D.C.: Congressional Quarterly, 1979.

Congressional Quarterly's Guide to Congress. 3d ed., Washington, D.C.: Congressional Quarterly, 1982.

Corwin, Edward S. *Court Over Constitution.* Princeton: Princeton University Press, 1938.

_____. *Doctrine of Judicial Review.* Princeton: Princeton University Press, 1914.

_____. *The Twilight of the Supreme Court.* New Haven: Yale University Press, 1934.

Cushman, Robert Eugene. *Leading Constitutional Decisions.* New York: Appleton-Century-Crofts, 1955.

Davis, Horace. *A Judicial Veto.* Boston: Houghton Mifflin, 1914; reprint ed., New York: Da Capo Press, 1971.

Ervin, Sam J. Jr. *Role of the Supreme Court: Policy Maker or Adjudicator.* Washington, D.C.: American Enterprise Institute for Public Policy Research, 1970.

Forte, David F. *The Supreme Court in American Politics: Judicial Activism vs. Judicial Restraint.* Lexington, Mass.: D. C. Heath, 1972.

Frank, John P. *Marble Palace: The Supreme Court in American Life.* New York: Alfred A. Knopf, 1958.

Freund, Paul A., gen. ed. *History of the Supreme Court of the United States.* New York: Macmillan, 1971, 1974. Vol. I: *Antecedents and Beginnings to 1801,* by Julius Goebel; Vol. V: *The Taney Period, 1836-1864,* by Carl B. Swisher; Vol. VI: *Reconstruction and Reunion, 1864-1888, Part One,* by Charles Fairman.

Friedman, Leon and Israel, Fred L., eds., *The Justices of the United States Supreme Court, 1789-1969.* 5 vols. New York: R. R. Bowker Co., 1969, 1978.

Harris, Richard. *Decision.* New York: E. P. Dutton & Co., 1971.

Hughes, Charles Evans. *The Supreme Court of the United States.* New York: Columbia University Press, 1928.

Jackson, Robert H. *The Supreme Court in the American System of Government.* Cambridge: Harvard University Press, 1955.

_____. *The Struggle for Judicial Supremacy: A Study of a Crisis in American Power Politics.* New York: Random House, Vintage Books, 1941.

Krislov, Samuel. *The Supreme Court in the Political Process.* New York: Macmillan, 1965.

Madison, James; Hamilton, Alexander; and Jay, John. *The Federalist Papers.* Introduction by Clinton Rossiter. New York: New American Library, Mentor Books, 1961.

Moore, Blaine F. *Supreme Court and Unconstitutional Legislation.* New York: Columbia University Press, 1913; reprint ed., New York: AMS Press, 1968.

Morgan, Donald G. *Congress and the Constitution.* Cambridge: Belknap Press of Harvard University Press, 1966.

Murphy, Bruce Allen. *The Brandeis/Frankfurter Connection.* New York: Oxford University Press, 1982.

Murphy, Walter F. *Congress and the Court.* Chicago: University of Chicago Press, 1962.

Post, C. Gordon. *Supreme Court and Political Questions.* Baltimore: Johns Hopkins University Press, 1936; reprint ed., New York: Da Capo Press, 1969.

Pritchett, C. Herman. *The American Constitution.* 3rd ed., New York: McGraw-Hill, 1977.

_____. *Congress vs. the Supreme Court, 1957-1960.* Minneapolis: University of Minnesota Press, 1961; reprint ed., New York: Da Capo Press, 1973.

Schlesinger, Arthur M. Jr. *The Politics of Upheaval.* Boston: Houghton Mifflin Co., 1960.

Schmidhauser, John R. *The Supreme Court and Congress: Conflict and Interaction 1945-1968.* New York: Free Press, 1972.

Scigliano, Robert G. *The Supreme Court and the Presidency.* New York: The Free Press, 1971.

Warren, Charles. *Congress, The Constitution and the Supreme Court.* Boston: Little, Brown, 1925.

_____. *The Supreme Court in United States History.* 2 vols. Boston: Little, Brown, 1922, 1926.

Articles

Berger, Raoul. "The President, Congress and the Courts." *Yale Law Journal,* May 1974, pp. 1111-1155.

Chase, Harold W. "The Warren Court and Congress." *Minnesota Law Review,* March 1960, pp. 595-637.

Edgerton, Henry W. "The Incidence of Judicial Control Over Congress." *Cornell Law Quarterly,* vol. 22, no. 3, 1937, pp. 299-348.

Ervin, Sam J. Jr. "The Gravel and Brewster Cases: An Assault on Congressional Independence." *Virginia Law Review,* February 1973, pp. 175-195.

Frank, John P. "The Historic Role of the Supreme Court." *Kentucky Law Journal,* Fall 1959, pp. 26-47.

Gimlin, Hoyt. "Challenging of Supreme Court." *Editorial*

Research Reports, 1968, vol. 2, pp. 741-760.

Hankin, C. A. "The Supreme Court and the New Deal." *Editorial Research Reports*, 1935, vol. 2, pp. 413-428.

Hankin, Gregory. "The New Deal in the Courts." *Editorial Research Reports*, 1934, vol. 2, pp. 347-362.

Hochman, Charles B. "The Supreme Court and the Constitutionality of Retroactive Legislation." *Harvard Law Review*, February 1960, pp. 692-727.

Shaffer, Helen B. "Separation of Powers." *Editorial Research Reports*, 1973, vol. 2, pp. 691-708.

Stencel, Sandra. "Burger Court's Tenth Year." *Editorial Research Reports*, 1978, vol. 2, pp. 681-700.

Swindler, William F. "The Supreme Court, the President and Congress." *Comparative Law Quarterly*, October 1970, pp. 671-692.

Putney, Bryant. "The President, the Constitution and the Supreme Court." *Editorial Research Reports*, 1935, vol. 1, pp. 339-470.

Ulmer, S. Sidney. "Judicial Review as Political Behavior: A Temporary Check on Congress." *Administrative Science Quarterly*, March 1960, pp. 426-445.

Vetter, George M. "Who Is Supreme: People, Court or Legislature? Role of the Supreme Court in the History of Judicial Supremacy." *American Bar Association Journal*, October 1959, pp. 1051-1055.

Worsnop, Richard L. "Supreme Court: Legal Storm Center." *Editorial Research Reports*, 1966, vol. 2, pp. 701-720.

Government Publications

U.S. Congress. Library of Congress, Congressional Research Service. *The Constitution of the United States: Analysis and Interpretation*, Washington, D.C.: Government Printing Office, 1973; together with the 1976 Supplement, 1977.

Subject Index

Index of Cases

RECEIVED
JA...
Mission College
Learning Resource
Services